D0821363

Henry James

—the Lessons of the Master

Henry James—

WILLIAM VEEDER

the Lessons of the Master

Popular Fiction and Personal Style in the Nineteenth Century

THE UNIVERSITY OF CHICAGO PRESS

CHICAGO AND LONDON

WILLIAM VEEDER is associate professor of English and Humanities at the University of
    Chicago. He is the author of *W. B. Yeats: The Rhetoric of Repetition* and is now
    coediting *The Girl of the Period*.

The University of Chicago Press, Chicago 60637
The University of Chicago Press, Ltd., London

Library of Congress Cataloging in Publication Data

Veeder, William R.
    Henry James: the lessons of the master.

    Bibliography: p.
    Includes index.
    1. James, Henry, 1843–1916—Criticism and
interpretation.
PS2124.V43   813'.4   75-8957
ISBN 0-226-85223-7

In literature we move through a blest world in which we know nothing except by style, but in which also everything is saved by it.

Henry James

Contents

Preface

> While men often throw away irreplaceable wealth, they not
> infrequently escape what seemed inevitable dangers, not knowing
> that they have done either nor how they did it.
>
> C. S. Lewis

Acknowledgments

Few things are harder to do than to express gratitude without making the thanked parties vaguely wish they were elsewhere. I had planned to avoid awkwardness by borrowing grace from my betters.

> Think where man's glory most begins and ends,
> And say my glory was I had such friends.

In the meantime, however, these lines from Yeats have become so associated with the dreary politics of 1972 that I cannot let them be a party to the goodly company I must thank. If, in turn, I resort simply to a litany of names, it is because those names have blessedly proved almost as extensive as my needs. The University of California at Berkeley, for photocopy funds; the University of Chicago, for research time and stenographic funds; the National Endowment for the Humanities, for a Younger Humanist Fellowship; the International Museum of Photography (Eastman House) for their generous and friendly help with the Coburn materials, especially Chris Hawrylak, William Jenkins, Martha Jenks, Robert Sobieszek, and Robert Doherty. Teachers and Colleagues: Robert Bloom, Wayne C. Booth, Merlin Bowen, John G. Cawelti, Elizabeth K. Helsinger, Marcia Jacobson, Jerome J. McGann, David Marcus, Sharon Meltzer, James E. Miller, Jr., Michael Murrin, Elder Olson, Mark Schorer, Robert E. Streeter, Napier Wilt; and with particular thanks to Joel Snyder, who directed me toward Eastman House and since then has provided repeated and patient assistance. My family: who watched and prayed; and particularly my mother, who helped so substantially with statistical data and has become in the process a most respectable Jamesian. And finally, for my wife Mary, who has not only borne the heavier half of our supposedly equal burden but has also managed to live a life of scholarship and service: this book.

Photographs

In 1953 Alvin Langdon Coburn wrote to Joseph J. Firebaugh that he intended to publish some fifty letters from Henry James "together with some hitherto unpublished photographs of the novelist."[1] Coburn, one of the century's greatest photographers, lived until 1966 but did not, so far as we know, carry out his plan to publish the letters and photographs. Today the letters are not among the extensive effects which Coburn willed to Eastman House.[2] Fortunately, the photographs are.

Coburn first photographed Henry James in 1905, for *Century Magazine*. Then, in June 1906 Coburn came to Lamb House and James sat (and stood) for a series of portraits. One of these became the frontispiece for the first volume of James' New York edition, another appeared in 1913 in Coburn's *Men of Mark*, and a third in Peter Buitenhuis' *The Grasping Imagination* in 1970. The rest have remained unpublished until now. These seven photographs (following page 186) capture both the delicacy and the power of Henry James, the grace of his hands and the facial expressions which vary in mood but consistently bespeak the master. Coburn was later to say in *Men of Mark*:

I have not attempted to do anything eccentric in the way of
portrayals, but I have studied my men and their works with enthusiasm, and in each instance I have tried to catch and reveal the elusive
something that differentiates a man of talent from his fellows, and
makes life worth while, worth struggling with towards ever greater
understanding.[3]

Pleased with the June portraits, James contracted with Coburn for twenty-three more frontispieces, and the young artist returned to Lamb House on July 3. The subject that day was the house itself. Of Coburn's six prints, one appeared in *The Awkward Age* volume, and a second was supplied by Coburn for Leon Edel's *Henry James: The Treacherous Years, 1895–1901*. The other four photographs, including the remarkable view of the Lamb House staircase, are published here for the first time. The interior shots, with their emphasis on James' books, indicate Coburn's desire to preserve and evoke the ethos of the literary master; the garden view conveys the beautiful repose surrounding the garden-house where James dictated much of his best late work.

At their July 3d meeting, the two artists also had another task—to plan for the remaining frontispieces. James gave Coburn detailed instructions for trips to France and to Italy (and eventually sent him supplementary letters). The instructions, though thorough, were often general enough that Coburn must have experimented considerably with scenes and camera angles. For example, James wanted a *porte cochère* for *The American*.

"Once you get the type into your head, you will easily recognize specimens by walking in the *old* residential and 'noble' parts of the city . . . .
having got the notion, go back and walk and stare at your ease."[4]

With comparable instructions for other frontispieces, Coburn must have
brought back many prints for James to pick from. What happened to the
unused photographs? From the hundreds of Coburn envelopes (some
inscribed in his own hand) at Eastman House I found three negatives
which seem to conform to various of James' instructions and were
apparently made by Coburn around 1906. I have included the three
prints[5] here, along with the instructions they adhere to so faithfully. But
the rest . . . These photographs would offer us the chance to study that
rare event—creative collaboration, selection, and rejection by masters of
different media.

> Early in November Henry James came up to London and we gloated
> together over my prints. Though sixty-three years old, H. J. was like a
> boy, always displaying unquenchable and contagious enthusiasm over
> every detail concerning these illustrations. This made it a joy to work
> with him. That is the splendid thing about an artist, whether his
> medium of expression be pigments, or sounds, or words, or even the
> Art of life, he does not "grow up," grow stale, or lose freshness of
> outlook; and Henry James was a true artist in this respect. He never
> lost the capacity to see things with that freshness of vision, as they are
> beheld by the very young or the very wise.[6]

Beaumont Newhall, a long-time friend of Coburn, has said that the great
photographer threw away nothing. So, possibly, the precious negatives
will emerge somewhere, someday. For now, however, we can be
thankful to have come upon artworks which, combining with and far
outshining a critical study of James, provide us another perspective on
the master.

Texts

With "popular" novels I have chosen recent reprints or standard
editions whenever possible; frequently, however, I have had to accept
what dusty shelves offered. With James, unrevised texts (or rather texts
revised only between the serial and first hardcover edition) are essential
to my study of his development. Where these texts are available in
paperback, I have tried to pick editions likely to remain in print. For
Watch and Ward I have had to resort to the initial *Atlantic* pages; for
Roderick Hudson, to the first American edition of 1875.

Novels Popular and Great

AB J. G. Lockhart, *Adam Blair* (Edinburgh, 1963) [1822].
CUF Rhoda Broughton, *Cometh Up as a Flower* (London, 1899) [1867].

DD   George Eliot, *Daniel Deronda* (New York, 1960) [1876].
EV   Oliver Wendell Holmes, *Elsie Venner* (Boston, 1885) [1861].
GA   ———, *The Guardian Angel* (New Jersey, 1970) [1867].
HR   Charlotte Yonge, *The Heir of Redclyffe* (London, 1854) [1853].
In   Baroness von Tautphoeus, *The Initials* (London, n.d.) [1854].
Ish E. D. E. N. Southworth, *Ishmael; or In the Depths* (New York, n.d.) [1864].
LL   Honoré de Balzac, *Louis Lambert* (Paris, 1961) [1832].
LM   George Sand, *La Mare au diable* (Paris, 1890) [1846].
LR   Victor Cherbuliez, *Le Roman d'une honnête femme* (Paris, 1882) [1866].
P   Charlotte Brontë, *The Professor* (New York, 1969) [1857].
R   Elizabeth Gaskell, *Ruth* (New York, 1967) [1853].
StE Augusta Jane Evans, *St. Elmo* (New York, 1867).
V   Charlotte Brontë, *Villette* (New York, 1972) [1853].
WWW Susan Warner, *The Wide, Wide World* (New York, n.d.) [1850].

Books by and about James
Amb *The Ambassadors* (Boston, 1960) [1903].
Ame *The American* (New York, 1952) [1877].
AN   *The Art of the Novel*, ed. R. P. Blackmur (New York, 1934).
AS   *The American Scene* (New York, 1967) [1907].
CT   *The Complete Tales of Henry James*, ed. Leon Edel (Philadelphia, 1961–62).
E1   Leon Edel, *Henry James: The Untried Years, 1843–1870* (Philadelphia, 1953).
E2   ———, *Henry James: The Conquest of London, 1870–1881* (Philadelphia, 1962).
EL   *Selected Letters of Henry James*, ed. Leon Edel (London, 1956).
FN   *The Future of the Novel*, ed. Leon Edel (New York, 1956).
FrP *French Poets and Novelists* (New York, 1964) [1878].
Ha   *Hawthorne* (New York, 1966) [1879].
HJL *Henry James Letters*, ed. Leon Edel (Harvard, 1974).
JF   F. O. Matthiessen, *The James Family* (New York, 1947).
LL   *The Letters of Henry James*, ed. Percy Lubbock, 2 vols. (New York, 1920).
MY   *The Middle Years* (New York, 1917).
Nb   *The Notebooks of Henry James*, ed. F. O. Matthiessen and Kenneth B. Murdock (Oxford, 1947).
NSB *Notes of a Son and Brother* (New York, 1914).
NY   *The Novels and Tales of Henry James*, "The New York Edition" (New York, 1907–9).
PE   *The Painter's Eye*, ed. John L. Sweeney (London, 1956).

PL   *The Portrait of a Lady* (New York, 1963) [1881].
PoP   *Portraits of Places* (Boston, 1884).
PS   *Parisian Sketches*, ed. Leon Edel and Ilse Dusoir Lind (London, 1958).
RH   *Roderick Hudson* (Boston, 1875).
SA   *The Scenic Art*, ed. Allan Wade (New York, 1957).
SB   *A Small Boy and Others* (New York, 1913).
WS   *Washington Square* (New York, 1959) [1880].
W&W *Watch and Ward*, *Atlantic Monthly*, August–December 1871, pp. 232–46, 320–39, 415–31, 577–96, 689–710.

        Periodicals
AL   *American Literature.*
ALR ˙ *American Literary Realism.*
AM   *Atlantic Monthly.*
CE   *College English.*
CLQ   *Colby Library Quarterly.*
ES   *English Studies.*
G   *Galaxy.*
MFS   *Modern Fiction Studies.*
MLN   *Modern Language Notes.*
MP   *Modern Philology.*
Na   *Nation.*
NAR   *North American Review.*
NCF   *Nineteenth Century Fiction.*
REL   *Review of English Literature.*

Introduction

> In him we see the culmination of all the forces of the last half of the century.
>
> *Bradford Booth*

> The best part of a writer's biography is not the record of his adventures but the story of his style.
>
> *Nabokov*

The lessons of the master: what Henry James learned, and what he taught. The materials that James received from various traditions and the ways that he transformed those materials into great art, are my subject. Or rather, my subject is how conventional materials, received and gradually transformed, contribute to the meaning of James' novels.

By the conventional materials of fiction we generally mean elements of plot and character—how the villain stalks the heroine, what color her hair is. Such elements are, as many readers have noted, basic to James' fiction throughout his long career, and I study them in detail in chapter 2. Another element of James' art is also indebted heavily to conventional practice. And this debt critics have largely ignored. The debt of his style. As James outfitted his characters from a common fund of types and gestures, he also shaped his style from a common fund of dictional and syntactic usages. What that fund was, I will attempt to define now. We can then go on to study the development of James' style and characterization, and how these elements work together in his fiction.

Few readers today assume, as the nineteenth century largely did, that fiction is an artless art. And yet, despite two decades of work by serious critics, most readers today still give little heed to style as one of the basic components of the art of fiction. We continue, at least implicitly, to accept the traditional assumption that *poetry*, but not *prose*, is "that which is lost in translation." Against the assumption here—that content is separable from form in prose works—Henry James protested to a French translator.

How much I feel that in a literary work of the least complexity the very form and texture are the substance itself and that the flesh is

1

indetachable from the bones! Translation is an effort—though a most flattering one!—to *tear* the hapless flesh, and in fact to get rid of so much of it that the living thing bleeds and faints away. . . . The small Boy . . . is locked fast in the golden cage of the *intraduisible!*

(*EL* 136)[1]

The small boy is one with his golden cage; content is one with form, in prose as in poetry. Because the agent of an action in literature cannot, like an agent in life, affect us directly, the language which renders the action becomes itself an action. That language helps shape our responses to each scene and thus contributes indispensably to the scene's meaning —whether our point of view is the narrator's or a character's.

He [Fireblood] in a few minutes ravished this fair creature [Laetitia], or at least would have ravished her, if she had not, by a timely compliance, prevented him.[2]

Our experience here is not the character's. Fireblood simply copulates. We first think that he has raped Laetitia; then, "or at least would have ravished her" suggests that she has escaped; finally, after "compliance," we realize that "prevented" actually means "she assented." A simple statement of the event—"Fireblood and Laetitia copulated"—would not have induced us to make the mistake which contributes so much to our experience of Fielding's several-layered lesson. By *discovering* through language the paradox that "prevented" means "assented," we experience the more general awareness that moral pretension hides fundamental corruption. This awareness, in turn, contributes to our acceptance of the basic thematic paradox of *Jonathan Wild the Great*—that worldly greatness precludes true moral greatness.

To establish how much our experience of Fielding's sentence resembles reading great fiction of any era, let us turn briefly to a passage from an apparently very different book.

It [Paris] hung before him this morning, the vast bright Babylon, like some huge iridescent object, a jewel brilliant and hard, in which parts were not to be discriminated nor differences comfortably marked. It twinkled and trembled and melted together, and what seemed all surface one moment seemed all depth the next.

Here in *The Ambassadors*[3] our viewpoint is the character's. We move down through the passage, word by word, moment by moment, as Strether moves through Paris, event by event, day by day. Paris is cumulatively defined for us in our passage through the language as it is for Strether in his European sojourn. Initially we find our Puritan assumptions confirmed: Paris is Babylon. This a priori notion soon begins to erode, however. After Paris has become an "object" and then a "jewel," we discover that the jewel evinces not only the "hard"ness which we expect but also the opposite traits of evanescence and amorphousness. What is "hard" is not *hard*, and so becomes hard to define. Since what we are reading is itself a definition, we recognize that knowledge is less an a priori entity than an accretive process—Paris-Babylon-object-jewel-hard-not—and that even this process is not fully reliable because it remains open-ended and tentative. Nor does the next sentence restore convenient limits. After "twinkled . . . trembled . . . melted" indicate that even so apparently undifferentiated a thing as evanescence can entail differences upon differences, we then experience the opposite lesson. Differences fail to occur where we expect them: "surface" interchanges with "depth," antonyms become synonymous. And our Puritan equation of Paris and Babylon seems simplistic indeed. By not merely presenting us with statements of a character's thoughts, by making us instead experience a mind thinking, James' style sets our minds in motion too. We are moved by Strether's situation because his words are our Paris.

Different in their points of view, our two examples also differ in that Fielding's omniscient narrator fosters what James' passage tends increasingly to undermine—definiteness of judgment. All the more striking because of these differences, then, is the fact that both authors share a fundamental assumption about rendering action. Regardless of the definiteness of judgment sought, neither author is satisfied with simple propositional statement; both at their best go beyond assertion, to use language processively. Their language makes us discover their meaning. In fact, our individual consciousnesses are induced to combine with the text to *produce* meaning. As James himself said, when the art is great, "then the reader does quite half the labor" (*AM* 1866, 485). Like poetry, fiction is great, not for what it says, but for what it does. The meaning of a work of art is, finally, our experience of it.

Belief in the importance of style has not, however, fostered any consistently effective critical method. The basic difficulty is in defining style itself. Leo Spitzer's definition—style is deviation from the norm—has a fundamental cogency which makes it today the starting point for many stylistic analyses.[4] It has also evoked intelligent objections which we cannot ignore.

Much of the uneasiness has to do with the problem of establishing or even sensing a norm. . . . Barthes finds its identification with the current spoken language at once "excessive" and "insufficient," since on the one hand the spoken language is only one of several possible codes of stylistic reference, and on the other "the opposition of speech and writing has never been exploited to its ultimate end." . . . [Also] why assume, for example, that the *difference* between two corpora entitles us to say that one represents the norm and the other the deviant? . . . Or, again: Is it not the case that "regularities," that is, precisely non-deviant

linguistic elements in a text, seem often to be stylistic, whereas "many
deviations ... are not stylistically interesting"?[5]

This last objection shifts us from the problem of "norm" to the act of
deviation. Critics rightly warn that viewing art as "deviant" tends to
underrate its reliance upon the everyday features of language. Yet even if
we accept Halliday's alternative of "deflection,"[6] a third problem, implicit
in the others, remains. How does art deflect from whatever the norm is?
The apparently obvious answer—it deflects because of the author's
choices—raises questions about the nature of artistic choice. How choices
are limited by a writer's genre and period, and by "the unconscious nature
of the process of composition" is explored by Fritz Martini and Louis T.
Milic; Carl H. Klaus, citing four stylistically different passages from
Franklin, concludes that style indicates who the artist chooses to be.[7]
Even this type of choice is complicated, however. Barthes outlines
several ways in which we cannot avoid being translated by style into
selves other than our own: we adopt the expressions of earlier writers; we
adapt such traditional usages as maxims; we recast previous expressions
of our own.[8]

Issues so basic and perennially troublesome will never be resolved
entirely. Help is available, however, from a source that might once have
seemed unlikely. The waning of the war between New Critics and
historical scholars allows us to see that, salutary though the emphasis
upon close analysis has been, the new-critical ideal of careful, faithful
reading cannot in most cases be achieved solely by the new-critical
method of hermetical analysis. Historical scholarship is helpful to the
stylistic critic because it offers him, not an evasion (as his new-critical
forefathers thought), but a way of dealing, at least provisionally, with
the vexing norm-choice issue. From a knowledge of literary context can
come a sense of period style and of genre style which may allow the critic
to discuss how much an author's particular stylistic choices conform to
and deflect from other practice within his tradition. The best of applied
stylistic criticism has never ignored historical contexts, of course; it has
consistently realized that words have histories beyond etymology and
can only be experienced fully in terms of those histories. Thus Charles
Muscatine relates Chaucer to the mixed styles of the French tradition;
Jonas Barish places Ben Jonson in a hundred-year development of prose
comedy in England; Richard Bridgman discusses various writers in terms
of the increasing colloquialization of American style; and Morris Croll
and Leo Spitzer use their learning to place authors of many languages
within the continuum of Western literature.[9] In these and other cases, the
critics manage both to avoid making extravagant claims for their norms
and to demonstrate how often literary effect depends upon stylists
accepting and transforming their conventions.

Henry James invites and yet challenges stylistic study based upon a norm. He is related to so many traditions that Bradford Booth can justifiably claim "in him we see the culmination of all the forces of the last half of the century."[10] Although James' diversity has fostered important research into French, English, and American influences, a norm for his style remains elusive because the influence of national literatures is actually part of a larger, threefold process. As a writer coming to maturity after the Civil War, Henry James is necessarily affected by his period—the changes, stylistic and otherwise, which occurred so rapidly in America and had counterparts in England and France. Also, James inherits the conventional materials of his genre, the tradition of American, English, and Continental fiction. Finally, James can express his personal vision only by transforming conventions, by personalizing his period and genre materials.

Three forces interact, then. Period, genre, personal. Beginning to seek a norm for James' style in the genre element may seem ill-considered, for critics of fiction have been even less successful than drama or poetry critics in defining a canon of transmitted conventions, forms, rules. Although various Great Traditions and important influences have been argued for, we remain chary of claiming too much for such clearly specialized relationships. We may even doubt whether any major novelist can be normative, since becoming "major" necessarily involves an intense personalization of techniques and materials. All is not lost, however. Aware of potential dangers, we can look with some hope to the most consistently maligned and slighted works of the genre. Popular fiction.

To explain how works so slighted can qualify as normative, we must begin by establishing a provisional definition of "popular." A work is *not* popular simply because it sells well or is intended to sell well. Every "great" Victorian novelist dreams of best-sellers. And dreams come true with *David Copperfield*, *Henry Esmond*, *The Last Chronicle of Barset*, and *Middlemarch*. Hawthorne's famous phrase "a d———d mob of scribbling women"[11] was prompted precisely by his irritation at being outsold by Fanny Fern; Dickens panicked when *Martin Chuzzlewit* sold *only* twenty thousand copies; Henry James struggled his entire later life to regain the popularity which *Daisy Miller* had won him. If "popular" does not distinguish Hawthorne's desire for mass recognition and profit from Fanny Fern's, however, the word does nonetheless point up a very real difference between the two authors. In *The Sense of an Ending*, Frank Kermode's discussion of fictions may help us define that difference.

Men in the middest [*in mediis rebus*] make considerable imaginative investments in coherent patterns which, by the provision of an end, make possible a satisfying consonance with the origins and with the middle.... But they also, when awake and sane, feel the need to show a marked respect for things as they are; so that there is a recurring need for adjustments in the interest of reality as well as of control.[12]

"Reality" and "control." We read novels because—no matter how many other reasons also enter in—we enjoy the "control," the security which an ordered realm provides. On the other hand, unless we are totally bereft of mature skepticism, we also need some sense of reversal, some incursion of "reality," which qualifies our conventional expectations. "The interest of having our expectations falsified is obviously related to our wish to reach the discovery or recognition by an unexpected and instructive route" (18). What Kermode goes on to say about peripeteia can be applied to moments of reversal throughout a work.

> The more daring the peripeteia, the more we may feel that the work respects our sense of reality; and the more certainly we shall feel that the fiction under consideration is one of those which, by upsetting the ordinary balance of our naïve expectations, is finding something out for us, something *real*. The falsification of an expectation ... is a way of finding something out that we should, on our more conventional way to the end, have closed our eyes to.
>
> (18)

Since even popular novels provide, as I shall show later, more reversals and complications than highbrow critics have recognized, we cannot use "popular" and "great" as absolute categories. The difference is not of kind, but of degree. Fiction confronts us with a spectrum between the unattainable poles of the completely conventional and the absolutely nonconventional. Our question is then: to what degree does a novel which provides "control" also insist upon "reality," upon reversals which upset "the ordinary balance of our naive expectations"? The question is not whether a novel contains occasional, momentary reversals but whether it *sustains* reversals. By keeping the reversals infrequent and the endings happy, many novels minimize complexity. They provide, instead, the solace of platitude. The basic function of such fiction is to confirm the conventional assumptions and attitudes of its readers. On across the spectrum are novels which provide the security of formal control and which may well share moral and social attitudes with their readers—and yet do not function like platitudes. Instead these novels adapt conventions sufficiently to "things as they are" that we cannot "close our eyes" to the harrying reversals of reality. And so, without pretending to any absolute categories, we can call "popular" a novel which tends consistently to reaffirm basic conventions, and "great" a novel which manages consistently to transform those conventions into a personal, complicating vision of experience. Now any spectrum allows

for middle-ground, borderline cases. Interesting as these cases are
—is George Sand "popular," how about De Forest, how much of
Dickens is?—they cannot be taken up here. For my purposes, Fanny
Fern and E. D. E. N. Southworth are clearly .popular, and Nathaniel
Hawthorne and Henry James are clearly not.

Popular literature is thus normative by its very essence. It mirrors and
confirms the norms of its society. That Victorian popular fiction did
indeed mirror its readers' attitudes is established convincingly by the
sales of E. D. E. N. Southworth, Charlotte Yonge, and their many rivals
and imitators.[13] That these attitudes were shared by more than one
generation of readers is also documented readily. "From *The Vicar of
Wakefield* to *A Tree Grows in Brooklyn* the pattern has not varied
greatly."[14] Moreover, what is true of attitudes is true of technique.
Because they are espousing similar visions of reality (or unreality),
popular novelists tend to rely upon common stylistic devices. They share
these devices not only with their High Victorian contemporaries, but also
with both their predecessors in the eighteenth century and their succes-
sors in the 1870s. As Alexander Holder-Barell notes, "a comparison of
some such [common, everyday] metaphors in *Roderick Hudson* with
[*sic*] Edgeworth's *Castle Rackrent* and *Belinda* makes it obvious that
there is hardly any development to be noticed."[15]

Linking Henry James and Maria Edgeworth raises another question
about the normative quality of popular fiction. Granted that such fiction
embodied the attitudes and used the techniques which moved most
readers most often throughout the century: did major writers read their
popular peers enough to be influenced by them? The particular case of
James' voluminous knowledge of American, English, and French popular
fiction I discuss in chapter 1. For now we can say with certainty that his
great contemporaries knew the popular tradition nearly as thoroughly as
he. The same Hawthorne who raged against Fanny Fern and the "d——d
mob" wrote Fields again the following year to praise the latest best seller.
Its title was *Ruth Hall;* its author, Fanny Fern. Throughout the eighteenth
and nineteenth centuries, great writers feel toward the scribblers a
mixture of sympathy and antagonism. Fielding, Scott, Austen, Thackeray, Dickens, Eliot, Hawthorne, Melville, all spend much effort attacking contemporaries who mindlessly ape conventions. On the other hand,
what major author was not moved to tribute and tears by *Uncle Tom's
Cabin?* James himself remembers its advent "as if a fish, a wonderful
'leaping' fish, had simply flown through the air" (*SB* 160). Readers who
simplify James into a High Priest of Art may also find surprising his
judgments on other popular contemporaries. Charles Kingsley, for
example, James calls "a man of genius"; Charles Reade he finds (with no
pun apparently intended) "the most readable of living English novelists
. . . a distant kinsman of Shakespeare" (*Na* 1866, 116; 1867, 128).

So numerous, then, are the bonds between popular and great art that we should not attempt to separate them completely.

It is all too easy by overstressing their iconoclasm to give the misleading impression that the great novelists were out of tune with their times. Close study of major novelists in relation to minor ones reveals affinities at least as important as divergences.[16]

Affinities and divergences, debt to and personalization of conventional materials. Studying James' art in these terms is fostered by a fact of his biography. From James' first novel to his first major masterpiece, from *Watch and Ward* to *The Portrait of a Lady*, is a decade exactly: December 1871 to December 1881.[17] Since his next novel is nearly five years away, *The Portrait* does indeed end a stage of James' career. Two major influences, Flaubert and Eliot, had died in 1880; Mrs. James and Henry Sr. will die in 1882, and Wilkie soon after. James himself is approaching forty. Whatever he is to be, the period of precocity is over. Thus in the crucial decade 1871–81, we find isolated for study a nearly paradigmatic example of creative growth, a time when the apprentice, steeped in popular practice, moves hesitatingly and with lapses to those transformations which will alter the form of fiction.

More specifically, by comparing young James with popular scribblers, we can explain better our responses to *Watch and Ward* and *Roderick Hudson*. The stylistic techniques which James borrows most directly from popular practice are, in large part, the ones that thwart him most consistently. My aim is not of course to comment upon the effectiveness of these techniques in general or in the masterworks of particular periods; my study of epithets, for example, does not dispute that Homer achieved some success with verbal formulas. My aim is to study how Victorian scribblers and young James use hallowed stylistic techniques. By then examining these same techniques in *The Portrait of a Lady*, we can discover how much James has transformed the conventional materials of his genre, and how important they are to the effects of his masterpiece.

What we also discover is that analysis of style cannot account fully for James' development between 1871 and 1881. Words operate not only in the context of other words but also in the context of characters and their actions. Exploring the interaction of style and characterization[18] requires two distinct efforts. We must first establish that characterization involves an alchemy similar to the one which we have defined with style. Chapter 2 studies James' debt to popular methods of character portrayal: how his earliest novels incorporate conventional materials all too completely, and how he manages by 1881 to transform these same materials into great art. I say "these same materials" because I cannot agree with Karl Kroeber that "the 'originality' of a writer is in large measure the pattern of his rejections of tradition and conventions."[19] A writer is original insofar as he can revivify the conventions of his tradition by conveying his personal vision through the timeworn materials of his genre. As with James' style, we will see with his characterization that the alchemy of genre and personal elements—the affinities and the divergences—is indispensable to the meanings of his novels.[20]

Our second task, after studying their origin and development, is to show how style and characterization work together to produce effects in a single work. *Washington Square* is ideal for this purpose. It is not only James' first great novel; it is also a novel about how the individual and the artist relate to tradition. Using style here with "flat" characters, James moves us beyond romance to a thorough critique of social and literary conventions. Chapter 4 then studies how James uses style with a "rounded" character in *The Portrait* to render mental process effectively for the first time in his career. We are again involved with his debt to the popular tradition, for the scribblers (as well as such major novelists as Austen and Eliot) had long been attempting to render the workings of the mind. By examining stiff passages from *Watch and Ward* and popular novels, and by then comparing them with supple moments from *The Ambassadors*, we can set *The Portrait* in the context of James' development. This context helps us recognize the emergence of recurrent syntactic patterns which generate the illusion of a mind thinking and depend for their success upon James' achievement not only in chapter 42 (as critics often say) but repeatedly throughout the novel.

Before we begin studying the delicate alchemy of genre and personal forces in James' work, we should briefly discuss the third element which affected and was affected by his maturation. The period. As James' prose style was becoming supple enough to render the mind's relentless flow, the external world was itself in violent flux. Charles Dudley Warner recognized at the time that "the eight years in America from 1860 to 1868 uprooted institutions that were centuries old, changed the politics of a people, transformed the social life of half the country, and wrought so profoundly upon the entire national character that the influence cannot be measured short of two or three generations."[21] Together with the changes which historians invariably catalog—the rise of the steel industry, the mechanization of agriculture, the advent of labor unions, the substitution of petroleum for whale oil, the development of the typewriter, telephone, electric light, phonograph, gasoline engine, improved cameras[22]—such other exotic changes as the advent of the bustle in 1870 and the growing disenchantment with Modern Spiritualism throughout the decade, *all* indicate that James' milieu was changing as fast as his style. The rise of the "money power" and the expanding immigration affected social life drastically. Howells laments that since 1875 "men and women in the best company talk together of things which would not have been discussed during the second and third quarters of the century."[23] Although Howells' inveterate gentility must qualify this evaluation somewhat, critics then and now tend to agree that taste did decline as the new rich rose.

Intellectually, comparable changes and uncertainties appear. The impact of Comte, Spencer, Darwin, Mill, and Zola is repeatedly documented among the younger intelligentsia. That more general spiritual dislocation which appeared as James began writing and continued on into the Great War which he did not survive, is summed up admirably by R. H. Gretton:

> A Rip Van Winkle of 1810, waking into 1850, would have been completely bewildered by the steam-engine; but he might have passed the remainder of his life in conversation which he would have enjoyed and found reasonably familiar. A Rip Van Winkle of 1870, waking in 1910, while he would have grasped the principle of the motor car in twenty minutes, would never have been on conversational terms with his neighbors; he would have found that he did not know what they were talking about.[24]

This postwar time in America, this "period of hesitation and uncertainty, a curious blend of the old and the new,"[25] shows its mixed character especially in its use of words. Oratory, essay, history, drama, fiction: all are "mixed" genres in the Victorian period because all attempt, as the century progresses, to shuck off certain eighteenth-century and early romantic stylistic influences. These genres are also mixed in several, more particular senses. Each genre contains in any decade practitioners of both the old-fashioned and the "new" styles; each genre will frequently display in single passages both old-fashioned and new stylistic devices; each genre can claim for most of its innovations but mixed success, at best; and, finally, each genre in its struggles affects and is affected by the toils of the others. Today few critics still support the Brooks-Parrington thesis that Henry James was an ivory tower émigré aloof from the turmoil of his times. More and more we realize that James in his development and fiction—and especially in his early development and early fiction—experienced the same struggles as the writers whose work he knew well. Let us discuss briefly how the oratory, essay, history, drama, and fiction of this changing period related to the young apprentice of prose style.

Edmund Wilson argues that "a change in American style takes place in the middle of the century. The plethora of words is reduced; the pace becomes firmer and quicker."[26] Wilson goes on to discuss oratory. "Both Higginson . . . and Lowell . . . speak of Lincoln as the much-needed innovator in a terser less pretentious style" (639–40). Wilson effectively contrasts "The Gettysburg Address" with both Sumner's "The Crime of

Kansas" bombast and Everett's flowery display at Gettysburg. Although additional support for his thesis is available,[27] Wilson, by not citing contradictory evidence, suggests for plain style a triumph which postwar speeches do not substantiate. E. G. Parker, writing elegiacally in 1857, does indeed proclaim the end of the Golden Age of American oratory, but what Parker is lamenting is the decline of eloquence into bombast, not the rise of plain style.[28] Colloquial elements do enter public speaking from the West ("farmers should raise less corn and more hell") and from the urban proletarian movements, but even rural and proletarian oratory is, as Larzer Ziff has shown, very mixed stylistically.[29] Moreover, many heralded orators of the postwar period—whom Wilson does not mention at all—practice a style anything but plain. We need only think of the "oriental style" of prodigiously famous Bob Ingersoll.[30] Or there is William M. Evarts, probably the most noted legal orator of his day, who "took Cicero as the model . . . for the splendor and copiousness of his style."[31] Among politicians in the period when the bloody shirt waved, the eloquence of Albert J. Beveridge of Indiana was particularly esteemed; only at the turn of the century did Beveridge temper "what might be called 'the higher florid' [style]. . . . marked by thrilling climaxes."[32] In the South, prewar grandiloquence characterized two of the most famous postwar speakers. The boy wonder of Georgia, Henry W. Grady, "was most typical of the school of flowery speech, with Colonel W. C. P. Breckenridge of Lexington, Kentucky, a close second."[33] And so, although examples can be cited on both sides of the question, and although public speaking was, on the whole, chastened somewhat as it entered the twentieth century, it remained overall a definitely mixed medium. Henry James' complex connections with oratory I discuss in chapter 1; for now we should realize that James in his formative years experienced a tradition hallowed by the immense prestige of the Golden Age speakers and subject after the war to an uncertain blend of antiquated fanciness and plain style.

Both the essay and the history presented similar stylistic mixtures. The Victorian sages, especially Newman and Arnold in England and Emerson and Whitman in America, were seeking to replace rep-essive vestiges of later eighteenth-century style with a colloquial diction and syntax which would convey the experience of a mind thinking. In America particularly, the influence of the war, of newspaper prose, and of the generally accelerated pace of life produced a style which—in the essays of Higginson and Howells and in the memoirs of Grant, Sherman, and Sheridan—was blessedly less ornate and leisurely. (It was by his prose style, we must remember, that Grant first earned Lincoln's admiration.)[34] How uphill the stylistic revolution was, however, becomes clear when we contrast these individual triumphs with the intransigency of most essayists and editors. Committed to maintaining Genteel Standards, these writers preserved (with some slight amelioration) a style which embodied their standards. The following piece of literary criticism is at least as representative of day-to-day Victorian expository prose as Higginson or Grant is.

> To read "The Initials" is to call back the days of one's youth, when the future was rosy with hope, and when all things were fresh and beautiful. . . . We know no fiction, in fact, which we would sooner recommend, for while it will fascinate all who read merely for amusement, it will delight as well as improve those who seek for something even in a novel.[35]

Necessarily an amalgam of fact and insight, history was a particularly mixed mode in nineteenth-century America because its major practitioners were "literary." At their best, Prescott, Motley, and Parkman turned consciously away from the later eighteenth-century ideal of style.[36] Prescott allows "no *words, epithets, that do not make it [the text] clearer, or stronger. Figures* I dislike—unless they conduce highly to both these ends."[37] Instead the historians turn to three other genres.

> These writers compared history to drama almost as often as they compared it to painting. . . . It was the dramatic effect of Rubens' *Descent from the Cross* that Motley praised.
>
> (Levin, 19, 20)

Besides drama and painting, the other model for dramatic intensity was fiction itself. In structure the historians followed Abbé de Mably's injunction to pay "such attention to the development of events tending to this leading result, as one would in the construction of a romance";[38] in characterization they sought to replace abstract ideas with personages as "picturesque" as Walter Scott's. Instead of becoming fully dramatic, however, their histories remain stylistically mixed. Not only were their models mixed themselves, but the three writers—Parkman offending least—were sufficiently torn between their romantic and their New England inclinations that they never completely eschewed either Byronic rhetoric or intrusive moralizing.

James' relation to these great historians has never been adequately documented. The very atmosphere of his apprentice years was saturated with the presence and prestige of history writing. The monthly which first befriended him, the *North American Review*, "was almost as much a historical publication as a literary one from the twenties through the Civil War,"[39] and the *Atlantic* boasted Prescott as one of its founders. Moreover, James knew the great historians, and not only socially (it was Motley who first secured him admittance to the London Atheneum).[40] Twice before 1875 James reviewed Parkman's forest history.[41] In an early review of historical novels, James links Motley with Balzac in terms of fidelity to the dramatic situation (*Na* 1867, 126). As "literary" men who wrote fiction and criticism,[42] the American historians struggled with problems—reconciling fact and fancy, blending drama and commentary, mastering hyperbole, declamation, and tableau—which had obvious relevance for a literary apprentice contending with loose baggy monsters of his own.

Drama in the nineteenth century, though inevitably prey to the declamatory mode, did parallel the other genres in a movement to more colloquial, realistic style. Critics of both British and American theater agree about "theater's slow movement toward more realistic dramatic treatment in the second half of the century."[43] Style changed accordingly. Archaic, abstract diction and stiff, literary syntax give place gradually and grudgingly to more colloquial speech patterns. Jones' *The Silver King* marks an important step in this development, for, as Matthew Arnold noted, "the diction and sentiments do not overstep the modesty of nature."[44] Acting itself becomes somewhat chastened under the impact of Belasco's "subdued colloquial style" and "the quiet, natural acting of William Gillette."[45] These changes, of course, were not complete. Jones' heralded modesty of diction still allows poor beset Nellie to declaim, "Merciful Father, help me now!"[46] And the revisions which James himself makes for the play versions of *The American* and *Daisy Miller* and the stylistic traits which I study in chapter 1, all show how endemic to nineteenth-century prose the style and conventions of melodrama were.

Traditionally an uneasy and scarcely respectable blend of essay, drama, oratory, history, sermon, travel book, guide to morals and etiquette, tract and exposé, biography and autobiography, the novel after the Civil War became still more mixed. Its formal triumphs were, at best, qualified; and the disparity between its few innovators and its many practitioners was great. Among its formal triumphs were the increased sophistication of its rendering of mental processes and the addition to its prose of sufficient colloquial leaven to achieve what Wilson calls finely "the language of responsibility."[47] As a major contributor to both achievements, Mark Twain manifests how qualified the triumph was. For, as critics have noted and as Twain himself knew, his rejection of hollow official language was never complete and rarely sustained. De Forest and Howells, as lesser writers, reveal still more the failure of good intentions. De Forest's consistent call for an end to old conventions and style is consistently belied by his own fiction; and how far Howells' new realism ever gets beyond surface details and occasional colloquialisms is questionable. Moreover, as there are two Twains, De Forests, and Howellses, so the major new English novelist after the war also struggled to control and integrate two styles.

There is the Hardy who can recreate dialect speech with flawless
authenticity . . . and there is the Hardy speaking to "the quality" in
orotund sentences of laboured syntax and learned vocabulary. . . .
It is probably the second Hardy who is responsible for the most
spectacular stylistic lapses.[48]

The mixed quality of the period is compounded by the disparity
between fiction's few innovators and its many mindlessly conventional
practitioners. If Edmund Wilson can find some examples of "the language
of responsibility," Larzer Ziff has much more evidence for his definition
of postwar fiction as "the business of adding 'est' to verbs" (14). Harold
Martin may—heroically—manage to discover some instances of colloquialism in Thomas Bailey Aldrich (139), but John Tomsich convicts the
genteel writers with the voluminous evidence of their own timidity and
evasion.[49] Their attempts to check the changing times with a static,
Augustan vision perpetuated a brittle syntax and enervated diction
which, in turn, helped perpetuate what might be called a national state of
stylistic schizophrenia.

The two types of stylistic mixture which I have been defining—the
individual and the cultural—come together in one of the period's great
bagatelles. Mark Twain, capable of genteel maunderings but in "The
Double-Barreled Detective Story" proving his greatness, composes a
nonsense passage full of hallowed expressions unrelated by theme and
not always related by syntax. "Far in the empty sky a solitary esophagus
slept upon motionless wing; everywhere brooded stillness, serenity, and
the peace of God."[50] His readers loved it, of course.

Twain's greatest American contemporary also cannot resist parodying
the language and situations beloved of mass audiences.

A Romance in 3 volumes. By 'Arry Jeames, alias G. P. R. author of the
"beacon beacon beacon light" etc. Vol. I. Part I. Book I. Chap. I. The
morning broke! High into the vast unclouded vault of Heving rode the
Awb of Day. . . . and the jew on the vine-leaves which clothe with a
garment of sweetest verdure its fair encastled banks glittered with a
rarer lustre than e'er did priceless diamond on a proud bewty's neck.

Henry James here is seventeen (*EL* 40). Over the next years he finds
writing serious fiction more difficult than parodying bad work, and his
own serious efforts reveal, like most efforts of his contemporaries, an
uncertain mixture of old-fashioned and newer, more direct writing.

[Rowland] submitted without reserve to the great national discipline
which began in 1861. When the Civil War broke out he immediately
obtained a commission, and did his duty for three long years as a
citizen soldier.

                                                                    (*RH* 14)

Denotatively both sentences *say* the same thing. They *mean* differently, however, because we experience the clauses in different ways, like swimming through currents of various temperatures. "He immediately obtained his commission" corresponds simply and directly to the action involved; it has the "responsibility" of the style of Grant, Sheridan, and Sherman. On the other hand, the surrounding diction—"submitted . . . the great national discipline . . . citizen soldier"—rings hollow. We cease feeling Rowland's individual situation and confront an official stereotype whom we cannot care for. This stylistic mixture is what prevents us from studying James solely in terms of the great tradition: he does not begin writing with the finish of Hawthorne, Thackeray, or Flaubert. Although every epoch is mixed and transitional, and although every artist, especially in his early years, struggles with the old and new, Henry James reveals the particular uncertainty of the period in what even he admitted was a long apprenticeship.[51] He recapitulates much of the struggle which we have seen in oratory, essay, history, drama, and fiction. Coming to maturity at a time when style is increasingly terse and flexible, James cannot begin at the wave's crest; he must make again many of the century's mistakes and must conquer for himself what earlier artists had already won.

This process is particularly valuable for us to study because it is, finally, so paradigmatic. In his development from the school of popular fiction, James recapitulates the careers of most major Victorian novelists. Hawthorne and Dickens and Howells: how much their early work, *Fanshawe, Pickwick, A Modern Instance,* resembles James' attempts to use popular materials which he cannot quite believe in; how much these writers owe to the oratory, essay, history, drama of the period. From James' career we can learn a good deal about the development of the artistic consciousness in the nineteenth century. We may also recognize in his stylistic triumph the artist's human, moral triumph as well. For we can see the artist live out his belief that " 'literature was a game of skill, and skill meant courage, and courage meant honour, and honour meant passion, meant life' " (*Nb* 224). We will see him have the courage of his honest arrogance, as he makes good on a promise—Victorian son and brother.

> It is time I should rend the veil from the ferocious ambition which has always *couvé* beneath a tranquil exterior; which enabled me to support unrecorded physical misery in my younger years; and which is perfectly confident of accomplishing serious things. . . . If I keep along here patiently I rather think I shall become a (sufficiently) great man.
>
> (*E2,* 105)

1

Tradition and Style

> She didn't give their tradition up; she but made of it something new.
>
> *Henry James*

> Philosophicum illum proverbium non solum moribus sed etiam verbis esse necessarium: ne quid nimis. (This maxim is true not only for morals but also for style—nothing in excess.)
>
> *Alcuin to Charlemagne*

> I am convinced that I cannot exaggerate enough even to lay the foundation of a true expression.
>
> *Henry David Thoreau*

> To speak is to fall into tautologies.
>
> *Borges*

Called by his father "a devourer of libraries" (*E*1:94),[1] young Henry James read so widely and listed titles so randomly that we will never know all he devoured. The very incompleteness of the huge list which we can compile, however, confirms how thoroughly familiar James was with popular fiction. By the time of his last apprentice novel, *Roderick Hudson*, in the middle of the crucial decade, James had definitely read the following scribbling women:

Louisa May Alcott (*Moods* and *Eight Cousins; or The Aunt Hill*), Mary Elizabeth Braddon (*Lady Audley's Secret, Aurora Floyd*, and others), Charlotte Brontë (all the major novels), Mrs. E. R. Charles (*The Schönberg-Cotta Family, The Diary of Mrs. Kitty Travylyan, Winifred Bertram and the World She Lived In*, plus others), Mrs. D. M. M. Craik (*A Noble Life, John Halifax, Gentleman*, and others), Maria S. Cummins (*The Lamplighter*), Mrs. Rebecca Harding Davis (*Waiting for the Verdict, Dallas Galbraith*), Maria Edgeworth (*The Parent's Assistant* and others), Mrs. Frances Eliot (*The Italians: A Novel*), Mrs. T. Erskine (*Wyncote*), Mrs. Gaskell (*Cranford, Wives and Daughters*, and others), Mrs. C. Jenkins (*Within an Ace*, and others), Anne E. Manning (*The Household of Sir Thomas More, Jacques

Bonneval, or The Days of the Dragonnades), Hannah More (tales), Mrs. Oliphant (*White Ladies* and others), Ouida (*Signa: A Story* and others), Miss Elizabeth Stuart Phelps (*Hedged In*), H. E. Prescott (*Azarian: An Episode, The Amber Gods, The Rim, Sir Rohan's Ghost*), Mrs. Radcliffe (*The Mysteries of Udolpho* and the other major novels), Mrs. A. M. C. Seemuller (*Emily Chester, Opportunity*), Elizabeth Stoddard (*The Morgesons* and *Two Men: A Novel*), Mrs. Stowe (*Uncle Tom's Cabin, Old Town Folks, We and Our Neighbors*, and others), Miss Thackeray (*Miss Angel* and others), Baroness von Tautphoeus (*The Initials*), Miss L. B. Walford (*Mr. Smith*), Susan Warner (*The Wide, Wide World*), Mrs. A. D. T. Whitney (*The Gayworthys: A Story of Threads and Thrums*), Mrs. Henry Wood (*East Lynne*), Charlotte Yonge (*The Heir of Redclyffe, The Daisy Chain*).[2]

Anything but discriminating, James also read the popular male authors:

Thomas Bailey Aldrich (prose as well as verse), Bulwer-Lytton (the major fiction), Wilkie Collins (*Woman in White* and other short and long fiction), Frederick Swartwout Cozzens [alias Richard Haywarde] (burlesques), George William Curtis (various short pieces), Benjamin Disraeli (*Lothair* and other major novels), J. W. De Forest (*Honest John Vane* and others), A. J. Froude (*Short Stories on Great Subjects*), Julian Hawthorne (*Idolatry, Bressant*), Oliver Wendell Holmes, Sr. (*Elsie Venner, The Guardian Angel*), Charles Kingsley (*Westward Ho!, Two Years Ago, Hereward the Wake, Hypatia, Yeast, Alton Locke*), Henry Kingsley (*The Hillyars and the Burtons: A Story of Two Families*), G. A. Lawrence (*Guy Livingstone*), Captain Marryat ("several . . . productions"), "Ike Marvel" (short and long fiction), James Payn (*Lost Sir Massingberd*), George S. Phillips (*The Gypsies of the Danes Dike*), Charles Reade (*The Cloister and the Hearth, Never Too Late to Mend, Griffith Gaunt*, and others), Henry D. Sedley (*Marian Rooke*), Bayard Taylor (*John Godfrey's Fortunes* and other fiction), T. A. Trollope (*Lindisfarne Chase: A Novel*), Artemus Ward (tales), George Whyte-Melville (various pieces).[3]

Although James' immersion in what he later called "the fashionable trash of Victorian times" lessens somewhat after *Roderick Hudson*, he nevertheless mentions the following authors between 1876 and 1881:

Frank Lee Benedict (*St. Simon's Niece*), William Black (*Macleod of Dare, Madcap Violet, Princess of Thule, The Three Feathers, Adventures of a Phaethon*), Rhoda Broughton (*Cometh Up as a Flower, Joan*), Charles H. Doe (*Buffets*), Mrs. Annie Edwards (*Leah: A Woman of Fashion*), Julia Constance Fletcher (*Kismet, Mirage*), Mrs. Gore (both short and long fiction), Julian Hawthorne (*Garth*), Helen Hunt Jackson (*Mercy Philbrick's Choice*), J. G. Lockhart (*Adam Blair*), Laurence Oliphant (*The Tender Recollections of Irene Macgillicuddy*), Edmund Yates (short and long fiction).[4]

Incomplete as these lists necessarily are—both because James did not compile them himself and because they are drawn from barely half his long lifetime of reading—the lists do seem to confirm Cargill's sense of James as "the *widest*, if not the *best*, read American of his day."[5]

To understand how popular fiction influences James' early work, we must forgo the highbrow assumption that popular techniques are themselves inadequate or "bad." Clearly they have given pleasure to millions of readers for generations. The rub is, however, that popular practice achieves effects and reflects attitudes at variance with the effects and attitudes that James comes to revere most. Basically, Victorian popular fiction presents a static world of immutable truths. Instead of combining the pleasure of formal control with what Kermode calls "a marked respect for things as they are," such fiction aims simply at satisfying mass needs. Which are basically two. Primarily the average Victorian reader wants security, wants reassurance that God is in His heaven or at least that order remains on earth. Popular fiction provides this security by replacing "things as they are" with idealized situations and happy endings. "Everywhere in popular fiction there was a tendency to idealize or to shy away from what Mitchell has disparagingly called the 'definite, sharp business' of reality."[6] For a style to render and mirror their safely ordered unrealities, the scribblers use devices sanctioned by the revered equipoise of neoclassical literature—the distancing diction of generalized nouns and formulas, and a rigorously patterned syntax of antithesis and balance.

The second basic need of popular audiences—a craving for violent action and emotion—might seem opposed to the first. In fact, however, this need complements the need for security. With order assured and morality absolute, readers can safely indulge their all too human desire for excitation. Delight in hairbreadth escapes, touching deaths, violent confrontations—and in the style that goes with them—is justified by that man of the people, Diderot. "We must have exclamations, interjections . . . we call, we invoke, we shout, we sigh, we shed tears, we laugh loudly. No refined wit, no epigrams, none of these prettily turned thoughts; that is too far from simple nature."[7] Although stylistic extravagance is, as Diderot notes, antithetical to the pretty equipoise of neoclassical epigrams, these two very different styles appear together consistently in Victorian popular fiction. And in James' early novels. His reviews belittle the popular needs for violent extravagance and pretty unrealities, but his early fiction relies consistently upon the two styles that reflect and satisfy these needs.

Why? Two styles so different can appear together consistently because both styles contribute finally to a single effect. The language of extravagance so distorts actions and the language of equipoise so controls them that, in Kermode's terms, our eyes are closed to things as they are. Especially when authors do not insist upon countering reversals, we escape too far from the intransigence of daily life and enter a world of words breathtakingly gaudy and reassuringly precise. James' gradual transformation of the styles of extravagance and equipoise is thus more than an aesthetic act (if there is such a thing). As he makes his prose his own, James is facing life more directly. He is combining Kermode's "control" and "reality." By gaining enough control over conventional materials to upset "the ordinary balance of our naive expectations," James manages both to open our eyes to things as they are and to provide us with the pleasurable security of formal order. Style is thus an act of love. It teaches and consoles.

The language of extravagance and the language of equipoise: we can best understand James' use and gradual transformation of these styles if we compare his practice with his popular peers'. Because of his huge reading, any comparison can remain manageable only if the number of normative works is limited severely. So, I refer primarily to three novels which James had definitely read by 1871—those favorites *The Heir of Redclyffe* by Charlotte Yonge, *The Initials* by Baroness von Tautphoeus, and *The Wide, Wide World* by Susan Warner.[8] Then, to establish how representative of the popular tradition these works are, I draw often upon two best-sellers which James apparently had not read—*St. Elmo* by Augusta Jane Evans and *Ishmael* by E. D. E. N. Southworth. Occasional examples also come from other popular novels which James knew, particularly Holmes' *Elsie Venner*, Cherbuliez' *Le Roman d'une honnête femme*, Charlotte Brontë's *Villette*, and Mrs. Gaskell's *Ruth*.

The great objection to words is
they are always oversaying
things.

W. D. Howells

Extravagance

Especially since Henry James, Sr., was, in Edward Emerson's
words, a "master of the superlative," Henry James, Jr., grew up in a
milieu alive with heightened language. "His childhood taste for the bigger
than life, the garish"[9] was part of the young nation's hunger for enormities
of every kind. By 1877 James can present a protagonist who "had sat with
Western humorists in knots, round cast-iron stoves, and seen 'tall'
stories grow taller without toppling over" (*Ame* 98). The first critic to
convincingly locate James within the American tradition of tall talk was
Constance Rourke, who saw him "grounded in the Yankee fable."[10]
D. W. Jefferson has expanded upon this notion. "A feeling for the 'tall
tale,' a delight in 'building high,' is, of course, one of the great assets of an
American narrator. And James can be thoroughly American in this
respect."[11] If this position has a weakness, it is its failure to overcome our
suspicion that the cosmopolitan James did not know the tall tale
tradition well enough to be influenced strongly by it. Rourke answers
this objection partially by stressing that "during James's boyhood the
streets of New York were alive with the color of the California
adventure" (188). Recently, still stronger evidence has appeared. Charlton Laird has shown convincingly that extravagant talk did not, in fact,
begin as a frontier phenomenon. Citing John Russell Bartlett, "who can
probably be called the first serious student of American English," Laird
notes that "Bartlett was aware of verbal exaggeration in his day, but he
was inclined to attribute it to the bad taste of relatively few parvenus, not
to the American ethos in its frontier manifestation."[12] Laird's research
confirms Bartlett's judgment. Reading newspapers from the decade
before Henry James' birth, Laird finds that "frontier braggadocio . . .
may be no more than the vaporings of lively journalists" (356). And not
frontier journalists either. "What was frontier journalism like? . . .
pallid, moral, conventional, conservative, and dull. . . . of wit, even of
blatant braggadocio, there was almost none" (369, 363). Rather, it is an
eastern editorial which is discussing verbal extravagance in 1839.

"The Editor of the *Philadelphia Gazette* is wrong in calling
absquatiated a Kentucky *phrase*. . . . It may prevail there, but its

origin was in South Carolina, where it was a few years since regularly derived from the Latin, as we can prove from undoubted authority."

(362)

Laird then points the moral.

One might notice here that South Carolina was by no means the frontier in the 1830's, that at least one editor recognized the word as a Latin coinage, and that the folklore was apparently already growing that this sort of thing was characteristic of Kentucky.[13]

And so, extravagant as frontier speech undoubtedly is (especially after the 1830s), there is enough tall talk in the eastern papers of James' omnivorous youth to feed his boyish love of extravagance. By the time James begins writing for publication, the American tradition of tall talk and tale is part of his critical and artistic vocabulary. In 1866, for example, he criticizes a popular author's use of "the traditional Sam Slick dialect," and in 1876 he criticizes a popular character for "speaking a barbarous dialect of the 'American humour' family" (*Na* 1866, 248; 1876, 372). In turn he promises Howells "some tall writing" (*HJL* 444). In 1878 James refers in one of his own stories to "American humour," and in 1879 discusses "[our] national gift, that 'American humour' of which of late years we have heard so much" (*CT* 2:254; *Ha* 48).

James' actual use of the style of extravagance, however, involves considerably more than these references suggest. The young apprentice was open, not only to American tall talk, but to several other sources of verbal exaggeration. The stage, for instance. Young Henry's attendance at the leading theaters of the day is well known; the plays he thrilled to were splendidly hyperthyroid. Speaking in "luscious superlatives," Heroes and Heroines were "bedecked with all kinds of superlative virtues."[14] Nor were the Heroes and Heroines of popular fiction less superlative. From the eighteenth century onward, the "boisterous exaggeration . . . and schoolroom idealism"[15] of the heirs of Samuel Richardson were sanctioned by Richardson's own, if less boisterous, hyperbole.

> Her conversation how instructive! how sought after! The delight of persons of all ages, of both sexes, of all ranks! Yet how humble, how condescending! Never were dignity and humility so illustriously mingled! . . . her shape was so fine, her proportion so exact, her features so regular, her complexion so lovely, and her whole person and manner so distinguishedly charming, that she could not move without being admired and followed by the eyes of every one though strangers, who never saw her before.[16]

In Victorian times, womanly perfection is championed not only by the best novelists (usually writing at their worst), but also by successive Poets Laureate.

> And now I see with eye serene
> . . . .
> A perfect Woman, nobly planned,
> To warn, to comfort, and command;
> And yet a Spirit still, and bright
> With something of angelic light.
> (Wordsworth, "She Was a Phantom of Delight")

> "But if you be that Ida whom I knew,
> I ask you nothing: only, if a dream,
> Sweet dream, be perfect."
> (Tennyson, *The Princess*)

Sufficient as these sanctions would have been for popular writers, perfection (and a style to render it) also boasted one other, supreme sanction.

> Be ye therefore perfect, even as your Father which is in heaven is perfect.
> (Matt. 5:48)

Religion itself encouraged the tendency to extreme statement in authors who were for the most part stridently Christian and who, denominational or not, wrote with expressly didactic ends. Since God was in his heaven, all was right with the next world. "Perfect" indeed. In *The Heir of Redclyffe*, Guy's "soul was with Him with whom dwell the spirits of just men made perfect. . . . Guy was perfectly happy" (2:210, 211). Alice in *The Wide, Wide World* is " 'perfectly' " happy on her deathbed because she is about to achieve the book's ideal—to " 'join the spirits of the just made perfect' " (457, 292). This heavenly perfection is officially denied to men on earth, of course.

> "Oh, I don't keep His commandments!" said Ellen, the tears running down her cheeks.
> "*Perfectly*, none of us do. But, dear Ellen, *that* is not the question."
> (*WWW* 253)

In practice, however, the word "perfect" does characterize certain earthly lives. Guy's death beatifies Amy, who "wished to make her mother share the perfect peace" (*HR* 2:222). Indeed God's " 'perfect law' " can be followed on this earth " 'when a child of God lives as he ought to' " (*WWW* 249).

As a reviewer Henry James repeatedly criticizes stylistic extravagance. He connects verbal excess with moralistic stridency, even when the writer (as in the case of Vernon Lee) is not expressly religious. "Moral passion.... has put certain exaggerations, overstatements, *grossisse-ments*, insistences wanting in tact, into your head" (*EL* 239). Giving to actors, critics, poets the same message—that "the touch of life is lighter" (*EL* 238)[17]—James saves his most graphic image for novelists. "To endeavor to fortify flimsy conceptions by the constant use of verbal superlatives is like painting the cheeks and pencilling the eyebrows of a corpse" (*NAR* 1865, 276). On the positive side, James' model, as early as 1874, is Turgenev. "His rare discretion serves him, and rescues him from the danger of exaggerating" (*FrP* 233).

Before we study how James in his early fiction fails to heed his own admonitions against exaggeration, we should examine one last admonition to the same effect, one which critics have largely ignored and which comes from a most unlikely quarter. The popular tradition itself. In *The Heir of Redclyffe* everyone learns the value of moderation. Guy's tendency to get " 'perfectly beside himself with anger' " (1:11) soon leads him to a " 'foolish exaggeration' " (1:69) which he must apologize for. Since he is the increasingly ideal protagonist, Guy learns the lesson of moderation more quickly than the other main characters. When Mr. Edmonstone judges Guy precipitately, Philip "defended Guy from the exaggerations" (1:280). Guy then repays the favor, "defending Philip against the exaggerated abuse" of Mr. Edmonstone and Charlie (2:64). As the Edmonstones continue to struggle with exaggeration, Philip's inner conflict comes increasingly to the fore. Unconsciously jealous of Guy, Philip repeatedly makes judgments so sweeping that we are distrustful. " 'I wish to be perfectly just.... he [Guy] was habitually ex-tremely imprudent' " (1:38, 2:63). The enormity of his exaggerations strikes Philip only after Guy's death, when he recognizes in his vicious sister's words an "exaggerated likeness of his own self complacent speeches" (2:254). Brought to a more moderate vision, Philip still cannot achieve Guy's moderation. " 'Over-worked in parliament, doing nothing in moderation' " (2:326), Philip can carry on only because Laura has sufficiently outgrown her exaggerated idolization of him that "there was far more peace and truth before them than when she believed him infallible, and therefore justified herself for all she had done in blind obedience to him" (2:353).

In *The Initials*, the theme of moderation appears even before page one, for the title page quotes the *Ladies' National Magazine* that "this novel ... has nothing forced or exaggerated about it." Although this statement is itself exaggerated, its moral is exemplary enough to receive the ultimate sanction—"his mother said that moderation should be observed in all things" (*In* 88). No mama's boy, the villainous Raimund declaims, " 'I desire nothing more than that matters should come to extremities' " (264). Fair Hildegarde, who "went from one extreme to the other" (158), is fortunate enough to find in the gallant Hamilton a " 'judge, Mentor, or whatever you please, for I am convinced that you only dislike me just enough to see my faults without exaggerating them' " (175). Likewise in *St. Elmo* an authority figure warns, " 'Take care, Gordon, I notice that of late you seem inclined to deal rather too freely in hyperbole' " (423–24).

Thus, insofar as Henry James manages in his earliest novels to affirm moderation and the middle way, he has learned not simply from major novelists[18] but from the popular tradition as well. In *Watch and Ward* Roger and Nora begin with ideas of love as exaggerated as Laura's. Roger wonders, " 'how can I have for her [Nora] that charm of infallibility, that romance of omniscience, that a woman demands of her lover?' " (325).[19] Nora, likewise, is initially extravagant. " 'It's very well for her to talk about life-long devotion and eternal gratitude. She doesn't know the meaning of words' " (326). What words mean is what each character must learn, for all the characters tend to overstate and overreact. "Mrs. Keith repented of this extra touch of zeal" with Hubert and "was frightened at her work" with Nora (590, 596). Romantic Nora's own extravagant diction—"she wished to do something [for Roger] . . . not only to prove, but forever to commemorate, her devotion" (587)— generates in us an uneasiness which the facts soon justify. Nora is falling for handsome Hubert. But misfortune soon teaches her better. Recognizing in Hubert's portrait a "superficial" man (706), she can then appreciate the truer beauty of Roger's homely features. *Roderick Hudson* points a similar moral. Homely Rowland, who, "as we know, was not fond of exploding into superlatives" (165), survives to woo (if futilely) the faithful Mary, whereas extremity-prone Roderick plunges Byronically into the abyss.

1

Aware of the inadequacy of extreme reaction and expression, popular writers and early James cannot, alas, resist the gaudy splendor of hyperbole. To study their practice I will use both of the basic methods of stylistics: quantitative and qualitative analyses. The quantitative approach to style—with its paraphernalia of statistics and computers—has achieved few striking successes and has met justified scholarly resistance. Distrust of numbers and of the pseudo-sciences should not, however, blind us to the importance of quantity. Critics too often seem to make mountains out of a single line or usage. Although the brute fact of frequency is no absolute guarantee, a technique important to the meaning of a work and basic to the mind of an author will—generally— recur with some frequency and at important moments in the work. This assumption is particularly central to my study because I want to demonstrate the *extensiveness* of James' initial commitment to popular practice. If quantitative analysis cannot, by itself, establish this commitment, it can make a beginning strong enough to justify more detailed analysis of the *quality* of James' hyperbole. Moreover, data can help us account for our reading experience. Repeated immersion in extravagant, hollow language must affect our response to a text. James would not have referred later to the "disgraceful and disreputable style of *Roderick Hudson*" and would not have called the novel "quite *vilely* written" (*LL* 2:55) if its qualitative inadequacy had not been quantitatively abundant.

The abundance of extravagant language in popular fiction derives from three related but distinct techniques. One is the bunching of intensifiers with certain themes. Is any ear good enough to distinguish Baroness von Tautphoeus in *The Initials* from Henry James in *Roderick Hudson?*

> Remarkably pretty . . . . "superlatively handsome" . . . . "so very handsome" . . . . "perfect model of female loveliness" . . . . "most beautiful" . . . . "very handsome" . . . . "perfectly beautiful" . . . . a perfect Hebe . . . . extremely pretty . . . . "singularly handsome" . . . . "very good-looking" . . . . so remarkably handsome . . . . perfect face and figure . . . . "remarkably handsome" . . . . "very good-looking" . . . . "very pretty" . . . . "uncommonly good-looking" . . . . "very beautiful" . . . . "very pretty . . . very handsome" . . . . never . . . so lovely . . . . very pretty . . . . so fresh and beautiful . . . . "very handsome" . . . . "never . . . so pretty" . . . . "very pretty" . . . . "very beautiful" . . . . "the handsomest girl."

> Remarkably handsome . . . . admirably chiseled . . . . most beautiful . . . . "most beautiful" . . . . "wonderfully beautiful" . . . . remarkably beautiful . . . . very becoming . . . uncommonly pretty . . . . wonderfully beautiful . . . . extraordinary beauty . . . . divinely beautiful . . . . perfect face . . . . "most beautiful" . . . . incomparably beautiful . . . . never . . . so beautiful . . . . "most beautiful" . . . . "wonderfully pretty" . . . . most beautiful . . . . "greatest beauty" . . . . strikingly beautiful . . . . "very beautiful" . . . . "most beautiful" . . . . "most beautiful" . . . . "very beautiful" . . . . "what a beautiful person" . . . . "most beautiful" . . . . "most beautiful" . . . . "the loveliest of women" . . . . extremely handsome . . . . a supreme beauty . . . . "never . . . so beautiful" . . . . "too beautiful" . . . . the purity of her beauty . . . . "impossible beauty" . . . . exquisite beauty . . . . more beautiful than ever . . . . "incomparably beautiful" . . . . admirably handsome.

James' assertions of perfect beauty (the second group)[20] resemble the Baroness' so thoroughly because he is sharing more than simply her tendency to exaggerate. He is using the *same* exaggerations. Especially when we recognize how many other heightened expressions James shares with the popular tradition—"perfect stillness," "perfectly grave," "perfectly conscious," "perfectly unconscious," "perfect weather," "remember perfectly"—we see that the diction of extravagance is not only unconvincing in itself. It is repetitious and conventional enough to be almost formulaic.

Fortunately for James, *Roderick Hudson* marks his last infatuation with perfect beauty. Already in *The American* he is qualifying the heroine's pulchritude. " 'She [Claire] is not a beauty, but she is beautiful, two very different things.' . . . if she was beautiful, it was not a dazzling beauty" (37–38, 83). In *The Portrait* Isabel Archer's beauty is presented even more tentatively. "Nineteen persons out of twenty (including the younger sister herself) pronounced Edith infinitely the prettier of the two; but the twentieth, besides reversing this judgement, had the entertainment of thinking all the others a parcel of fools" (32). We do not doubt which judgment is correct, of course. Besides the appeal to our instinctive snobbery, James is now capitalizing upon our instinctive distrust of hyperbole. "Infinitely the prettier" is sweeping enough to seem ill-considered, and we opt for Isabel. Although this preference is repeatedly seconded by characters throughout the novel,[21] James manages to make each expression of praise so symptomatic of its speaker—as with Caspar's " 'the most beautiful young woman of her time' " (33–34)—that the very absence of express narrative endorsement qualifies the superlative sufficiently. Moreover, the word "perfect" appears in *The Portrait* with only one physical feature: hands "of a perfect shape—a shape so perfect" (162). Beautiful hands are, of course, a trait conventional with heroines. As early as 1713, the expression "the finest Hand of any Woman in the World" recurs three times in the five pages of *Spectator 113;* in 1866 Isabelle, the heroine of *Le Roman d'une honnête femme,* has "de belles mains" (87). To recognize how complex James has become by 1881, we need only realize that the perfect hands in *The Portrait* are Madame Merle's. Conferring the heroine's trait upon the *femme fatale* transforms a conventional extravagance sufficiently that we experience the unexpected reversals and troublesome truths of daily reality.

In James' early novels, however, the quantitative effect of verbal overkill is exacerbated by a second technique—bunching intensifiers at various moments in the action. When Hamilton in *The Initials* loses his way in the Alps

> the valleys were in the deepest shade. . . . [He heard] a sharp sound, perfectly incomprehensible to him. . . . By this time he had lost all idea of where he might be, and although extremely unwilling to increase his distance from the *châlet,* he saw the absolute necessity of still climbing. . . . [though] perfectly unacquainted with the irregularities of the mountain.

All this occurs in less than half a page (52). Unfortunately, James can just about match such popular concentrations of intensifiers.

[Mrs. Hudson] must have been a very girlish bride.... she probably had looked terribly frightened at the altar. She was very delicately made.... [her hair] was of extraordinary fineness.... She was excessively shy, and evidently very humble-minded.

(49)

Possibly because he senses how unconvincing this stereotypic Mother is, James attempts to *assert* an intensity that only the dramatic reality of an achieved character could convey. This assertion is symptomatic, in turn, of James' general tendency to bunch superlatives in those situations which he avoids or effectively minimizes in later fiction—long descriptions, towering confrontations, appearances of darling children, dogs, etc.

Intensifiers bunched with particular situations and with particular themes contribute, in turn, to a third way in which hyperbole affects the reading experience—by total cumulative presence.

"A perfect blossom" .... "in a perfect transport" .... perfectly feminine .... perfectly ignorant .... perfectly sparkling .... so perfectly new and delightful .... "perfectly exhausted" .... perfectly natural .... perfectly truthful .... perfectly appalled .... perfect ease .... perfect lull .... perfectly cool .... a perfectly serenely happy present .... "perfect confidence" .... perfectly still .... perfect horror .:.. perfect health .... "perfectly well" .... perfectly awful .... "perfectly well" .... perfectly unconscious .... "perfectly conscious"* .... "perfectly unacquainted" .... perfectly quiet .... "quite perfectly" .... perfectly petrified .... "perfectly free" .... perfectly bare .... perfectly incomprehensible .... perfectly unacquainted .... perfectly right .... perfectly insensible .... "perfectly" .... perfectly inconceivable .... perfectly thunderstruck .... "perfectly obdurate" .... "perfectly serious" .... "perfectly quiet" .... "thinks him perfection" .... "perfectly original" .... "perfectly well" .... in perfect keeping .... perfectly understood .... "you speak English perfectly" .... most perfect good-temper .... "perfectly unaffected" .... "so perfectly ... so perfectly" .... perfect impunity .... perfect confidence .... "perfectly irresistible" .... perfectly harmless .... "perfect reconciliation" .... perfectly explicit .... perfectly crimson ear .... perfectly unconscious .... perfectly stunned .... perfectly calm .... perfectly dark .... perfectly conscious .... perfectly calm .... perfectly serious .... perfectly reassured .... "perfectly amiable" .... "perfect impunity" .... perfectly independent .... perfect satisfaction .... perfectly unknown .... "perfectly desperate" .... "perfectly contented" .... most perfect composure .... "perfectly" .... "perfectly well informed" .... most perfect sincerity .... "perfect tactician" .... "perfectly indifferent" .... perfectly immovable* .... "perfect epitome" .... perfectly

unhappy .... the perfection of his constancy .... perfectly simple
.... the perfection of an attitude .... perfectly succeeded ....
perfectly inoffensive .... "perfect monster" .... "the perfect truth"
.... "perfect good faith" .... "it's perfect" .... perfectly irregular
.... the perfect hush .... perfect purity .... perfection .... a perfect
good conscience .... physical perfection .... brought it to perfection
.... so perfect an example .... "the perfection of form ... the perfection of spirit" .... "perfect beauty" .... "a perfect surprise" ....
perfectly grave .... "perfectly" .... perfect response .... perfect face
.... "perfectly frank" .... extraordinary perfection .... "the perfection" .... "perfectly happy" .... the perfection of her features ....
perfectly characteristic .... perfectly attuned .... perfectly willing
.... perfect success .... "perfectly free" .... "to perfection" .... "too
perfect" .... "be perfection" .... "perfectly respect" .... perfectly
satisfactory .... "perfection" .... "perfectly secure" .... perfectly
portionless .... "perfectly" .... perfect gentleness .... perfectly
unflattered .... "deuced perfect" .... "perfection" .... "perfectly"
.... perfectly indifferent .... perfect absoluteness .... "perfectly
well" .... "perfect vacuum" .... the most perfect feminine model
.... perfectly void .... perfect indifference .... perfect moon ....
perfect docility .... perfectly contemplative .... perfectly unconscious .... perfect oblivion .... perfectly indifferent .... perfect
immobility .... perfectly sane .... perfectly reasonable .... perfect
sincerity .... perfectly remembered .... perfect statue .... "perfectly
serious" .... "perfect egoist."

The asterisks above separate *The Heir, The Initials,* and *Roderick Hudson.*[22] A few of the "perfect"s in James' novel function in ironic or comic or conversational ways (as we will see); and I have, of course, exacerbated matters by grouping the "perfect"s together. On the other hand, I have illustrated only one intensifier. Besides the 72 "perfect"s in *Roderick Hudson,* the word "passionate" appears 70 times; "extremely," 57; "extraordinary," 38; "magnificent," 37; "terrible," 29; "immense," 28; " absolute," 24; "excellent," 23; "fantastic," 19. By using these and still other intensifiers,[23] James removes the action too completely from the realm of recognizable experience. In popular fiction this effect is intended. We escape into the perfection which we crave or into the casuistic extreme which points the sharpest moral (Holmes says "of course I shall choose extreme cases to illustrate the contrast" [*EV* 15]). With James even the early novels are more serious business. F. R. Leavis maintains that "the sustained maturity of theme and treatment qualifies the book [*Roderick Hudson*] as a whole to be read at the adult level of demand in a way that no novel of Thackeray's will bear" (130). Leavis does not overstate James' intentions: clearly the young novelist took his themes with a young man's seriousness. But Leavis does overrate *Roderick Hudson* (and wildly underrates Thackerary) in terms of treatment. What

we have already seen and shall study soon, indicate that we cannot take *Roderick Hudson* so seriously as Leavis says. The style keeps exiling us to a glittering realm of violent extravagance. Since we do not have this experience with *The Portrait*, a quantitative comparison of the intensifiers in James' fiction between 1871 and 1881 can reveal much about his development.

Comparison reveals, for example, that some of the most violent and extravagant words in *Watch and Ward* and *Roderick Hudson* are mercifully absent from *The Portrait*. Among these are: craven, damnably, frantic, frenzied, miraculous, preposterous, ravenous, stupendous, stupefied, superhuman, unalterably, unbounded, inestimable, inexpungeable, infallible, infinitesimal, insurmountable, invincible, unpardonably. Further, quite a few of the most numerous and meaningless intensifiers decrease significantly betwen 1875 and 1881 (table 1).[24] The decline is significant indeed. Tables 2 and 3 tell different tales, however. Not only do some intensifiers recur with approximately the same frequency; others actually proliferate. Moreover, if we compare the elegant *Portrait* with *St. Elmo, The Heir, The Wide, Wide World* and *The Initials*, we see that the novelist who relies most frequently upon the "popular" device of proliferating intensifiers is Henry James. In the four tables we thus have a paradigm of how a great artist deals with his tradition. We do not find that complete abandonment of conventional practice which total deletion of, say, the word "perfect" would indicate. Rather than to abandon or entirely reconstitute, James, like other major

TABLE 1

	W&W	RH	Ame	PL
extraordinary	6	27	12	11
fantastic	0	13	6	1
magnificent	0	26	16	4
passionate	104	48	13	18
terrible	16	20	25	7

Note: Numbers in tables 1–4 indicate incidence per 100,000 words. The actual figures in each novel are given in the corresponding tables in note 24.

TABLE 2

	W&W	RH	Ame	PL
absolute	12	17	7	10
excellent	20	16	18	14
exquisite	6	11	9	9
extremely	40	40	57	34
remarkable	6	14	19	14

TABLE 3

	W&W	RH	Ame	PL
immense	10	20	20	24
perfect	50	57	50	71

TABLE 4

	PL	StE	HR	WWW	In
extraordinary	11	3	2	2	12
fantastic	1	6	1	1	1
magnificent	4	4	4	1	2
passionate	18	9	11	22	19
terrible	7	8	8	1	2
absolute	10	6	10	5	6
excellent	14	0	14	10	18
exquisite	9	6	3	2	1
extremely	34	4	16	9	26
remarkable	14	6	5	4	9
immense	24	14	1	1	9
perfect	71	36	28	30	24

novelists, chastens and transforms. From the beginning, he recognized what Richard Chase calls "the latent extravagance of his imagination"; and, had young Henry by some chance overlooked this tendency, his brother William was there to remind him ("it will be a good thing for you to resolve never to use the word 'supreme' ").[25] On the other hand, James never wavers in his commitment to the superlative. In 1865 he can sympathize with Trollope's determination to avoid Kingsley's bombast and yet can conclude that Trollope has erred as seriously at the opposite extreme. "The most that can be said of the affairs of this lady's [Miss Mackenzie's] heart is that they are not ridiculous. They are assuredly not interesting. . . . Why should we batten upon over-cooked prose while the air is redolent with undistilled poetry?" (*Na* 1865, 52). In the same year James takes up directly the Kingsley brothers' hollow paeans to "human nobleness."

> In the ordinary course of life it [human nobleness] does not come into play; it is sufficiently represented by courage, modesty, industry. Let the novelist give us these virtues for what they are, and not for what no true lover of human nature would have them pretend to be, or else let him devise sublime opportunities, situations which really match the latent nobleness of the human soul.
>
> (*Na* 1865, 22)

Sublime opportunities, the air redolent with poetry . . . Forty years later James remains confident enough of his ability to recognize the basic "virtues for what they are" that he can still champion the superlative in life and in art.

> The extraordinary is most extraordinary in that it happens to you and me. . . . nothing counts, of course, in art, but the excellent; nothing exists, however briefly, for estimation, for appreciation, but the superlative.
>
> (*AN* 257, *FN* 118)

James' lifelong task, then, is not to purge his instinct for the superlative but to discover techniques that allow him to combine the Kingsleys and Trollope, to make us experience the extraordinary within the confines of the credible. Although critics have noted various aspects of James' success,[26] no one has explained how he manages to move from the ineffectual hyperbole of *Roderick Hudson* to the compelling splendor of *The Portrait*. A quantitative study can only begin such an explanation. Securely grounded in the factual data, we must now go on to examine carefully the *quality* of the intensifiers which James retains. I focus on "perfect" because its proliferation in *The Portrait* indicates James' increasing tendency to scrutinize certain basic Victorian concepts. "The perfect lady" is, as scholars have demonstrated,[27] the commonly acknowledged ideal of the nineteenth century.

Amiable, angelical woman, beings on whom nature has stamped the image of perfection.

Watterson, here in *Glencarn*, makes being a woman sound very attractive indeed. Neal in *Keep Cool* seems to agree. "She is woman, perfect woman . . ." But then the rub comes. ". . . helpless, lovely, and shrinking as a sensitive plant."[28] What perfection costs womankind—we shall tally this cost later—is any chance for complete development. As Mrs. Jameson notes, "Coleridge, as you will remember, has asserted that the perfection of a woman's character is to be *characterless*."[29] To bolster this suspect ideal of perfection, both literature and religion are called upon. Ruskin says of Shakespeare that "there is hardly a play that has not a perfect woman in it";[30] sentimental drama and fiction from the eighteenth century onward combine with the humanitarian wing of Christianity to advocate "the perfectability of man." Heroines, as Brown notes, "were invariably perfectionists; their favorite occupation was 'stepping heavenward'" (183). As Henry James works throughout the crucial decade to perfect his formal artistry, he comes increasingly to recognize that perfection is not of this world. The sublunary affairs which concern him most are "all comically, all tragically" mundane. Increasingly incapable of facile hyperbole (and of the moral whitewash it involved), James examines "perfection" in *The Portrait* as part of a sustained critique of Victorian life which I study in chapter 2. His decade-long concern with "perfect" allows that word to represent much which we cannot study fully now—an emblem of James' instinct for extravagance and of his determination to achieve the language of responsibility.

2

Beginning with James' most popular practice will help explain both the weakness of his first novels and the way he eventually converts that weakness into strength.

In repose Lawrence may have looked stupid; but as he talked his face slowly brightened by gradual fine degrees, until at the end of an hour it inspired you with a confidence so perfect as to be in some degree a tribute to its owner's intellect, as it certainly was to his integrity.

(W&W 232)

The first clause, even with its "may," undercuts Lawrence fiercely. Almost immediately, however, we are expected to feel "a confidence so perfect." Since we do not, James' sentence fails to evoke a single complex response or even two separate but somehow complementary ones. The sanguine assertion of perfection remains unconvincing in itself and fails also to temper the overly severe first clause. Polarization into severe and sanguine extremes is particularly harmful to James' early work because extremes which cannot moderate one another in the same sentence have even less chance of success when they appear separately. James is often severe, for example, with his Byronic sculptor.

"She [Mrs. Hudson] . . . looks at me, when I displease her, as if I were a perfect monster of depravity. . . . I care only for perfect beauty. . . . there's a perfect vacuum here!" And he tapped his forehead.

(RH 37, 106, 394)

Especially with no moderating forces in evidence, Roderick's limitations seem so egregious—the "perfect"'s icing the cake—that he passes beyond the bounds of our sympathy.

James evokes little more sympathy when he goes to the opposite extreme and, like a popular novelist, sanguinely proclaims characters "perfect." *The Wide, Wide World* tells us, for example, that " 'Ellen Montgomery is a *perfectly* well-behaved child.' . . . 'I never saw a more perfectly polite child.' . . . 'perfectly lady-like always'. . . . 'and perfectly child-like'" (435, 494, 570). When Nora Lambert in *Watch and Ward* returns from Europe, "here she stood, a woman turned, perfect, mature, superb. . . . 'My dear Mr. Lawrence, she's perfect'" (577, 579). Since James' spokesmen here, Hubert and Mrs. Keith, are established authorities on the female charms, we must accept their word. Nora is perfect. She may need a bit more seasoning, but when this is provided by wicked New York, Nora makes Roger's dream come true indeed—"he had determined that she should be a lovely woman and a perfect wife" (320). We cannot, of course, feel the joy appropriate to this dream-fulfillment because the whole process of perfection has been too patently a wish-fulfillment, a mere assertion. In James' next novel, however, the perfect woman is more intriguing.

Like Roger, Mrs. Light intends to mold a child into a perfect woman. " 'I was determined she should be a perfection'" (RH 226). James is still apprentice enough to grant half of Mrs. Light's dream. We are told of "a

blooming oval of perfect purity.... [Christina's] perfect face"; "the
extraordinary perfection of her beauty .... the perfection of her features
and of her person" (87, 161, 169, 180–81) are beyond question. Her mind
and her spirit are another matter, however. Christina's combination of
perfect beauty and perfect capriciousness makes her resemble a *capricciosa* who influenced James strongly, Hildegarde of *The Initials*. In both
novels the suitors aspire to the same goal—to "make her mind as perfect
as her form" (*In* 175). The eventual success of Hamilton makes *The
Initials* seem simplistic. Roderick's failure, on the other hand, does not
necessarily assure to Christina Light the complexity of James' later
heroines. Unlike Isabel Archer or Maggie Verver, Christina is prevented
by her secret parentage from being "free" to choose her husband. Thus
her dilemma derives, not from her own personal limitations (as with
Isabel and Maggie), but from forces external to her. The Sinister
Compulsion introduces the black-white morality of melodrama. Christina is not finally imperfect enough for tragic responsibility.

Christina *is*, however, *capricciosa* enough to become James' first great
character. And his use of "perfect" shows him part way toward
discovering how to create admirable yet believable figures.

"She could be perfectly happy in poverty."
"She would make too perfect a princess."

(177, 221)

We do not respond to these contradictory evaluations of Christina as we
did to "Lawrence may have looked stupid" and "a confidence so perfect."
The evaluations of Christina are not demeaning or impossible in
themselves, and they are confirmed by our experience of the *capricciosa*
in action. Thus, with Christina, James achieves mystery for the first time.
Moreover, this " 'girl wantonly making light' " (222) taxes James' style in
ways which promise greater mystery still. "Light" can mean several
things—brilliance, mere cleverness, irreverence, even moral insuffi-
ciency. Like Christina in dramatic situations, the pun which is her name,
Miss Light, can sustain multiple and even contradictory interpretations
simultaneously. After *Roderick Hudson*, James manages increasingly to
achieve comparable ambiguity with other aspects of his language,
particularly the word "perfect."

"Perfect" and other superlatives necessarily evoke in serious readers an
ambivalent response. We wish for perfection, yet we cannot really
believe in it. Having appealed primarily to wish-fulfillment with Nora,
James comes increasingly to capitalize upon our skepticism about
perfection. Even this practice is not, however, entirely unknown to
popular authors. As Philip enters in *The Heir*, Charlie is asking his sister,
" 'What is your opinion of perfect heroes?' ... 'Here comes one,'

whispered Amy to her brother, blushing at her piece of naughtiness" (*HR* 1:33). Later, although Amy says, " 'I can't afford to lose my faith in my sister's perfection, or Philip's, especially now,' " she does lose it, for Laura's secret engagement to Philip has long since meant that there "could never be the perfect freedom that they enjoyed before the avowal of their sentiments" (2:148, 1:322). Thus when James qualifies his "perfect" characters, he is not so much abandoning popular practice as adapting what popular authors could not bring themselves to sustain.[31] For, if Amy loses Laura and Philip as perfect ideals, she still has the memory of Guy as her "faultless model" (2:148);[32] and she herself becomes a model for others. Fortunately, James cannot allow himself this consolation as he matures through the second half of the crucial decade. The very word which oversimplified his early novels proves two-sided enough now to enrich his subsequent fiction.

The American might, in many ways, seem all too like its predecessors.[33] Like Roger and Mrs. Light, Christopher Newman wants a perfect woman; like Nora and Ellen, Claire is declared perfect by a knowledge-able man and woman. What distinguishes *The American* is that James manages quite consistently now to encourage our skepticism about perfection. Having already suggested its limitations by page 3,[34] James uses Noémie Nioche to establish the two-sided nature of "perfect."

> "Oh, it [the painting] shall be finished in perfection; in the perfection of perfection!" cried mademoiselle; and to confirm her promise, she deposited a rosy blotch in the middle of the Madonna's cheek.
>
> (5)

Although we do not yet know that Noémie will spot her own cheeks with rouge like the stained virgin she is (53), we are made immediately aware of the gap between perfection and claims for it. That this disparity will especially concern Paris women is suggested when Noémie is called "a perfect Parisienne" (11). And so when Mrs. Tristram applies to Claire the very words of Mrs. Keith—" 'She is perfect' " (38)—we do not react to Claire as we did to Nora. Especially with Tom Tristram's encouragement, we, paradoxically, remain more committed to the story because we are less than fully committed to its heroine. "Perfect" is not reduced to a simple assertion because both sides of the word seem warranted by context.

Newman likewise begins somewhat wary. "This was the proud and beautiful Madame de Cintré, the loveliest woman in the world, the promised perfection" (39). Even as he falls in love, Newman undergoes "temperate raptures" (123) which spare us the single-minded infatuation of Roderick and popular swains.

> He remembered what Mrs. Tristram had told him of her "perfection."
> . . . The presumption, from the first moment he looked at her, had

been in her favor. And yet, if she was beautiful, it was not a dazzling beauty.

(83)

Although it would be reading the novel backwards to claim that we already foresee Claire's inadequacy and collapse, we are reacting ambivalently to her.[35] We continue to do so even when Newman begins sounding like Roger or Hamilton—" 'you are just the woman I have been looking for, except that you are far more perfect' " (117). In this and other outbursts we attribute the hyperbole to Newman, not to James, because the novel itself continues to encourage our skepticism about perfection. When Valentin says, " 'I have never seen a woman half so perfect.... She is extremely perfect' " (103, 200), he is speaking of two different women. Intending to praise Claire unreservedly and Noémie with much qualification, Valentin increases our awareness of the complexities of perfection itself. And finally, of course it is the violent who bear it away. With Valentin dead, Claire entombed, and Newman alone, Noémie reappears in her "Parisian perfection" (345). The distance we have come is marked by how much and how little "perfect" means to us here.

The Portrait of a Lady opens amid perfection—on "the perfect lawn" during "the perfect middle of a splendid summer afternoon" (5).[36] Although James achieves a true idyll here, the moment, like a flower, derives its perfection partly from its transitoriness. Shadows are lengthening, "slowly" (5) but inevitably. "An eternity of pleasure" it is, but only "from five o'clock to eight" (5). We revere the moment so much because our afternoon perfection is set in the context of that approaching night in which no man can work. And so, although we cannot yet know the fate of these partakers of the *fête-champêtre*, we are not ultimately surprised when the old man and his son are dead, the lord has grown heavy and strange, and the young lady who entered the greensward laughing has left it for horror in the eternal city.

Within this context of perfection limited and ephemeral, *The Portrait* presents a hyperbole-prone heroine who learns two lessons about the nature and possibility of the "perfect." To signal immediately his heroine's tendency to extremism, James introduces Isabel in emblematic colors. "Her white hands ... folded upon her black dress" (18). Isabel's tendency to extravagant diction—among her first words are " 'so lovely .... too enchanting .... adorable' " (16)—is soon undercut gently by the novel's most exemplary figure.

"I have never seen anything so beautiful as this," she declared.
"It's looking very well," said Mr. Touchett.

(18)

Such gentle corrections do not temper Isabel, however. "Her conversation ... gave a large licence to violent statements.... [She] often praised profusely" (56, 71). As Henrietta is satirized when "she knew perfectly in advance" what she would find in Europe (49), so Isabel seems equally naive but much more endangered when she says that meeting the experienced Europeans " 'will suit me perfectly' " (54). In her quest for "perfect freedom," Isabel is aspiring to the ideal of popular fiction's and James' major characters.

> [Hamilton is] "perfectly free to choose"
>
> *(In* 31)
>
> [Nora demands] "perfect independence"
>
> *(W&W* 690)
>
> [Newman says,] "I am perfectly free"
>
> *(Ame* 23)

Isabel's progress toward painful wisdom is marked by a series of sweeping judgments which make us uneasy in proportion to her confidence. She is as confident, for example, that the Misses Molyneux are "very original" (70) as she is years later that their brother "was certainly . . . a contented man. . . . British politics had cured him; she had known they would" (353, 355). Her own life has seemed equally simple. "The fine things a rich, independent, generous girl . . . might do were really innumerable. . . . how easy it now promised to become for herself" (207, 312). No wonder that Osmond need only feign simplicity to win Isabel. Although she recognizes that "perfect simplicity was not the badge of his family," she accepts a suitor who declares, " 'it is perfectly simple' " (236, 287).

Isabel is no Roderick Hudson, however. She complicates our response because she not only proclaims perfect freedom and pronounces sweeping judgments; she also does the opposite—indicates a mature awareness of human limitation and of the consequent need for moderation.

> "Never?" said Lord Warburton.
> "I won't say 'never'; I should feel very melodramatic."

> "If you look for magnificent examples of anything I shall disappoint you."
>
> (74, 139)[37]

Moreover, Isabel cedes to Madame Merle not only the Heroine's perfect hands but also the accomplishments conventionally reserved for those hands. "When Madame Merle was neither writing, nor painting, nor touching the piano, she was usually employed upon wonderful morsels of picturesque embroidery" (177). Especially in light of his famous catalog of Isabel's limitations (48), James cannot be convicted, as some critics claim, of trying to force upon us a perfect ideal. Rather he has quite clearly created an admirable but flawed heroine whose very limitations make her both more convincingly "real" than Nora or Claire and more believably excellent than either. We experience enough sustained qualification that the judgment " 'she is beautiful, accomplished, generous.... very clever and very amiable' " (222) does not seem extravagant or facile; we can even believe Henrietta's " 'you were exceptional' " (262). Moreover, when the unqualified expression of Mrs. Keith and Mrs. Tristram does appear in *The Portrait*, the " 'she is perfect' " (214) is highly qualified indeed. The "she" is Pansy. We do not experience her as we did Ellen or Nora because Pansy's very perfection prevents her from being our ideal.[38] Osmond's daughter is a perfect doll because she at sixteen can never be anything more.

Isabel can, however. She can earn a measure of greatness by learning two distinct lessons about the "perfect." One we encountered in *The American*. We are repeatedly shown in *The Portrait* that what appears perfect is not so. Mrs. Touchett's speech was "perfectly veracious . . . but not as perfectly timed" (189); with the Countess "one got on . . . perfectly if one observed a single simple condition—that of not believing a word she said" (259); and even at the end, relations are no easier, for Henrietta may hold Caspar "with an intention of perfect kindness" but his final stare shows anguish and bewilderment (545).

Isabel learns about such perfection. Discovering the real nature of Osmond and her marriage, Isabel tries in her honesty and stubbornness not to shift the blame melodramatically onto others. " 'I was perfectly free' " (306). Even her subsequent realization of how much her own blindness worked against her must be qualified, however. "If ever a girl was a free agent, she had been. A girl in love was doubtless not a free agent" (374). And so, when Isabel says still later, " 'I was perfectly free' " (450), she achieves a greatness beyond Christina Light. Isabel blames no one, and she affirms individual responsibility in the face of her awareness of how limited the individual actually is. She can then suffer further tempering of her romantic extremism. Originally confident that Henrietta's relations with Bantling were "perfectly innocent," she eventually discovers them not "completely original" (190, 522). Having sweepingly decided that dying "was the most perfect of all" rest (516), Isabel hears dying Ralph say, " 'dear Isabel, life is better; for in life there is love. Death is good—but there is no love' " (530). And so, when Caspar says melodramatically, " 'you are perfectly alone' " (542), Isabel has already learned better. " 'I don't think anything is over' " (531). Ever.

These moments, some of the greatest in James' canon, teach the lesson which we learned in *The American*. *The Portrait* also undertakes a second examination of perfection, however. Besides learning to distinguish the "perfect" from claims to it, Isabel comes to question the very value of perfection. She rejects Lord Warburton, for example, because " 'he was too perfect.... I am not perfect myself.... his perfection would irritate me' " (137, 138).[39] She thus is susceptible to Osmond. "He was not perfect—far from it" (226). This unlikely admission appeals to Isabel because she has already questioned being "too perfectly the social animal that man and woman are supposed to have been intended to be" (178). Isabel here is criticizing Madame Merle, not for pretending to the ideal, but for the very limitations of that ideal. When Ralph applies to Madame Merle the now loaded expression " 'she is perfect,' " he can add without non sequitur, " 'she pushes the search for perfection too far' " (232).[40] This criticism would be meaningless to popular novelists because their characters aspire to a perfection divine and therefore infinite. Since James is of the secularists' party, however, his "perfect"s lack transcendental sanction and thus can, like anything mundane, become inordinate. The limitations of mundane perfection come home to Isabel when she discovers in Osmond precisely what she rejected Warburton for. "Perfectly consistent with the best breeding" (242) characterizes even Gilbert's shyness. On the other hand, James no more allows "perfect" to become one-sided with his villain than he did with his heroine. Osmond is not simply pretending to society's ideal of surface perfection; his demeanor holds up creditably under fire. He confronts Goodwood with a "perfectly modulated voice" (466); he speaks twice of "his perfect intimacy with his wife" (468); threatening to banish his sister, "he looked perfectly good-humoured" (492). Thus in quest of an alternative to society's ideal, Isabel finds herself bound to society itself. Gilbert Osmond is a perfectionist.

3

The portrait of Isabel, which begins to emerge as we study James' use of language, gains detail and intricacy throughout chapters 1 and 2 and is complete only when we examine her mental processes in chapter 4. We can add to the portrait by understanding that James' debt to popular practice goes beyond using hyperbole with character traits; like the scribblers, James also uses extravagant language with characters' achievements and with their speech itself.

Roderick Hudson achieves extraordinary success intellectually, socially, and artistically. By concentrating upon James' attempt to make credible the chief of these achievements—Roderick's art—we will find both a paradigm of James' practice with other achievements and, more important, an explanation of why the popular mode of presenting action fails to move serious readers of fiction today.[41] Attempting to make great achievement credible, James, like popular writers, makes incredible assertions of potential. As Leigh in *St. Elmo* "gave promise of eminence in his profession" (105) and as Philip "seemed likely to distinguish himself [in Parliament] according to the fondest hopes ... [of] Laura" (*HR*

2:310), so "certainly, among the young men of genius who, for so many ages, have gone up to Rome to test their powers, none ever made a fairer beginning than Roderick" (94). To convert potential into achievement, popular heroes need endurance and "genius." Fortunately for Roderick Hudson and unfortunately for *Roderick Hudson*, James endows his sculptor with plenty of both. Roderick "could draw indefinitely upon a mysterious fund of nervous force, which outlasted and outwearied the endurance of many a sturdier temperament.... [Roderick] looked indefatigably" (21, 84). The very word indefatigable characterizes such popular worthies as Ellen, who "was indefatigable" (*WWW* 475), Guy, who "persevered indefatigably" (*HR* 2:143), and Isabelle la sérieuse, who studies "Max avec une infatigable attention" (*LR* 83).[42] Before discussing how these apoplectic labors affect our reading experience, we should note the second requisite for great achievement.

"Genius" is attributed to Roderick repeatedly. The nearest any of these come to redemptive irony is "the essential salubrity of genius" (200); unfortunately, however, it is the salubrity which Rowland is wrong about, not the genius. Such genius, plus endurance, puts both popular and Jamesian characters on the road to great achievement. As Ellen "went forward steadily and rapidly" (*WWW* 348) and Laura "prospered beyond her hopes (*HR* 2:190) and Isabelle's artiste "fit un chef-d'oeuvre" (*LR* 194), so "Roderick ... brought it [the statue] to rapid completion. ... The work was rapidly finished .... [his mother's portrait] was taking a very happy turn" (*RH* 135, 161, 322). With the finished products, James, like popular writers, resorts to allusion and sweeping assertion.

> [Roderick's statue] reminded Rowland in its homely veracity, its artless artfulness, of the works of the early Italian Renaissance.
>
> (*RH* 33–34)
>
> [Edna's song was] solemn as the Hebrew chant of Deborah, and fully as triumphant.
>
> (*StE* 7)

Sweepingly Rowland asserts that Roderick's Drinker achieves "the perfection of an attitude" (17) and that his later Adam is "physical perfection" (95).[43] Nor can we read in needed undercutting here by assuming that infatuation has colored Rowland's judgment, for we are assured that "a good judge here and there has been known to pronounce it [the Adam] the finest piece of sculpture of our modern era" (95).

Such artistic—and intellectual and social—achievements indicate not only how much James' characters resemble popular counterparts, but why the whole popular mode of presenting action fails to move serious readers today. James renders scenes as he did "perfect" traits: he asserts. Irony is not at issue here because Roderick's eventual failure does not qualify what is asserted about his statues; and his intellectual and social prowess, however qualified, seems still too facile and coyly done. Thus we do not experience represented actions; we confront words that assert the existence of such actions.

She had something wonderfully winning and fascinating about her.
(*HR* 1:181)
Il y avait en lui je ne sais quoi qui le sauvait toujours du ridicule.
(*LR* 313)
"He has the ineffable something that charms and convinces."
(*RH* 271)

That ineffable something is just what popular fiction omits. We cannot experience Amy's " 'perfect blossom' " (*HR* 1:3) or James' "delicate plant of radiant hue" (*RH* 238) because we quite literally cannot see them. Moreover, this substituting of word for thing, of hyperbolic assertion for experience of the object, derives from a sentiment deeper than mere love of verbal tinsel.

A neat specimen of tattooing . . . . That superb blush . . . . hideous
. . . . admirably touching and noble . . . . magnificent movement.
(*W&W* 330, 429; *RH* 33, 367, 481)

Here, and in much popular writing, the language is inadequate because detail has been replaced by evaluation. Avowedly didactic, popular fiction was primarily interested, not in making us see, but in making us better. Thus the author's main task was to *judge* the event, so that we would be elevated or warned. James, of course, inveighs from his earliest criticism against such didacticism, but once again his practice lags behind his theory in 1875. *St. Elmo's* readers are dazzled by "a glory that was dazzling" (304) because the word of Augusta Jane Evans is good enough for them. In *Roderick Hudson*, we are not struck by a "strikingly beautiful" face (290)—or statue—because James' novel is sufficiently serious that mere words are not good enough for us.[44]

The Portrait is good enough, for several reasons. Achievements are still marked by superlatives, but often the "remarkable talent" is for journalism (49), the "remarkable aptitude" is for mechanics (107), the "remarkable knowledge" is of Paris (201). When "exquisitely" characterizes the productions of a gifted hand, James is referring to penmanship (80). Some achievements *are* considerable, of course. But the very fact that "remarkable intelligence" (300) and "extraordinary charm" (393) are credited to the villain and his helper, qualifies the superlatives enough, here. And what about Isabel?

Although some critics find her overpraised, James clearly does strive to make his heroine attractively qualified. He not only satirizes Isabel gently as a "prodigy of learning" (46), he also tempers her "genius." See how much Isabel resembles Roderick initially: a " 'young person of genius in want of encouragement and patronage' " (*PL* 40). She is presented quite differently, however. Whereas Roderick's "genius" is affirmed repeatedly by authorities, Isabel's "genius" is never insisted upon more strongly than this first time. And even here, both the qualified use of the word (Lily clearly means not Michelangelesque powers but an unchanneled potential) and the dramatic context (eccentric Mrs. Touchett repeating fond Lily's effusion) make the statement acceptably tentative. It becomes still more so when Mrs. Touchett adds, " 'it may be that Isabel is a genius; but in that case I have not yet learned her special line' " (40). These and other reservations[45] qualify Isabel sufficiently that we share Ralph's eagerness to " 'find out her special line' " (41). Since she, like Dorothea Brooke and most nineteenth-century women, has only the "special line" of marriage, her husband will determine whether that line draws out her genius or binds it tight. The answer?

"Does she [Isabel] take the opposite line from him?"
"In everything."

(332)

When Isabel finally " 'has a line sharply marked out' " (481), that line necessarily leads away from Gilbert Osmond. For, as Dorothea Brooke is stifled by Casaubon's limitations, Isabel finds herself bound to a man with " 'a genius for upholstery' " (356). That we have moved from Roderick to reality becomes especially clear when Countess Gemini is soon called " 'a fool whose folly had the irresponsibility of genius' " (414). Roderick too was irresponsible and foolish, but his perfect statues compensated; by 1881 no such glittering unrealities remain. The change is not primarily in subject matter, of course. James now sustains a consistently more sophisticated view both of his subject and of what makes an action convincing experientially.

4

Speech that out-Heroded Herod—or in *Watch and Ward*'s terms "out-Fentoned Fenton" (700)—was an extravagance encouraged by an age which "considered such luminous eloquence an essential property of all literature."[46] Particularly in America. Already in 1834 Dr. Daniel Drake is asking, "ought not the literature of a free people to be declamatory?"[47] In fact American (and French and English) drama, fiction, and oratory all did rely upon declamatory eloquence, and all influenced Henry James. His stylistic endeavor throughout half a century will be, not to purge aureate influences and write in plain style, but to create an elaborate style which is more than simply declamatory.

In the dramas which young James loves, for example, the thrilling tirades and protestations gain additional intensity from a special loftiness of purpose.

> "They are sermons in dialogue," an American periodical said in 1787 of contemporary plays. "If they are not a true picture of life, they show, at least, what life itself ought to be." This description was accurate for the whole melodramatic tradition that followed.
>
> (Grimsted, 229)

Failure to resolve this paradoxical tension between the need to preach truth and the obligation to depict life truthfully, does not of course prevent drama from continuing to preach eloquently. Besides timeless advice about avoiding seducers, the various decades voice particular messages—from abolitionist and teetotaling plays to such later works as *Shore Acres*, "which, like *Sag Harbor*, produced in 1899, is a kind of sermon on the evils of land speculation."[48] Sermonizing, and its paradoxical tensions, are not restricted to drama. Pious preachment was one of the practices which James reacted against most strongly in the fiction of his immediate predecessors, popular and great.

> Mrs. Stowe did not much care to read novels; the sermon was undoubtedly the literary form by which she had been most deeply influenced. . . . she cannot always refrain from making them [Negro characters] think and talk a little too much like preachers.
>
> (Wilson, 33, 40)

Wilson's wry tone notwithstanding, Mrs. Stowe is a very representative Victorian. "The reading of sermons was perhaps the most popular of their [the early and mid-Victorians'] literary pastimes."[49] Further, Mrs. Stowe is not only representative of popular women novelists who frequently come from clerical households and who invariably defend virtue with eloquent preaching; she also resembles an equally representative but very different novelist, Thackeray.

> A few years ago I should have sneered at the idea of setting up as a teacher . . . but I have got to believe in the business, and in many other things since then. And our profession seems to be as serious as the parson's own.[50]

Popular novelists at their most eloquent and great novelists at their least enduring share the podium with another, very influential group. "To a degree that we have lost sight of, oratory was then the basis for other forms of writing."[51] As a main attraction at July Fourth celebrations and famous trials, as parlor entertainment, as standard newspaper and lyceum fare, as a disproportionate share of our publications, eloquent speeches thrill the century—Walt Whitman as well as black slaves, Macaulay and the literary historians no less than the habitual group around the perennial soapbox. Elocution lessons are standard in school curriculums and repeatedly dramatized in novels; even the irregularly educated Henry James, Jr., spends one afternoon a week in 1858 "declaiming eloquent pieces from 'Sargent's Standard Speaker' " (*LL* 1:7).[52] Especially since his father knew many of the sages and Brahmins and was himself a lyceum and July Fourth speaker, young Henry receives declamation as a familial as well as a national legacy. In 1870 he claims to be sufficiently "reconciled" to America that "I ought to be a formidable rival to the most popular fourth of July lecturers" (*HJL* 246); in 1903 he can still urge William, with the pride (and the irony?) of a younger brother, to be "a Niagara of eloquence" in his Concord address (*LL* 1:422). So it is not surprising that Henry James' early work contains "passages of sheer delight for declamation."[53]

Such simple joys are complicated. Drama, sermon, novel, oration, all present in their eloquence a moral dilemma which James has to face. Twain must too.

> What Clemens was after was the very reverse of oratory: he worked to exclude every rhetorical effect, every symptom of confident declaration. . . . Clearly this desire to invert all established canons of oratory is involved in the inversion of the pastoral situation.[54]

From every side the roar of genteel moralizing challenges the consciousness of Twain and James. Their task is to show moral failure without failing morally, to stage man's drama without falsifying man's experience. Since probity, for each artist, is inseparable from form, each seeks a speech truly his own. To learn how James gradually transforms conventional ventriloquism into personal expression, we must begin with his dialogue extravagances.

In his first two novels the word "eloquent" occurs at least twenty-six times.[55] We have difficulty responding to the eloquence for two main reasons—either we do not experience it, or we do. Since what we do not actually hear is as unconvincing as James' other assertions of great achievement,[56] we can concentrate upon the declamations which we must listen to. In *Roderick Hudson*, for example, James apparently does not demur when Rowland calls one of the following outbursts "eloquence" and the other "over-trenchant." Which is which?

> "I have been idle, restless, egotistical, discontented. I have done no harm, I believe, but I have done no good."

> "I thought you would help me, you and Mary; that's why I sent for you. But you can't, don't think it! The sooner you give up the idea the better for you. Give up being proud of me, too!"

> (39, 386)

Rowland-James espouses the "cruel eloquence" of the second passage with the vague "there was something in the ring of Roderick's voice, as he uttered these words, which sent them home with convincing force" (386). To us, however, both passages seem self-indulgent and hollow. Nor are we convinced later by the assertion that "Roderick had been wandering among formidable abstractions" (394), for we have just experienced the unformidable vagueness of

> "My work's over. I can't work—I haven't worked all winter. If I were fit for anything, this sentimental collapse would have been just the thing to cure me of my apathy and break the spell of my idleness."

Our problem with such passages is not simply that Roderick rants too much. James is resorting to the popular tactic of asserting what he cannot make experiential. By repeatedly insisting upon Roderick's eloquence, Rowland compounds our irritation at the rant itself, for we feel that our arm is being twisted. And when we encounter such additional coercions as "Roderick began to talk . . . with his usual vividness. . . . he talked as well as ever, or even better" (127–28, 414), James' sculptor, like St. Elmo and other ranters of the popular tradition, perishes in the gulf between narrative intent and reader experience.

The dilemma for James and the popular tradition involves more than the issue of asserted vocal prowess, moreover. The nineteenth century struggled consistently with two related but distinct forms of eloquence. Often Victorian scribblers and early James perpetuate a technique old-fashioned by the end of the eighteenth century—turning dialogue into "a series of epic harangues."[57] James was especially prey to the charms of such harangues because his homeland was famous for the "big, old-time orating and banqueting type of American citizen."[58] Thus Tocqueville's observation is undoubtedly accurate—"an American cannot converse, but he can discuss; and his talk falls into a dissertation."[59] To establish both that James' early characters tend to dissert and harangue and that he has learned to modify this tendency by 1881, we can focus on one group of quotations.

> Roderick . . . declared that America was good enough for him, and that he had always thought it the duty of an honest citizen to stand by his own country and help it along. He had evidently thought nothing whatever about it, and was launching his doctrine on the inspiration of the moment. The doctrine expanded with the occasion, and he declared that he was above all an advocate for American art. He didn't see why we shouldn't produce the greatest works in the world. We were the biggest people, and we ought to have the biggest conceptions. The biggest conceptions of course would bring forth in time the biggest performances. We had only to be true to ourselves, to pitch in and not be afraid, to fling Imitation overboard and fix our eyes upon our National Individuality. "I declare," he cried, "there's a career for a

man, and I've twenty minds to decide, on the spot, to embrace it—to be the consummate, typical, original, national American artist! It's inspiring!"

(RH 30)

[Newman] finally broke out and swore that they [the United States] were the greatest country in the world, that they could put all Europe into their breeches' pockets, and that an American who spoke ill of them ought to be carried home in irons and compelled to live in Boston.

(Ame 29)

"You [Ralph has been making fun of Henrietta] will never be serious. I like the great country stretching away beyond the rivers and across the prairies, blooming and smiling and spreading, till it stops at the blue Pacific! A strong, sweet, fresh odour seems to rise from it, and Henrietta—excuse my simile—had something of that odour in her garments."

Isabel blushed a little as she concluded this speech.

(PL 87)

Early in each novel, James presents protagonists who get fervidly patriotic. His tactic differs considerably in each case, however. Since Newman's passage is barely one quarter the length of Roderick's, Newman is not exposed long enough to pass beyond the innocent to the ridiculous. His enthusiasm is further muffled because he never bursts into direct discourse. And Newman ends with wit—making him more than just a ranter and giving us more to experience than simply his limitations. In *The Portrait* James, reserving "forensic triumphs" (295) for Lily's comic husband, loud Edmund, puts definite curbs on Isabel's extravagance. For one thing, her topic on page 87 is not America per se; she is standing up against cosmopolitan levity for ideals which we cannot dismiss lightly (friendship, intellectual seriousness, *and* love of country). She evinces, also, a self-awareness which tempers her patriotism. During her speech she adds " 'excuse my simile' " and acknowledges Henrietta's limitations; afterwards, she blushes. As for her patriotic outburst itself, its restriction to four lines is probably a milestone in American oratory, although its transcontinental sentiment is certainly not unprecedented.

As grandiloquent perorations kept the eagle in constant flight from the Alleghenies to the Rockies, a folk-adage declared that its shadow had worn a trail across the basin of the Mississippi.

(Matthiessen, Renaissance 22)

Even here, however, James tempers Isabel's eloquence by omitting the eagle and by the simple candor of " 'I like the great country.' " Thus when Ralph finds her blush "very becoming" and declares, " 'you are a woman of imagination,' " he is not coercing us as Rowland did. We feel rather that our experience of Isabel is confirmed by a judicious character.

These three passages cannot, of course, make James' development from 1875 to 1881 into a simple progression. Ranting, especially at moments of stress, still obtrudes in *The American*; and speeches sometimes get long in *The Portrait*. But Newman and Isabel for all their faults move us as Roderick for all his virtues does not, partly because we experience their faults less protractedly and find their language enjoyable in itself. Other factors are also operating by 1881, but before we concentrate upon eloquence in *The Portrait*, we must define a second type of popular rant in James' early novels.

"The litanies of petitions"[60] which beset eighteenth-century popular fiction remain conspicuous in Victorian novels. In *Le Roman* Max expressly reproves the languishing coquette for " 'vos désolantes litanies' " (155). To suggest how much James' characters sound like popular stereotypes and like one another, I will group various litanies below in terms of the syntactical construction they repeat. Try to distinguish the characters and their authors.

"I'm selfish, I'm vain, I'm anything you please."

"I'm poor, I've my way to make, I'm on the world; but I'm an honest man."

"I am silly, I am ignorant, I am affected, I am false."

"I am glad for your sake, and I am glad for mine; and I am glad, too . . . "

"I wondered at myself; I sneered at my idiotcy [*sic*]; I cursed my mad folly."

"I feel weary, I feel angry, I feel like crying."

"I am not complaining of them; I am simply stating a fact. I am very sorry for them; I am greatly disappointed."

Is any ear good enough to distinguish Hubert from George from Christina from Ellen's mother from St. Elmo from Christina from Roderick?* Or even Henry James from the "d—d mob"?

"To find my poor boy so handsome, so prosperous, so elegant, so famous . . . "

"She is so proud, so sensitive, so scrupulous, and yet so boundlessly ambitious."

"You see there is so much danger, and so little profit, so much romance, and so little vulgarity."

"This priest . . . was so truly useful to his pupil, so complaisant to his vices, so good a calculator of every sort of force, so deep when it was necessary to play some human trick, so young at table . . . "

The first litanist is Mrs. Hudson; which one is Balzac? I include him

*W&W 590, 334; RH 235; WWW 24; StE 317; RH 189, 325.

here—last, after *St. Elmo's* Hammond, and *The Initials'* Baron*—to suggest how much the "great" novelists in France (and in England) retain and thus sanction the potentially hollow syntax of litany.

> He knew that he couldn't marry her, that he shouldn't, that he wouldn't.
>
> (*W&W* 594)
>
> "I am corrupt, corruptible, corruption!"
>
> (*RH* 371)

Indicating how much litany appealed to James' passion for the feel and roll of sheer language, these extreme examples seem almost grammar book paradigms. They are also paradigmatic of the danger inherent in litanies. If the novelist, apprentice or otherwise, cannot make the syntactic patterns seem the expression of a particular character, then the patterns take over and we lose what we value most in James' fiction—the inidividual consciousness. Especially at times of high emotion, the ornate and long-familiar patterns of litany tend to preclude spontaneity and thus reduce the character's emotion to the prepackaged passion of the stage tirade.

The outburst itself, however, is what James comes eventually to question. Granted that fiction must present the profoundest human moments: do these occur in litany and harangue, or in the silence of the night? This dilemma too has roots in the popular tradition. As that tradition can repudiate exaggeration and then exaggerate or can remand perfection to eternity and then create "perfect" characters, so mid-Victorian scribblers cannot maintain a single attitude even toward The Word. Despite all its harangue and litany, fiction has traditionally been wary of eloquence. Reflecting a Low Church aversion to aureate language, the novel goes on record in favor of plain style. Whether we contrast the forthright speech of Richardson's heroines with the gilded guile of their seducers, or listen a century later to Hamilton prove his affection ("'I cannot rave like your cousin'" [*In* 396]), the basic assumption abides: truth needs not the embellishment of art. This attitude is summed up well in *Ishmael*. Three elaborate, manipulative styles are defined and dismissed.

> The first of these [lawyers], Mr. Wiseman, was distinguished for his profound knowledge of the law, his skill in logic, and his closeness in reasoning; the second, Mr. Berners, was celebrated for his fire and eloquence; and the third, Mr. Vivian, was famous for his wit and sarcasm. . . . In vain Wiseman appealed to reason; Berners to feeling; and Vivian to humor. . . . Wiseman's wisdom was found to be foolishness; Berners' pathos laughable; and Vivian's humor grievous.
>
> (464, 472)

*RH 299–300; StE 195; In 369; FrP 86.

Ishmael defeats this trio of giants and "their old, familiar, well-worn styles" (472) because he is "a new orator among them, with a fresh original style" (470). His secret? " 'I have made some notes; but for the rest I shall trust to the inspiration of the instant.'. . . 'for the rest "it shall be given ye in that hour, what ye shall speak," ' said Beatrice earnestly" (463).[61] Truth is God's gift, and needs not man's ornament. Moreover, the need to disseminate God's truth makes plain style indispensable. As Hannah More opines, "if people were ever so wise and good, yet if they had not a simple, agreeable, and familiar way of expressing themselves, some of their plain hearers would not be much the better for them."[62] Not on his way to any plain-style soapbox, but definitely moving away from hollow rhetorical eloquence, Henry James learns from the scribblers as well as from the sages. By 1881 he has even gone so far as to question the probity of plain style itself.

In his first two novels James is already aware that too much eloquence cannot be taken seriously. When Roger proposes "with manly elo-quence" (*W&W* 235), Miss Morton "smiled at this fine talk" (236). James is also smiling when Roderick's fit of eloquence "nearly swamped the gondola" (*RH* 84) and when various characters undercut his declama-tions repeatedly (108, 208, 209). Then, with *The American*, James makes an important advance, for the characters most readily eloquent here are *not* the main figures. Besides the appropriately named Miss Finch, who "discoursed brilliantly, not only during the entr'actes, but during many of the finest portions [of *Don Giovanni*]" (221), the figure who most nearly matches Roderick's supposed fluency is Valentin Bellegarde. Valentin clearly is *not* Roderick, however. The Frenchman does not have the title role and does provide us complex enjoyment.

> [Newman] "I suppose you have swallowed all those fine words you used about her [Noémie] the other night. You compared her to a sapphire . . ."
> "I don't remember," said Valentin, "it may have been to a carbuncle!"
>
> (223)

Since a carbuncle is a boil as well as a gem, Valentin's pun shows him sufficiently aware of his pleasant limitations that we may well regret his passing more than Roderick's.

> "I couldn't go into business, I couldn't make money, because I was a Bellegarde. I couldn't go into politics, because I was a Bellegarde—the Bellegardes don't recognize the Bonapartes. I couldn't go into litera-ture, because I was a dunce. I couldn't marry a rich girl, because no Bellegarde had ever married a *roturière*."
>
> (*Ame* 93)

"I couldn't be a shopkeeper. I can't be a doctor, it's a repulsive
business. I can't be a clergyman, I haven't got convictions. . . . I can't be
a lawyer; I don't understand—how do you call it—the American
procédure."

(*PL* 200)

In the second passage Ned Rosier echoes Valentin in the first. Clearly,
however, the languishing swain plays an even less major role in 1881
than he did in 1877. After *Roderick Hudson* James concentrates upon a
different type of hero-talker.

Christopher Newman is, we are told, a plain-style man of the people.
With "a relish for ungrammatical conversation" he likes to "gossip" on
"rail fences" (47). Thus we are not surprised when he cannot profess his
love in eloquent, Roderick style.

He made no violent love to her—no sentimental speeches.

"So what I say is not mere gallantry and compliments and nonsense—I
can't talk that way, I don't know how, and I wouldn't, to you,
if I could."

(*Ame* 163, 117)

On page 117, however, Newman is denying the oratorical manner in an
oratorical manner. His " 'can't . . . don't . . . wouldn't' " litany resembles
the "couldn't . . . shouldn't . . . wouldn't" of *Watch and Ward*. Not only
does such mechanically patterned eloquence occur elsewhere in *The
American*, but James even resorts to the device of summing up Newman's
speech with assertions of its effect. "This passionate sally" (296) follows

"I want to bring them down—down, down, down. . . . They took me
up into a high place and made me stand there for all the world to see
me, and then they stole behind me and pushed me into this bottomless
pit, where I lie howling and gnashing my teeth!"

The "down" litany echoes Richard II's " 'Down, down, I come; like
glistering Phaeton' "; being taken to a high place and being hurled into the
pit recall both Christ's temptation and Satan's fate. All of which is too
fancy for a plain-style boy from San Francisco.

The break with litany and harangue which *The American* begins soon
spreads by 1880 to the genteel world of *Washington Square*. Catherine
Sloper is a plain-style protagonist beset by rhetoricians. At their least
venal, the rhetors are comic.

[Mrs. Almond] "I thought a lovelorn maiden was always scenic."
[Dr. Sloper] "A ridiculous widow is more so. Lavinia has made
me a speech."

(81)[63]

In predictable litany Lavinia descants upon Morris. " 'He is very handsome; he is very clever; he expressed himself with a great deal—a great deal of felicity' " (34). This litany seems especially untrustworthy because Morris has already expressed himself. " 'What a delightful party! What a charming house! What an interesting family!' " (29). Thus the very syntax of litany, echoing Morris' (and Lavinia's) hollowness, takes on thematic significance.

Despite the comic inanity of his style, however, Morris is finally different from those languishing swains, Roger-Roderick-Valentin-Ned. Morris is a rhetorician who causes profound hurt. For, alas, Catherine also thinks him eloquent. "He was saying clever things . . . when Morris kissed her and said these things—that also made her heart beat" (32, 66). Catherine's plight is especially serious because she is beset, from the other side, by another rhetorician whom she also loves. Her father. "She admired his neatness and nobleness of expression" (73). Since neat Sloper abhors Lavinia's frothy excesses and Morris' melodramatic ardor, we should have no trouble distinguishing his icy self from them.

> "Have you no faith in my wisdom, in my tenderness, in my solicitude for your future?"
>
> "That you should be reasonable . . . that you should take counsel of worldly prudence, and submit to practical considerations; that you should agree to—a—separate."
>
> "I have nothing to do with your sentiments, your fancies, your affections, your delusions."
>
> "On the question of my reputation, of my relations with your father, of my relations with my own children . . ."
>
> (110, 177, 114, 152)

The similarity here (Sloper speaks the first and third sentences, Lavinia and Morris the second and fourth) does not derive, like the similarity of James' earlier litanists, from his inability to provide individual characters with individual voices. Rather the conventionality of Sloper's eloquence is James' very point. All three characters—despite their surface differences and their presumptions to the contrary—*are* much alike. They share the rhetoric of litany because they all treat Catherine as an object of power.

Thus James in the crucial decade learns not only to avoid rhetorical excesses but also to capitalize upon our traditional distrust of wily rhetoricians. In 1881 he then carries his examination of eloquence one step further. The eloquent artificers in *The Portrait* wrap themselves in the verbal mantle sacred to protagonists and assume the virtues of plain style. First, there is Madame Merle.

" . . . what have I got? Neither husband, nor child, nor fortune, nor position, nor the traces of a beauty which I never had."

(184)[64]

In this mixture of litany syntax and plain-style candor, the candor makes Isabel receptive. If the litany makes us uneasy here and earlier (174, 181), we cannot yet be certain that Madame Merle is lying. Nor do subsequent revelations disprove her statement here entirely, for she has indeed lost Pansy without gaining wealth or rank and without replacing the husband she never loved. Unlike the rhetoricians of popular literature, then, Madame Merle is not simply a liar; she keeps our response ambivalently sympathetic by combining eloquent litany with plain-style candor. In turn, the consequences of using language for unhallowed ends are increasingly suggested by the syntax itself. Madame Merle's lies may succeed temporarily, but she knows the price of turning life into litany. " 'What do you call one's life?' asked Madame Merle. 'One's appearance, one's movements, one's engagements, one's society?' " (220). And when even this litany life of meaningless great-house visits is imperiled, Madame Merle resorts again to the syntax which captivated Isabel once. " 'Now don't be heroic, don't be unreasonable, don't take offence' " (476). She fails, of course, and is exiled to America, where her sad half-truths will be sadder still.

Osmond suffers less.

"I am very sorry for Catherine."

(*WS* 81)

"I am sorry for Miss Archer!"

(*PL* 222)

The seducer in *The Portrait* echoes the heroine's only ally in *Washington Square*. Such plain-style forthrightness and sympathy help prevent Gilbert Osmond from becoming simply the embodiment of evil. On the other hand, putting the traditional comment of sympathy into the villain's mouth allows James to create a more terrible seducer. Osmond's onslaught seems particularly conscious and inhuman after he proves human enough to enter into the plight of his prey. His duplicity and litany resemble Madame Merle's, for, as she had " 'neither husband, nor child, nor fortune,' " he says, " 'I have neither fortune, nor fame, nor extrinsic advantages' " (287). Which is true. Rather than lie, Osmond makes the truth into a lie by using it to misrepresent and to seduce. The litany form continues to signal his hollowness both when he describes his " 'perfect' " conjugal situation (" 'we read, we study, we make music, we walk, we drive—we talk even' " [469]), and when he explains away his treatment of Pansy (" 'a young girl should be fresh and fair; she should be innocent and gentle. . . . she will have her books and her drawing; she will have her piano' " [490]). His litany here is part of that "mesh of fine threads" (495) which has caught and bound Isabel. She eventually moves beyond Osmond's eloquence because she, like the reader, learns about extravagances of speech.

Isabel begins as a complex speaker. That her famous " 'personal independence' " declaration is both noble and inadequate James signals when he adds, "whatever there was of grandeur in this speech moved Caspar Goodwood's admiration" (149). Her subsequent litanies in praise of Madame Merle contrast with Ralph's litanies which call into question Madame Merle and the litany form itself.

> She was rare, she was superior, she was pre-eminent. . . . [Isabel] envied the talents, the accomplishments, the aptitudes of Madame Merle.
>
> (174, 175)
>
> "She is too good, too kind, too clever, too learned, too accomplished . . . . [Upon the character of everyone else you may find some little black speck] but on Madame Merle's, nothing, nothing, nothing!"
>
> (232, 233)

We tend to side with Ralph and apprehension, of course, but we do not lose hope because Isabel proves capable of qualifying her own litanies. "He [Warburton] was pleasant, he was powerful, he was gallant, there was no better man than he. But her answer remained" (268). Unfortunately Isabel cannot also manage to qualify her litanies with Osmond —cannot, that is, until too late.

> "He [Osmond] knows everything, he understands everything, he has the kindest, gentlest, highest spirit. . . . no property, no titles, no honours, no houses, nor lands, nor position, nor reputation, nor brilliant belongings of any sort. It is the total absence of all these things that pleases me."
>
> (321)
>
> A mind more ingenious, more subtle, more cultivated, more trained to admirable exercises, she had not yet encountered. . . . She had thought it so large, so enlightened, so perfectly that of an honest man and a gentleman. Had he not assured her that he had no superstitions, no dull limitations, no prejudices that had lost their freshness?
>
> (394, 395)

On page 321 the superlatives arrayed in litany help suggest the extremity of Isabel's delusion. Although the language of extravagance on pages 394 and 395 also denies as it affirms, James' tactic is different here. The point now is not that he sees what Isabel cannot, but that she sees what she could not earlier. Her disillusioned retrospection provides the necessary qualification. "She had a vision of him—she had not read him right" (393).

Isabel has shared the rhetoricians' litanies not because she, like they, is practicing deception consciously, but because she, like us all, is partially deceived about herself. The alternative to her romanticism is not any simple, plain-style realism, however. The spokesmen for plain style are Osmond and Mrs. Touchett. "He never forgot himself" (323) and she lapses into "no exaggeration" (189) even at her husband's death. When Lydia says dryly of dying Ralph, " 'it has not been a successful life' " Isabel must add, " 'no—it has only been a beautiful one' " (525). A balance of head and heart, of plain and poetic styles, constitutes the ideal so lacking in the extreme practices of James' earliest novels. In *The Portrait* such a middle way is expressly espoused. "Ralph, with his experimental geniality, suggested, by way of healing the breach, that the truth lay between the two extremes" (88). As he perceives how the genial experiment of his behest to Isabel had produced deadly earnest results, Ralph becomes still more humanely a figure of the middle way. "He wished to discharge his mind. But he wished also to be superlatively gentle" (318).

This state of the qualified superlative is what Isabel also achieves. Eventually capable of imagining two sides to Madame Merle, she wonders "whether the most discreet of women might not also by chance be the most dangerous" (446). Extremes then come together as Isabel recognizes the mixed nature of our common humanity and must temper her moment of revenge. "What remained was the cleverest woman in the world ... knowing as little what to think as the meanest" (509). Isabel's growth beyond the easy extravagance of her early superlatives parallels James' own. By 1881 he has managed to make his superlatives mean contrary things simultaneously. Osmond has real excellences, as Isabel has real faults; and the standards of judgment are themselves seriously questioned. Undercutting and affirmation coincide because only then does style achieve that true moderation which, free of extravagance yet committed to the superlative, is the language of responsibility.

Even moderating control, however, can involve dangers. Equipoise is no more ideal *in itself* than extravagance. To see how Isabel (and James) learn to avoid the limitations of too simple control, we turn now to the style of equipoise.

The rhythms of the early James
are old-fashioned, almost
eighteenth-century.
                    Edmund Wilson

Equipoise

Toward the eighteenth century James felt an ambivalence which critics have never defined adequately.

No other age appeals at once so much and so little to our sympathies, or provokes such alternations of curiosity and repugnance. It is near enough to us to seem to partake of many of our current feelings, and yet it is divided from us by an impassable gulf. . . . It is peopled with men and women whose style of dress inspires both admiration and mistrust.

                                                            (*FrP* 291)

James' ambivalence appears clearly in his attitude toward Samuel Johnson. Mentioning the Great Cham no less than fourteen times before 1881, James can praise Johnson for his "authority" and "affection for London" and his prose for its "vigorous brevity"; yet James can also recognize Johnson's "conversational brutality" and can lament that we have been "too long the victim of the purely Johnsonian view [of Chesterfield]" (*SA* 10; *FrP* 72; *SA* 10; *Na* 1876, 182; 1875, 262).[65]

In general, James' most consistent praise of the *bon temps* goes to the English prose masters. Perennially esteemed in America, these masters received special attention during young Henry's formative years because Thackeray's first lecture tour " 'has given start to a Swift, and Congreve, and Addison furor.' "[66] In 1858 James first reads *The Vicar of Wakefield;* in 1878 he praises "Goldsmith's delicate and humorous masterpiece, whose charm is almost wholly the exquisite narrative style" (*SA* 114); in 1900 James is still charmed enough to write an introduction for the novel.[67] After living so happily in Newport, that "corner of the eighteenth century that had lingered into the nineteenth" (*E*1:139), James chooses as his first London residence a Georgian house on "Bolton Street. . . . which had an eighteenth-century air about it. Fanny Burney had lived a few doors away at No. 11, the 'Old Pretender' had once lodged there."[68] By this time James has read Addison, Boswell, Chesterfield, Congreve, Franklin, Gibbon, Goldsmith, Johnson, Reynolds, Steele, Swift, Walpole, Lady Mary Wortley-Montague. Moreover, traditionally eighteenth-century stylistic devices reach James not only directly but also through the influence which the *bon temps* exerts upon American and English culture at every level.

54

For most cultivated Americans in the Victorian period, the eighteenth
century remained a time of elegance and authority.[69] It is no accident, for
example, that those American tourists Henrietta Stackpole and Isabel
Archer plan in their London visit to "find out where Doctor Johnson
had lived, and Goldsmith and Addison" (*PL* 117). American attitudes
toward language up to the Civil War remain predominantly eighteenth-
century. The major grammarians are Noah Webster and Lindley Murray,
who draw almost entirely upon neoclassical theories, and Goold Brown,
who surpasses these men in some important ways but "culturally . . .
never got much beyond the classical horizon that his father had shown
him as a boy."[70] As for style itself, numerous examples and contemporary
testaments support Furness' statement that to "many generations of
Americans . . . the *Spectator* was held up as the supreme model of prose
style" (63). In James' particular case, four of his favorite novelists are
profoundly committed to the eighteenth century—Jane Austen, Thackeray, Howells, and the writer whom young James probably resembles
most, Nathaniel Hawthorne.[71] Having said that "there is always a little of
the Dr. Johnson" in Hawthorne, James then notes "that Hawthorne has
paid to Boswell's hero (in the chapter on 'Lichfield and Uttoxeter,' in his
volume on England) a tribute of the finest appreciation" (*Ha* 53). See, in
fact, how much Hawthorne sounds like Henrietta and Isabel when he
says, "I think that what interests me most here [in England] is the London
of the Queen Anne age—what Pope, *The Spectator*, Defoe, and down as
late as Johnson and Goldsmith have mentioned."[72] This biographical
interest is reflected in Hawthorne's style, as two very different critics
note.

> The influence of the Augustans (and a salutary influence it was) is seen
> everywhere in his writings: his prose was firm-textured like theirs; he
> had their sense of structure, and their penchant for criticism and satire.

> Hawthorne's balance between confession and evasion is reflected in
> his style, whose distance and abstraction are often confused with
> Augustan serenity. The meditative poise, the polite irony, the anti-
> theses, the formal diction, and the continual appeal to sentiments that
> are generally shared, all serve to neutralize the dangerous knowledge
> that lies at the bottom of his plots.[73]

The lingering attractiveness of the eighteenth century is also felt
strongly by the mass reading public, as sales figures indicate. In Victorian
England "one street-seller told Mayhew that nothing sold better than
eighteenth-century prose classics, from Addison to Goldsmith"; as for
America's standard fare, "Goldsmith they read, and Hume, and *The Swiss
Family Robinson*, and Blair's *Rhetoric*, and on Sunday the Bible."[74]
Eighteenth-century poetry remains so popular in both countries that not
only *Night Thoughts* and the *Essay on Man* endure, but even Watts'
verse "was widely diffused and lasted for a hundred and fifty years or

more."[75] Popular writers' conscious (and unconscious) debts to the eighteenth century are so numerous[76] that we must attempt to understand why. Whatever the neoclassical stylistic devices of generalized diction, pointed syntax, personification, and epithet may have meant to the neoclassical masters, to nineteenth-century popular writers they mean security. The security, first, of sanction. This is how educated gentlemen wrote in the most gentlemanly of times. More profoundly (if more sentimentally), the neoclassical style provides the security of equipoise: an ordered and intelligible cosmos; truths universal in range and acceptance. Sanctioned by acknowledged masters and carried on by Victorian writers of authority (though often at their least enduring), neoclassical stylistic devices suffer at the hands of the scribblers what neoclassical ideas suffer from in the heads of the scribblers—all are simplified, rigidified, deified. Popular writers and early James use the language of equipoise in ways which make the diction too vague and the syntax too tidy. By 1881 James has learned to control both diction and syntax enough to make them contribute to his (and our) emerging portrait of Isabel. First, techniques which tend to create dictional vagueness.

1

Establishing the continuity of the neoclassical ideal of stylized diction, James Sutherland quotes Addison's admonition that " 'a poet should take particular care to guard himself against idiomatic ways of speaking' " and then quotes Johnson defending Pope's diction on the ground that " 'knowledge finds no willing reception till it be recommended by artificial diction.' "[77] These prose masters defend poetic diction because prose, as much as verse, was committed to the artificial, the generalized, the abstract. The age, as Jean Hagstrum says, "found the generalized diction, the personifications, and the abstract ideas of reflective and didactic poetry to be emotionally and aesthetically evocative."[78] Hagstrum could, almost as well, be speaking here of Victorian times, for the generalizing and abstracting techniques which moved eighteenth-century readers[79] are still flourishing a century later in the fiction of early James and his popular compeers.

Personification, for instance.

Age will perform the promises of youth.

Grace will surely lend a generous hand to nature.

Duty and Love seemed to signal a truce.

Pride . . . steps in to our defence.

Discretion drew a long breath.

Pleasure sat on all faces.

The first and fourth examples are from Johnson and Pope; the second and fifth from *Watch and Ward;* the third and last from *St. Elmo* and *The Wide, Wide World.*[80] So self-conscious of and so addicted to personification is the Victorian popular novel that *The Initials* can present "perfect personifications of German beauty. . . . 'a better personification of a pretty, naughty child' . . . . 'vulgarity personified' . . . . the personification of gratitude" (10, 12, 72, 91). James follows the popular practice of personifying both actions,

> defeated self-interest smirked horribly,
>
> the Cavaliere's shrewdness exchanged a glance with Rowland's,
>
> the anguish of remorse clothed itself in tangible forms,

and reactions,

> weariness mastered her,
>
> fatigue conquered memory and sorrow,
>
> "gentle sleep will take her revenge."

In each case agency is denied.* The individual is replaced by a trait or humor. Which is what popular authors want: they distance any threat by making the situation impersonal, and they increase significance and appeal by making the action or reaction universal. In James' fiction, however, personification removes precisely what interests us most—the particular character and his fate. Personification, moreover, is only one of several neoclassical devices which reduce action to expression. Other types of tired language in James' early fiction are the formula, the epithet, the noun entity, the cliché, and circumlocution.

Of the many formulas derived from the eighteenth century and beloved of Victorian scribblers, Henry James' favorite is "heart."

> In her alarm her heart had chosen.
> [In her alarm she had chosen]
>
> Pain and pleasure, at once, possessed Nora's heart.
> [Pain and pleasure, at once, possessed her]
>
> (W&W 243, 588)[81]

In each case our concern is for Nora, and in each case "she" or "her" is what "heart" displaces in the sentence. Instead of the plight of a particular individual, James gives us a standardized formula, a pre-digested pill which usage has guaranteed safe and effective. Rather than evoking an emotion, the formula provides an occasion for emotion, for the coalescence of any and all heartfelt associations. This tactic mars scenes in James' early novels for several reasons besides the most

---

*W&W 703; RH 218; AB 163; W&W 691; StE 40; HR 2:167.

obvious—that it panders to bathos. One reason is quantitative. Despite the abundance of formulas in such perennial best sellers as Homer and Racine, fifty-eight "heart"s in ninety-one pages do not make poor *Watch and Ward* into an *Iliad* or a *Phaedra*, especially since "heart" is by no means James' only formula.[82] Moreover, formulas are particularly prominent at moments of high intensity. "Roger's heart rose to his throat. . . . Nora's heart began to beat" (327, 338). The literal aspects of the formula—and even James' earliest fiction is too serious to slight any aspect of the language completely—introduce ghastly and ludicrous suggestions into serious scenes. The figurative aspects, in turn, tend especially to convert action into expression because the formulaic word occurs so often in formulaic phrases. "[Roger] felt a certain sinking of the heart . . . . [Nora] felt a most unreasoned sinking of the heart . . . . Nora's heart sank . . . . Nora's heart sank" (243, 692, 693, 696).

Formulas also limit agency in another way. With their obviously sentimental origins and sanctions, "heart" and other saccharine expressions control experience by sugar-coating it. The same readers who glow warmly when a house in *The Heir* is called "a perfect little snuggery" (1:336–37) also tingle when the glares of Mrs. Keith and Hubert are called "a dainty crossing of blades" (*W&W* 587). James is fond of the saccharine formula "sweet"—"his growing sense of her sweetness bade fair to make him bungle his naughtiness" (*W&W* 331)—but an especially conventional use of "pretty" is what confirms James' early tie to the tradition of sugar and spice.

> She had a very pretty trick of suddenly turning her head . . . . Fenton was a pretty fellow enough . . . . [Hubert] had a very pretty firmness of manner . . . . such pretty elements of success . . . . it seemed a very pretty joke . . . . a very pretty heritage of prohibitions . . . . "must be a very pretty fellow" . . . . "a very pretty fortune" . . . . had made a very pretty show.
>
> (*W&W* 235, 329, 416, 419, 420, 421, 585, 593, 702)

How completely a saccharine expression can control actions is evident when James (and popular writers)[83] have recourse to "tussle." Imagine with what security the Gentle Fair caught their breath when "Roger expected a tussle" (*W&W* 700) or when "there was a lively tussle, but he [Rowland] gained his case" (*RH* 14) or when Rowland's hat rolls away "in vague symbolism of an actual physical tussle" (288). Vague indeed.

Epithet is another major device by which eighteenth-century writers, Victorian scribblers, and young Henry James turn action into expression. In the *bon temps* Alexander Pope wrote of the Man of Ross, Mackenzie of the Man of Feeling, and Joseph Warton distinguished between A Man of Wit, A Man of Sense, and A True Poet. Such practice is particularly

influential in Victorian times because it is also sanctioned by theater—
and not only the upper-class theater from Wycherley to Sheridan. The
father of melodrama, Réné Pixerécourt, reveals his sentimentality "in the
very texture of his language, as witness those recurring epithets which are
such a distinguishing mark of his style—*père tendre, ami généreux,
amant fidèle, époux sensible,* and the like"[84] Such epithets flourish in
English and American plays, particularly in the first half of the nineteenth
century. Drink, for example, "is called 'the deadly compound,' 'the
destructive bowl,' 'the envenomed cup,' and 'the poisoned chalice.' "[85]
Prose writing in the nineteenth century thus experiences the double
influence of drama and the established neoclassical mode.

> Much that is bad in nineteenth-century romantic writing—English and
> American—can be put down to the plague of unemployed epithets
> which settled on literature and robbed it of much of its ability to pay
> any clear-eyed, simple, trenchant attention to the empirical facts
> of the world.
>   (Tanner, 151–52)

Determined to write a "sunny" novel after *The Scarlet Letter,* Nathaniel
Hawthorne controls his gothic imagination by using (among other
neoclassical devices) a steady barage of epithets. "The gentlemen of
worship . . . . the man of patches . . . . the man of conventionalities . . . .
the man of root-beer . . . . the urchin of elephantine appetite . . . . the
man of flesh."[86] Since young Henry James was open to all the influences
of the period and considered *Seven Gables* Hawthorne's finest novel, we
should not be surprised to find in two consecutive pages of an early tale
"a man of refined tastes . . . . a man of observation . . . . a man of action
. . . . a man of culture and of society" (*CT* 1:236–37). In *Watch and Ward*
we find "a man of tremors and blushes . . . . a man of delicacy . . . . a
man of taste . . . . a woman of perceptions . . . . a man of culture . . . . a
woman of spirit" (234, 417, 424 [twice], 430, 704). The effect of such
epithets—aside from their profusion—is exemplified by our response to
Nora's German houseguest. Appearing suddenly from nowhere and
vanishing soon without mention, Fräulein Lilienthal seems all the more a
plot contrivance because James follows the popular practice of concentrating epithets with young ladies. As "the musical stranger" and "the
gentle Fräulein" (584), Miss Lilienthal suffers the fate of virtually
everything that James applies epithets to.* She lacks that minimum
particularity essential to catching and sustaining our interest.
    A third device with neoclassical sanction controls and overcontrols
action in a related, but different way.

---

*Nora herself is called "a fair stranger" (577). We also find "the fair sex. . . . a fair
Papist. . . . fair beauties" (415, 585, 592).

Ramblers were addressed to those only "whose passions left them leisure for abstracted truth, and whom virtue could please by its naked dignity." "Abstracted truth" and "naked dignity" are phrases of moral meaning, but they suggest the type of literary style that most appropriately should convey such truth and express such dignity.

(Hagstrum, 85)

"Abstract truth" and "naked dignity": noun phrases like these occur frequently in eighteenth-century masterpieces, in popular fiction, and in early James. For lack of a better name I will call them noun entities. As Johnson speaks of "abstract truth" and "naked dignity," Victorian scribblers write of "disinterested friendship" and " 'natural dignity,' " and James of "dutiful demureness" and "cosmopolitan Occidentalism" (*In* 160; *HR* 1:67; *W&W* 323, 330). James tags both physical qualities ("the beauty of natural movement" [*RH* 17]) and psychological states ("the inexpugnable instinct of paternity" [*W&W* 238]). Before attempting to explain why the noun entities which obviously succeed in neoclassical masterpieces fail with James and the scribblers, we should note the frequency of the device in Victorian fiction. Find *Watch and Ward* below, keeping in mind that it is one fifth the length of popular novels.

That sweet curiosity of little girls . . . . her childish innocence and grief . . . . her childish sweetness . . . . her childish sense . . . . childish colors . . . . that subtle divining process common to illiterate children . . . . the air of a child who has been much alone . . . . her primal sense of things . . . . elfish gravity . . . . the shambling and sheepish state of girlhood . . . . the frank perspicuity of childhood . . . . shambling childhood . . . . that charming girlish moment . . . . the broad freedom of childhood . . . . the very genius of girlhood . . . . her formless girlhood . . . . her sensitive youth . . . . childish keenness . . . . dutiful demureness . . . . tentative daughterliness . . . . youthful brightness . . . . the careless gaiety and the light immediate joys of girlhood . . . . a young girl's passion for novels . . . . the lost graces of youth . . . . her girlish good will . . . . girlish heart . . . . the fount of her virgin sympathies . . . . boyish vagueness of outline . . . . girlish frankness . . . . the mental pinafore of childhood . . . . little-girlishness . . . . departing childishness . . . . hungry virginal days . . . . her girlish *épanouissement* . . . . a school-girl's primness . . . . the shrinking diffidence of childhood . . . . girlish freshness . . . . childish simplicity . . . . a simple maiden of common gifts . . . . the slender, angular, neutral grace of youth and freshness . . . . tender slip of girlhood . . . . her maiden's fancy . . . . maidenly reserve . . . . virginal faithfulness . . . . her helpless childhood . . . . fervid youthful parting . . . . filial solicitude . . . . girlish *brusquerie*.

Womanly finesse . . . . her tender feminine promise . . . . poor little uprooted germ of womanhood . . . . housewifely gossip . . . . lady's

peaceful domestic genius .... motherly science .... woman's heritage
of garrulity .... the feminine charm .... the pliable innocence of early
maidenhood .... womanly cunning .... woman's estate .... an
almost feminine voice .... the half-concessions, the reserve of freshness, the fugitive dignity, of gently nurtured womanhood .... the
woman's peace-making art .... feminine right .... a tender matronly
smile .... blooming maturity .... the ladyish gossip .... feminine
impedimenta .... motherly unction .... maternal ardor .... feminine riddles .... the miseries of young ladyhood .... a sumptuous,
ladyish air .... sisterly graciousness .... that sense of feminine
appeal which to a man who retains aught of the generosity of manhood
is the most inspiring of all motives .... air of remote widowhood ....
maternal care .... maternal care.

They are all from *Watch and Ward*, of course. And are only part of the
total.[87]

Granting, then, the impact of such profusion, how else do noun
entities affect the reading experience? James uses entities as though the
qualities which they refer to are static and universal. "That natural
reserve of the altered mind" (*W&W* 578) suggests that all altered minds
are one "mind" and have one response—reservation—which is "natural."
In so epistemologically static a world the names of things stand for the
things themselves. The writer need only point. He takes us into his
confidence, for example, and refers knowingly to "one of those dark rich
toilets of early winter" (592). Or he uses the "that which" construction;
we are presumed to know "which" thing is meant once the author states it
is "that" one.

That wholesome discretion whose .... that tempered Roman glow
which .... that natural reserve of the altered mind when confronted
.... that serene good grace which .... that circumspect jealousy with
which ....
(*W&W* 234, 429, 578, 582 [twice])

James also turns action into entity by his use of articles. When Fenton's
partner in *Watch and Ward* is raving to cronies, "several of them sat ...
listening with a half-bored grin" (693). "Several" men can have "a" grin
because James is imagining a general mental set, not a specific dramatic
situation. James also uses the definite article to create noun entities, as
when Roger tours the hemisphere "so that he might know the range of the
feminine charm" (320). Since "the" feminine charm implies a single reality
which *is* feminine charm and can be learned, we move from a fictional to
a fictitious situation. This also happens when James omits articles. At a
crucial moment in *Watch and Ward*, Mrs. Keith is "stirred by vague
conjecture" (697). "A" vague conjecture would keep the moment particular, specific; omission of the article anthropomorphizes "vague

conjecture" and depersonalizes the moment. Once again James is destroy-
ing what interests us most in his scenes—the individual character.

> When a very little girl becomes the happy possessor of a wax-doll,
> she testifies her affection for it by a fond manipulation of its rosy
> visage. . . . we would compare Miss Prescott to such a little girl. She
> fingers her puppets to death. "Good heavens, Madame!" we are
> forever on the point of exclaiming, "let the poor things speak for them-
> selves. What? are you afraid they can't stand alone?"
>
> (*NAR* 1865, 271)

What we must recognize here is not simply that James does in *Watch and
Ward* what he criticizes Miss Prescott for doing in *Azarian*. More
important is the fact that a novelist can fatally finger his puppets by
overcontrolling his style as well as his plot. The words themselves can
thwart the character. "Good heavens, Sir!" we repeatedly exclaim, "let
the poor creatures live, live, live! And let your language conform to
them, however they become." Such an admonition does not reduce
James' early fiction to ill-shaped prototypes of the late. Already with
Miss Prescott in January of 1865 James is announcing his commitment to
the integrity of the character. From the middle of the crucial decade
onward he moves away from stylistic overcontrol, and comes increasingly to recognize how fluid experience is for him, how much his basic
sense of language and character differ from the static epistemology and
techniques of popular fiction. Before tracing James' movement toward a
new epistemology in the years between 1876 and 1881, however, we
must study two other early devices which, like noun entities, overcontrol
the action by referring us to sanctioned alternatives. Cliché and
circumlocution.

The atrophy which noun entities represent had touched almost all
aspects of literary language by the late eighteenth century. Much
mid-Victorian fiction is still affected by it.

> "Force of character" . . . . "his heart was set" . . . . held his peace . . . .
> quivering with indignation . . . . beguile the time . . . . strength of will
> . . . . wounded to the quick . . . . not one whit . . . . the very brow of
> the beetling crag . . . . laughed the speaker to scorn . . . . "the horns of
> a dilemma" . . . . threw her arms round him . . . . heaving a deep
> sigh . . . . fits of laughing . . . . a flood of tears.

> Bathed in blood . . . . in great distress . . . . cracked with a great report
> . . . . to lie awake at night trying hard to fix in his mind the happy
> medium . . . . mused ever and anon . . . . the lion's share . . . . to check
> the headlong course . . . . feasted her fill . . . . took heart again . . . .
> lining his pockets . . . . at her fingers' ends . . . . failed to appreciate
> . . . . [his] head swam.

Clichés are so endemic to popular novelists and early James (his are the second group here and are only part of tiny *Watch and Ward*'s total)[88] that they consistently vitiate the action. Worse still, they seem to cluster at crisis moments where James most needs convincing language, and least gets it. Roger's crucial illness, for instance, "went from bad to worse . . . . strength and reason were at the lowest ebb . . . . [Roger] had taken a marked turn for the better, and was out of the woods" (582, 583, 587). By converting a threatening event into familiar words, popular writers control the event sufficiently that their audiences can enjoy both a sense of security and whatever is delightful about the event (and mid-Victorians found illness immensely attractive). In James' presentation of Roger's illness and in many scenes like it throughout the early novels, however, the patient perishes from overattention, and is mummified in verbiage.

Circumlocution functions like cliché, but less crudely, in James' early fiction. Some simple examples do appear. Whereas Boswell wittily calls sexual interplay "the wars of Paphian Queen,"[89] James tritely calls Nora's seamy milieu "the scenery of Bohemia" (*W&W* 241). We can, of course, have fun with an age that skirted piano legs and preferred "white meat" to "breast" (at least in public). E. Douglas Branch finds fair game in the foremost American poetess of the time.

> In Mrs. Sigourney's autobiography occurs a reference to "a quadruped member of our establishment which has not been mentioned, and is, I suppose, scarcely mentionable to ears polite. Yet I never could understand why it should be an offense to delicacy to mention the name of" —and she trails off into a circumlocution, for not even in her private diary would she write the word "hog."
>
> (137)

The major problem which circumlocution causes James is not so simple, however. He rarely shies from the facts of life that his plots entail. Rather, circumlocution hurts James as it hurts the best of the popular tradition—in control of tone.

> [Nora] smiled with a kind of tentative daughterliness through the traces of her recent grief.
>
> (*W&W* 325)
>
> [Mrs. Hudson] empty-handed save for the pocket-handkerchief in her lap, which was held with an air of familiarity with its sadder uses.
>
> (*RH* 47)

James' gentle readers would feel all the more in on orphaned Nora's plight because they are in on the fact that "traces of her recent grief" means "tears"; to us, however, the circumlocution joins with the mindless noun entity "tentative daughterliness" to make the orphan's already conventional situation seem too literary and arch.[90] What about Mrs. Hudson? At times James can clearly smile at this "doting mother"

(413). But since even the hard-boiled Gloriani rhapsodizes over " 'the prettiest wrinkles in the world' " (330), we are uncertain about our reaction to that handkerchief. Should we be touched by what its "sadder uses" are, or should we be feeling the irritation that we actually do?

Moreover, even when James is clearly intending wit (as he tries to do with most of the devices we have studied), he has trouble like popular writers.

He wore a little dead black moustache, which, at first, you would have been likely to suspect unjustly of a borrowed tint.

His hair was arranged in a faultless manner—unless, perhaps, it had a *little* too much of the tallow candle.

In each case the seducer is undercut wryly. Sounding so much like Susan Warner, however, means that James (in the first passage)* also suffers from a borrowed tint, of the lamp. His difficulties increase when we cannot be certain that he is intending wit. Roger, for example, "spoke of Nora with lowered tones, with circumlocutions, as some old pagan of an unveiled goddess" (698). How wry is James intending to be here? As the languishing lover, Roger has been undercut earlier; but the situation here is dire, and the novel itself, as we have seen, shows Nora just about perfect enough to warrant reverence from Roger and us. Popular circumlocutions, like clichés and noun entities, point to a reality which we all espouse or all agree not to mention; young James, partially emancipated from this arch realm, points often to . . . to what indeed?

Watch and Ward is a mixed beginning because James already knows that another mode of presentation (and, by implication, another epistemology) is possible and even advisable. Hubert says of truth, " 'if you can get it in the concrete, after shivering all your days in the cold abstract, it's worth a bit of a compromise' " (585). Replacing "the cold abstract" with "the concrete" involves more than simply a dictional preference. Hubert is espousing an epistemology radically different from the Augustan ideal of static laws which Victorian scribblers perpetuated in grossly simplified form, and defended ardently. In *St. Elmo*, for example, Edna scorns those who "unblushingly violated hearth-stone statutes and the venerable maxims of social decorum" (559). James himself appears at times in *Watch and Ward* to share this rigidly ordered world view. When Miss Sandys' blush precedes her smile, for example, "this was not the order of nature" (428). Although Nora confronts momentarily an "appalling hush of the harmonies of life" (690), her marriage restores these harmonies, for life as it were. Roger also finds

*W&W 330; WWW 262.

harmony, not only in the marriage, but earlier in nature herself—"he was appealing from his troubled nerves to the ordered quietude of the stars" (335). Especially in such a context, James' personifications, formulas, epithets, noun entities, clichés, and circumlocutions all function as stylistic equivalents (and thus as apparent espousals) of the neoclassical ideal of ordered, regularized life.

Hubert's words about "concrete" truth show that James knows of another, quite different epistemology. As a critic, James repeatedly reproves writers for applying to fluid experience a rule-making mind and a style appropriately rigid. He says in 1874 that "all rigid critical formulas are more or less unjust" (*FrP* 219); in 1876, "with all respect to French pulpit eloquence. . . . I turned, before long, a deaf ear to the categories of virtue and vice—it was like the dreadful nomenclature of chemistry" (*PS* 42). A quarter-century later James articulates more fully his distrust of general rules.

> It is so often the make-believe that we are all but driven comfortably to generalize—so great is the convenience of a simple law. The law, however, ceases to be simple from the moment even one book in five hundred does appeal, distinguishably, to a critical sense. The case, though of the rarest, occurs, and it thereby deprives the conscientious student we have postulated of the luxury of a hard-and-fast rule.
>
> (*SA* 304)

The rare or the rule: James' preference is clear enough in 1901, and it is clearer still six years later when he receives his copy of *Pragmatism* and makes to William his famous profession of faith. "All my life I have (like M. Jourdain) unconsciously pragmatized. You are immensely and universally *right*" (*LL* 2:83). Although Henry's pragmatizing may well have been quite unconscious during much of the crucial decade, his dissatisfaction with "the cold abstract" indicates how early he was inclined toward another epistemology. His attempt to capture the mind's evanescent processes we will study in chapter 4. For now we must realize that James, seeking throughout the decade for his own personal style, manages increasingly after *Roderick Hudson* to avoid rigid abstraction and to achieve a more pictorial and personal style. His progress is threefold. He uses neoclassical devices less frequently; he counters their deadening abstractness by increasing the number and specificity of his images; and, most important, he transforms many of the remaining devices by capitalizing upon their potential for evoking complex response.

The facts of frequency are more difficult to compile here than they were with the language of extravagance (see table 5). The devices most readily counted indicate both James' early similarity to popular writers, and his movement away from them by 1881.[91] Even here we must be careful, however. Since personification appears primarily in mental

TABLE 5

	W&W	RH	StE	HR	WWW	In	Ame	PL
personification	78	13	16	9	9	3	6	4
formula: "heart"	140	47	153	63	98	16	39	22
formula: "pretty"	124	34	25	22	23	30	63	27
entity: girls, women	152	20	47	13	4	9	3	10

Note: Numbers indicate incidence per 100,000 words.

process situations, it tends not only to linger in *The Portrait* but also to appear in modified form in the later style. Vernon Lee finds that James' late pronouns "become a sort of personification";[92] and Holder-Barell notes "the personification of Strether's 'inner sense' " (85). Data about epithet, circumlocution, and cliché must be still more tentative because these devices depend upon dividing lines somewhat arbitrary and personal. But the presence of the three devices in even James' late style is unquestionable. With epithets, for example, James may, as Matthiessen suggests, "still have been indulging, unconsciously, in the family habit of 'attaching other than usual significances' when he read his peculiar catch-all meanings into such epithets as 'splendid,' 'prodigious,' and 'sacred' " (*JF* 107). Circumlocution also remains evident in the late style, not only because "the circumloquacious flourish ... amused him in his late manner" (*JF* 74), but because James' congenital diffidence continued to affect his life and art. He can in fact praise forthrightness about sex with the expressions "the great relation between men and women, the constant world-renewal" (*FN* 39). The continued presence of these three devices in the late style and the difficulty of counting their appearances in the early fiction must not, however, obscure the fact that the devices are definitely less frequent and less harmful by 1881.

The quantitative decline of neoclassical devices is also manifest in James' revisions. Repeatedly (though not with rigorous consistency) James deletes abstract and vague expressions, as when he cuts from *Roderick Hudson* the noun entities "youthfulness of temperament .... sense of beauty .... ineffable candor .... tragic shrug .... stoical pleasure." Yet, extensive as it is, deletion cannot do enough by itself. Repeatedly James replaces generalized expressions with images which we must interpret ourselves. For example, he replaces the personification "giving alarming pledges to ennui" (*RH* 82) with the image "he was eating his cake all at once and might have none left for the morrow" (*NY* 90). Likewise, the entity "hopeless confidence" (*RH* 313) becomes "he would remain ... taken for granted ... as a good cellar, with its dusky supporting vaults, is taken for granted in a sound house" (*NY* 344). At their best, images can replace whole passages of ineffectual devices.

And he looked at him with his eyes of such *radiant lucidity* that *one* might have said (and Rowland did almost say so, himself) that it was the fault of *one's* own grossness if *one* failed to read to the bottom of *that beautiful soul.*

(*RH* 200, my italics)

And he looked at him out of such bottomless depths as might have formed the element of a shining merman who should be trying, comparatively near shore, to signal to a ruminating ox.

(*NY* 223)[93]

James can add images with such effectiveness in 1907 because he has been strongly committed to them for so long. In fact, *The Portrait* not only depends less upon neoclassical devices; it also manages consistently to generate mystery through images which make us readers do quite half the work. Since I discuss *The Portrait's* imagery in chapter 4, let us simply call to mind a few of the novel's great pictorial moments: Daniel Touchett acknowledging that his wife finds him " 'of no more use than a postage stamp without gum' " (14); inquisitive Henrietta with the "large, polished buttons" of her eyes or mannish Henrietta as " 'a thorn on the stem of his rose' " (78, 115); Raph's dying face "still as the lid of a box" which is surely his coffin (528); the aptness of Ralph imaging Osmond as " 'a faded rosebud' " or the irony of Osmond applying " 'strong as an English portmanteau' " to the man who would later try to carry off Isabel (318, 456); Isabel's response to Ned selling his bibelots—"it was as if . . . he had had all his teeth drawn" (486). *Watch and Ward* and *Roderick Hudson* contain few images of such force and complexity because only by the end of the crucial decade has James fully accepted the challenge which he would articulate years later.

> The real "fun" of the thing would have been exactly to sacrifice my comparative platitude of statement—a deplorable depth at any time, I have attempted elsewhere to signify, for any pretending master of representation to sink to—without sacrificing a grain of what was to be conveyed.
>
> (*AN* 137)

The real fun of transcending mere statement involves more than simply avoiding neoclassical devices and adding strong images. James must do with the style of equipoise what he did with the style of extravagance: transform weak conventionalities into powerful fiction by capitalizing upon their potential for thematic significance.

Circumlocution, for example. The popular novel traditionally used euphemisms to soften the awful reality of death.

> The rigid sleeper . . . . Aaron Hunt had indeed fallen asleep, to wake no more . . . . Mr. and Mrs. Dent slept side by side . . . . Felix slept his last sleep.
>
> (*StE* 14, 27, 33, 567)

In *The Portrait* James refers euphemistically to death at least ten times.[94] "The great rest" (7), appearing in the context of the Gardencourt idyll, demonstrates the power of that moment—that even death can be transformed. We do not mistake *The Portrait* for *St. Elmo*, however. James has so clearly established the transitoriness of the idyll that we know another reality and thus another death abide when the ceremony of innocence ends. " 'You have lately lost your father' .... '[he has] gone to his reward' " (19, 40). Speaking now outside the ceremony of innocence are people much aware of sublunary realities. Ralph Touchett's intimate knowledge of mortal illness does not prevent him from using a euphemism to show kindness to the bereaved, while his mother cuts through conventional pieties and expresses wry disapproval of the deceased. Isabel must learn to combine both habits of mind, both uses of language. After marriage to Osmond has removed her from the ceremony of innocence, Isabel thinks of Daniel Touchett "sleeping under English turf, the benevolent author of her infinite woe!" (393–94). Fond of the old man and yet aware of what he cannot now undo, Isabel manages to express sentiment without sentimentalizing. The euphemism "sleeping" may soften the awfulness of death, but in the next clause paradoxical life reappears with an awfulness which words cannot hide.

Isabel moves still further from conventional simplifications when Countess Gemini tells her both about Osmond's dead wife,

"what was more natural than that she should have left behind a pledge of their affection,"

and about dead M. Merle,

"M. Merle had rejoined—I won't say his ancestors, because he never had any."

(501, 502)

Especially in the context of "what was more natural," the circumlocution on page 501 echoes with the falsity of Pansy's paternity *and* implicates society at large. For Osmond is, in effect, parodying accepted Victorian practice: covering up Pansy's parentage has its stylistic equivalent in society's insistence upon speaking euphemistically about so natural a process as conception and birth. In turn, faced with the whitewash of socially sanctioned circumlocutions, Isabel must learn from the Countess on page 502. She must see through conventional verbiage to the unlovely reality beneath. Dying Ralph then teaches the ultimate lesson. When Isabel, like a popular novelist, tries to soften his situation with " 'this is not death, dear Ralph,' " he replies, " 'Not for you—no' " (530). This reply is particularly devastating because Ralph himself has, apparently, just encouraged a euphemistic attitude with " 'I have all eternity to rest' " (529). What makes Ralph's euphemism beautiful and Isabel's false—and by extension all euphemisms beautiful or false—is the degree of aware-ness involved. Ralph can echo the "great rest" of the opening idyll because he has achieved in death that comic acceptance which reconciles horror and communion and transforms his language accordingly.[95] It is to this condition that Isabel aspires.

Epithets and noun entities also bear increasing thematic weight as the decade progresses.[96] As early as 1872 James has characters saying,

> I beheld the fair musician. . . . I have called her fair, but the word needs explanation.

> My fair cousins in Rome,—"fair" is for rhetoric; but they were excellent girls.

> (*CT* 2:379, 3:241)

By the time of *The American*, James can suggest the inadequacy of epithets without commenting directly and can make that inadequacy function thematically. Noémie Nioche in her opera box is called "its fair occupant" (232). Our experience of her "perfection" has already been complex enough to prevent "fair occupant" from functioning here as "fair stranger" did with Nora. Since epithets are conventionally used with genteel ladies, James need only apply "fair occupant" to Noémie—and let us recognize the disparity between her pretensions and society's ideal. By avoiding the explicit statements of 1872, James assures us the experience of recognition.

Both Ralph and Isabel make comparable discoveries in *The Portrait*. Ralph expects Henrietta to be the conventional journalist who will gush professionally at Gardencourt's splendors. To emphasize the inadequacy of such conventional stereotyping, James puts Henrietta beyond the effusion of epithets and other ejaculatory formulas.

> [Henrietta] delivered herself of none of the little ready-made ejacula-tions of delight . . . was but little addicted to the use of conventional phrases.

> (82)

Epithets with Henrietta's beau teach Isabel the opposite lesson. As we have seen, Isabel calls Henrietta's relation with Bantling "unique"; the epithets applied to Bantling, however, have a decidedly stock quality— "an amiable bachelor . . . . 'a man of courage' . . . . 'the good Bantling' . . . . the good Bantling . . . . the gallant ex-guardsman" (131, 155, 156, 202–3). This tension between Isabel's assumptions and the narrator's language is resolved late in the novel. As Isabel is forced to recognize the all too ordinary quality of the relationship, Bantling is called "the gallant bachelor" (518). The epithet assures his perennial excellence as bachelor or husband, but it also precludes much uniqueness. Isabel (and we) learn that assumptions too unconventional can mislead as badly as Ralph's too conventional expectations.

Comparably sophisticated effects can occur with noun entities.[97] Having lavished entities most profusely upon children and ladies in *Watch and Ward*, Henry James not only restricts severely the number of entities in *The Portrait*. He uses the remainder to add to our portrait of Isabel. Early we encounter "childish voices .... the manner of children .... a hundred childish sorrows," plus "the elation of liberty and the pain of exclusion" (23). Since the last two entities refer not to great issues but to Isabel's absence from grade school, and since the first three are not treated with the tearful reverence of the popular tradition, James utilizes potentially hollow expressions to create a complex tone which presents Isabel wryly, yet tenderly. Then, what James takes lightly with children becomes more serious with grown women. The Misses Molyneux retain "the smile of childhood" (70). What does the expression mean, since children's smiles are surely as various as adults'? James could have written "smiled as children often do," or something better. We realize, however, that the entities which once deadened his apprentice work are now functioning thematically. The very inadequacy of the entity suggests gently the Misses Molyneux's limitations; we cannot find in their cloistered virtue the complex attractiveness of true maturity.

Female inadequacy (and the entities which render it) become increasingly important as *The Portrait* proceeds, for Isabel and Pansy are both dangerously innocent. When Madame Merle disparages Isabel's ties to " 'the aspirations of your childhood' " (186), the abstractness of the entity captures well the romantic unworldliness and ineffectuality which Isabel must outgrow. Later, when Isabel persists in judging with "the presumption of youth" (299), the set expression reflects her lack of supple, mature awareness—especially since we have just met the embodiment of protracted childhood. Pansy does the honors of her father's house, not with the grace of a budding young woman, but with "the wide-eyed conscientiousness of a sensitive child" (291). Rather than protest (as we would have with early entities) that the conscientiousness of sensitive children is as manifold as the children themselves, we recognize the aptness of James' entity here. The set expression suggests how arrested Pansy's development is and will remain. The convent which finally immures her is only the architectural counterpart of Pansy's perennial childhood and of the noun entities which express it.

Pansy's plight and Isabel's increasing maturity are also reflected in James' sophisticated use of saccharine formulas.[98] Although no irony is apparent in *Watch and Ward* when James, like popular authors, says, "Miss Morton's niece was a very pretty child" (235), he finds himself increasingly concerned with the *limitations* of prettiness. In the "pretty professions" of Valentin's sister-in-law (323), for example, we sense a disparity between promiscuously pretty words and the beauty which is truth. In *The Portrait* James moves closer still to the questionable core of Victorian obsession with prettiness, for he is now presenting not a promiscuous French aristocrat, but a sixteen-year-old girl. Pansy may make a "pretty little speech" (327) and have "eyes the prettiest in the world" (375), but such compliments are qualified terribly by the social criticism which underlies them. Gilbert Osmond, that slave to Victorian ideals, has so retarded his daughter in the process of making her an ideal pretty child that she has only one chance left for happiness—to become a porcelain figure with Ned as her shepherd. This possibility is real, for Ned too is called "very pretty" (487). But having reduced Pansy to Ned, Osmond must also deny her to him because another social ideal—the grand marriage—charms Osmond powerfully. Thus pretty Pansy is not cloying like popular heroines; she is touching. Helpless and (except for Isabel) hopeless, the Victorian child has passed through the looking glass, for life as it were.

"Pretty" is also applied to Isabel, especially in the early pages. She grows to a more complex beauty as she outgrows her reliance upon the pretty set-speeches conventional with pretty heroines. To such language she is very prone.

> Her [Madame Merle's] nature spoke none the less in her behavior because it spoke in conventional language. "What is language at all but a convention?" said Isabel. "She has the good taste not to pretend, like some people I have met, to express herself by original signs."
>
> (178)

To her suitors Isabel repeatedly says the wrong things. Which are, conventionally, the correct things. For example, after she has refused Warburton, she says,

> "You will live to marry a better woman than I."
> "Don't say that, please," said Lord Warburton, very gravely. "That is fair to neither of us."
>
> (101)

Warburton is primarily protesting, not Isabel's refusal as such, but the conventionality of her response. By not treating him as an individual, Isabel is turning his crucial moment into melodrama. The scene itself is not melodramatic because James is not the one slipping into formulas now; rather, he achieves high art by making the scene an examination of the melodramatic consciousness.[99] Isabel, we must notice, has not yet matured beyond the color scheme which we recognized in her first scene and which is still emblematic of a melodramatic proclivity for simplification. "A white dress ornamented with black ribbons" (92). Over the next four hundred pages Isabel will struggle to make herself be and feel and say, not what she should as a pretty heroine, but what she should as a human being.

Although the next proposal scene still finds Isabel speaking inadequately, she can, at least, catch herself at it. "Isabel looked away while she spoke these words, for she knew they were of a much less earnest cast than the countenance of her listener" (143). She even manages to avoid with Caspar the pretty words of conventional consolation that wounded Warburton. " 'I won't say that I shall always remain your friend, because when women say that, in these circumstances, it is supposed, I believe, to be a sort of mockery. But try me some day' " (145). When Osmond proposes, however, Isabel is only half able to deal with the uniqueness of this suitor. She can answer "at last, in a tone of entreaty which had nothing of conventional modesty." But she also says, " 'I don't know you' . . . and then she coloured, as she heard herself saying what she had said almost a year before to Lord Warburton" (287). When Osmond then admits his own conventionality (288), Isabel's disbelief establishes the connection between her inability to respond uniquely and her inability to determine the uniqueness of others.

When Isabel does learn of Osmond and the world, she adopts that stiff silence which Victorians admired in Roman matrons and which was as conventional to Beset Heroines as pretty set-speeches were to Courted Heroines. Isabel writes to Ralph, "but her letters told him nothing that he wanted to know" (361); to Warburton, " 'she will never complain' " (368). Eventually Isabel does, of course, manage to move beyond "superficial embarrassment" (519) and superficial silence. Opening to Henrietta (450) and to Ralph (531), Isabel achieves the development which Henry James himself has managed—to move beyond mindless formulas to personal expression. Isabel even manages to reach, like Strether and James' other great protagonists, that communion which lies beyond language altogether. "She begged him [Ralph] to be quiet now. 'We needn't speak to understand each other,' she said" (532).

2

The neoclassical devices studied so far tend to make early Jamesian and popular diction too abstract and general. Other devices, primarily syntactic, make the writing seem tidy and reductive. Once again, the sanctioning ideal derives ultimately from the eighteenth century. Joseph Trapp states that

> among the many Embellishments of Writing, few are attended with
> greater Beauty than *Antitheta*. The Reason is obvious, because
> Contraries illustrate, and recommend each other by Comparison. . . .
> When the Thoughts are thus set against each other, they appear with
> Energy, and strike the Mind with redoubled Force.
>
> (Hagstrum, 167)

Balance, of course, shared syntactic primacy with *antitheta*,[100] and not only in neoclassical England. French plays and essays relied traditionally upon witty uses of balance, antithesis, paradox, and epigram. Such polished perfection constitutes a kind of standard for James both in his early criticism,

> these agreeable "notices" [of] M. Sarcey.... are gracefully and often lightly turned; occasionally, even, the author grazes the epigrammatic,

and in his early novels,

> [Roger] uttered perhaps no epigrams, but he gave, by his laughter, an epigrammatic turn to the ladyish gossip of his companions.
>
> (*SA* 71, *W&W* 427)

A taste for epigrammatic pointing and contrast also reaches James from the popular tradition. For a style to emphasize its black-white contrasts, melodrama drew both upon the Augustans and, somewhat incongruously, upon the romantics who were prone not only to haranguing but to haranguing in neat periods. In fact, when James states his reservations about pointed style—and he has definite reservations in the crucial decade—he singles out the highly pointed prose of that arch-romantic, Victor Hugo.

> We get immediately the romantic formula, the short cut of antithesis, the vital spark, for a conspicuous example, of the theater of Victor Hugo. The antithesis is a short cut because it ignores shades and lives on high contrast.... shades are thus transitions and links; and, transitions and links being comparatively quiet things, the deep joy of the close observer, the romantic effect will have none of them. This is what makes one extreme seek another.
>
> (*SA* 320)

That the extemity-prone romantics and melodramatists could share with the cool Augustans the syntax of antithesis and balance may seem incongruous, but it is a fact, and a fact which affected American fiction. "The Augustan tradition of serried banks of balanced clauses ... still [in the nineteenth century] finds occasional expression ... in the novels of passion, where balanced clauses serve as restraints on the otherwise uninhibited excesses of declaration, protest, ecstasy, grief, and romantic despair."[101]

Popular writers, thus encouraged on three sides in their black-white habit of mind and style, found a final sanction in Christianity itself. In best orthodox fashion, Ellen is taught that judgment "will be a dreadful day to all but those whose names are written in the Lamb's book of life" (*WWW* 252). Besides the sheep and the goats, *The Wide, Wide World* also offers the polarities of "soul and body" (66) and of "earth or ... heaven" (40). In *The Heir*, Charlie refers expressly to " 'the saying about

fools and angels' " (2:348) and his father can say with a straight face that
" 'it was only Philip, who would persuade me black was white' "
(2:45).[102] So habitual are popular antitheses that the words "contrast"
and "contrary" appear more than once every ten pages in *The Initials*.[103]
And John, the authority figure in *The Wide, Wide World*, sounds like
Joseph Trapp when he says, " 'you know we enjoy anything much more
by contrast' " (498).

Many of James' early antitheta seem to betray a sheep-goats mentality.
In *Watch and Ward*, he refers to "good men and bad" (336). Although he
deletes this sentence in 1878, James cannot salvage a novel conceived so
consistently in polar terms. For example: "in proportion as other people
grew hot, he [Hubert] grew cool" (417). Here the charm of contrast has
clearly overcome any instinct for dramatic credibility; the barometric
precision of "in proportion" and the pointed syntax are too neat for a
work which is not a Popean satire or a Johnsonian apologue. Comparison with other genres is particularly relevant here because the nineteenth-
century novel is, as Bradford Booth notes, "a form which has never
totally abandoned characteristics of the essay" (74). In James' particular
case, many scholars have noted that he matures as an essayist-critic
considerably before he emerges as a major fiction writer. He tends,
especially in the first half of the crucial decade, to apply to the materials
of fiction an epigrammatic prose like Sarcey's. The outcome is often
unhappily essay-like.

> The uses of things that please and the charm of the things that sustain
> .... you had already passed from measuring contours to tracing
> meanings .... not so good as to fail of the proper picturesqueness, nor
> yet so bad as to defeat the proper function .... if their interview had
> been purely painful, he wished to ignore it for Miss Garland's sake;
> and if it had sown the seeds of reconciliation, he wished to close his
> eyes to it for his own .... if constancy is the flower of devotion, reci-
> procity is the guarantee of constancy .... it had been more than civil-
> ity and yet it had been less than devotion.
>   (*RH* 15, 50, 215, 408, 413, 437)

When James intends his antitheses to control moments of dramatic
violence, he often succeeds only in making the characters seem mechanical. "[Roger] held her [Nora] for a moment as close as he had held his
hope, and then released her as suddenly as he had parted with it" (596).
And in dialogue this style sounds, not like French theater, but like an
unconscious parody of the epigrams of Sardou or Dumas *fils*.

> "If he shouldn't, it would do you no good; and if he should, it would
> do him none."
>   (*W&W* 579)

> "I have as little power to do one as I have desire to do the other."

"I might be bad by nature, but I needn't be by volition."

(*RH* 368, 369)

Extreme pointing also causes a second, related difficulty. When James writes of a "force ... which you hardly know whether to denominate humility or pride" (*W&W* 424), we wonder why the force is not a mixture of humility *and* pride. We wonder this often, for James repeatedly makes antithetical what could only be a less tidy mixture in the real-life world he purports to present. "The instinct of free affection alternating ... with the dim consciousness of measured dependence" (334) bears little resemblance to the intricate workings of the mind and bears too much resemblance to the work of popular authors.

> A cold fit naturally succeeds a hot one. . . . this oscillation of the spirits in extraordinary men appears to be more or less a law of nature.

So long as Charles Reade can be satisfied with this "oscillation" theory, and Mrs. Henry Wood with "the rules of contrary," and the Baroness with the "spirit of contradiction,"[104] the disruptive elements of their worlds can be seen as alternating, as sequential, and thus as ultimately safe. Good or Bad, Good then Bad: simple polar elements are isolated, and can thus be controlled.

But what about Good *and* Bad? Despite substantial evidence against him, Henry James does not, like his popular peers, seek to ignore the untidy, mixed aspects of life. He is willing to go beyond contrast to complexity. Not Good or Bad, but Good and Bad; not alternate but simultaneous. His ideal is to make diverse elements "somehow hang together" (*AN* 75), hang together in our minds, as they do in our lives, simultaneously.[105] As with most of James' ideals, the problem here is primarily formal.

> Half as an entreaty, half as a threat . . . . half shrinking, half eager . . . . one half respect and the other half self-denial . . . . half modesty and half philosophy . . . . half cousin, half hostess . . . . half sitting, half lounging . . . . half impulsive, half deliberate . . . . half Italian and half French . . . . half sardonic, half good-natured . . . . half anxious and half angry . . . . "half like a Madonna and half like a *ballerina*" . . . . half excavated and half identified . . . . half fearful, half shameful . . . . half bleak and half pastoral . . . . half irritated, half depressed.
>
> (*W&W* 233, 584, 587, 701; *RH* 3, 47, 73, 106, 113, 122, 175, 318, 432–33, 443, 469)

Here mixture is asserted. Clearly, however, the relentless precision of "half-half" functions, not to blend the polar elements, but to emphasize their polarity. Nor does James manage to suggest a mixture when he actually uses the word "mixture," as in "a singular mixture of the rough and the smooth" or "a singular mixture of brutality and finesse" (*RH* 8; *CT* 2:243). Determined to go beyond the safe contrasts of his popular peers, James is nonetheless continuing to use the popular technique of sharply pointed assertions. His dilemma here is part of his lifelong effort to fashion a personal style. By 1908 James had moved so far from tidy antitheses (without forsaking his "rich passion ... for extremes" [*AN* 31])[106] that Owen Wister criticized him for going too far in the opposite direction, for attempting to achieve actual simultaneity of effect. "He is attempting the impossible ... to produce upon the reader, as a painting produces upon the gazer, a number of superimposed, simultaneous impressions. He would like to put several sentences on top of each other."[107] Whatever we think of the late style, its quest for simultaneity of effect begins in the 1870s, and part of the impetus is James' growing uneasiness about pointed style.

This uneasiness appears most obviously in James' reviews. He can praise Turgenev's "A Correspondence" as "the most perfectly epigrammatic of our author's stories" (*FrP* 245) and can say of Dumas *fils* that "his concentration, all confidence and doctrine and epigram, is the explanation of his extraordinary force"; yet James can also recognize that the epigrammatic glitter of Dumas *fils* is not all gold, that "the epigrams, the *tirades*, the aphorisms, [are] by this time rather drearily familiar" (*SA* 278, 51). Such divided allegiance James cannot sustain indefinitely. The scales eventually tip. He may seem to equivocate when he says of the English and French imaginations that "the one beholds a great many shadows and the other a great many lights" (*FrP* 81), but he concludes, finally, that the French, for all their glittering luminescence, lack profundity.

> Looking about afterward at the usual little French landscapes on
> Goupil's walls, with their high average of superficial cleverness, we
> were not arrested in the reflection that there is something inherently
> superior in the English sentiment of landscape, when it has really
> mastered its means. It has a story to tell—it has a mystery (sometimes
> very slender) to reveal.
>
> (*PE* 102–3)

The key word here is mystery. Believing that "in the arts, feeling is always meaning" (*PE* 185), James comes increasingly to realize that feeling is conveyed not by the glittering antitheses of Dumas *fils* and Victor Hugo, but by a synthesis like Tintoretto's.

> He has an eye for that which, for want of a better name, we may call
> the *mystery* of a scene, and that under his treatment its general expres-
> sion and its salient details are fused into the harmony of poetry itself.
>
> (*PE* 48; James' italics)

To the ideal of synthesis (if not, finally, to an ideal of mystery), the popular tradition contributes its share. " 'I have the double pleasure of giving them [woodcocks] to mamma, and of eating them afterwards' " (*WWW* 58). Having your cake and eating it too is endemic to the suspect religiosity of popular fiction.[108] "Duty" prepares Ellen for "pleasure" because mid-Victorian Christianity's emphasis upon our failings is more than outweighed by its belief in our perfectability. Meliorism is the word of the day. Although some goats remain exemplarily goats, the educative power of the Word makes real the possibility of redemptive balance. See how Charlotte Yonge's syntax mirrors her meaning when Guy struggles "to prevent himself from losing in gladness the balance he had gained in adversity" (*HR* 2:92). Guy reaches greatness of moral balance, not by extirpating, but by harnessing his potentially violent impulses; Ellen's comparable greatness comes from moderating a pride which can then make her self-reliant; and St. Elmo directs into that proper channel, the church, the energies which had once made him satanic. Mirroring the divine oneness, such human syntheses constitute the scribblers' ideal.

Moreover, these syntheses do not always seem simplistic in popular fiction. Occasionally we experience a complexity analogous to that of our daily lives.

"Tell him," said Miss Fortune, coloring. . . .
"I was wrong," said Ellen.
"And I was right," said Miss Fortune. . . . "Why, you said you were wrong," said Miss Fortune, "that's only half of the business; if you were wrong I was right; why don't you say so. . . . "
"I said I was wrong," said Ellen, "and so I was; but I never said you were right, Aunt Fortune, and I don't think so."

(*WWW* 188)

The sheep-goats mentality (of Miss Fortune) is clearly criticized; and, in Ellen's ambivalent awareness (that one person can be wrong without the other being right), we experience genuine complexity. These two techniques occur also in *The Heir*. The sheep-goats mentality is criticized in Philip's vicious sister, "dealing her letters into separate packets of important and unimportant" (2:279). The complexity of ambivalent awareness also appears effectively.

"Yes. No. That is, I *have* no ideas."

"Yes—no—I don't know."

The second speaker here is Laura from *The Heir* (2:314); the first is Lambert Strether (*Amb* 364). Like great writers, Miss Yonge makes us experience the movement of Laura's mind from pole to pole to that uneasy middle ground where most of life occurs. That James was capable of such moments in *Watch and Ward* and that he reached great art with them by 1881 will be the subject of the rest of my chapter.

In *Watch and Ward* James uses both the techniques which we saw in *The Wide, Wide World* and *The Heir.* After poor Roger reveals his sheep-goats mentality with

"I don't know . . . whether he's an honest man or a scamp,"

James undercuts such simplicity with

Whether or no he was an honest man remained to be seen; but on the face of the matter he appeared no scamp.

(329)

By denying one polar term and then declining to affirm the other, James *suggests* complexity as "half-half" never can.[109] He also makes us experience the ambivalent awareness of characters who refuse to accept tidy polarities.

"Is that philosophy, or indifference?" said the young man [Roger].
[Nora] "I don't know that it's either; it's because I know you're so good."

[Nora] "Do you mean that he's [Fenton] an impostor?"
[Roger] "The word is your own. He's not honest."

(*W&W* 324, 335)

In each example, a simple antithesis (philosophy-indifference, impostor-honest) becomes complex because the terms of the contrast are themselves questioned. The character and the reader share the experience of seeking, not to affirm one easy extreme, but to recognize the claims and inadequacies of both poles.

What James accomplishes in dialogue here he manages to achieve with his narrative prose in *The American.* For instance, "after a brief further exchange of words, there had been an exchange of cards. M. Stanislas Kapp was very stiff" (236). *Antitheta* is now functioning thematically. The stiff, formal syntax mirrors that formal, gentlemanly code which reduces life to black-white affairs of honor and eventually reduces Valentin Bellegarde to the grave. Throughout the novel, the limitations of rigid social forms are suggested by James' use of formal syntax. The Bellegardes' party is a good example. The serene assurance which derives from an exalted place in an absolute hierarchy is reflected both in the syntax used with the duchess ("monumentally stout and imperturbably serene" [211]) and in the syntax of her equally formal speech (" 'charmed, dear friend; charmed, monsieur' " [212]). The whole aristocratic gathering has this same serene assurance.

There were large, majestic men, and small, demonstrative men; there were ugly ladies in yellow lace and quaint jewels, and pretty ladies with white shoulders from which jewels and everything else were absent. Every one gave Newman extreme attention, every one smiled,

every one was charmed to make his acquaintance, every one looked at
him with that soft hardness of good society which puts out its hand
but keeps its fingers closed over the coin.

(214)

Even without the last image, the very language of the passage would
suggest the limitations of aristocratic society. The balanced "every one"
clauses are as stiff as the phrases which greet Newman and as the
etiquette which handles him without an embrace. How out of place
rough Newman is in this neat world appears when

"I came here on purpose to see you," said Newman in his bad
French, offering to shake hands. And then, like a good American, he
introduced Valentin formally: "Allow me to make you acquainted
with the Comte Valentin de Bellegarde."
Valentin made a bow which must have seemed to Mademoiselle
Noémie quite in harmony with the impressiveness of his title.

(140)

In harmony Newman is not. His handshake is too casual; his introduction too stiff. Although we do not want him to ape superficial French
elegance, we do lament his alternation between inadequate extremes—
especially since we have already learned that synthesis is possible.

Is she [Claire] grave or gay?" asked Newman.
[Valentin] "She is both; not alternately, for she is always the
same. There is gravity in her gayety, and gayety in her gravity."

(103)

Because the simultaneous presence of contraries is what we do not
experience to any great extent with Claire, Valentin's fine words here
remain largely assertion. They do, however, define the complexity
which James desires for his protagonists. Although he fully masters the
techniques for conveying this complexity only with the late style which
Wister criticized, James has, by the end of the crucial decade, come a
long way from the stiff antitheses of *Watch and Ward*. Saving some of his
techniques for chapter 4, let us study how James uses pointed syntax
to make us experience in Isabel Archer that simultaneous presence
of contraries which constitutes, for him, the highest refinement of
consciousness.

James succeeds with Isabel partly because he manages to relate her to a
definition of form which develops throughout the novel and which
helps us to judge her development and our own. Chapters 1–3 establish
two different types of formalism. The stately, precarious balance of the
ceremony of innocence is reflected in and preserved by not only the
qualified "perfect"s and the careful euphemisms but also the syntax itself.
"Part of the afternoon had waned, but much of it was left.... [the

house] had a name and a history" (5, 6). Instead of the barometric overprecision of the "in proportion" in *Watch and Ward*, we find now a "gallery of charming proportions, which had a sitting-room at either end of it, and which in the evenings was usually lighted" (43). Such equipoise is presided over by the gentle spirit of Daniel Touchett, who, even in death, manages to join contraries and thus to sustain the possibility of true harmony. "His face was the face of the dying, but his eyes were the eyes of Daniel Touchett" (166).

The other spirit which presides over the beginning of the book is more angular. As we shift from the Gardencourt idyll of chapters 1–2 to the background pages of chapter 3, the prose shifts from the balanced syntax of Daniel Touchett to the sharp antitheses of Lydia. We learn immediately that her character "although it was by no means without benevolence, rarely succeeded in giving any impression of softness. Mrs. Touchett might do a great deal of good, but she never pleased" (20). With words as sharp as her judgments, Lydia says that breadsauce "looked like a poultice and tasted like soap" (21). On this one page she is associated with "law . . . . reason . . . . system . . . . fixed . . . . consistent . . . . so extremely definite." With "neither beauty nor vanity. . . . without coquetry and without any great elegance" (20, 21), she finds life's issues sufficiently clear-cut that " 'the two words in the language I most respect are Yes and No' " (254).

Using antithesis and balance with such control in his opening pages, James begins to teach Isabel (and us) about the nature of form. The fact of his control encourages us to believe in the possibility of genuine order; but the difference between Daniel's and Lydia's types of order makes us apprehensive about any system so tidy as hers. We also tend to trust Daniel's alternative because of another stylistic device which James uses to create Isabel's milieu. Chapter 1 of *The Portrait* contains several explicit puns.

> [Mr. Touchett] "I can't tell till I feel."
> "Perhaps some one might feel for you," said the younger man [Ralph], laughing.
> "Oh, I hope some one will always feel for me!"

> [Mr. Touchett] "He's [Ralph] a very good nurse—for a sick-nurse. I call him my sick-nurse because he's sick himself."

> "Were you ever sick, Lord Warburton?" his father asked.
> Lord Warburton considered a moment.
> "Yes, sir, once, in the Persian Gulf."
> "He is making light of you, daddy," said the other young man.
> "That's a sort of joke."

> (8, 9)

Critics who have noticed these obvious puns have neither established that puns recur throughout the rest of the novel[110] nor, more important, explained *why* James relies upon puns so heavily. In chapter 1, after Warburton says to Daniel, " 'you told me the other day that I ought to "take hold" of something,' " Ralph quips, " 'you ought to take hold of a pretty woman' " and Warburton comes back with " 'I will lay hands on one as soon as possible' " (11, 12). Once the pretty woman becomes Isabel, sexual double entendres are directed at her. Ralph's, " 'she touches nothing that she doesn't adorn' " prompts Warburton's, " 'it makes one want to be touched, Miss Archer,' " and she must reply, " 'be touched in the right sense, and you will never look the worse for it' " (61). Even marriage does not protect Isabel from sexually ambiguous language, for Osmond "had told her a week before that it was indecent she should go to him [Ralph] at his hotel" (399). By discussing a dying man and his cousin-nurse in terms of a conventionally adulterous situation, Osmond perversely shows us how sexual puns—and by extension all puns—function in *The Portrait*. Women are threatened not only by men's questionable intentions but also by the generally ambiguous and unstable nature of experience itself. Language reflects the unreliability of appearances. With their multiple interpretations, words indicate how meaning varies with point of view. Since any consciousness committed to a Yes-No tidiness is endangered in so fluid a world, the heroine's task is clear. She must develop the ability to sustain, like a pun, contrary attitudes simultaneously; she must, like Daniel Touchett and his syntax, balance oppositions in harmonious oneness. She must, in short, approach the condition of James' style.

To reveal how far Isabel moves from a neatly antithetical mind and style, James contrasts her with two other American women.

> Henrietta expressed the opinion that American hotels were the best in the world, and Mrs. Touchett recorded a conviction that they were the worst.
>
> (88)

Lydia's stiff style emphasizes her emotional limitations. When, for example, she returns home after long absence, she thinks of her sick son after "her house and her conservatory" (35). The second "her," unnecessary to the literal meaning here, emphasizes the self-fulness beneath Lydia's plain-style veneer. "She inquired scrupulously about her husband's health and about the young man's own" (35). Lydia is not unloving, but the needlessly exact balance of the "about"s suggests the scrupulous precision of a duty which never flowers into self-transcending love. When Ralph dies, "she was stiff and dry-eyed" (534).

Henrietta would at first glance seem very different from Lydia, for the reporter's voluble emotionalism sends her skittering after every will-o'-the-wisp.

82 *Tradition and Style*

"You [Ralph] have acted on Isabel Archer." . . .
"I have been absolutely passive."
"You are too passive, then."

"You [Ralph] are laughing worse than ever." . . .
"I assure you I am very serious." . . .
"Now you are too serious."

(111, 113)

Ultimately, however, a consciousness so prone to instant polarities is not very different from Lydia's Yes-No mentality. Henrietta wonders " 'whether you [Touchetts] consider yourselves American or English. . . . once I knew, I could talk to you accordingly' " (78). She later tells Ralph that Caspar " 'is just the opposite of you' " (113). And when Henrietta in her good-hearted American simplicity encounters Bantling's well-meaning British simplicity, see James' syntax.

This simplicity was none the less honorable on either side; it was as graceful on Henrietta's part to believe . . . as it was on the part of her companion to suppose . . .

(202)

Isabel initially resembles Lydia and Henrietta dangerously. Like Lydia she can be "stiff" and "dry" (50, 279); like Henrietta, she can, as we will see, reverse her field all too quickly. Our experience of Isabel's limitations is complicated, however, because James can now make balanced and pointed syntax function thematically with her.[111] For example, Isabel, anticipating Warburton's proposal, "wished both to elude the intention and to satisfy her curiosity" (94). The precise syntactic balance mirrors Isabel's have-your-cake-and-eat-it-too attitude and thus indicates James' awareness of and judgment upon such selfulness as nothing in *The Wide, Wide World* did when Ellen gave away the woodcocks and ate them too. Similarly, Isabel's definition of Madame Merle—"a woman of ardent impulses, kept in admirable order" (163)— reflects in its tidy syntax an innocence which encourages our traditional distrust of mysterious European Madames.

By using syntax to *suggest* Isabel's tendency to oversimplify, James conveys her limitations delicately enough both to avoid coarseness like Roderick's and to make credible her eventual maturation. Lydia, Henrietta, and syntax help chart Isabel's progress.

[Lydia] "I suppose you are one of the daughters?"
[Isabel] ". . . It depends upon whose daughters you mean." . . .
"And are you the prettiest?"
"I have not the least idea," said the girl.
"I think you must be."

(25)

However aware Isabel actually is of her beauty, she distrusts from the beginning those tidy formulations which satisfy Lydia Touchett. Later, when flighty Henrietta resorts to paradox—" 'I never saw an ugly man look so handsome' "—Isabel must complicate this simplification. " 'He is very simple-minded,' said Isabel. 'And he is not so ugly' " (90). When she defends England against Lydia and then attacks it with Ralph (57), Isabel is showing her tendency to swing like Henrietta between poles; often, however, there is an important difference. Whereas Henrietta must know whether the Touchetts are English or American, Isabel can answer the question " 'whether you are a liberal or a conservative' " with " 'I am both' " (68). During the Civil War she neither feels stiff partisanship nor fluctuates between the sides, but rather is moved by "the valour of either army" (33). Characterized by oxymorons—("delicious pain . . . . pleasant pain . . . . ardent coldness" [285, 286, 308])—Isabel justifies Ralph's contention that " 'you are many-sided' " by the mature moderation of " 'if one is two-sided, it is enough' " (139). Isabel thus manages at times to sustain a simultaneous awareness of contraries. She can see that love "was the tragical side of happiness; one's right was always made of the wrong of some one else"; with Henrietta, "Isabel was irritated by her friend's interference, but even in the midst of her irritation she tried to think of what truth this declaration could represent" (323, 153).

Despite such promising two-sidedness, Isabel "was far from understanding the contradictions among her own impressions" (109). Thus, when she meets Osmond, she cannot deal with *his* contradictions—as the sharply antithetical syntax indicates.

> It was hard to see what he meant, for instance, by saying that he was gloriously provincial—which was so exactly the opposite of what she had supposed. Was it a harmless paradox, intended to puzzle her? Or was it the last refinement of high culture? Isabel trusted that she should learn in time; it would be very interesting to learn.
>
> (242)

Confronting the opposite of what she supposed, Isabel can only imagine alternatives of "a harmless paradox. . . . Or . . . the last refinement of high culture." The truth, of course, is somewhere between. Osmond's admission is less high culture than smug urbanity, and it is more dangerous than a mere paradox. Unfortunately, Isabel does not see the danger. What seems "interesting" here seems so again when she next makes polar oppositions.

> Isabel scarcely understood him; it seemed a question whether he were joking or not. Why should a man who had struck her as having a great fund of reserve suddenly bring himself to be so confidential? . . . his confidences were interesting.
>
> (245)

Osmond, of course, is neither joking nor being so confidential as Isabel imagines. Later still, her increased affection prompts increased polarization—"'You know everything and I know nothing'" (285). And finally, the terrifying non sequitur in one last, counterpointed sentence foreshadows the destruction of innocence. "Osmond had the attachment of an old acquaintance, and Isabel the stimulus of new, which seemed to assure her a future of beautiful hours" (325).

Beautiful, Isabel's future is not. What it *is*, critics have debated ceaselessly. So much ink and blood have flowed over the issue of why Isabel preserves the "form" of her marriage[112] that what we need now is not one more explanation but a more sustained commitment to the reading experience. Criticism tends to polarize because we do not apply to the analysis of literature what we have experienced in the literature itself. As the style of equipoise, the style of extravagance, and James' reviews all show, "form" for him is not static. Tintoretto achieves mystery by combining the general and the particular; Turgenev joins the ideal and the real. Such simultaneous coalescence of opposites is what James means by form. It is less a static state than an ongoing process. Imagine two circles, one inside the other. The outer circle, our aesthetic experience, must be whole and complete; we must feel the aesthetic pleasure of formal cloture. On the other hand, the inner circle of thematic issues must remain incomplete. Such issues as the relation of freedom and necessity, the nature of Victorian society, the possibility of sexual fulfillment, can escape simplification only by remaining issues, by not rigidifying into the propositional resolutions beloved of popular literature. The tension between these two circles—the inner one broken and pushing ever toward diffusion, the outer kept shapely by this threatening pressure—constitutes the major excitement in James' fiction and, indeed, in most great literature.

Processive form can, in turn, constitute our critical model. James praises "the art of not thinking singly." This art is what his art should teach us. Like a pun, our response to Isabel must sustain multiple and at times conflicting elements. We can never approach this state until we dismiss (once and, let us hope, for all) the notion that Isabel Archer is James' ideal. She is not. He said only that he was much struck by the image of a particularly engaging young woman.[113] When he adds that "she would be an easy victim of scientific criticism, if she were not intended to awaken on the reader's part an impulse more tender and more purely expectant" (48), James is insisting on both sides of the coin. Critics hostile to Isabel have been goaded to their stridency by the long-standing and still continuing tendency of some readers to whitewash the idol. Yet the hostile critics can put us off too. In demonstrating Isabel's inadequacies—her sexual fears, her tendency to superficiality, her condescension, cruelty, and pig-headedness—they lay bare her viscera with an absence of human sympathy which often seems righteous and even vicious. Their fierceness can prompt interpretations as extreme and uncongenial as the other camp's sentimentality can. If we can acknowledge Isabel's humanity, we will sustain the bond of human sympathy even as we face up to the limitations of flesh and blood. We will master the art of not thinking singly and will, in turn, be better able to appreciate James' heroine and art for what they are.

We will appreciate, above all, a profoundly qualified notion of freedom. Even the moderately qualified notion of Matthiessen and others[114]—that Isabel is free in her discovery of the limitations of freedom—is not two-sided enough. After acknowledging external restrictions, this position tends to allow Isabel unrestricted inner freedom; making her finally self-sustaining entails the possibility of a still quite idealized status. As Isabel cannot attain perfect physical beauty or complete external freedom, she cannot accomplish full spiritual freedom either. Her limitations and indeterminateness remain part of a portrait necessarily unfinished. Her flaws are not and cannot be perfectly synthesized away at the end. We see that in the days and years which continue beyond the book's close she will continue to struggle. And she will never entirely succeed, for James cannot believe nature that free.

It is in light of this permanent ambivalence that I take up, in chapter 2, the sexual and maternal aspects of Isabel's return to Osmond and Pansy. We will see then both the self-serving aspects of her flight from sex to Pansy *and* the immense social pressures for that flight, pressures which hostile critics have not acknowledged and which make *The Portrait* part of the continuing Victorian debate on the Woman Question. We will better appreciate James' use and transformation of character types if we examine them in terms of what his style has taught us—to not think singly. With this awareness we are also better able to take up now another aspect of Isabel's return to Osmond—her choice of form as form, the epistemological aspect of Isabel's reaffirmation of marriage.

Some critics feel that her espousal of the form of marriage makes Isabel as hollow a formalist as Osmond himself. Granted that Isabel has shown tendencies in this direction, we can recognize (and indeed insist upon) these tendencies and yet interpret her final affirmation differently. Isabel, in espousing the form of marriage, is in fact practicing the art of not thinking singly. A form which can become rigid and reductive is, paradoxically, her only means to true complexity. When Osmond insists upon the form of marriage, he is insisting that his wife should reflect his ideals and wishes. He uses the image of the mirror several times. But as a mirror reflects, it also reverses. By returning to Osmond, Isabel is his other half in two senses: she remains his mate and yet she remains *other* with regard to his "hideously unclean" (398) ideas. Only in this dual role can Isabel avoid being one with her husband. As adulteress she would reflect his hideously unclean *monde;* as servile wife she would be his lifeless reflection indeed. As mate and yet opponent she manages, like a pun, to sustain multiple interpretations simultaneously. Again we have, then, two circles. The inner, unresolved issue of Isabel with her life yet to live pushes out against the potentially deadening form of her marriage to Osmond. This processive relation redeems, in turn, the very language of Osmond's *monde*. Amid verbal ambivalence and double entendre, Isabel accepts the face value of her vows both to Osmond at the altar and to Pansy in the convent. In the process she does not falsify language into the propositional truisms of popular fiction, because the two vows are irreconcilable. Isabel is and must remain the focus of oppositions.

With her limited freedom and with all her undeniable flaws, Isabel is thus admirable and moving. She is, in fact, moving *because of* her limitations. She appeals precisely not by her ideality, but by her humanity. Seeing how far she still has to go, we are yet struck by how far she has come. In the partial quality of her self-transcendence, she is one of us; in the extent of her transcendence, she surpasses most. Her commitment to the good as she sees it, yet her failure to achieve "the good," make her finer than her *monde*. She is finally serious in the most admirably comic of ways.

Isabel's synthetic achievement is, in turn, Henry James'. He, as well as she, has had to struggle to overcome the limitations of extravagance and equipoise. She can approach the condition of his style because she can never reach it. James justifies his concern with artistry by his awareness that life is not art. Paradoxically, it is the artless scribblers who make life "perfect." James can polish his style without fear of affectation because his sense of life's obduracy increases with the luster of his art. Thus, in his style, James embodies the moral value of his tale. I use the word "moral" as James did when he said of Delacroix, "I am not ashamed to say that I like him in part for his moral tone" (*PE* 185). James in his fiction cannot resort to simple propositional assertion, as his popular compeers can. Technique must thus become vision. James' form approaches synthetic completeness in proportion as we are moved to embrace what his artistry reveals as our earthly good. Insofar as we are able to acknowledge and appreciate the apparent contradictions of our reading experience without succumbing to any easy indiscriminateness, we become one with the novel. We recognize the redeeming other side to what we might neatly dismiss, and the limiting other side to what we might extravagantly affirm. We finally accept life for what it is and, in accepting, bless it.

2 🐚

Tradition and Character

Saints and devils are not tragic.
Robert B. Heilman

I knew she could play any part. . . . I didn't understand that she
would play two at the same time.
Henry James

"Je crois enfin dans les âmes pures, et peut-être dans le monde
entier, Dieu n'a pas d'une autre ennemi que lui-même; mais je
crois aussi que je ne prêcherai jamais sur ce texte ni chez les
Indiens ni ailleurs."
Victor Cherbuliez

She had been humanized, to his view, by the mere accidents of
flesh and blood.
Henry James

To study characterization in light of style, we should begin by
recognizing that these two elements, apparently so different, are similar
both in their origins and in the way their effect upon James' fiction
changes between 1871 and 1881. First, their origins. As James shapes his
style from a common fund of language, he also outfits his characters (in
varying degrees) from a common fund of gesture and type. Moreover, as
James draws for stylistic devices upon both major and popular writers,
so the debt of some of his characters to Hawthorne, Eliot, and other
masters should not obscure his substantial borrowings from the popular
tradition.

It has long been recognized that his plots are mainly reworkings
of such never-fail formulas as seduction with sentiment, and his
characters have their origins in the villains, heroes, and poor little
rich girls common to novelists of all ages. His special genius is to take
materials of the ordinary novel and transform them by his advanced
technique.[1]

Although his "advanced technique" is operating successfully by 1881, the
characters in his early fiction often suffer, like his style, from the

limitations and uncertainties of popular practice. Here, for example, are excerpts from the first two dramatic scenes which James created as a novelist.

> [Roger meets Mr. Lambert, who] walked straight to the table in the center of the room, and poured out and drank without stopping three full glasses of ice-water, as if he were striving to quench the fury of some inner fever. He then went to the window, leaned his head against the cold pane, and drummed a nervous tattoo with his long stiff finger-nails.... His face was as white as ashes, his eyes were as lurid as coals.... His open waistcoat displayed a soiled and crumpled shirt-bosom, from whose empty button-holes the studs had recently been wrenched. In his normal freshness the man must have looked like a gambler with a run of luck.

> [Roger proposes to Miss Morton.] There glimmered mistily in the young man's brain a vision of a home-scene in the future—a lamp-lit parlor on a winter night, a placid wife and mother, wreathed in household smiles, a golden-haired child, and, in the midst, his sentient self, drunk with possession and gratitude.... Miss Morton addressed herself to her niece's tapestry, and as her lover went on with manly eloquence, glanced up at him from her work with womanly *finesse*.
>
> (*W&W* 233, 235)

In the first scene, the explicit definition of the character's type— "gambler"—is not effectively complicated by the absence of "normal freshness," for Mr. Lambert's rumpled condition is also stereotypic. The detail of the soiled studless shirt, the Byronic traits of burning eyes and inner fever, the conventional metaphor "white as ashes" and the conventional gestures of drumming a tattoo and leaning against a window, and the mechanicalness of the sequence walked-poured-drank-went-leaned-drummed—all these traditional elements combine expectedly to compose that favorite of melodrama, the Doomed Driven Man. And we are not amused.

The second scene functions quite differently. Although Roger's ideal of domestic harmony is as conventional as Mr. Lambert himself, James here is clearly undercutting that conventionality—with "glimmered mistily" and "his sentient self, drunk." Then, the equally conventional marriage proposal is, as we saw in chapter 1, qualified wryly by "manly eloquence" and by Miss Morton's subsequent smile.

Together these two scenes indicate that James' characterization, like his style, begins basically "mixed." At times he sees through what at other times he tries to present more or less straight. Thus James is caught at the beginning of his career in a dilemma endemic to American fiction.

The double falsity of many American heroines . . . arises out of the
compounding of the inadequacy of the sentimental prototypes by the
writer's lack of faith in them.

(Wilson, 274)

James' mixed method of characterization, like his mixed style, derives in
part from the mixed nature of popular practice and in part from his own
still greater ambivalence toward his materials.

One of the paradoxes of popular fiction is that a genre which
consistently sacrificed the aesthetic to the didactic remained so self-
consciously *literary*. Not only do the scribblers refer frequently to
famous authors and to how things happen in novels and plays, they even
manage to gain enough distance from their conventional materials to
undercut them.

"Disappointed affections, broken hearts, early graves, are more
terrible."
"Fudge!" was the word that rose to Hannah's lips.

(*Ish* 39)

In *Elsie Venner* Holmes pokes fun at "the flat-chested and cachectic
pattern which is the classical type of certain excellent young females,
often the subjects of biographical memoirs" (291). In *The Heir* irony
touches romantic lovers (2:101), the young poet (1:121), and even " 'the
sister with the spine complaint' " (1:229).

Despite such complexity, however, popular novelists are unwilling to
sustain their irony. E. D. E. N. Southworth can admit that "it was only
the same old story" and yet can go right on

—of the young girl of fortune marrying a spendthrift, who dissipated
her property, estranged her friends, alienated her affections, and then
left her penniless, to struggle alone with all the ills of poverty to bring
up her three little girls.

(*Ish* 453)

The same old story indeed. But Mrs. Southworth continues to spell it out
for a full paragraph because pathos is so endemic to the situation that
reiteration only confirms how universal—and thus how pathetic—the
situation is. More sophisticated than Mrs. Southworth, Oliver Wendell
Holmes can nonetheless say, "it was the old story. A poor country-
clergyman dies, and leaves a widow and a daughter" (*EV* 93). Worse still,
what Holmes parodies in students' compositions—

that youth exhaled, like the dewdrop from the flower, ere the sun had
reached its meridian; that life was o'ershadowed with trials; that the
lessons of virtue instilled by our beloved teachers were to be our guides
through all our future career

(95)

—these popular sentiments and situations are the very ones which Holmes ultimately resorts to for pathos in his novel.[2] Likewise in *The Heir*, characters who mock the notion of conventional lovers shed, at the proper time, tears and *sentence* over such lovers; jokes are made about "the sins of the fathers," but Guy worries strenuously about this curse and eventually succumbs to it.

These and other turnabouts do not, finally, create great fiction. Like style, characterization can aim for simultaneity or alternation of effect. A popular character generally "seems the effect of two successive impulses of the author's imagination."[3] Not good and bad, but good then bad. Because they do not intend, finally, to make us experience life's contrarieties, the scribblers do not attempt to create a Hamlet who is mad and yet lucid, an Emma Woodhouse who is both valuable and dangerous. Moreover, whatever the effect might be of the scribblers' occasional (and often apparently inadvertent) turnabouts, the effect is in fact minimal because the two alternatives are not really given an equal chance. We never seriously doubt the worth of romantic lovers or the pathos of the invalid because popular novelists do not seriously question the genteel presuppositions which sell their books.

Like his popular compeers, Henry James not only uses traditional materials but uses them self-consciously. In criticism and fiction throughout the crucial decade, he evokes conventional representations.

> looking like an old Venetian print . . . . [like] a lithograph on a music sheet . . . . the old prints of the figures in the conventional Italian farce . . . . the Italy that we know from the still engravings in old keepsakes and annuals, from the vignettes on music-sheets and drop-curtains at theatres.
>
> (*SA* 11, *PE* 151, *FrP* 53, *RH* 423)

He refers with equal ease and consistency to basic character types.

> The traditional tutor of our old novels and comedies . . . . the old stage *soubrette* . . . . the Belle au Bois Dormant . . . . the ravishing young widow and the romantic young artist . . . . a classic *valet de théâtre* . . . . the Belle aux Cheveux d'Or . . . . a shepherd and shepherdess in a bucolic poem . . . . a *belle brune* . . . . like a pair of ravishers in a German ballad . . . . like the heroine of an Eastern tale . . . . a servant in an old-fashioned comedy . . . . the ideal 'gallant' Frenchman of the old type . . . . the *oncle de comédie* . . . . the familiar combination of the wife, the lover and the husband . . . . the little country cousin . . . . one of those slouched sombreros which are the traditional property of the Virginian or Carolinian of romance . . . .

the heroine of a serial in a magazine . . . . the regular old *oncle de comédie*.

> (*CT* 2:131, 132, 258–59, 323
> [twice]; 3:31, 94, 164, 222, 338;
> 4:225; *FrP* 157; *W&W* 337; *Ha*
> 100, 111; *RH* 22; *PE* 169; *SA* 17)

Also like his popular compeers, James goes beyond self-consciousness to a critical use of conventional materials. His own ambivalence is more sustained and complete, however. Let us first study his statements in reviews and essays; we can then devote the rest of this chapter to examining how James, as a novelist, handles the two basic components of characterization—gesture and type.

Readers who exaggerate James' fastidiousness fail to recognize how much he delighted in the great, histrionic figures of the stage. In 1875 he says of Irving's Macbeth, "his best moment is his rendering of the scene with the bloody daggers—though it must be confessed that this stupendous scene always does much toward acting itself" (*SA* 37). Later, he can relish Salvini's Othello. "He falls into a chair on the left of the stage, and lies there for some moments, prostrate, panting, helpless, annihilated, convulsed with long, inarticulate moans. Nothing could be finer than all this" (*SA* 174–75). Yet finer moments James *can* imagine. In the final paragraph of a later review he defines Salvini's effects as "mainly of a coarse kind. . . . he paints his pictures with a big brush" (*SA* 190).* The big brush is coarse because Salvini's conventionalized histrionics remain too consciously artful to evoke the complex concern we feel in real-life or lifelike situations. Already in 1875 James can say

> there is always a certain langour in our intellectual acceptance of the grand coquettes of fiction . . . we always seem to see the lady pushing about her train before the foot-lights, or glancing at the orchestra-stalls during her victim's agony.
>
> (*FrP* 232)

James thus finds Millais lacking what Hawthorne excells in.

> M. Millais paints her [Mrs. Langtrey] as if he meant her to pass for the heroine of a serial in a magazine.
>
> (*PE* 169)

> They [Hawthorne's tales] are moral, and their interest is moral; they deal with something more than the mere accidents and conventionalities, the surface occurrences of life.
>
> (*Ha* 64)

---

*James adds that "fortunately his stroke is wonderful."

James' phrasing in the Hawthorne passage is important. Morality is not antithetic to the conventional; it entails more than the conventional. What more is needed? The popular tradition provides in extremes what is *not* needed. In 1875 James notes that the theater audience "does not go with the expectation of seeing the mirror held up to nature as it knows nature—of seeing a reflection of its actual, local, immediate physiognomy. The mirror, as the theatres show it, has the image already stamped upon it—an Irish image, a French image, an English image" (*SA* 22–23). At the opposite extreme from the overly generic is the overly particular. In 1880 James criticizes "a public which passes from the drawing-room to the theater only to look at an attempt, at very best imperfect, to reproduce the accidents and limitations of the drawing-room" (*SA* 135).

Instead of inadequate extremes, an artist must join the particular and the general in that imaginative synthesis which James found in the style of Tintoretto. In terms of characterization, two artists achieve the ideal blend. Of Velasquez James says in 1874 "that his men and women . . . [are indebted] to his conception of them quite as much as to their real appearance" (*PE* 84). Having praised Turgenev for his "commingled realism and idealism," James adds that "abstract possibilities immediately become, to his vision, concrete situations" (*FrP* 224). Thus, avoiding the superficiality of either conventional melodrama or petty realism, Turgenev achieves with his characters that coalescence of opposites which is the "moral."

> The scene, the figures [in "Hélène"], are as present to us as if we saw them ordered and moving on a lamp-lit stage; and yet, as we recall it, the drama seems all pervaded and coloured by the light of the moral world.
>
> (*FrP* 224)

Resembling the stage is not harmful if fiction entails more than conventional elements, if it incorporates the profound realms of consciousness. Then our consciousness is also engaged. James thus does with characters what he did with style—does not abandon the popular tradition but transforms it. James bases his strategy for characterization upon our knowledge of conventions because our expectations will then be sufficiently one-sided that he can make us experience the other, ambivalent, implicating side of character, and life.

> What Shakespeare does to Richard himself serves not to make him any less a villain but to modify, in more ways than one, the straightforward response to him.[4]

The late eighteenth century loved
a fine gesture.
J. M. S. Tompkins

Gesture

J. M. S. Tompkins establishes convincingly that gesture is a major feature of the popular arts a full century before James enters his crucial decade. Sanctioned by "a society very ready to weep and tremble and to take credit for doing so" (113), flamboyant gesturing is further recommended to later eighteenth-century novelists by the example of their great predecessors, particularly Fielding with his background in theater, Richardson with his "studied record of movements" (349), and Sterne's more sentimental and comic use of "that hieroglyphic of a lifetime, the habitual gesture" (52). Two other genres are also influential.

> Eighteenth-century novels and romances . . . . are stagey; for they certainly include some shoddy fragments of the technique which tragic actors found necessary in the great theatres of the period, or rather of that technique as debased by strollers and barnstormers.
>
> (352–53)

Besides borrowing from drama, later eighteenth-century novelists owe a large and readily acknowledged debt to the striking poses and settings of Claude, Rosa, and other "picturesque" painters.

> The method applied equally to landscape and to figures, and its vogue was perhaps strengthened by the absence of illustrations in English novels; perhaps also by the belief, occasionally expressed by critics and novelists, that painting is a more expressive art than writing.
>
> (356)

In mid-Victorian times surprisingly little has changed. Not only does emphatic gesturing remain a staple of theater and fiction, but painting remains a major storehouse for both to borrow from. Probably theater's most famous borrowing is Douglas Jerrold's.

> Jerrold's inspiration for *The Rent-Day* was two well-known paintings by Sir David Wilkie. Jerrold proudly represented these paintings in stage tableaux: the picture entitled "The Rent-Day" in the opening scene, and "Distraining for Rent" in the opening and closing scenes of Act II. Walter Jerrold reports that the audience greeted the opening scene with "rapturous applause . . . as an exact reproduction of Wilkie's popular picture." Sir David Wilkie wrote to Jerrold that his

"inventive fancy has created . . . all the living characters and progres-
sive events of real life" suggested by the pictures.

(Bailey, 259)

Although painting's influence upon "great" Victorian fiction has been
discussed by Mario Praz and Peter Conrad, critics have not defined
adequately the comparable debt which popular fiction owes to the plastic
arts.[5] When Charlie in *The Heir*, for example, is asked how Philip and
Charlotte are getting along, he replies, "'A good deal like the print of
Dignity and Impudence'" (1:99). Guy wishes always to remember Amy
"like one of those peaceful spirits, with bending head, folded hands, and
a star on its brow, in the *Paradiso* of Flaxman" (1:296). Reliance upon
famous art works shades off into a still more widely used device.
"'Nothing I admire so much as a graceful figure at a spinning-wheel'" (*In*
398). Tableau is a staple of popular fiction because meaning and hence
moral evaluation are endemic to the pose itself. Many paintings and
illustrations and their immense moral force flash upon us when we
encounter such tableaux as The Byronic Outcast:

> he found himself seated on a rock which crowned the summit of one of
> the hills, his handkerchief loosened, his waistcoat open, his hat thrown
> off.

Or Motherhood:

> overhung by the long shoots of the roses, Amabel's close cap and small
> head were seen against the deep-blue evening sky, as she sat in the
> summer twilight, her little one asleep in her cot.

(*HR* 1:268, 2:311)

Postponing two questions—why the Victorians rely so heavily upon
gestures and how "Victorian" is Henry James in this regard—we can
readily document that James too loved a fine gesture. In painting, drama,
and fiction. As art critic, James repeatedly praises "an especial truthful-
ness of gesture" (*PE* 85). In 1875, for example, he admires

> a remarkable success. . . . Nero is seated, leaning forward, with his
> elbow on the back of his chair, and his hand over his mouth, watching
> the contortions of a slave who, extended on the pavement, is expiring
> in agony before him. Beside him, and nearer the spectator, is seated the
> horrible Locusta, descanting upon the properties of her dose, her face
> turned toward him and her arm, with a strangely familiar gesture,
> lying across his knee.

(*PS* 139–40)

Mastery of gesture and tableau is also what James praises actors for. He
applauds Irving's Hamlet because "few actors . . . can rest a well-shaped
hand on the hilt of a sword in a manner more suggestive of the models of
Vandyke"; as Andromaque, Miss Bernhardt "bends over her classic

confidant like the figure of Bereavement on a bas-relief" (*SA* 140, 92).
With fiction James often singles out moments that depend upon conventional gestures. To exemplify "the way in which M. Turgénieff almost
invariably appeals at the outset to our distinctively moral curiosity, our
sympathy with character," James cites a passage in which the hero
"'threw himself into a chair by the chimney-piece, and covered his face
with his hands. . . . He got up, went back to the fireplace, sank into his
chair again, and covered his face with his hands'" (*FrP* 237, 238).

The power which James feels in the gestures of fiction, drama, and
painting, he also wants readers of his own fiction to feel. Lamentably
many of his attempts are either too assertive, too mechanical, too
violent, or some combination thereof. For example:

> drumming on the back of his sofa . . . . drummed a nervous tattoo with
> his long stiff fingernails . . . . beat a hurried tattoo with the heel of his
> boot.

> resting her forehead against the glass . . . . leaned her head against it
> [the windowpane] . . . . leaned his forehead against the cold pane.

How readily Mr. Lambert (in the second and last examples)* blends in
with his popular peers. When we add to these gestures the others that
James relies relentlessly upon—blushing, weeping, frowning, glaring,
staring, pacing nervously, whistling nervously or exuberantly, wringing
hands, fixing eyes, falling on knees, going hat in hand, putting handkerchief to brow—we discover one reason for the inadequacy of certain
scenes in James' early novels. Like the style in these scenes, the gestures
are so conventional that they *assert* emotion rather than evoke it. Instead
of the character giving meaning to the gesture, the gesture has its
meaning so rigidly prescribed by convention that the character merely
personifies it. We encounter "Worry" or "Despair," not a worried or
despairing individual. What might be powerful in emblem books or other
genres is lethal in James' fiction. Mystery rigidifies into formula.

A second, more express type of assertion occurs when:

> Roger frowned; the conversation . . . was too much for him,
> <div align="right">(<i>W&W</i> 324)</div>

> he [Roderick] simply shook his head several times, in dogged negation,
> <div align="right">(<i>RH</i> 387)</div>

> he [Hammond's] hands clasped behind him, as was his habit when
> engrossed by earnest thought.
> <div align="right">(<i>StE</i> 330)</div>

Since any gesture, no matter how conventional, is a visual emblem, we
can participate at least to the extent of recognizing what the emblem
stands for. This small experience is abbreviated, however, when James

---

HR 2:44; *W&W* 233; *StE* 121; *HR* 1:278; *In* 233; *W&W* 233.

and popular writers explain, as they do in the examples above, what the image stands for. Our recognition lasts only a moment before the assertion of meaning replaces our perception of it. Yet even such a moment—"blushing and squeezing his hat as if in an agony of embarrassment" (*In* 32)—allows more participation than "silent and obsequious, with his hat raised to his lips" (*Ame* 211). At least in *The Initials* we encounter the gesture first, so that a fleeting recognition can occur. By *beginning* with "silent and obsequious," James reduces the already conventional gesture to the status of a proof, a detail added to substantiate the prior assertion of meaning. And when this assertion replaces the gesture entirely—replaces it with the word "gesture" or "attitude"—then we are denied any chance of doing half the work. We are simply told what to feel when Christina flings her hands apart with "an admirable gesture" or when Nora moves "with a gesture of eloquent simplicity" or when Amy's "nervous capricious rapidity of motion and gesture, gave her an air of girlish *brusquerie* which was by no means without charm" (*RH* 368, *W&W* 706, 708).

Besides being at times overly assertive, James can also make gestures seem mechanical when he, like a popular novelist, multiplies them in either of two ways.

> [Roderick] sat for some moments with his elbows on his knees and his head in his hands . . . . [Roderick] was sitting with his elbows on his knees and his head in his hands . . . . Roderick was sitting with his elbows on his knees and his head in his hands . . . . [Rowland] was sitting with his head in his hands and his elbows on his knees . . . . [Cavaliere] was sitting with his elbows on his knees and his head in his hands . . . . [Roderick] leaning his elbows on his knees and holding his head in his hands.
>
> (*RH* 35, 77, 277, 287, 374, 384)[6]

Already stereotypical, this gesture is repeated so relentlessly that the characters blend into one another, and become little more than automatons. A different, but equally unfortunate, mechanicalness occurs when

> he strode over to the fireplace, flung himself into the chair, leaned forward with his head in his hands, and groaned audibly.
>
> He drew a chair from the side of the room, flung himself upon it, stampt his foot twice against the floor, smote his breast with an air of inexpressible vengeance, and taking a paper from his pocket, held it at arm's length, and burst into tears.

Stringing conventional gestures together gives the character an impossible jerkiness and reveals just how antiquated this technique is. The popular hero in the second quotation,[7] whom Mr. Lambert resembles so obviously and unfortunately (*W&W* 233), was jerking mechanically

across the pages of a novel nearly a century before James began writing!
   These last examples, with their "flung" and "burst," also manifest a
third basic liability of Jamesian and popular gestures.

> The young man sprang up with alacrity . . . . they flung themselves on
> the grass . . . . Roderick sprang to his feet . . . . one long leg flung over
> the other . . . . springing up . . . . He sprang up . . . . it sprang from his
> lips . . . . flung open the gates of his eloquence . . . . flung down his
> tools . . . . he sprang up . . . . flung the instrument down . . . . fling
> himself back . . . . Christina then sprang to her feet . . . . flung it behind
> him . . . . Roderick flung himself into an arm chair . . . . Rowland
> sprang up . . . . flung her arms . . . . he flung himself into a chair . . . .
> flung their odorous promise . . . . he flung himself in the sun . . . .
> Christina flung off her burnous . . . . she flung herself into a chair . . . .
> flung them [arms] apart . . . . "if I flung everything to the winds" . . . .
> he had flung himself upon a sofa . . . . Mrs. Hudson flung herself upon
> his neck . . . . he sprang up . . . . he flung himself down . . . . he sprang
> to his feet . . . . he flung himself down . . . . Rowland sprang out . . . .
> as if the billows of the ocean had flung him upon the strand . . . . had
> flung herself.
>
> (*RH* 20, 29, 32, 47, 65, 88, 93,
> 105, 114, 200, 201, 238, 239
> [twice], 246, 281, 282, 284, 286,
> 287, 343, 368 [twice], 370, 383,
> 418, 459 [twice], 466, 470, 472,
> 479, 481)

Maybe we should be grateful for small favors. *Roderick Hudson* is less
violent than some popular novels; *The Initials,* for example, repeats the
one gesture of springing at least forty-one times in four hundred pages!
Even gratitude has it limits, however. The kangaroo quality of "spring"
and "fling" in *Roderick Hudson,* plus all the bounding and scrambling
and throwing and bursting, plus the way various characters share in the
violence quite indiscriminately—all this mayhem reduces James' novel at
times to the point of ludicrousness.[8]
   Inadequate as conventional gestures seem today, we must realize that
James and the scribblers dissatisfy us for different reasons. Popular
gestures, like popular stylistic devices, are not "bad" in themselves. Their
success with their audiences is indisputable. Understanding why they
succeed and why the Victorians rely so heavily upon visual emblems will
help explain the problematic effect of conventional gestures in James'
own fiction. Let us start with a sentence from *The Wide, Wide World.*

> She [Mrs. Montgomery] understood far better than her husband what
> Ellen's feelings were, and could interpret much more truly than he the
> signs of them.
>
> (65)

The interpretation of signs. Biblical exegesis is a hallowed Christian practice, and its application to profane subjects has been long standing and honorable. French painting of the seventeenth century (especially LeBrun and his followers) and eighteenth-century English essayists from Addison to Johnson give detailed renderings of the soul's manifestations in face and gesture—the look of rage, the smile of a friend. In mid-Victorian times, the popular mind could still find convenient correspondences between physiognomy and vice.

> The temperance man of *The Drunkard's Warning* orders the offender to "look at your bloated features, drooping eyelids, trembling joints, fetid breath, and say, drunkenness, this is thy work!"

> [Sex] manual writers cautioned girls never to handle their sexual organs, for, while it gave temporary pleasure, the habit left "its mark upon the face so that those who were wise may know what the girl is doing." . . . [for boys] the ravages of masturbation were "written in the countenance."[9]

With everybody reading away, art and life merge in revealing ways. So sturdy an American businessman as George E. Putnam bases his decision to publish *The Wide, Wide World* solely—he never read the dog-eared manuscript—upon the intuition of his mother, who "believed in mystical signs, in portents, in the double meaning of spiritual symbolism."[10] Not all Victorians maintain proper reverence, of course.

> None so keen as these young misses to know an inward movement by an outward sign of adornment . . . there is not an end of ribbon or a turn of a ringlet which is not a hieroglyphic with a hidden meaning.
>
> (*EV* 516)

With the words "know an inward movement by an outward sign," Holmes is clearly parodying the orthodox definition of a sacrament—a visible and outward sign of inward, spiritual grace. Although Holmes is justifiably ridiculing the romantic silliness of finding tremendous signifi-cance in every trivial event, we should not suppose that the sacramental view of reality lingers in the nineteenth century only as a butt of jokes. Romantics as different as Emerson and Baudelaire build upon the theory of Correspondences which Swedenborg developed from traditional Chris-tian typology; Carlyle and Whitman refer frequently to nature as "hieroglyph"; and as Michael Davitt Bell demonstrates, "the romantic historian was, in essence, applying typology to history."[11] To many individuals in High Victorian times, the world remains a storehouse of hidden meanings to discover. Not only does so apparently irreverent a novel as *Pelham* contain the expression " 'the outward and visible sign of an inward and *spiritual grace*,' " but Bulwer also discusses "the curious investigator into the initials of things."[12] One of the century's best sellers, *The Initials*, centers upon the very act of deciphering the initials A. Z., the alpha and omega. Popular novelists can take their tasks so seriously because the act of reading is for them—quite literally—the act of life itself.

> The strong hieroglyphics graven as with iron stylet on his brow. . . . if I did not *know*, at least I *felt*, the meaning of those characters, written without hand.
>
> > (*V* 206)
>
> I thought he was trying to read my character . . . he might see lines, and trace characters, but he could make nothing of them; my nature was not his nature, and its signs were to him like the words of an unknown tongue.
>
> > (*P* 15)

To regard life as a matter of reading and translating is especially natural to Protestants because the very essence of their religion is (supposedly) the individual's interpretation of The Word. With salvation itself at stake, sign-reading becomes obsessive in popular fiction, as almost any novel of the period will demonstrate.

> "Of what are these things the signs and tokens" . . . . how could inn-servants and ship-stewardesses everywhere tell at a glance . . . . "read that countenance" . . . . she studied me long . . . . he laid himself open to my observation . . . . there was language in Dr. John's look, though I cannot tell what he said . . . . I traced in the gesture . . . . the strong hieroglyphics graven as with iron stylet on his brow . . . . if I did not *know*, at least I *felt*, the meaning of those characters, written without hand . . . . I read in it no common mastery of the passions . . . . he did not read my eyes . . . . he left signs of each visit . . . . I felt a longing to trace . . . the signs . . . . in this sign I read a ruffled mood . . . . the multitude have something else to do than to read hearts and interpret dark sayings . . . . Madame Beck read the riddle . . . . I know some signs of the sky; I have noted them ever since childhood.
>
> > (*V* 2, 54, 61, 64, 92, 134, 168, 206
> > [twice], 216, 309, 332, 387, 404,
> > 436 [twice], 480)

Thus in popular fiction, conventional gestures and their interpretations are part of the whole didactic cloth. If these signs are unmoving today, it is because we cannot accept a whole epistemological-moral system. The universe does not seem sacramental to us; typology solves few problems. This unbridgeable gap does not, however, explain how conventional gestures affect James' fiction. Such gestures do, to be sure, seem old-fashioned here too. But this inadequacy is compounded by its opposite—in James' fiction conventional gestures are manifestly *not* part of the whole cloth. James can refer many times in his early tales to the reading of signs.

I read this for the most part in the severe humility . . . . it seemed to
say—this lingering virginal eyebeam—in language easily translated,
Thou art the man! . . . the outward signs of his mission . . . . "you'll
read the enigma" . . . . Philip flattered himself that he could read very
small signs . . . . to deal in signs and portents . . . . her pale face . . .
spoke most forcibly . . . . its wild disorder told me how he had raved
. . . . I knew the signs and symptoms . . . . To read the full meaning
of his attitude . . . . I watched . . . for the signs and portents.

(*CT* 1:166; 2:37 [twice], 43, 47,
87, 223, 368, 401; 3:114, 324)

He can even echo *The Wide, Wide World's* assertion that women are
better sign-readers than men. But the truths that his seers come increasingly to discover are not, finally, the a priori propositions that conventional gestures embody. James can no more take over whole the gestures
of the popular tradition than he can be satisfied with the style of
equipoise. Meaning for him is not general. Its source is not God eternal
or Newton's harmonious cosmos but the individual struggling for the
truth of a full consciousness in a moment of time. Thus gesture must
function like style itself. Having praised an actress in 1872 for "an
intonation in gesture as eloquent as if she had spoken it" (*SA* 6), James later
says still more explicitly of the pantomimist:

What are his motions, what is his play of face, but so many tones and
syllables, so many signified mute words, all making sentences and with
the sole difference of their being addressed to the mental instead of the
physical ear. Language is not the less in question for its but *appearing*
to be uttered.

(*SA* 214)

As a language, gesture must *suggest*, must make us experience the
particular and often contradictory meanings of a specific dramatic
moment. This use of gesture does not, on the other hand, isolate James
entirely from his popular peers. Like them, he still presumes that
meaning abides beneath appearances. For him, too, gesture is the word
made flesh. Thus, James does with gestures what he did with style: rather
than eschew popular practice, he transforms it enough to take us below
the surface, to the mystery.

To learn how James transforms the basic liabilities of his early
gestures—how he avoids seeming too violent, mechanical, and assertive
—let us begin with violence (table 6). Clear again are the similarity
between early Jamesian and popular fiction, and the decline in James'
grossissements by 1881.[13] His new control is achieved through two basic
techniques, as we can see with "fling" and "spring." The few "fling"s

which remain in *The Portrait* function metaphorically. Instead of characters flinging themselves around ridiculously, we find huge old trees which fling down their shade (6), and Caspar's "hard, slow American tone, which flung no atmospheric color over propositions intrinsically crude" (303). To appreciate how the switch to metaphor can control an otherwise melodramatic scene, we need only remove the "as if" from the following sentence. "Isabel ... and Ralph ... stood for a moment looking at each other as if he had flung down a defiance or an insult" (319). With "spring" James' control is equally firm, but it is not asserted through metaphor. Isabel and Countess Gemini each spring up. With Isabel we read "she said gently, as if the anger with which she had just sprung up had already subsided" (320). At the time of her actual rising, however, we encountered simply "she rose quickly" (319). Only as Isabel calms the scene does James suggest the full passion resident in it. He is thus doubly successful. He provides us the experience of intuiting how strong Isabel's emotion actually was; yet he saves his heroine from any demeaning, jack-in-the-box violence. A jack-in-the-box does appear, however. "The Countess threw herself hastily backward, tossing up her clasped hands.... [and] sprang from her chair" (416). In so finely controlled a novel, these gross gyrations are not a vestige of popular practice. James is now exploring the social consequences of such practice, such violence. Countess Gemini's erratic behavior is as mindless and finally random as her flights among lovers and social realms. Her flailing about will not cease until she has struck Isabel with words which themselves reveal the random and violent doings of polite society.

TABLE 6

	W&W	RH	StE	HR	WWW	In	Ame	PL
fling-spring	32	27	19	15	21	23	6	3
burst	12	9	2	7	18	7	5	4

Note: Numbers indicate incidence per 100,000 words.

Unlike violence, mechanicalness is difficult to represent in tables, but James' increased refinement by 1881 is evident here too. We encounter in *The Portrait* no mechanical series like Mr. Lambert's walk-poured-drank-went-leaned-drummed and no obviously repeated gesture like Roderick's elbows-on-knees-and-head-in-hands. James does still repeat gestures, however, and one example of repetition will indicate how the mechanical can become meaningful.

[Osmond] "What have you made of her [Pansy]?"
The sister dropped her eyes a moment.
"A good Christian, monsieur."
Her host dropped his eyes as well; but it was possible that the movement had in each case a different spring.

(213)

We participate in this moment because the conventional gesture of lowering eyes gains meaning with repetition. Since the maker of the gesture is now establishing its significance, that significance necessarily becomes problematic. We must intuit it from what we discover about the character. The ambivalence is, in turn, increased by James' use of "possible." The once-assertive narrator now declines to tell what the gesture means; at best he will only suggest the possibility of multiple meanings.

Thus the third liability of James' early gestures, their overassertiveness, is also effectively transformed by 1881.

When it [the piano concerto] was finished she [Isabel] felt a strong desire to thank the player, and rose from her seat to do so, while at the same time the lady at the piano turned quickly around, as if she had become aware of her presence.

"To think of you [Caspar]?" Isabel said, standing before him in the dusk. The idea of which she had caught a glimpse a few moments before now loomed large. She threw back her head a little; she stared at it as if it had been a comet in the sky.

$$(159, 542-43)^{14}$$

Although the "as if" construction functions in most popular and early Jamesian fiction to assert the narrator's intention unequivocally,[15] James can now capitalize—as he did with "fling"—upon the ambiguity inherent in "as if." On page 159 he suggests that Madame Merle is behaving, not spontaneously, but as if she were spontaneous. By not asserting that her behavior is artful, James allows us, or rather forces us, to deal with the ambivalent gesture as Isabel must confront the ambivalent Madame. On page 543 the "as if" gains additional ambivalence because James joins it to an image. He avoids the deadening effect of an assertion because the comet forces us into an interpretative role. Whether Isabel's idea of Caspar's love is a bright epiphany (like Pierre's comet in *War and Peace*) or is a portent of disaster (like the comets in Shakespeare), we cannot tell at this moment. And if the portent *is* evil: is it so because Caspar comes advocating divorce or because Isabel will, we presume, refuse him?

Narrative assertion is most deadening when, as we saw earlier, the word "gesture" or "attitude" replaces a specific gesture entirely. As table 7 indicates,[16] the sharp decline of the asserted "gesture" in *The Portrait* is not matched by "attitude," for James is now capitalizing upon the potential ambivalence of this word. "Attitude" can mean both a physical posture and a mental state, and the two may not coincide. For example, when Ralph and Isabel are quarreling about her choice of Osmond, "Ralph blushed as well; his attitude embarrassed him. Physically speaking, he proceeded to change it" (318).

TABLE 7

	W&W	RH	StE	HR	WWW	In	Ame	PL
gesture	8	15	3	4	1	3	8	2
attitude	2	25	1	1	1	0	12	17

Instead of simply presuming upon an automatic response to the word "gesture," James now explores the moral consequences of society presuming upon automatic responses to adopted "attitude"s. By attitudinizing, the *grand monde* enacts a specious melodrama in pantomime.

> They were sitting in an attitude of unexpressed expectancy; an attitude especially marked on the part of the Countess Gemini, who, being of a more nervous temperament than Madame Merle, practiced with less success the art of disguising impatience.
>
> (246)

Although Osmond and Isabel are not included in "they" here, both husband and wife are inescapably part of the social pantomime. After Osmond has righteously declared that Pansy must return to the convent, Countess Gemini exclaims, " '*En voilà, ma chère, une pose!*' But if it was an affectation, she [Isabel] was at a loss to see what her husband affected" (490). The question of Osmond's attitudinizing has arisen earlier, of course. At their first meeting, Isabel noted "that light, smooth slenderness of structure which made the movement of a single one of his fingers produce the effect of an expressive gesture" (242). While we wonder whether this gesture indicates a sensitive gentleman or an artful poseur, Isabel confidently recognizes "the signs of an unusual sensibility." The various possible meanings of "unusual" here mirror the ambiguity of Gilbert's attitude. Language and posture then interact again later to confirm our worst fears. After three years of marriage

> Osmond stood before the chimney, leaning back, with his hands behind him; he had one foot up and was warming the sole.... [Ned] went up to shake hands with him. Osmond put out his left hand, without changing his attitude. "How d'ye do?"
>
> (338)

With his sinister left hand and with words as coarsely casual as his raised foot, attitudinizing Gilbert will never warm that soul of his.

Isabel's concern with social forms makes her prone to attitudinizing like Osmond, Madame Merle, and Countess Gemini.

> She dropped on her knees before her bed, and hid her face in her arms.
>
> She was not praying; she was trembling.... she wished to resist her excitement, and the attitude of prayer, which she kept for some time, seemed to help her be still. She was extremely glad Caspar Goodwood was gone; there was something exhilarating in having got rid of

him. As Isabel became conscious of this feeling she bowed her head a little lower; the feeling . . . was a thing to be ashamed of—it was profane and out of place.

(151)[17]

Isabel feels uneasy enough at the disparity between her physical and mental attitudes that we hold out hope for her. A disparity does exist, however. Kneeling but not a prayer, Isabel lacks spiritual communion with her fellow mortals. The pose which controls her physical and psychic agitation does not redeem the mental attitude which causes that agitation; indeed she eventually rises with a continued enjoyment of "her power" over Caspar (152). This disparity between physical and mental attitudes corresponds, in turn, to an ambivalence which Victorians felt toward the supposedly sacred act of kneeling. Beneath their submission to the ideal of woman's submission, the scribbling females harbored subversive dreams. As Helen Papashvily has shown, the dream of castrating the oppressive male is enacted over and over in popular fiction (77–94). St. Elmo's total abasement before Edna Earl is a good example. Less extreme, but still more power-oriented than most Victorians would have admitted, is the dream which Isabel shares with many heroines— " 'a young man with a moustache going down on his knees to you' " (186). This dream soon comes true for Isabel.

> She had wanted to see life, and fortune was serving her to her taste; a succession of gentlemen going down on their knees to her was by itself a respectable chapter of experience.
>
> (253)

Isabel's exaltation, human though it is, prevents her from experiencing full communion with men and indeed with mankind. Living out the dreams of all too many Fair Readers, Isabel may kneel after Caspar's visit, but she kneels in triumph. And, at least by implication, in revenge.

Only in this context does the reappearance of Isabel's "attitude" assume its full meaning.

> She sank upon her knees. . . . "What is it you did for me?" she cried, her now extreme agitation half smothered in her attitude. She had lost all shame, all wish to hide things.
>
> (529–30)

Thus Isabel transcends the meanness of spirit which fostered both her early exultation with Caspar and her subsequent silence about her marriage. A new danger abides now, however, at the opposite extreme. Kneeling can mean the woman's abasement, even when it has earlier signified her hegemony; Edna Earl prostrates herself before St. Elmo once she has humbled him. Isabel, however, falls on her knees, not before

Osmond or even before Caspar or Warburton, but before Ralph. Although Ralph cannot remedy events, he is nonetheless the proper person to kneel to because Isabel is no longer attitudinizing like the *grand monde* or like the Stage Heroine who acknowledges her Lord and Master or proclaims herself an Honest Woman or begs for return to the Paternal Hearth or evokes pity upon Her Babes. In her drama of consciousness Isabel transforms a stage posture into a meaningful experience because she is ready to acknowledge the moral consequences of a melodramatic attitude.

How these consequences affect Ralph becomes clear when James goes on to transform another stock element of deathbed scenes. Ralph's conventional " 'you have been like an angel' " (529) echoes Isabel's earlier, unconventional " 'I am not an angel of any kind' " (442). How much Isabel does fit the Victorian ideal of angel is then complicated further when Ralph adds, " 'you know they talk about the angel of death. It's the most beautiful of all' " (529). Although Victorian fiction did allow for a Death Angel as well as a Household Angel,[18] novelists almost never achieve the complexity which James does here. Usually the Fair Beauty as Death Angel represents the beauty of the Sufferer's afterlife. Not only is Ralph's salvation unmentioned, however, but dark Isabel is his death angel in a more sinister way. She has killed him. I agree with critics who see that Isabel holds Ralph in life; whether or not he could withstand his illness indefinitely, Ralph stops wanting to once he discovers that the drama of Isabel's life has turned to tragedy. In confessing to Ralph her unhappiness, Isabel is acknowledging the prideful, naive attitude of mind which prevented her from recognizing his wisdom; she is also accepting the consequences of what her marriage has done to them all. Kneeling now is a spiritual, almost liturgical, experience because the gesture earns its significance as Isabel earns communion. Humble now instead of humbling, she can open herself more fully to Ralph's love, and love him more fully in return. Thus I cannot agree with critics who say that this scene might come from any of a hundred bad plays. The basic components do derive from the popular tradition. But, like the conventional language of euphemism and romantic exaggeration which we have seen qualified in this scene, James so transforms a conventional "attitude" and its accompanying paraphernalia that the drama can become primarily inward. We get down to the mystery, and are moved as we are not in a hundred bad plays.

> The heroines of fiction are of a race
> so mixed that there is no finding out
> just where they come from.
> *William Dean Howells*

Type

James' portrait of Isabel gains intricacy from his use and transformation of character types. Villains as well as heroines are important here because the promising young woman is threatened both by the dominating male and by the author who cannot make that male more than a straw-man. In creating his portraits of Osmond and Isabel, James mixes many elements from popular and great novels. This mixture, or rather its effects upon our reading experience, must be defined carefully. Female characters from James' early novels reveal how soon his practice becomes mixed and how the nature of that mixture changes; then, after studying the complex mixture that is Gilbert Osmond, we can concentrate upon Isabel as she grows from her heterodox heritage and from intercourse with her husband.

1

In *Watch and Ward*, Nora Lambert shares many traits with the conventional Orphan-Heroine. As the foundling in *The Heir* wears "shabby-genteel mourning" (1:260), Nora wears "shabby, pretentious mourning" (237); she also finds comfort in that traditional property of orphans, the keepsake. After the usual play at "romps" and shyness before handsome men, Nora matures into a young woman who engages in the mandatory knitting scenes, adorns her beautiful throat with the conventional ribbon and pearls, and knows the operas—*Il Trovatore* and *Der Freischütz*—mentioned in *St. Elmo* and *The Initials*.

Besides these ties to the popular tradition, Nora so strongly resembles one particular heroine—Hildegarde—that *The Initials*, and not Sand's *La Mare au Diable*, is probably the novel which James borrowed from most in *Watch and Ward*. As Hildegarde "sat at her window, long after dusk, trying to discover him [Hamilton] in every tall dark figure she saw" (385), so "late in the afternoon . . . Nora sat by the window, waiting for Roger to come" (415). Before these protagonists manage to bear their Fair Ladies to the altar, rival suitors intervene. Hildegarde is discovered by Hamilton "in her cousin's arms. She was not struggling . . . while Raimund, not in the least disconcerted by his presence, passionately kissed her two or three times" (290). Nora lets *her* cousin embrace and

106

kiss her in Roger's presence and, when Roger exits, the cousin "still holding her, showered upon her forehead half a dozen fierce kisses" (339). Although Nora, like Hildegarde, remonstrates belatedly and dismisses the bold cousin, both women continue to proclaim to the jealous protagonists a strong, if chaste, affection for the cousins who are their only male relatives. These cousins, in turn, reveal their vile intentions eventually—trapping their women in rooms, barring the doors, and threatening their reputations (*W&W* 704–5; *In* 297–98). The very act that frees Hildegarde from her pursuer has, years before, left Nora open to hers, by making her an orphan.

> . . . a figure lying on the ground, which, when Hamilton approached, he found to be the corpse of her cousin! He must have shot himself through the mouth, for the upper part of his head, hair, and brain were scattered in frightful bloody masses around. A more hideous object could hardly be imagined.
>
> (*In* 295)
>
> . . . an astonishing scene. In the middle of the floor lay a man, in his trousers and shirt, his head bathed in blood, his hand grasping the pistol from which he had just put a bullet through his brain. . . . Roger recognized, in spite of his bedabbled visage, the person who had addressed him in the parlor.
>
> (*W&W* 236)

Numerous and specific as these similarities are, they also establish how much both Nora and Hildegarde resemble the innumerable Beset Heroines of stage and fiction. Meditative vigils, smoking corpses, vile seducers, sickbed nursing, eventual wedlock: *The Initials* provided James not with inspiring innovations but with an attractive packaging of conventional types and situations. In turn, James' own heroine is sufficiently conventional that few modern readers find her interesting.[19] Our problems with Nora do not end with her conventionality, however. Determined to get away from "the everlasting young man and young woman," James creates relationships so bizarre that he *increases* our difficulties in responding to Nora.

Central here is the Ward-Guardian situation. It occurs quite frequently in Victorian literature. Like Silas Marner, Roger is humanized by contact with a young girl; like guardians in many eighteenth- and nineteenth-century popular works, Roger initially opposes his ward's marriage; and then—in a rarer but by no means unprecedented move—he marries her himself. Seeking specific sources, Oscar Cargill finds the prototypes for Nora-Roger in the young girl-older man situations of *La Mare au Diable* and *The Guardian Angel*. In fact, however, neither Marie in *La Mare* nor Myrtle in *Angel* is a ward, and the older man in Holmes' novel feels no sexual attraction for his young girl. More generally, even when traditional

Ward-Guardian relationships do involve coercion or marriage, they rarely introduce the erotic elements which appear in *Watch and Ward*. For, despite the critical tendency to relegate James to an ivory tower, few novelists face the facts of Victorian domestic relations more directly than Henry James. Fashioning a perfect wife is one of the obsessions of the period. And although we must wait until *The Portrait* to take up this issue fully, we can establish now that James begins his novelistic career commenting upon the salubrity of Victorian family life.

The idea of fashioning a perfect wife comes down from Rousseau and Maria Edgeworth and finds its classic formulation in Ruskin.

> You have first to mold her physical frame, and then, as the strength she gains will permit you, to fill and temper her mind with all knowledge and thoughts which tend to confirm its natural instincts of justice, and refine its natural tact of love.
>
> (62)

Ruskin's decidedly suspect attachment to little girls and his failure in wedlock might, in themselves, call his advice here into question. But we should not be hasty. There is, for example, the love of the twenty-three-year-old E. W. Benson for his Minnie. She is eleven. And theirs is a success story. They eventually marry, produce children of talent, and Benson himself becomes Archbishop of Canterbury. Even this marriage, however, reveals the dangers inherent in the Victorian obsession with young girls. Benson was so dominating that Minnie, especially meeting him so early, was never able to love him as he loved her or to develop fully her own considerable talents. And many relationships fare worse than the Bensons. J. A. Symonds' struggles with homosexuality, for example, lead him to fifteen-year-old Rosa Engle and then to unhappy marriage with Catherine North. Still more like James' Roger Lawrence is Holman Hunt. As Roger takes a girl from decidedly Bohemian circumstances and determines to make her a perfect wife, so

> Annie [Miller], a very beautiful but unrestrained and uneducated young girl whom Hunt had rescued from the London slums, was to have turned art into life. Hunt made her his protégée, arranged for her to have lessons in elocution, dancing and deportment, and to be cared for and watched over during his two-year absence in the Near East. Upon his return he expected to find a changed Annie, metamorphosed by her lessons in decorum and the example of the *Awakening Conscience* into a prim, proper and submissive lady whom he would take as his wife. But Annie had too much spirit for that. In defiance of Hunt's instructions she kept company with a notorious rake and a fashionable prostitute, and she sat for Rossetti and Boyce. . . . Hunt finally admitted his failure.[20]

If *Watch and Ward* does not examine Victorian domestic relations as thoroughly as *The Portrait* will do, James' first novel does reveal how randy the specific act of raising a perfect wife can be. Nora finds herself in situations unsavory, puzzling, and—though not unknown to Dostoevski and *fin de siècle* writers—peculiar enough to make the characterization in James' first novel mixed indeed.

The opening pages, for example, present strangely rum doings.

"Nora," he said, "come here."
She stared a moment, without moving, and then left the sofa and came slowly towards him.... "Do you remember my taking you last night in my arms?" It was his fancy that, for an answer, she faintly blushed.... He put his arm around her waist.... he drew her towards him and kissed her.

(238)

These lines would not be out of place in *Fanny Hill, My Secret Life,* and other traditional pornographic tales in which the woman is called before the male, talked to about sexual doings, and then embraced. James' scene reenacts this situation, but with one difference. The woman is twelve.

She was aroused by feeling him again at her bedside, kissing her, fondling her.

(237)

The stock situation of the Surprised Maiden is clear enough, but the male here is her father. Thus what we find in James' two scenes is anything but the towering and finally orthodox passion of a George Sand novel. Mr. Lambert, destitute and beset, is on his way to suicide; Roger has just had his third marriage proposal rejected. James' novel opens not with Sandian passion, but with male inadequacy. Unlike Germain in *La Mare au Diable* or Gyles Gridley in *The Guardian Angel,* Roger turns to Nora because he has failed with a woman his own age; unlike those men, Roger seeks both a conjugal *and* a paternal bond. The intricacies of this bizarre mixture—male uncertainty, inadequacy, desire, guilt, and woman's response to them—are revealed gradually through intricate patterns of erotic imagery.

James leaves little doubt about the phallic potential of Roger's rivals. Hubert, with his "slim, erect, inflexible *Ego*" (415), towers "upright" in the pulpit (422) and imagines himself (incredibly) "erected into a mouthpiece of the spiritual aspirations of mankind" (581). George, with his "manful hardness," rises tall and attractive against the sunset (337). George, however, is eventually defeated by Nora so completely that his last act is to slump impotently in a chair. When Nora then confronts Hubert, "she saw him, growing ... infinitely small in the large confidence of her gaze, rise in a perfect agony of impotence" (707). Nora, in turn, manages to rise to the occasion. "She rose and bridged this dizzy chasm" (707).

Her phallic gesture here is one of many throughout the novel, for James consistently reverses traditional male and female symbols.[21] Nora can rise above impotent Hubert at the climactic moment because she has been a better man than her suitors from the beginning.

> High above the level horizon now, clearly defined against the empty sky, rose this little commanding figure.
>
> (240)

Young Nora unmans Roger with her mental powers. "Roger was forever suspecting her of a deeper penetration than his own, and hanging his head" (325). Especially in the context of such male inadequacy, Roger's daydreams seem not only chauvinistic (and pornographic) but downright pathetic.

> Roger caught himself wondering whether, at the worst, a little precursory love-making [by George] would do any harm. The ground might be gently tickled to receive his own sowing; the petals of the young girl's nature, playfully forced apart, would leave the golden heart of the flower but the more accessible to his own verticle rays.
>
> (331)

George, unwilling to do Roger's tickling, "turned, therefore, upon his charming cousin the sunny side of his genius" (331). George's initial success is emphasized in the revisions. "Nora was fast overtaking herself in the exhilarating atmosphere of her cousin's gallantry" becomes "Nora was expanding in the sunshine of her cousin's gallantry" (332). Then, to show Nora responding similarly to Roger's other rival, handsome Hubert, James changes "she felt herself drifting toward an answering freedom of confidence" to "she felt herself beginning to expand" (416). Hubert, in turn, apparently fulfills Roger's dream by descending like Jove upon Nora-Danae, his face "transform[ed] . . . into a dazzling focus of light" (422).

All is not lost, however. When someone is eventually "tickled," it is Hubert, by Mrs. Keith (589). Confronted with male inadequacy, Nora can become her own sun because she contains within herself the rays which her suitors pretend to. Her eyes, with "a sort of arrested, concentrated brightness, a soft introversion of their rays, . . . retained their collected light. . . . Now and then the lids parted widely and showered down these gathered shafts" (238, 323). Sufficient without male sunshine, Nora blooms in an act of parthenogenesis.

> It was as if she had bloomed into golden ripeness in the potent sunshine of a great contentment; as if, fed by the sources of aesthetic delight, her nature had risen calmly to its uttermost level.
>
> (577)

Roger, who has been unmanned throughout, manages finally to join Nora in "the joyous brightness of the day" (709). Although he has likened himself to an "unmelted ... polar iceblock" (424), has felt "unsunned" when Nora refused his proposal (700), and has seemed to her "eclipsed" (595), Roger is, nonetheless, credited by the knowledgeable Miss Sandys with a potential for better things. " 'He is not a shining light perhaps ... but he has the real moral heat that one so seldom meets' " (425). This moral heat makes him finally boil over when Nora is threatened. "Passing his handkerchief over his forehead" (709), Roger can sweat with the intensity of his purpose. He does not "rescue" Nora because she has done that herself; but he can at least manage to get out in the sunshine—his rivals are both indoors at the moment—when Nora is ready to be married.

This capacity to act links Roger and Nora with the popular tradition, for the scribblers would emphatically agree that "in man or woman the capacity then and there to *act* was the thing he most relished" (695). That the dominant force is *Nora* makes James' novel still more orthodox. The reversal of sexual symbols throughout popular fiction derives from the scribblers' basic belief that women can (and will) rise to the occasion when their men fail to.[22] When James applies male symbols to women, he is not being simply idiosyncratic and perverse.

He is not, on the other hand, being simply conventional. The erotic passages in *Watch and Ward*—Hubert erected and Nora tickled and everyone caressing her long thick hair—are obviously more bizarre than what most popular fiction presents. A conventional heroine seems to have strayed into reminiscences of Sade. To explain this mixture, Dupee and later critics have concluded that naive James simply did not recognize the erotic nature of his materials.[23] The precision of James' image patterns and the consistency of the male-inadequacy theme indicate, however, that any naiveté is probably not James'. On the other hand, he *is* guilty of a failure of recognition. Doing with his imagery and characterization what we have seen him do with his style ("in repose Lawrence may have looked stupid"), James is failing to gauge the degree of our disaffiliation. Compare

> Nora came in. Her errand was to demand the use of Roger's watch key, her own having mysteriously vanished. She had begun to take out her pins and had muffled herself for this excursion in a merino dressing-gown of somber blue. Her hair was gathered for the night into a single massive coil, which had been loosened by the rapidity of her flight along the passage. Roger's key proved a complete misfit, so that she had recourse to Hubert's. It hung on the watch-chain which depended from his waistcoat, and some rather intimate fumbling was needed to adjust it to Nora's diminutive time-piece. It worked

admirably, and she stood looking at him with a little smile of caution
as it creaked on the pivot

(*W&W* 418)

with

"I am perfectly aware that I myself am as rusty as a key that has no
lock to fit it. It polishes me up a little to talk with you—not that I
venture to pretend I can turn that very complicated lock I suspect
your intellect of being!"

(*PL* 239)

Or

the ground might be gently tickled to receive his own sowing; the
petals of the young girl's nature, playfully forced apart

(*W&W* 331)

with

her mind was to be his—attached to his own like a small garden-plot
to a deer-park. He would rake the soil gently and water the flowers; he
would weed the beds and gather an occasional nosegay.

(*PL* 398)

Or

the central pivot of his being continued to operate . . . the slim, erect,
inflexible Ego

(*W&W* 415)

with

His egotism lay hidden like a serpent in a bank of flowers.

(*PL* 396)

Osmond's intentions are less honorable when he uses the lock-key image
than Hubert's were with an actual key, yet the effect in *The Portrait* is
not gross. Similarly the phallic chauvinism of Osmond's raking and
watering is all the more sinister for the absence of any crude tickling; and
the phallic egotism which we see in Hubert on page 415 is sufficiently
transformed in the later novel that James can *suggest* effectively the
phallic and even demonic quality of Osmond's far greater egotism. Thus
the difference between *Watch and Ward* and *The Portrait* derives less
from James' growing awareness of sexual themes than from his growing
ability to control those themes. The difference is not one of intention, but
of execution. With a heroine too conventional and with situations too
bizarre, James' mixed characterization does not produce the effects he
intends. In his next novel, James takes a major step forward. Without yet
managing to provide his young woman with a completely effective
situation, he does achieve in her character a compelling mixture of traits.

Christina Light resembles strongly the coquette of a novelist whom James began reading in the 1860s and was still mentioning in 1914.[24] The novelist is Victor Cherbuliez; the coquette, Emmeline de Mirveil of *Le Roman d'une honnête femme*. The connections between Christina and Emmeline not only increase our awareness of James' debt to Cherbuliez; they also help us understand how James first transforms a conventional type into a great character. Like Christina, Emmeline is "light." After Emmeline herself refers to " 'mes légèretés,' " the narrator confirms the fact. "Avec l'exagération ordinaire des caractères légers . . . elle donna des marques d'humilité" (290). James intends to raise the same issue with Christina. " 'Think of a girl wantonly making light of such a chance as hers!' " (222). Although Cherbuliez' word "léger," like James' "light," has a variety of meanings, *Le Roman* does little to exploit the connotations and possible ambiguities. Emmeline is flighty (and of somewhat light virtue), and little more. In *Roderick Hudson*, Christina's mind and conduct are sufficiently complex that, as we saw before, several and possibly all the connotations of her last name—brilliance, mere cleverness, irreverence, moral inadequacy—may obtain. To appreciate fully how James' light woman (and thus his fiction) differ from Cherbuliez', we must begin by establishing similarities.

Like so many melodramas and popular novels, *Le Roman* and *Roderick Hudson* have, as one of their themes, the education of young women. Both Emmeline and Christina are raised by their mothers for grand marriages.

"Sa mère avait toujours été sérieusement convaincue que l'éducation d'une fille est achevée quand on lui a appris à jouer de la prunelle et à pêcher à la ligne un mari."

(287)

"What sort of education," Rowland asked, "do you imagine the mother's adventures to have been for the daughter?"
"A strange school! But Mrs. Light told me, in Florence, that she had given her child the education of a princess. In other words, I suppose, she speaks three or four languages, and has read several hundred French novels."

(149)

To emphasize the inadequacy of such educations, both novelists introduce widowed, provincial parents who raise daughters in ideal fashion. Cherbuliez' M. de Loanne and James' Cecilia provide the discipline, education, and affection which makes their daughters princesses, not by marriage, but by personal superiority. The ill-educated coquettes, in turn, continue to need guidance. They receive it, in conventional fashion, from old duenna types, Madame d'Estrel in *Le Roman* and Madame Grandoni in *Roderick Hudson*.

Each coquette visits her guide four times. As Christina "burst into uncontrollable sobs and flung her arms upon Madame Grandoni's neck" (282), Emmeline has " 'ces accès de pleurs' " and " 'se jeta à mon cou' " (146, 292). Although the young women threaten dire actions, the older women are not taken in. Hearing Emmeline cry, " 'je me tuerai,' " Madame d'Estrel "n'avait pas précisément peur" (286); learning that " 'sometimes she thought of taking poison,' " Madame Grandoni recommends that Christina " 'come and see me instead. I would help her about as much, and I was, on the whole, less unpleasant' " (177). Despite her superior wit, Madame Grandoni resembles Madame d'Estrel in the way she chides her young charge, then soothes her, then advises patience. One effect of this advice is that both coquettes turn ascetic. Christina apparently becomes a Catholic, and Emmeline, who already is one, takes the next step and "parlait de se retirer au couvent" (146). This, in turn, alters their appearance. Christina " 'put on a black dress and a black lace veil' " (336), while Emmeline dons "une robe brune montante . . . l'air et la tournure d'une béguine" (286–87). These changes are soon changed again because they are effects of the larger and essentially unchanging capriciousness of both women. As extremity-driven Christina moves, like a pendulum, between two religions, two lovers, laughter and tears, so Emmeline's affairs are off and on, like her moods.

> "Elle partit d'un éclat de rire auquel succéda un de ces accès de pleurs. . . . riant, pleurant . . . tour à tour regrettant son mar-quisat et se félicitant de n'avoir pas épousé ce *monstre d'homme*."
>
> (146, 344)

Such changeability does not indicate mere flightiness, however. Capriciousness means that the woman possesses the potential for alteration, for transcending her bad education.

> "I have had a horrible education. There must be some good in me, since I have perceived it, since I have turned and judged my circumstances."
>
> (261)

As Christina can transcend herself enough to judge Mary Garland fairly, so Emmeline manages to do justice to a more serious rival, the wife of her ex-lover.

> "Je persiste à croire qu'elle est moins jolie que moi . . . mais il y avait dans son air, dans son maintien. . . . Que vous dirai-je? Il se passa en moi quelque chose de bien étrange: pour la première fois de ma vie, je me jugeai."
>
> (289–90)

Especially since Emmeline has, like Christina, also recognized the evil of *her* education, the French coquette earns the kind of sympathy—" 'il y a toujours quelque chose de rare dans une âme qui a la force de se juger' " (290)—which Madame Grandoni and Rowland Mallet repeatedly express for Christina.

It is this very issue of sympathy which finally distinguishes James from Cherbuliez. In presenting his characters, Cherbuliez maintains the basic sheep-goats distinctions of melodrama. "Un poëte a dit qu'il y a deux sortes de femmes, les *poupées* et les *natures*" (148). Since a coquette is necessarily a *poupée* in this schema, Cherbuliez allows Emmeline few moments which could justify sympathy from other characters or could elicit sympathy from us. In fact Emmeline never really has a chance. Lest she seriously challenge the heroine (as Christina does Mary Garland), we are assured that " 'cette femme ne vous va pas à la cheville du pied' " (135). Lest Emmeline gain our sympathy as a woman abandoned by her lover, she is made to admit that Max had never given her any cause for hope (288). And, having undermined her irrevocably with

"une si grande maxime dans une telle bouche m'aurait fait rire, si je n'avais eu envie de pleurer. On eût dit une perruche s'essayant à répéter un air de bravoure,"

(146)

Cherbuliez cannot even let Emmeline retire from the novel with dignity. " 'Si frisottée, si pimpante, si folle et si jolie' " (345).

Thus a character with potential for change and complexity—the *capricciosa*—remains bound within the safe confines of the conventional type. James, however, explores the ambiguities which a melodramatist like Cherbuliez ignores. Having stressed repeatedly in his reviews that characters must be allowed the weakness of their strengths and the strength of their weaknesses, James rejects the convenient distinction between *poupées* and *natures* and insists instead upon a "mixed" characterization. Christina lives up to the ambiguities inherent in her last name and in the *capricciosa* type because James makes us see her from several viewpoints. One way to do this is to combine character types. In *Le Roman* a figure enters accompanied by two people and preceded by a poodle which later wears a pink ribbon. The similarity to Christina is obvious[25]—but Cherbuliez' character is not Emmeline. It is M. de Malombré, whom Emmeline loathes. By giving to Christina both Malombré's fantastic dog and his passion for observation,[26] James adds strangeness and heightened consciousness to the coquette type. We have seen also that "perfect" is convincingly applied both to Christina as " 'princess' " and to Christina as " 'happy in poverty.' " Since the Beautiful Princess and the Domestic Angel are two very different types, James has managed to create a character mixed enough to sustain multiple interpretations.

Interpretation is all the more difficult because the authority figures in *Roderick Hudson* cannot make up *their* minds about Christina. " 'She said in so many words, that her mother was an immoral woman. Heaven knows what she meant. . . . I don't think she either means all she says, or, by a great deal, says all that she means' " (177–78). Although Rowland agrees with Madame Grandoni here and elsewhere, their opinions would, by themselves, be only assertions. To be effective these opinions must corroborate feelings of comparable ambivalence which James' scenes have made us experience.

> "When the prince says a brilliant thing, it would be a pity to lose it," said the young girl. "Your servant, sir!" And she smiled at him with a grace that might have reassured him, if he had thought her compliment ambiguous.
>
> (211)

Ambiguous her compliment surely is, for Christina can respect neither the prince's charms nor her mother's fawning before aristocracy. James' language then increases the ambiguity. Since "might" is conditional, it is potentially self-denying; that Christina's smile might be reassuring introduces the possibility that it might not be. Christina is capable of such complex behavior because " 'there's nothing I cannot imagine' " (258). She thus undermines rigid notions of language and reality. When Rowland simplistically asks, " 'are you sure,' " she can reply, " 'sure is a good deal to ask' " (369). She has a fine ear for paradox—" 'it is what they call a marriage of reason. . . . that means, you know, a marriage of madness' " (335). But Christina's ambivalence is sufficiently complete that it cannot be captured by the simple polarities of paradox. Finding that life means " 'playing with shadows more or less grotesque' " (254), she verges at times upon the enigmatic. Since many of the best examples are lengthy, I will quote only one.

> "Be something,—something that, in looking at, I can forget my detestable self! Perhaps that is nonsense too. If it is, I can't help it. I can only apologize for the nonsense I know to be such and that I talk—oh, for more reasons than I can tell you . . . I am very capricious. . . . Now I have an idea that you would make a useful friend—an intimate friend—a friend to whom one could tell everything. For such a friend, what wouldn't I give!"
> Rowland looked at her in some perplexity. Was this touching sincerity, or unfathomable coquetry? . . . "I feel weary, I feel angry, I feel like crying. I have twenty minds to escape into my room and lock the door and let mamma go through with it as she can. By the way," she added in a moment, without a visible reason for the transition, "can you tell me something to read?"
> Rowland stared, at the disconnectedness of the question.
>
> (188, 189)

Is Christina being merely capricious, or is she truly haunted by her mother's dreams and her own loneliness, or is her behavior a mixture of both emotions? The ambivalence is increased by suggestions before and after this scene that Christina herself does not always know. " 'I think she's an actress, but she believes in her part while she is playing it.' . . . she herself was evidently the foremost dupe of her inventions" (176, 251).

A final source of ambiguity derives from the novel's point of view.

> Rowland suspected that after she had got into it [the fiacre] she disburdened herself, under her veil, of a few natural tears.
>
> (241)

Because we experience Christina's actions, not directly, but through the consciousness of Rowland Mallet, we can never be certain how "natural" she is. We wonder not only whether she is serious and whether she knows for certain but also whether Rowland is correct. Unable to answer confidently any, let alone all, of these questions, and yet secure in the artistic control manifest by an ambiguity consistently threefold, we respond to Christina as to no previous character of Henry James.

> "She has bothered me half to death," he [Rowland] said, but somehow I can't manage, as I ought, to hate her. I admire her, half the time, and a good part of the rest I pity her."
>
> "I think I most pity her!" said Madame Grandoni.
>
> (337)

We do too. Christina combines and elicits emotions so contradictory that we experience in her a complexity analogous to life itself. She carries us beyond the melodramatic need to divide *poupées* from *natures.* For the first time, James' fiction makes inescapable the primacy of suffering. Christina is one of us.

We must not, however, overrate her as an artistic achievement. Although Christina as a character escapes most of Nora's limiting conventionality,[27] she does not escape the limitations of an all too conventional plot-situation. The Sinister Compulsion which denies her the freedom to choose her husband is melodramatic, not because it derives from popular literature, but because it is inadequately transformed in *Roderick Hudson.* How James can achieve a complexity of situation comparable to Christina's complexity of character, his next novel shows.

The luridness of *The American*'s last chapters is not so unrelieved as critics suggest. Even late in the novel James manages to keep a conventional situation pleasurably "mixed." Let us first establish how conventional his basic materials are. In later eighteenth-century fiction and drama we repeatedly find, as Varma notes, "an aged and garrulous maid who has locked up in her heart many a secret of the family legend"; these revelations frequently involve a "mysterious manuscript [which] . . . contains the detailed confession of some foul murder" (114, 59–60). In the nineteenth century, writers often appropriate details from contemporary tabloid scandals. As early as 1816, Pixerécourt writes a play that "dealt with the attempt of a provincial family of some eminence to place blame upon an old servant for a murder committed by one of its own members";[28] as late as 1859 George Eliot, of all people, uses newspaper accounts in "The Lifted Veil," the tale of a servant girl and a man about to be poisoned.

Thus it is hardly unconventional for James to have an old servant reveal a letter which convicts an aristocratic family of a poisoning *en province*. Moreover James seems to play *up* the melodrama. He not only uses the moonlit castle and chilling diction (" 'killed . . . . distracted wooer . . . . curse . . . . mutilate . . . . potion . . . . grotesque . . . . inquisitor' " [277, 279, 284]), but he also calls attention to the similarity between his situation and tabloid accounts. "Newman felt as if he had been reading by starlight the report of highly important evidence in a great murder case" (305). Why this *emphasis* upon the conventional quality of the situation? Is James simply, as some critics say, resorting once again to the opiate of melodrama? Or do the actually quite unconventional aspects of his scene stand out most effectively against a conventional backdrop?

Early in the scene Newman asks, " 'are you a Catholic, Mrs. Bread?' . . . 'No, sir; I'm a good Church-of-England woman, very Low' " (292). The Low Church righteousness and Anglophilia of Mrs. Bread contrast humorously with the traditional seriousness of such scenes. Mrs. Bread is again comically incongruous later when "she reminded him of an ancient tabby cat" (301). A comparable incongruity—not mere conventionality —is what characterizes the events of the scene itself. We learn, for example, that Mrs. Bread "was dressed with unwonted splendor" because " 'I was never out in the evening before, sir' " (292). What James is suggesting here becomes clearer when he speaks of "this preconcerted interview, in a remarkable locality, with a free-spoken millionaire" (297). In so intimate a situation we find the woman saying, " 'You are not quite faithful, sir. . . . you have enticed me up into this strange place. . . . is it the solemn truth you are speaking?. . . I see you have your idea, and I have no will of my own. . . . Well, you have done what you would with me, sir, and I suppose you will do it again. You *must* take care of me now' " (294, 295, 298, 310). In the process, Newman with "all his native shrewdness" has adjured, " 'I won't say a word that shall be disagreeable to you' " and has readily promised " 'you shall come and live with me. You shall be my housekeeper, or anything you like' " (297, 294, 296). When Mrs. Bread, on the verge of giving over the letter, asks, " 'so you are serious, sir, about that,' " Newman replies, " 'about your living with me? Why of course' " (309).

All this is, obviously enough, the language of seduction. That James recognizes the incongruity of making the servant girl seventy, is clear when he describes the trysting place as "favorable to quiet conversation, as probably many an earnest couple, otherwise assorted than our friends, had assured themselves" (292). Otherwise assorted, indeed. And otherwise than conventional is James' mixing of Servant-Hero revelation scene and Servant-Rake seduction scene. Since Mrs. Bread imagines herself in the romantic situation of having a man's will worked upon her, and since Newman consciously uses all his arts to get what he wants from her, the different but equally obsessive overearnestness of the characters prevents a comparable seriousness on our part and thus fosters a comic perspective. James' control of conventional situations allows us to experience simultaneously the intensity and the silliness of Newman's Byronic revenge.

Although James cannot sustain this simultaneity of effect throughout the finale of *The American,* he does mark here a definite stage of development. Having shown, even in *Watch and Ward,* a desire for mixed characters and situations, he transformed conventions sufficiently to achieve a genuinely complex character with Christina Light and a comparably complex situation with Mrs. Bread. His task now is to *sustain* such situations with a complex heroine. To do so, to avoid the Sinister Compulsion still evident in *The American,* James must create a villain complex enough to make us experience what compels the heroine.

2

Critics who discuss Gilbert Osmond as a gothic villain have not done him justice, in several senses. Before explaining why, we should look briefly at the still more problematic efforts of those critics who do not heed Osmond's origins at all. A case in point is his name.

> Osmond may be derrived [sic] from either Old English, in the sense of "protection of God," "divine guardian," or Medieval Latin, with the possible gloss "world mouth." James may of course have known neither suggested etymology: I like to think he knew both.[29]

Although Quentin Anderson's suggestion of "fixed and dead, boney or of the earth" and R. W. Stallman's *"the world"*[30] are less far-fetched, these critics also miss the chief significance of Osmond's name. They too are exploring etymology rather than the literary tradition. Name borrowing is frequent in all literary genres and is particularly common in the faddish and somewhat *sui generis* mode of gothic fiction. Railo says, for example, that "the names of most characters [in Shelley's *Zastrozzi*] are copied from *The Monk* and from *Udolpho"* and that "names like Theodore and Conrad [from Southey's *Joan of Arc*] suggest affinities with Walpole's romanticism."[31] Among many other borrowings we find the name "Manfred" in Walpole, then in Byron, then in Mary Shelley; "Oswald" comes down from Shakespeare to Clara Reeve, and on to *The Borderers, Corinne, Rokeby*; Clara Reeve herself gives to an old servant the name "Joseph" which will reappear in *Wuthering Heights*.

James' names, particularly during the crucial decade, derive often from the literary tradition.[32] "Roderick," for example, is highly romantic— with Scott's gloomy and passionate Roderick Dhu, his "The Song of Roderick," Southey's *Roderick, the Last of Goths*, Poe's Roderick Usher, and Hawthorne's Roderick Elliston. Besides several possible predecessors for Miss "Lambert," Miss "Sandys," Miss "Morton," Mrs. "Keith," "Valentin," and Mrs. "Montgomery,"[33] there are at least six names in *The Portrait* that derive directly from traditions which James knows. "Pansy," for example, is more than simply another flower name for young girls, like Daisy or Flora. *Pansy* was a children's magazine which began its enormously popular run in 1873.[34] By giving to his marriageable young woman a name which readers associated with children, James emphasizes how arrested his Pansy's development is. The name "Stackpole" has a complicated history. James Stackpole was an American art critic prominent in Henry James' boyhood; more famous still was Ralph Stackpole, who towered so tall on the American stage in the 1830s that "like Paul Bunyan and Pecos Bill, Stackpole was a folk-hero."[35] As an art critic with heroic pretentions to self-sufficiency, Miss Stackpole fares widely and well in the world, but she settles finally for wedlock and a balding bantling; anything but a folk-hero, "Ralph" is nonetheless the novel's representative male, for he and Caspar and Osmond and Warburton all fail to control experience when it matters most, when the heroine is concerned.[36] "Isabel" derives directly from Cherbuliez' "Isabelle la sérieuse," and ultimately from that archetypic Beset Heroine, Isabella of *The Castle of Otranto*.

Which brings us to the name "Gilbert Osmond." "Gilbert" is the Champion of the Wrong in Walter Scott; *Gilbert Gurney* is a once-famous Dandy novel.[37] Appropriate as these overtones are to *The Portrait*, the primary association of the name "Gilbert" is with artists. Besides Gilbert Stuart, one of the major illustrators for the *London Journal* during the 1850s and 1860s was named Gilbert. Fiction not only provides such popular examples as the painter Gilbert in *The Wide, Wide World*, but Henry James himself in "The Story of a Masterpiece" presents "a young artist named Gilbert" (*CT* 1:262).

"Osmond" is still more traditional. Seeking a name for his villain in *The Castle Spectre*, Monk Lewis may well have gone back (consciously or unconsciously) to a bloody and exotic drama of the British theatrical past, *Osmond, the Great Turk*.[38] For certain we find in Lewis' perennially popular play several details so similar to details in *The Portrait* that we should examine them. *The Castle Spectre* contains, for example, a "knave" named Gilbert (I i). His master is "Osmond. . . . the very antidote of mirth" (I i). In his pursuit of the heroine, Osmond is thwarted both by "the Portrait of a Lady" (III iii) which swings back to reveal a convenient passage-way and by the lady of that portrait, who comes back (as a ghost) to save her daughter from incarceration by Osmond. Before the Beset Heroine escapes, however, she endures a dark night "allowed you to reflect upon your situation" (III iii). (I cannot resist adding that the heroine's duenna exclaims, "oh gemini" [III iii].) After *The Castle Spectre* we find the romantics christening characters "Osman" and "Osmyn" and the name "Ormond" appearing in both Maria Edgeworth and Charles Brockden Brown. In America the name Osmond itself appears as early as 1804, in Alicia La Fanu's *Lucy Osmond*. This story of betrayed heroines, inadequate guardians, and sudden fortunes is then followed in the 1830s by a terrifically successful play, *Lucy Leslie, the Cottager's Daughter; or, The Maid, the Mother and the Maniac*. Here "poor Lucy is shot down by her betrayer, Osmond, when he learns she is not, as he has been led to believe, the heiress to fifty thousand pounds."[39]

Such ties with traditional villains are then strengthened by one other name in *The Portrait*. When villainous characters become famous, later authors create genealogical lines, not only by borrowing names directly, but by echoing them unmistakably. For reasons less than clear (and notwithstanding such evident counter-examples as Mary, Marlowe, Mariana, Maud, and others), the names of villainous characters frequently begin with "M." Among males the most infamous are Mephistopheles, Manfred, Marmion, Melmoth, Montini; the lesser, Maldoni, Manfrone, Mervyn, Morosini, Montalt, Markheim, Mesardus, Manuel, Montraville, Monsieur le Monte, Lord Mountfalcon (and Mrs. Mount) from *Richard Feveral*, Monmouth, Moriarty, Melveric of *Death's Jest-Book*; plus, of course, Machiavelli, who is mentioned twice in *The Portrait* (240, 457) and is transformed in *Griffith Gaunt* to "she-Machiavel" (160). Among women (besides the Maid, Mother, and Maniac), there are Mary Magdalene, Medusa, Messalina, Malevola, Matilda, Marquise de Merteuil of *Les Liaisons dangereuses*, Stephen Hunt's *Melinda the Murderess*, the Mysterious Mother, and Charlotte Bury's *The Manoeuvering Mother*, those bad educators Mrs. Mowbray from *Adeline Mowbray* and Miss Monflathers from *The Old Curiosity Shop*, Dickens' Miss Miggs and Mrs. Mann and Trollope's Miss Melmotte, Lady Audley's maiden name of Miss Maldon, plus such promiscuous women of Henry James as Marie de Mauves (1874) and Mora Montravers

(1909). Interestingly, everyday reality seems intent upon substantiating this literary tradition, for three of the period's most infamous women are the murderesses Maria Manning and Mrs. Maybrick and the incendiary Maria Monk.

Madame Merle's connection with villainy extends beyond her initials, of course. That the vile seducer had a female helper is established in fiction at least as early as Squire B and Mrs. Jukes; but that he and the lady were themselves lovers is an innovation of Monk Lewis. Matilda in *The Monk* is willing not only to be Ambrosio's mistress but to procure him other mistresses once his ardor for her has cooled. Walter Scott then borrows Lewis' situation. When Marmion tires of Constance, she, like a good Matilda-figure, is willing to help him win Clara.[40] By 1850, according to Praz, the daughters of Matilda have become an established type in fiction and verse.[41] This jibes with Michael Booth's contention that drama in "the last half of the nineteenth century saw the villainess or adventuress really come into her own as an important melodramatic character"; especially since the West End audience had become higher class, "an elegant villain and fashionable adventuress were therefore necessities" (156, 163).

Among the necessities of conventional villainy which Madame Merle possesses, one is suggested by her last name.[42] Matilda was a witch with magic powers. Although her literary progeny are not often actual witches, *femmes fatales* do continue to behave bewitchingly. Cherbuliez' "Mme. Mirveil" clearly suggests "merveille," a marvel; Christina Light is twice called a " 'sorceress' " (340, 341); in *Ishmael*, Miss Merlin boasts " 'I'm a witch, and know people's secret thoughts' " (193).[43] Madame Merle is both enchanting and prescient. When she first encounters Isabel, she captivates the young woman with music woven out of the dusk. Madame Merle is, in turn, prescient enough to impress the tough-minded Osmond and Lydia Touchett. Osmond exclaims, " 'how you guess everything' " (224); Lydia, who reproves Madame Merle for being " 'too fond of mystery' " (161), still addresses her as " 'you who know everything' " and admits that " 'she can do anything' " (254, 310). Two other conventional details are her past and her smile. "Just as the Byronic hero's origin was often said to be mysterious and extremely noble, so, too, was the origin of the Fatal Woman."[44] Like Osmond, Madame Merle can be mistaken for royalty; like his shrouded past, hers hides passion and deception. Consequently, when she smiles, her mouth

> drew itself upward to the left side, in a manner that most people thought very odd, some very affected, and a few very graceful. . . . her thoughtful smile drew up her mouth more than usual toward the left corner. . . . her mouth [was] drawn up to the left. . . . Madame Merle's mouth rose to the left. . . . [she] smiled in the left corner of her mouth.
> (162, 255, 331, 333, 473)

The crooked curl of the villain's sardonic smile derives, as Thorslev shows, from Milton's Satan and reappears in Byron, Scott,[45] and in virtually every popular novel that I know, including *The Heir, The Initials, St. Elmo,* and *The Wide, Wide World.* Madame Merle's smiles are sinister, not only because they, like Osmond's handshake, are associated with the left, but because they, like her name and powers and origins, are conventional enough to place her in the tradition of villainy.

We do not experience Madame Merle as we do conventional *femmes fatales,* however. Among James' many transformations of the type, we have already seen that Madame Merle possesses the perfect hands and the skills with needle, brush, and pen which usually characterize the heroine. Merle's colors too are complicating. "She ... [was] dressed in dark blue satin, which exposed a white bosom" (164). However appropriate to her passionate past the erotic quality of the white is here, we recognize that James has associated his Madame with the blue and white colors conventionally reserved, not for the daughters of Matilda, but for the Madonna of Christianity and the heroines of fiction. Even Madame Merle's name is not simply conventional. Critics have long known that her first name was "Geraldine" in the serial and that James changed it in the hard cover edition to "Serena." Why "Geraldine"? Tribble suggests an echo of "Emmeline" (de Mirveil). We hear a much stronger echo when we recall one of Matilda's greatest daughters, the Geraldine of "Christabel." Revising away so sinister an association is part of James' effort to avoid with *The Portrait* the luridness of his earlier works.

"Ah, Gertrude,"—and his voice fell—"you are a great enchantress!"
(*CT* 1:195)

"Serena" suggests Madame Merle's smooth social surface. Grief and rage and cunning still abide in the depths of the adventuress and her actions, but her (and James') moderation assures a complexity which evokes our deepest interest.

How much this fundamental transformation affects our reading experience becomes clear when we compare Madame Merle with the literary character whom she probably resembles most. Lydia Glasher in *Daniel Deronda.* Both women are past their first youth; each has borne progeny to the heroine's eventual husband; and, in a small but substantial detail, Madame Merle is associated with a cracked teacup as Mrs. Glasher is with a cracked flute. Consistently, however, James moderates the luridness of his Other Woman. For example, the theme of " 'How changed' " is conventional with the type. (In *East Lynne* Isabel, after her adultery, illegitimate child, and disfigurement in a train wreck, returns home in a chapter entitled—not surprisingly—"Change and Change.") Lydia Glasher's appearance undergoes a dramatic, not to say melodramatic, change. She was once "exceedingly handsome" (111) and

now is so wasted by the flames of passion that "her chief thought of herself
seen in the glass was, 'How changed!' " (255). Madame Merle, however,
was apparently never a great beauty and in middle age is plump and
attractive enough not to be an evident object lesson.[46] A comparable
difference appears with these women's children. Lydia having *four* babies
by the Byronic male is slightly ludicrous. Moreover, that she attacks
Gwendolen's marriage on behalf of the children's good name is more
simplistically melodramatic than the impossible situation of Madame
Merle's marrying off her lover to save her child.

    Madame Merle's plight is especially touching because James also
transforms one of the *femme fatale*'s most basic traits. Instead of merely
asserting her prescience melodramatically as E. D. E. N. Southworth
does with Miss Merlin's " 'I . . . know people's secret thoughts,' " James
reveals with Madame Merle the tragic consequences of such knowledge.
When the words " 'she knows everything' " reappear late in the novel
(502), the issue now is not prescience or even power. Madame Merle
knows enough to know that her own daughter does not care for her. In
turn, Madame Merle can never know enough; savoir faire cannot avail in
the worst of lost causes. This fact increases Isabel's compassion and ours
when she has triumphed so completely that "what remained was the
cleverest woman in the world . . . knowing as little what to think as the
meanest" (509). Because the theater of conflict is finally internal, the
drama of consciousness moves us deeply. Madame Merle is, in fact,
capable of some of the greatest lines in Victorian fiction. " 'The tragedy is
for me. . . . Have I been so vile all for nothing. . . . You are very
unhappy, I know. But I am more so' " (484 [twice], 515). It was ever
thus. Madame Merle, like most of her fatal sisters, fails to win the
Byronic man. "She must pay the price of aspiring to the place she has no
right to, and he must remain gigantically alone."[47]

    How gigantic Osmond finally is, and even how alone, we can only
determine by accepting the fact of his conventional origins and then
doing him justice as no critic yet has. By justice I mean acknowledging, as
we did with Madame Merle, the twofold nature of his makeup: that
Osmond evinces more conventional traits than scholars have recognized;
and that he is more extensively and successfully transformed than readers
tend to allow. Let us study this twofold mixture by beginning with
conventional traits of appearance and temperament.

> I tremble when I see that horrid man—
> He carries on his brow the badge of vice,
> That narrow cheek, that keen but sunken eye
> That black complexion, all denote the villain:
> His scowl is dreadful as a winter's blast,
> His hate is deadly—O beware the man![48]

James' first Byronic suitors had the chiseled features and extreme handsomeness conventional to the type. Hubert Lawrence "was a singularly handsome youth.... his features were cut with admirable purity" (245); Roderick's face "was remarkably handsome. The features were admirably chiseled and finished" (21). By 1880, James has not abandoned such conventionalities, but he is using them differently. Morris Townsend, for example, "had features like young men in pictures; Catherine had never seen such features—so delicate, so chiselled and finished—among the young New Yorkers" (*WS* 30). That we *have* seen such features does not mean failure for James now, because he is no longer attempting to espouse what he cannot take seriously. While Catherine is charmed, we doubt the adequacy of so picturesque a suitor.

James' task is more difficult with Gilbert Osmond. Osmond must be attractive enough to keep us sympathetic with Isabel during her infatuation, and yet his inadequacy and thus her limitations must still be established. "He had a thin, delicate, sharply cut face" (211). Although we are happily spared any extreme handsomeness, we recognize definitely the Byronic face, and its attractiveness for Isabel. Repeatedly noting how "sensitive" and "delicate" he is, "Isabel had never met a person of so fine a grain. The peculiarity was physical, to begin with" (242). As Catherine Sloper thinks that Morris "had features like young men in pictures," Isabel admits that "a certain combination of features had touched her, and in them she had seen the most striking of portraits" (393). Osmond also has the trimness and litheness appropriate to Byronic figures. Although he might at first seem distinguished from them by not being tall, the type was actually, in its origins, of only average height. Byron and Brummell both fit the description of the Corsair—"No giant frame sets forth his common height" (I ix); and the foremost successor of these archetypes, Lermontov's Pechorin, is of "medium height" and even "smallish."[49] Osmond also has the "foreign, traditionary look" (211) conventional with men who speak several languages and are apparently of mixed blood. Finally, although seducers are traditionally swarthy, we can find at least as early as *East Lynne* in 1861 the epigram " 'that man is as false as he is fair' " (12). Like Pechorin and Grandcourt, Gilbert Osmond is beguilingly "fair" (211).

On the other hand, since his features seem "overdrawn, retouched" and his face "looked too pointed" (242, 211), the signs of affectation and narrowness (and even diabolism) are also carefully established. Affectation is suggested, too, by Osmond's dress. Although the Byronic Dandy became associated with flamboyant clothes, Brummell's taste was actually severe, so severe in fact that one of his maxims was " 'the severest mortification which a gentleman could incur, was to attract observation in the street by his outward appearance.' "[50] This attitude becomes positively subversive by the time of Bulwer-Lytton's *Pelham*.

[Maxims]
7.
To *win* the affection of your mistress, appear negligent in your costume.
(178)

Thus we cannot credit Osmond with too complete an indifference to the
things of this world (including an heiress' fortune and person) when we
learn that "he was dressed as a man dresses who takes little trouble about
it" (211). Again that "as." Does Osmond take little trouble with his
clothes, or does he dress as though he took little trouble? In the context of
his other Byronic associations, the ambiguity is ominous indeed.

Ominous too is Osmond's hair. When we first meet Morris Townsend,
he, like Roderick Hudson and innumerable passionate men, has dark
clustering locks to run fingers through.[51] Twenty years later Townsend's
"clustering locks had grown thin. . . . how long ago it was—how old she
had grown" (202, 203). The point here is not ugliness (Catherine, in fact,
finds Morris "still remarkably handsome" [202]). What James achieves is
the unmasking of a specious dream. Balding lays bare the inadequacy of
a type of virility that had charmed many besides poor Catherine. In *The
Portrait* James desires a comparable revelation. But unlike George Eliot
who makes Henleigh Grandcourt quite bald, James wants neither to lay
bare Isabel's suitor this crudely nor to depart from convention so far.

The thick curling hair that clung in glossy rings to his temples was
turning grey.

The hair, still dense, but prematurely grizzled, had been cropped close.

Gray hair does not signal patriarchal wisdom here. St. Elmo (in the first
quotation [149]) and Gilbert Osmond (211) are too young to have earned
the snowy locks of revered grandparenthood. Premature graying traditionally signifies moral inadequacy, the attrition of a too fiery youth.[52]
This attrition does not, however, necessitate a loss of virility; St. Elmo's
hair is still "thick" and Osmond's is twice called "dense" (211, 242). Thus
the older man with dense graying hair is as traditional and dangerous as
his lustrous-locked young counterpart. In fact he is more dangerous to
Isabel. Not only does she lack Catherine's opportunity of seeing through
a balding man, she does not even confront a man with telltale ringlets
like St. Elmo. Wily Osmond has his hair "cropped close."

Of all the Byronic villain's features, the most important is the eyes.

The glance of the Wandering Jew, whose sinister power Lewis has so
well expressed, is a special characteristic of romantic, saturnine persons,
from Eblis (the Oriental Lucifer of *Vathek*) onward, increasing in
significance as a source of mysterious influences as attention is drawn
to the general possibilities of power in the human eye.
(Railo, 198–99)

From the Bleeding Nun to Elsie Venner's Lamia-like power and on to
W. S. Gilbert's parody (the mesmeric male in *Engaged* is incapacitated by
pinkeye), the puissance and attractiveness of fatal charmers has glowed
out through the eyes. After using the flashing eye crudely in *Watch and
Ward* and *Roderick Hudson*,[53] James manages in *The Portrait* to suggest
real power. We are told initially that Osmond has a "luminous,
intelligent eye, an eye that expressed both softness and keenness" (211).
Since the "keen" eye traditionally indicates a high intelligence capable of
piercing prey, the fact that Osmond's eyes are also "soft" may seem
anomalous. Actually, however, the trait derives from Byron himself—
"Yet there was softness too in his regard" (*Lara* I xvii)—and is carried on
by Ouida and other popular writers. James uses the conventional
"softness" to prevent us from pigeonholing Osmond too readily. If
Gilbert's softness may indicate a tendency to moral laxness, it may also
indicate a capacity for tenderness. Or some mixture. We cannot know
yet. And we are especially disinclined to condemn Osmond outright
because we have already encountered an "eye, a little too keen perhaps in
her graver moments, [which] had an enchanting softness when she
smiled" (43). Not only is the heroine characterized by the same keen-
softness as her suitor, but Osmond offers an explanation of why both
qualities are desirable in a mate. "What could be a finer thing to live with
than a high spirit attuned to softness? For would not the softness be all
for one's self, and the strenuousness for society?" (323–24). If the suitor's
questions allow of more than one answer, and if the heroine's keen-
softness functions as much to call her into question as to redeem him, the
similarity between Osmond and Isabel does nonetheless incline us to
withhold final judgment until married life has tested each mate.

> She dreaded the power of his lustrous, mesmeric eyes.
>
> She was quite sure from that one look into his eyes that he was a
> person to be feared.
>
> He had never before felt the keenness of this gentleman's eyes.

Disillusioned after three years of marriage, Osmond loses his ambiguous
softness and any suggestion of tenderness, and blends in (his is the last
quotation)* with traditional villains. At this point in a popular novel, the
scribbler would allow us the solace of a facile dichotomy. As the villain is
reduced to the "keen," the heroine would achieve the "soft"ness of a True
Heart. In James' scene, Ned does encounter the heroine soon. "She gave
him, straight in the eyes, a look . . . keener than he liked, and he took
himself off" (347). James' refusal to simplify Isabel here is matched in the
second half of *The Portrait* by his continued determination to keep our

*StE 326; WWW 286; PL 338.

judgments of Osmond complex, to prevent any simple attribution of moral laxness.

To Isabel "it was as if he had the evil eye; as if his presence were a blight" (391). Made credible by its metaphoric quality, the attribution of evil to Osmond is kept tentative because the accuser is not the narrator, but a character. In blaming Osmond's evil eye, Isabel is failing to recognize how much she herself is to blame for her plight. This use of point of view does not exonerate Osmond, of course. But it does keep before us the fact that all characters share responsibility for the chaos of their lives.

"The man you have married has a withered heart."

"You have not only dried up my tears; you have dried up my soul."

"Il a d'ironiques sourires qui me glacent le coeur."

Action had been . . . transformed by the blight of her husband's touch.

In each case, the evil-eyed Byronic male blights and is blighted by his life-denying urges. But only James' passages (the second and the fourth)* capitalize upon the potential ambivalence of a dramatic situation. When the wronged women in *Daniel Deronda* and *Le Roman* accuse their Byronic men, the situation is strictly conventional—woman's word is trustworthy. But when Madame Merle and Isabel accuse Osmond, the validity of their claims cannot hide the advantages which each woman derives from her accusations. Madame Merle is not facing the fact that she, as much as Osmond, has always been dry enough of soul to serve society before all things. And Isabel is soon forced to recognize that the action which Osmond has questioned is indeed "irreflective" and that "he was after all sincere, and that this, as far as it went, was a merit" (496).

Besides basic physical attributes, Osmond shares with the Byronic tradition a fundamental dualism of temperament. He is prone both to violence and to lethargy. His violence is, of course, restrained by his abhorrence of "scenes." As Osmond's face displays no flaring nostrils or cloven brow, he will neither fight duels nor thrash horses. Moreover, he avoids scenes as well as abhors them, for surface display is not his mode. Osmond wins by wile and indirection. Since his is a world where things are not as they seem, he shifts with the chimerical scenery, minimizing the overt signs of villainy.

Yet for all his quiet, Osmond *is* violent. "What she [Isabel] was afraid of . . . was simply the violence there would be in going when Osmond wished her to remain" (498). In fact, James, by controlling coarseness as carefully with Osmond's actions as with his physiognomy, manages to

*DD 267; PL 481; LR 144; PL 496.

associate a nonhistrionic villain with the most violent aspect of the Byronic temperament—the abyss-prone, peak-aspiring instinct.

He stood at the highest point, where the precipice was most abrupt. ... [He] began to climb higher, and was soon out of sight.

[He] climbed with an ease and lightness which surprised his companions.

His friends frequently saw him skirting the edge of plunging chasms, loosening the stones on long, steep slopes, or lifting himself against the sky, from the top of rocky pinnacles.

Roderick (in the third quotation) is virtually indistinguishable from Guy and Hamilton because his climbing is as conventional as his tossed locks.* Worse still, the matched scenes in *Roderick Hudson*—Roderick climbs for a flower for Christina (239) as Rowland does for Mary (427)— resemble many scenes in other novels. Grandcourt in *Daniel Deronda* plunges his horse down a ravine to grab a flower for Gwendolen as Max de Lestang in *Le Roman* plunges his horse down a ravine to grab a flower for Isabelle; in *The Heir* Guy saves Amy on the cliff edge where she has gone after a flower as Hamilton saves Crescenz on a similar cliff in *The Initials*. In all cases the flower-cliff scenes demonstrate not only male prowess but also female subjugation. Like Gwendolen and Isabelle, Christina is forced to express fear and admiration for her height-defying suitor.[54]

Osmond's conquest of Isabel begins on his hilltop. James does not, however, attempt to redeem the juvenility of cliff escapades by condoning boyish impetuosity.[55] Rather, he perfects a more promising use of the gulf which he found in both popular and great authors.

"As you say, Hubert's a gulf. I never sounded it."

Nora felt as if she had taken a jump.... she rose and bridged this dizzy chasm.

(*W&W* 595, 707)

Metaphor makes the villain himself an abyss, and the heroine a climber. Although the metaphor in *Watch and Ward* lacks intensity because Nora's plight never really becomes a cliff-hanger, the basic situation— woman confronting the void of male inadequacy—gains real power by 1881.

"You're unfathomable," she [Madame Merle] murmured at last. "I am frightened at the abyss into which I shall have dropped her!"

Osmond gave a laugh....

"You are quite unfathomable," she repeated.

(263)

*HR 1:337, 2:116; In 51; RH 426.

Isabel is especially prey to the violence of a fall because she has always engaged in brinksmanship.

> Edward [Rosier] told her [Isabel] that he was "defended" by his *bonne* to go near the edge of the lake.... He took a great interest in Isabel, and remembered perfectly the walk at Neufchatel, when she would persist in going so near the edge.
>
> (198–99)

By introducing the abyss theme with a humor which absolves him from any histrionic simplicity, James can then use the metaphor in earnest. His heroine, envisioning Italy as a land of beauty and promise, stands poised on the brink of the Mediterranean. "Whenever she strolled upon the shore with her cousin . . . she looked awhile across the sea, with longing eyes. . . . She was glad to pause, however, on the edge of this larger knowledge" (207). Isabel's temptation is thus Edenic—to taste of knowledge. Osmond is not only associated with Satan, like most Byronic males;[56] he also possesses that fund of enormous knowledge which makes tempters so attractive to innocents. " 'You know everything,' " Isabel tells him (285). Compare, in fact, her " 'you know everything, and I know nothing' " (285) with " 'papa . . . knows everything' " and " 'papa knows everything . . . and I know nothing.' " Our difficulty distinguishing Isabel from Pansy (343) and Nell (*CUF* 168) indicates both how traditional the heroine's abasement before male wisdom is, and how similar the functions of Suitor-Husband and Father are. For certain, Osmond, like the Father of Lies, knows how to tempt Isabel-Eve. " 'He wants me to know everything' " (317).

So fall she does.

> She had suddenly found the infinite vista of a multiplied life to be a dark, narrow alley, with a dead wall at the end. Instead of leading to the high places of happiness . . . it led rather downward.
>
> (391)

Unlike Nora, Isabel's fall is real and irretrievable; unlike Roderick, she is denied the easy escape of death. Because her fall is mental and not physical, Isabel must confront the abyss again and again.

> A gulf had opened between them over which they looked at each other.
> . . . it seemed to him that at last the gulf between them had been bridged.
>
> (391, 428)

Like Nora, Isabel has bridged her chasm. The difference between the heroines' resulting situations, however, reveals how James has transformed the conventional gulf metaphor by 1881. The "them" on page 391 is Isabel and Osmond; on page 428, "them" is Isabel and Ralph. Unlike *Watch and Ward, The Portrait* does not allow marriage to round out the drama with a circle and a song, for Isabel can bridge her gulf with Ralph only by widening her gulf with Osmond. The transformation of violent action into graphic metaphor makes us experience what James believes so deeply—that our ordinary lives can be as precarious and breathtaking as any melodrama. The transformation also makes Osmond part of a long and notorious tradition, from Faustus and Milton's Satan on to the Monk, Manfred, Melmoth, and many more abyss-bound villains. Osmond too plunges eventually into the gulf. "He was going down—down; the vision of such a fall made her almost giddy" (444).

Or rather . . . what we actually have here is not Osmond plunging like his forebears, but rather his wife *imagining* that plunge.[57] In fact Osmond's violence comes to us largely through Isabel's often melodramatic consciousness. Having admitted that "he was not violent, he was not cruel" (392), Isabel thinks later "he had not been violent, and yet there was a violence in that. There was a violence at any rate in something, somewhere; perhaps it was only in her own fit of weeping" (447). Without minimizing the fact that Osmond uses quiet power in a thoroughly coercive—and therefore violent—way, James forces us to recognize how violent other characters can be and, more important, how personality traits can be projected upon an individual by the melodramatic minds of others. James continues complicating our judgments in this way when Caspar, like Isabel and Madame Merle earlier, judges Osmond Satanic. "It seemed to him for a moment that Osmond had a kind of demoniac imagination" (468). That we do not dissent here means we are pulled up especially short later when Caspar repeats his contention.

"Your husband's a devil!"
She [Isabel] turned on him as if he had struck her. "Are you mad?"
(542)

Caspar's charge of demonism, like Isabel's and Madame Merle's, is self-serving, for it justifies divorce or adultery. Our recognition of this is particularly striking because the character who has most encouraged us to simplify Osmond into a demon—Isabel—is now the one insisting that any such denial of basic humanity makes *us* the inhuman ones. Lest his heroine, in turn, seem too free from sulphur herself, James also shows how universal one basic desire of Satan is. When Isabel says, " 'I know nothing about revenge,' " and Osmond replies, " 'I do' " (494), the situation of innocence confronting diabolism is conventional enough. But soon we find

that Madame Merle had lost her pluck . . . this in itself was a revenge. . . . Isabel's only revenge was to be silent still—to leave Madame Merle in this unprecedented situation. She left her there for a

period which must have seemed long to this lady. . . . Isabel would
never accuse her, never reproach her; perhaps because she never
would give her the opportunity to defend herself.

(508–9)

That Isabel admirably forgoes the full fury of the revenge open to her[58]
must not obscure the fact that she does get revenge. James never allows
the sheep to become so white or the goats so black that we lapse into the
simplistic vision which allows villains to behave as they do.

Osmond's ties to the Byronic tradition are particularly strong because
James endows him with *both* aspects of the conventionally dual temperament—not only a penchant for violence but also the opposite inclination,
to ennui. That Osmond is bored, indolent, aloof, misanthropic, and
ironically amused at the folly of other men is evident enough; that he
shares these traits with Grandcourt, Max, St. Elmo, and other conventional misanthropes since Satan and Byron is also clear. Part of his charm
for Isabel is, in fact, what has charmed heroines since Desdemona. " 'She
loved me for the dangers I had pass'd, / And I loved her that she did pity
them' " (*Othello* I iii 167–68). The Heroine's traditional sympathy for
Suffering Males appears in James as early as *Watch and Ward*. Nora is
attracted to George because " 'women have a fancy for an outlaw. You
turned me out of doors, and Nora's heart went with me' " (699); she is
also attracted to Hubert, who "had . . . a slightly jaded, overwearied
look, certain to deepen his interest in female eyes" (416). By 1880 such
showy suffering and the heroine's sympathy for it are mocked when Dr.
Sloper says of Morris, " 'Ah, he has had misfortunes? That, of course, is
always interesting' " (56). To avoid undercutting his suitor and susceptible heroine so thoroughly in *The Portrait*, James sets the Byronic
sufferer in a more complex context.

> He was like a sceptical voyager, strolling on the beach while he waited
> for the tide, looking seaward yet not putting to sea.
>
> (393)
>
> What lonely straggler looks along the wave? . . .
> "'Tis he—'tis Conrad—here—as wont—alone."
>
> (*Corsair* I vi)[59]

James does not present his Byronic tableau until we can see Osmond's
reclusive and misanthropic instincts in the context of his other, very
different desires for social position and esteem. How, in fact, can this
Byronic misanthrope say truthfully, " 'I am convention itself' " (288)?
Answering this question is indispensable to understanding Osmond's
complex mixture.

So far we have been treating the villain as a single static figure. Set in
historical perspective, this figure is set in motion, for he undergoes a

sustained evolution from 1780 to 1880. In the later eighteenth century the villain was just that, villainous. But with Mrs. Radcliffe, Lewis, Scott, and Byron comes the villain-hero. Although this appealing creature does not entirely replace his more single-minded forebear, our sympathies are now, in repeated cases, with the swarthy sufferer. This change comes in part because the villain shows increasingly a delicacy of feeling which can even approach the artistic.

> Refined by the touch of Byron's hand, Schiller's Robber was eventually to become Jean Sbogar, the polyglot brigand, musician and painter.
>
> (Praz, *Agony*, 78)[60]

Violent escapades still characterize the Byronic figure, of course, and violence retains its appeal in the "Newgate" novels of the 1830s and '40s and in the "sensation" fiction of the 1860s and '70s. Toward the end of the crucial decade, however, Henry James can say that "Europe was getting sadly dis-Byronised" (*CT* 4:90). Scholars tend to agree. "Burning ardor is, at this period, merely conventional. . . . the Miltonic Lucifer is no longer heroic, as in Byron. . . . the trouble is that the foaming cataract had itself become a cliché."[61] Although the escapades of mountaineering and rant seem antiquated in *Roderick Hudson*, Roderick possesses, like Byron himself, another side.

> Here and there, over it [the floor], certain strongly perfumed flowers had been scattered. Roderick was lying on his divan in a white dressing-gown, staring up at the frescoed ceiling. The room was deliciously cool, and filled with the moist, sweet odor of the circumjacent roses and violets. . . . He was smelling a large white rose . . . lying there like a Buddhist in an intellectual swoon, whose perception should be slowly ebbing back to temporal matters.
>
> (359)

Replete with pride and infinite sensitivity but without the coarseness of cliffs and rant, one of Byron's many personalities enters fiction with Disraeli and Bulwer and remains a major vehicle for the Decadents and *fin de siècle*. It is the Dandy.

> Romanticism, at the source of its inspiration, is chiefly concerned with defying moral and divine law. That is why its most original creation is not, primarily, the revolutionary, but, logically enough, the dandy.
>
> (Camus, 50)[62]

The Dandy fascinates, haunts, obsesses the nineteenth century, because he embodies most of the period's contradictory impulses. He is all things to all men, yet ever an outsider.

> Politically, the dandy appealed to both the reactionary and the revolutionary, as a man of the past or man of the future. . . . His

arrogant superiority was an affirmation of the aristocratic principle,
his way of life an exaltation of aristocratic society; but his terrible
independence proclaimed a subversive disregard for the essentials of
aristocracy.

(Moers, 13, 17)

The Dandy is also subversive to the aristocracy because he espouses
social standards with a rigor that even high society cannot measure up
to. For all his libertine tendencies the Dandy is a kind of ascetic. He
makes rules for life, makes life in fact a kind of art.

The dandy creates his own unity by aesthetic means. But it is an
aesthetic of singularity and of negation. . . . From romanticism
onward, the artist's task will not only be to create a world, or to exalt
beauty for its own sake, but also to define an attitude. Thus the artist
becomes a model and offers himself as an example: art is his ethic.
With him begins the age of the directors of conscience.

(Camus, 51, 53)

Since ordering the lives of other people necessarily involves violating
those people, the very conservatism of the Dandy's moral stance makes
him as much an enemy of society as his brother, the bandit.

Even Baudelaire's conformity has the odor of crime. If he chose
Maistre as his master, it is to the extent that this conservative goes to
extremes and centers his doctrine on death and on the executioner. . . .
[Lautréamont's] reasoning recapitulates the morality of a choirboy or
of an infantry manual. But conformity can be passionate, and thereby
out of the ordinary.

(Camus, 52, 86)[63]

Gilbert Osmond can derive from the Dandy tradition and yet say truthfully, " 'I am convention,' " because the Dandy feels the "burning need
to acquire originality, within the apparent bounds of convention."[64] As a
radical reactionary, the Dandy possesses enormous potential for evoking
ambivalent response. Barbey d'Aurevilly himself, the supreme apologist
for Dandyism, embodies the contradictions of the type. "He was always
to be the Byronic rebel. . . . In theory a faithful devotee of the Jesuits, in
practice he was a radical and independent Catholic."[65] In such a life we
see clearly that coalescence of opposites which has been the ideal and
achievement of much great literature. Amazingly, however, the nation
which created Dandyism created in its fiction no Dandy who realizes the
type's potential for ambiguity. Pelham's witty attacks may at first seem
shocking and even iconoclastic but they are, in fact, directed not against
basic moral truths but against moralizers who cannot stomach the
sternness of such truths. In *Vivian Gray* the Dandy's ends, unlike
Pelham's, are genuinely immoral; but Disraeli finally chastises Gray in

most laudable fashion, and basic moral attitudes remain unquestioned.[66] England was either too healthy or too frightened or both to create in fiction a Count D'Orsay. Why a Europeanized American could do so by making the Dandy a Europeanized American, we should attempt to understand.

Let us begin with Leavis' contention that "Osmond so plainly *is* Grandcourt" (113).[67] Plainly Osmond is not Grandcourt or Max de Lestang. Osmond is not an aristocrat. He looks the part and puts on airs, but he is not even high born for an American. Thus Grandcourt and Max are *not* Osmond: they are what Osmond aspires to. This distinction is fundamental. James goes back with his Dandy to the very origin of the tradition.

> The dandy, as Brummell made him, stands on an isolated pedestal of self. He has no coat of arms on his carriage (indeed, Brummell kept no carriage), no ancestral portraits along his halls (and no ancestral halls) . . . and no title but Mr. Brummell, *arbiter elegantiarum.*
>
> (Moers, 17–18)

Thus Osmond fits Mrs. Gore's definition of a Dandy: "a nobody, who had made himself somebody, and gave the law to everybody." By making his Dandy a commoner, James provides a psychological explanation for the disappointment and misanthropy which convention had made automatic with the type. Max and Grandcourt condemn the *grand monde* simply because they are disposed to find it inadequate; Osmond finds that *monde* inadequate because he is excluded from its inner sanctums. His motivation thus derives from the very nature of nineteenth-century international society. The extreme severity of his indictments depends—as Grandcourt's and Max's do not—upon the essential fact of his birth.

If Osmond clearly is not Grandcourt, he just as clearly is not a traditional Dandy, however. He is a widower with a teen-age daughter.[68] Now Moers is quite right that "a wife or child would be unthinkable" (18) for Brummell and his imitators. Especially as exemplified by the prototype for Gilbert Osmond, Francis Boott, the Paterfamilias seems to stand at the opposite end of the social and moral spectrum from the Dandy. How James could link these two types, and why he would want to, are two distinct questions. He *could* link them because the Dandy was inevitably protean.

> Baudelaire's three masks as divine, dandy, and demon are incompatible. Yet they derive from the same impulse, and they balance one another. When he pushed any one of the roles to its limit, it tended to merge with the others.
>
> (Beebe, 138)

The Dandy's tendency to combine roles so apparently polar as divine and demon is, then, precedent for the union of Dandy and Father—in Dickens' Mr. Turveydrop and in James' Mr. Osmond. Auden has called the Dandy the "religious hero turned upside down";[69] with James the Dandy is the ethical hero turned upside down, the Paterfamilias. Why James would want to make this inversion, is another question. Our answer will enable us to understand how Gilbert Osmond becomes the most subversive Dandy in English literature and how James uses him in an extensive critique of Victorian social life.

As a father, Osmond is a representative figure. " 'I have brought up my child as I wished, in the old way' " (326). He repeatedly articulates old school sententiae. " 'She is too young to have strong emotions. . . . she is too young to make journeys of pleasure. . . . Tell her she must love her poor father very much' " (229, 262, 288). At the time such *sentence* seems too easy to provide us much *solas*; but that the old school attitudes are downright horrific becomes clear as Osmond reveals his intentions.

"Convents are very quaint, very convenient, very salutary. I like to think of her there, in the old garden, under the arcade, among those tranquil, virtuous women. . . . several of them are noble. She will have her books and her drawing."

(490)

The Christian father values a proper religious atmosphere, the socially conscious parent seeks association with the upper classes, the aesthete imagines a life of art and literature—and the telltale word is "convenient." Beneath the velvet glove of old school truths is the iron fist of paternal will. This dichotomy reappears when Osmond says, " 'I set a great price on my daughter' " (349). The pearl of great price is an admirable standard indeed, but Osmond is actually referring to a sale price, of course. His dualism here derives from an awareness of society's basic paradox. " 'I think young girls should be kept out of the world' " (262). Society would agree with this piousness, and so would Ned Rosier. But when Ned offers a marriage that would assure Pansy's preservation from the social corruption, Osmond rejects him unconditionally. Osmond's pious words were again two-faced. For a great social marriage, a girl needs the purity which social life would spoil. Thus, the basic paradox: a girl is preserved from society for a while, so that she may be bound to it permanently. Purity is the surest means to corruption.

Old-school paternity—with its power to incarcerate a daughter until she can be sold into corruption—seems still more unsavory as Osmond reveals his attitude toward another aspect of marriage. When Pansy at sixteen has apparently no hint that Isabel and Osmond are engaged, Osmond says, " 'There seems to me something enchantingly innocent in that' " (326). When Isabel then suggests that Pansy may indeed have guessed, Osmond replies, " 'Don't say that; I should be disgusted if I believed that' " (327). Osmond's attitude reappears when Madame Merle is discussing Pansy's "relations" with Ned.

> "Pansy has thought a great deal about him; but I don't suppose you think that matters."
> "I don't think it matters at all; but neither do I believe she has thought about him."
>
> (345)

The traditional paternal obsession with female innocence seems especially perverse with Osmond because we see it in light of two earlier tableaux. First, the Holy Family pose: with Isabel sitting beside Pansy, Osmond "sat down on the other side of his daughter, who had taken Isabel's hand" (238). Tableau. Then the pose shifts slightly, to an equally conventional one—the child at her father's knee. "He ended by drawing her out of her chair, and making her stand between his knees" (238). As James can reveal a whole relationship by the small indecorum of having Madame Merle stand while Osmond sits, so his variation upon the child-father tableau is meaningful too. How often in the traditional tableau is the daughter "between" her father's legs? Especially when he "makes" her stand there? Especially when she is of marriageable age?[70]

Osmond's peculiarly mixed relation with Pansy reflects his own perverse mixture of character types and traits. Our task is not to divide up the traits and assign one to the Dandy and another to the Paterfamilias. Rather, we must recognize that the impossibility of making such tidy divisions is James' point. The will to power, its sexual aspect when women are involved, and the repressive insistence upon conventional standards—in all these traits, how do we tell the Father from the Dandy? "Unnatural and even sinister" are the terms which Henrietta Stackpole applies to the "girl of twenty" whom Osmond, the artist-father, has fashioned (451). We agree. In turn Osmond's sinister and even unnatural mixture seems to reflect a general, if hidden, ambivalence in the Victorian period itself. In an age when John Ruskin, Lewis Carroll, Burne-Jones, and, as Hamlin Hill has recently shown, Mark Twain, were all engaged in decidedly "curious" relations with *jeunes filles*, the fabulously popular "Elsie" books of Martha Finley were representing father-daughter relationships of

> rather questionable intensity. He "fondled her hair," he "pressed her lips again and again to his," he "folded her to his heart"; he "drew her to his knees" and kept her there hour after hour; he declared at least every other chapter, "You belong to me."
>
> (Papashvily, 171–72)[71]

Although two of Martha Finley's young women are named Fleda and Mysie, our chief concern is not her possible influence upon Henry James. Martha Finley is primarily important as a representative Victorian. The obsession with young girls and older men which we find in her fiction (and which we have seen in James' novels as early as *Watch and Ward*) is so widespread in Victorian times that even Rhoda Broughton's notoriously iconoclastic Nell can say, "There is no relationship so delightful as that between father and daughter when at its best. . . . I liked my father a hundred times better than Dick" (the appropriately named fiance [*CUF* 35, 158]).[72] Pansy Osmond is attracted to her father. Having asked in her first scene, " 'am I not meant for you, papa?' " (217), she becomes more assertive later. " 'If he were not my papa I should like to marry him' " (292). That Pansy cannot imagine the implication of her words (and feelings) here indicts old-school education. A training which appears rigorously moral has actually inclined both parties toward the ultimate taboo. When we discover eventually "that the poor girl had been vanquished" (512), we see that the power drives of the Paterfamilias have found release in a consummation devoutly to be abhorred.

Although the best British and Continental fiction examines the father-daughter relation more sophisticatedly than Martha Finley or Rhoda Broughton do, Henry James' emphasis upon the relationship shows him particularly American. As Michael Davitt Bell has demonstrated,

> patriotic historian romancers. . . . were torn between the patriotic impulse to idolize the founders and the romantic impulse to criticize them as enemies to independence. . . . these characters represent a tension, not so much within Puritanism itself as within the nineteenth century's *view* of Puritanism. . . . the Puritan father is harsh, bigoted, and intolerant in both his public and his private relations—in both the Puritan community and the world of the romantic marriage plot.
>
> (14, 19, 151)

Like the American romancers, James uses the father's conventional opposition to young love to make a commentary upon social authority. Moreover, the sexual unsavoriness which James finds in the father-daughter relation also appears in the popular American romances.

> The villain . . . is often literally associated with parental authority, having managed to deceive the fathers with respect to his true intentions. In one extended case the villain *is* authority. . . . the seducing villain can be, and often is, a narrow Puritan.
>
> (155, 156)

In turn, the heroine is doubly beset. Avoiding the ravisher proves finally easier than winning over the father *without openly rebelling against him*. Here is where the romancers become specious.

By remaining the dutiful daughter to the end, and by being rewarded at that end, the natural heroine allows these writers, as it were, to have their cake and eat it too. Like the heroines they are portraying, these writers can affirm the new society without repudiating the old.... we are simply expected to accept the magical transformation of Mr. Grey from intolerance to tolerance.... literary convention is *substituted* for historical analysis.

(168, 169)

How Hawthorne in *The Scarlet Letter* responded to the specious conventional heroine is then described by Bell in words which could be applied to Hawthorne's pupil, Henry James. "[He] thoroughly repudiates this convention.... But his repudiation is carried out by means of the very symbols that other writers used to *support* the convention" (184). Thus James has a darling daughter and ardent swain who persevere without rebellion against the paternal will, and fail in an appallingly unconventional fashion. All is not necessarily lost, however, and the enormity of Victorian paternity is not fully exposed, until a second conventional female type also encounters the flinty male.

With regard to a wife, Osmond is as idealistic and conventional as he was with his daughter. When Madame Merle proposes a new candidate, Osmond's reply is only half in jest. " 'Is she beautiful, clever, rich, splendid, universally intelligent and unprecedentedly virtuous? It is only on these conditions that I care to make her acquaintance' " (222).[73] After Isabel meets Osmond's standards initially, he decides to undertake that fashioning of a perfect wife which is both an important theme in early Jamesian fiction and a standard practice of Victorian males. Osmond feels confident with Isabel because he has already succeeded so well with Pansy. " 'She is made for the world' " (214) means that Pansy is ideally suited to the world because she had been so carefully fashioned for it. Osmond's hopes for a wife are not, however, founded on any error so gross as a simple equation of Isabel and Pansy. Recognizing that Isabel " 'was brought up on a different system' " of education and that she is " 'exceptional' " (262), he is not disconcerted. "If she was too eager, she could be taught to be less so" (281). Osmond then goes on to make a judgment so symptomatic of his attitude toward women that later unhappiness is inevitable.

Let it not, however, be supposed that he was guilty of the error of believing that Isabel's character was of that passive sort which offers a free field for domination. He was sure that she would constantly act— act in the sense of enthusiastic concession.

(283)

Rather than fail to recognize Isabel as the new active woman, Osmond refuses to accept the new as new. Seeing the new as old means that he sees this and any woman in terms of the conventional ideal. Women make concessions, women enthusiastically serve their lords and masters.

Expecting his wife to reflect the conventional ideal, Osmond is in fact expecting her to reflect himself—in ways which critics who have discussed the theme of reflection have not defined. To begin with:

> He would be proud of her in company, would dress her handsomely, and show her off in the best lights. But from the very hour that he felt his power over her firmly established, he would begin to remodel her after his own worldly pattern. He would dismantle her of her womanly ideals, and give her in their place his table of market-values. He would teach her to submit her sensibilities to her selfish interest. . . . "As the husband is, the wife is,"—he would subdue her to what he worked in.
> (*GA* 248)

> Her face . . . was a representation. . . . Ralph in all this recognized the hand of the master. . . . what he saw was the fine lady who was supposed to represent something. "What did Isabel represent?" Ralph asked himself; and he could answer only by saying that she represented Gilbert Osmond. . . . the motive was as vulgar as the art was great. . . . under the guise of caring only for intrinsic values, Osmond lived exclusively for the world.
> (*PL* 362, 363, 364)

Osmond shares with rakish Murray in *The Guardian Angel* the Dandy's traditional desire to make the world into an art work reflecting their own values. But James complicates conventional practice by once again introducing duality—this time playing upon the different meanings of "reflection." Osmond sends Pansy back to the convent " 'for . . . a little reflection'. . . . 'she must think of it [the world] in the right way' " (489, 491). Thus Osmond wants his victims to reflect upon his own attitude toward the world until they reflect it. "It," in turn, means both his attitude and the world since his attitude toward the world is the world's attitude toward itself.

Like Pansy, Isabel must reflect the appropriate social ideal. Since she, upon reflection, cannot, she reflects her husband only as a hollow perfunctory echo.

> [Osmond] "Your temper isn't good."
> "No—it's not good."
> . . . "I know he was an old friend of yours."
> "Yes; he's an old friend of mine."
> (386)

Since "Madame Merle's interest was identical with Osmond's" (474), their harmony is reflected verbally. Each says of Pansy, " 'she is a little saint of heaven.'... 'she is a little saint of heaven.' "* With Isabel, however, Osmond's echoes sound only more hollow as the marriage grows more dissonant.

> [Isabel] "He told me then that he meant to write to you."
> "He has never written to me." ...
> [Osmond] "He's an odd fish." ...
> [Isabel] "I have never had a letter from him."
> "Never had a letter?" ...
> "As you say, he's an odd fish."
>
> (436)

Given this issue of reflection, a phrase which we discussed earlier takes on additional meaning. When Isabel calls her decision to visit Ralph an "irreflective action," we see that she is not only acting spontaneously; she is also failing, as a model wife never should, to reflect her husband's thinking.

Even extreme disobedience cannot finally disconcert Osmond, however, because "reflection" involves one last complication. Although he pictures an ideal wife as a silver plate which reflects him, Osmond can survive the eventuality that she turns out to be "earthenware" (that is, human).

> "Your wife indeed may bore you, in that case; but you will never bore yourself. You will always have something to say to yourself—always have a subject of reflection."
>
> (469)

Saying over to himself his wife's imperfections, Osmond is in effect maintaining before himself his own perfection. Either way, earthenware or silver, the wife confirms his superiority. Thus Osmond the Victorian husband lives like a Dandy.

> "To live and die before a mirror:" that, according to Baudelaire, was the dandy's slogan.
>
> (Camus, 51)
>
> His solitude, his *ennui*, his love for his daughter, his good manners, his bad manners, were so many features of a mental image constantly present to him as a model.
>
> (*PL* 364)

Making unnatural the act of holding the mirror up to nature, Osmond, like all Dandies, aspires to godhead—to create all in his image and likeness. For such blasphemy the popular tradition punished the villain with final defeat. James transforms this righteous simplification in Osmond's last "scene" in the novel.

*Osmond speaks on page 246, Madame Merle on 507.

Osmond is the Outraged Husband. Granted that we do not find him so persuasive that we side against Isabel: is Osmond simply *playing* the conventional role, or is he sincere but responding in terms of conventional simplifications, or is he legitimately outraged? If our experience of him is too complex for any one of these alternatives to seem immediately adequate, if Osmond's behavior is an uncertain mixture, then we may well not want to interpret this "scene" in sheep-goats terms.

Osmond is a figure of unrelieved malignity, but scarcely

> a believable human being. . . . Osmond's absurd and degenerative cruelty destroys the credibility of Isabel's return. . . . he has become an almost apparitional figure of satanic power.
>
> (Levy, 46, 47, 49)

Every previous transformation of the conventional type combines with important features of Osmond's last scene to prevent our reacting this way. Previously, for example, Ned Rosier's melodramatic response to Osmond was reproved by both the narrator—

> in a palace, too, little Pansy lived—a palace in Roman parlance, but a dungeon to poor Rosier's apprehensive mind. . . . In a less preoccupied frame of mind he could have done justice to the Palazzo Roccanera—

and Isabel—

> "She won't enjoy being tortured."
> "There will be nothing of that."
>
> (336, 403)

This same Isabel who rejects Caspar's melodramatic characterization of Osmond as a devil also reproves Henrietta for a comparable oversimplification.

> "What does he do to you?". . . .
> "He does nothing. But he doesn't like me."
>
> (450)

Isabel is not exonerating Osmond here; not liking one's wife is a hard attitude, particularly on the wife. But Isabel is rejecting any lurid interpretation of the situation. Since she rejects luridness again in Osmond's final scene, we must do likewise. "In his wish to preserve appearances he was after all sincere, and . . . this, as far as it went, was a merit" (496). How "far" this is, we cannot measure with any crudely melodramatic standards.

Like the Paterfamilias, the Dandy sees himself as a social conscience.

> Precisely because the dandy was, for Baudelaire, a figure apart from life, irresponsible, idle, absorbed with self, he could serve as a moral

consciousness for the contemporary world. . . . [Balzac claims] "moral
superiority": it was a new and unusually earnest claim for dandyism.

(Moers, 283, 131)

It remained Dandyism's claim, for in "ce stupide dix-neuvième siècle" the Dandy deplored the abandonment of the old standards. We cannot dismiss Gilbert Osmond as simply villainous because he, as Father-Dandy, makes moral judgments of impeccable severity.

> "His mother, as I suppose you know, is in America, so there is no one to prevent him [from journeying to Rome]. . . . I think it was a most extraordinary time for Mrs. Touchett to choose for going to America."
> . . . "I believe his mother is at last coming back to look after him. That little lady is superb; she neglects her duties with a finish!"

Can we distinguish Gilbert Osmond from Lord Warburton?* If the member of the House of Lords, the liberal traditionalist, the defender of maiden sisters, the pure suitor—if he and the "Dandy-Villain" make identical judgments based upon the same code, we must be wary of dismissing Osmond's other judgments as simply villainous. Osmond objects to Isabel's journey not merely from dislike of Ralph (whose part in Isabel's fortune Osmond does not know of) or from indifference to woman's conventional duty to nurse. Rather, Osmond is distinguishing in terms of decorum between who should and should not nurse. Mrs. Touchett should. Judging Isabel's nursing " 'indecent' " (495), Osmond not only joins a long line of Dandies who judged social behavior, but in particular follows Henleigh Grandcourt, who lectures Gwendolen on what is "decent."

> "If you are to appear as a bride at all, appear decently."

> "It's very indecent of Deronda to go about praising that girl," said Grandcourt, in a tone of indifference.
> "Indecent!" exclaimed Gwendolen.

(*DD* 321, 442)

How do we respond to a judgment so complexly, if perversely, tuned? Do we experience here something of Pelham's realization that "villains have passions as well as honest men" (384)? To teach us how subtle we must be with Gilbert Osmond, James offers a clue. In his last scene, Osmond is, as many critics have noted, painting. Instead of concentrating upon the coin's significance, let us note the brushes. Initially they are called "fine" (493). Which is ambiguous. Are they brushes capable of refined beauty, or are they simply little? Osmond himself has, in turn, offered us a comparable range of possibility. How much refinement of

*Warburton (353, 354), Osmond (469).

feeling and how much littleness of spirit compose his difficult mixture? The clue which James provides is as subtle as our response must be. The last action that Osmond makes in the novel is to take "up one of his little brushes" (497). With the shift from "fine" to "little" James tips the scales, particularly since the diction here echoes Isabel's earlier exclamation, " 'Oh, Osmond, for a man who was so fine' " (445).[74]
"Little" also has additional significance.

> James makes an odd slip in writing, "The quiver of her *little* body ..."
> [italics mine]. Pansy is now twenty and can scarcely be described in
> this way. Evidently James is so possessed by his image of the tyran-
> nized child that he forgets that the exigencies of his story have
> brought Pansy to womanhood. The slip suggests how completely
> static a figure Pansy is.
>
> (Levy, 123)

James has made no slip, of course. Pansy is static, not because he has viewed her and made her that way, but because Osmond has. The first time we meet Gilbert, in fact, he says " 'I like little women' " (213). We learn subsequently that his former wife was a " 'little woman' " (500). The new Mrs. Osmond is another matter, however. What we learn first about Isabel physically—even before her prettiness—is that she is "tall" (15). When she meets Mr. Osmond, her full intellectual and spiritual substan-tiality is exactly what Isabel tries to minimize.

> She had effaced herself, when he first knew her; she had made herself
> small, pretending there was less of her than there really was.
>
> (393)

Thus when Osmond turns back to his little brushes, he is turning away from a type of woman too large to be dominated completely. It is appropriate that Osmond's ideal of "little women" echoes the title of Miss Alcott's famous novel, for Osmond's ideal is decidedly popular. That (virtually infantine) docility which Victorian society insisted upon as part of womanly perfection is espoused both by chauvinistic males like Gilbert Osmond and by the sentimental females whom Miss Alcott spoke for and to in *Little Women*. When Osmond turns away from substantial women, he is returning to what Madame Merle has already undercut. She says of his art, " 'as the only thing you do, it's so little' " (224). Linking the "little" artifact which Osmond the Father has fashioned (Pansy is expressly called "little" at least forty-nine times)[75] and the "little"ness of spirit which Osmond the Aesthete has revealed, Henry James passes judgment upon a whole way of life, the old order and its ideals and practices. "Art should be as hard as nails—as hard as the heart of the artist—a person who, *qua* artist, is an absolutely Roman Father."[76] Qua artist: this is the qualification which Henry James makes and which

Gilbert Osmond and society fail to observe. The Victorian Father treats human beings with a hardheartedness justifiable only with an artist's puppets. James' indictment is so sweeping because Osmond is not simply a Bohemian extremist; we cannot explain him as a Byronic aberrant and thus explain him away. As Paterfamilias, Gilbert Osmond abides at the heart of Victorian proprieties.

Joining Dandy and Father, James can thus disqualify both as figures of authority. The Dandy is only an Outraged Husband declaiming before the footlights of his self-esteem; the Father is finally dandiacal in the worst sense, retiring to the little realm of artifacts and disdain. James thus denies the pretensions of Baudelaire and the radicals even as he rejects the claims of traditionalists. Gilbert Osmond is the most subversive Dandy in English literature because he calls into question social morality itself. Pelham's gibes seem safe by comparison; *Pelham* attacks the indecent in the name of the decent. But Osmond the Father-Dandy judges " 'indecent' " that deathbed nursing which Victorians considered woman's highest calling. When Camus speaks of "the morality of a choirboy or of an infantry manual," he could as well be referring to the Father as to the Dandy. Madame Merle's criticism of Osmond—" 'You are more like a copy-book than I' " (484)—is directed at a capacity for sententiousness which combines the inflexible rigor of the infantry manual with the simplistic pietism of the choirboy. Copybook sentimentality undercuts Osmond's pretense to Byronic aloofness even as it underlies an idealization of women at best maudlin and at worst degraded and perverse. This link between Decadence and Victorian morality—between the sentimentalism of sickness and the sickness of sentimentalism—indicts two apparently polar attitudes as ultimately similar wills to power.

Through Gilbert Osmond, James thus takes part in an examination of values which continues throughout the nineteenth century and can be summed up in the question "What is a gentleman?" From *John Halifax, Gentleman* through *Modern Painters* and Newman's *Idea of a University*, the questioning continues. It is, once again, in Lermontov that the basic ambivalence finds its classic formulation.

"Listen, Monsieur Pechorin, I believe you are a gentleman."
I bowed.
"I am even convinced of it," she went on, "although your behavior is somewhat ambiguous."

(178)

This inability to distinguish the traditional gentleman from the dandiacal villain, this tension between the will to believe and the disconcerting evidence of the senses, affects even that ultimate Victorian inner sanctum, the family. What appalls us, for example, about the extensive discussion in the 1868 numbers of *The English Woman's Domestic Magazine* is that the periodical is anything but outré (like, say, *The Pearl*) and that its subject is not even sons, but daughters.

> Definitely pathological forms [of sexual urges] . . . were displayed in a lengthy correspondence in the columns of *The English Woman's Domestic Magazine* for 1868 on the vexed question "Ought we to whip our Daughters?" The volume of letters on this subject became so great that at last the magazine had to publish a special monthly supplement to contain them.
>   They supply us with evidence of a mass of sadism existing not merely in girls' schools but in the happy English home. Letters from victims as well as from parents and mistresses supply precise details, the numbers of strokes—twenty to fifty . . . the method—by strap, slipper or birch—(but the birch is preferable "as causing the more exquisite pain"); the tying down or the hanging up (for each has its advocates) of the victims, whose age runs from four to eighteen.
>   (Cunnington, 185–86)

Or we might witness the shocking fact (and the contemporary awareness of it) that many of the period's many horrific murders were perpetrated within the family circle by members of that circle—such killings by spouses as the Smethurst, Bartlett, and Maybrick cases, by servants like the notorious Kate Webster and F. B. Courvoisier or the wetnurses Mary Pratt and Elizabeth Gough, and by the physicians Palmer, Pritchard, and Cream.[77] Or we can cite that father of ten children, the aging Charles Dickens, dressed in dandiacal plaids and extravagant greatcoats and stalking the London nightlife of his imagination, pursued by Harthouse and Bradley Headstone. Or, finally, there are conjugal attitudes as horrendous as Gilbert Osmond's and as orthodox. When Thomas Bailey Aldrich writes (revealingly) to his mother "that he was most attracted to Lillian [his wife] when she was ill," he is only echoing that archconservative and antifeminist Eliza Lynn Linton. "She [the Real Woman] is never more charming than as an invalid or a convalescent." [78] In this line, however, nothing equals the Count D'Orsay (and is it not appropriate that the great Victorian Dandy reflects the period so well), who, after all the years of flamboyance and innuendo, can call Lady Blessington at her death " *'a true, loving mother to me!'* "[79]

Seeing Henry James as so thoroughgoing a social commentator—his involvement with the Woman Question we will take up soon—has not been the tendency of most criticism. Yet during James' own lifetime, William Dean Howells could handsomely praise him for "the wisdom of a rarely experienced witness of the world."[80] Howells intended no pun here on "rarely." If we tend to read the word in two senses today, we are responding to Van Wyck Brooks, C. V. Parrington, and many others who have criticized James as rarefied. Defenders tended for too long to stress only the compensations of his fiction's formal excellence. Now that the vogue of the Brooks-Parrington thesis has waned somewhat, we may see that the social commentary which appears in "The Point of View" (1882), *The Bostonians* (1886), and in subsequent works is—like most aspects of later James—grounded strongly in the crucial decade. In the very first chapter of *The Portrait*, James' most knowledgeable character says, " 'I believe things are getting more serious.... I am convinced there will be great changes; and not all for the better' " (11). Throughout the novel echo the phrases " 'radical' " (65, 67, 68, 69, 71, 276), " 'revolution' " (68), " 'new ideas' " (91), " 'now-a-days' " (65, 251), " 'everything that is really new' " (465). Scholars and historians have defined as particularly Victorian the period's sense of itself as transitional and critical. When Ralph Touchett calls Lord Warburton " 'the victim of a critical age' " (67), we recognize both that Warburton is suffering from the anxieties which plagued so many Victorians and that Henry James is clearly aware of the period's critical tendencies. Moreover, James himself, like sages on both sides of the Atlantic, takes part in the critical examination of Victorian social life. In 1879 he says, "the good American, in days to come, will be a more critical person than his complacent and confident grandfather" (*Ha* 125). Still earlier, James, criticizing the tendency to "squint at the truth instead of looking straight at it," refuses to restrict the blame entirely to the individual consciousness. "It seems to me that this fatal obliquity of vision inheres not wholly in any individual but is some indefinable property in the social atmosphere" (*HJL* 47). Thus the presence of social commentary in James' fiction should not surprise us, especially since such commentary came directly to him from two particularly hallowed sources. Henry James, Sr., was anything but complacent and confident, was in his touchingly remote way a consistent and often furious commentator upon the social and political scene. To an 1869 letter from Henry, Sr., Henry, Jr., replies revealingly.

> I am not prepared perhaps to measure the value of your notions with regard to the amelioration of society, but I certainly have not travelled a year in this quarter of the globe without coming to a very deep sense of the absurdly clumsy and transitory organization of the actual social body. The only respectable state of mind, indeed, is to constantly express one's perfect dissatisfaction with it—and your letter was one of the most respectable things I have seen in a long time. So don't be afraid of treating me to a little philosophy. I treat myself to lots.
>
> (*HJL* 187)

The second hallowed source of social commentary is the Victorian novel itself. The novelists whom James grows up admiring and imitating are serious social critics. Besides Flaubert, Dickens, and Eliot, there are the scribblers who relentlessly attack drink and slavery and sexual promiscuity. And novelists all across the spectrum unite in indicting the English treatment of children. The archetypical confinements of David Copperfield and Jane Eyre are followed for many Victorian Young Persons by marriages which Bulwer-Lytton calls "a marketing peculiar to ourselves in Europe and only rivalled by the slave-merchants of the East."[81] For Dickens, as Stephen Marcus notes, "the image of the delinquent or inadequate parent becomes the very paradigm of wickedness."[82] Attacking the evils of a whole society by revealing the inadequacies of domestic life is one of the great concerns of High Victorian fiction and is carried on by Meredith, Hardy, Howells, Twain, and innumerable scribblers. James' attempt to join this goodly company is in part revealed by his readiness to comment through his fiction upon the moral health of society. *The Portrait* explores, for example, the relation between domestic and political authority.

> "He [Warburton] owns about half England; that's his character,"
> Henrietta remarked. "That's what they call a free country!"
>   "Ah, he is a great proprietor? Happy man!" said Gilbert Osmond.
>   "Do you call that happiness—the ownership of human beings?"
> cried Miss Stackpole.
>
> (276)

Osmond refuses to be drawn out further, but his admiration for the proprietary is clear. As one of the novel's most conservative but least political men, Osmond does not reveal his proprietary drives by any direct links with such political conservatives as the ludicrous Mr. Luce (" 'they want to be kept down, sir, to be kept down; nothing but the strong hand—the iron heel—will do for them' " [197]). James is primarily intent, not upon burlesquing the mindless right-wing, but upon examining seriously the opposite and more dynamic political force, the radicals. Lord Warburton—and he should know—tells Osmond that England "was just the country for him—he would be sure to get on well there" (438). Warburton himself has surely prospered. Even politically " 'the world has come round to me' " (354). How far that world actually had to come, however, how radical Lord Warburton actually is, has long since been called into question by the reliable Ralph and Daniel Touchett.

> "He [Warburton] says I don't understand my time. I understand it certainly better than he, who can neither abolish himself as a nuisance nor maintain himself as an institution." . . . "He seems to want to do away with a good many things, but he seems to want to remain himself. I suppose that is natural; but it is rather inconsistent. . . . The radicals of the upper class . . . talk about changes, but I don't think

they quite realize. . . . Their radical views are a kind of amusement;
they have got to have some amusement."

(67, 68, 69)

For all of Warburton's liberated views, his treatment of women indicates
how much the proprietary instinct endures in great radicals of the upper
class. After Warburton ignores a question which his sister asks him in
public, she "looked ladylike and patient, and awaited his pleasure" (123).
Warburton takes good care of his sisters, and does eventually what they
wish; but how completely they await his pleasure, and how completely
the active role is his (" 'I never do anything,' said this young lady" [124])
is never in doubt. Such paternalistic domination is more sinister with
Osmond and Pansy. But James has already indicated that Warburton's
proprietorship can also be tinged with the sinister. As Isabel proves more
and more intractable in the proposal scene, Warburton begins "giving
short nervous shakes to his hunting-whip." Finally defeated, he "shaking
his hunting-whip with little quick strokes . . . walked rapidly away"
(102). Without overstressing Warburton's violence here, and without
underestimating his genuine tenderness toward Isabel, we can and indeed
must recognize the significance of the whip. In crises the traditional
lordly instinct surfaces—thrash what will not submit to proprietorship.
And Osmond? When he confronts *Ned's* intractability, Gilbert says, " 'he
ought to be horsewhipped' " (346). Linking the apparently polar figures
of conservative Osmond and radical Warburton, and linking within
Warburton the apparently polar roles of radical reformer and old-school
authoritarian, James comments socially as he does by linking the Dandy
and the Paterfamilias in Osmond himself. We see how thin the genteel
veneer is, how basic to the Victorian Male is the instinct for proprietorship, and how all class and political creeds share in this instinct. The
Victorian world is not what it pretends or imagines. And Henry James, in
the great tradition of his father and fellow sages and novelists, is
committed to telling the social truth.

James' critique of society in *The Portrait* remains convincing to the end
because his presentation of Osmond remains complex to the end. We feel
that Osmond is, finally, unreasonable and that Isabel's nursing is not
indecent; we may even feel that Osmond is, ultimately, a villain in ways
which Amerigo in *The Golden Bowl* is not. But certainly, James does not
fail in *The Portrait*, as he did with earlier villains, to heed the admonition
which Charlotte Brontë once jotted down in a special memorandum on
" 'villains'—'N.B. Moderation to be observed here.' "[83] Moderate, James
remains to the end. Osmond reveals his essential littleness sufficiently
that he does not fit the conventional formula—that the villain remains
"gigantically alone." Osmond is not gigantic. On the other hand, James
avoids the equally conventional righteousness of leaving his villain

simply alone and crushed. Because Osmond is finally the object as well as
the subject of his reflections, he can never be alone or lonely. Nor is he
crushed. By allowing the Paterfamilias to endure and presumably to
prevail, James establishes how complete the power of such figures is.
Osmond's enduring presence means that another guide figure—Isabel
Archer—is faced with an especially formidable task.

3

With the Heroine as Guide Figure, we can proceed as with Gilbert
Osmond. Define the type, then study the courtship and marriage. "A girl
deceived by villains is standard enough; as a girl self-deceived, Isabel
draws upon predecessors in George Eliot and Jane Austen." Donald
Stone's summary (209) of types here is particularly good because his two
clauses give due recognition to both popular and great influences. Critics
distort Isabel's situation when they either overemphasize James' debt to
major writers or forget Howells' admonition that the heroines of fiction
are too mixed for their origins to be defined precisely.[84] Both these
distortions appear in one brief example. When Isabel says, " 'a swift
carriage, of a dark night, rattling with four horses over roads that one
can't see—that's my idea of happiness,' " Henrietta Stackpole replies,
" 'You . . . say . . . that—like the heroine of an immoral novel' " (153).
R. W. Stallman speaks for several critics when he says, "the 'immoral
novel' (to identify it) is Flaubert's *Madame Bovary*" (14). My intention
here is not to quibble about a source (although James' passage does
differ from Flaubert's in basic ways).[85] Stallman makes " 'an' " immoral
novel into "the" immoral novel. Such overspecificity is reductive. It
denies the rich range of romantic reference which is as much James' point
here as the mere fact of Isabel's romanticism. Isabel has not read just
Madame Bovary, she has been saturated with the midnight rides of
innumerable popular and great heroines. The eighteenth century was
already so overrun with elopements, abductions, and wild carriage
chases—from Clarissa's archetypal flight to the first American copies in
Charlotte Temple and *The Coquette*—that these rides are the object of
parody by 1801.

> Dorcas. . . . changed her name to Dorcasina, romanticized every
> scoundrel she met and longed to elope in a chaise, declaring, ". . . it
> has been my supreme wish and expectation to realize the tender and
> delightful scenes so well described in these enchanting books."[86]

Isabel's dreams seem scarcely less romantic. Whether James knew *Female
Quixotism* or not, he did know *East Lynne* (definitely an "immoral
novel" by Henrietta's standards), where a heroine named Isabel flees in a
midnight coach with her lover. Isabelle in *Le Roman* is tempted three

times to fly from her home (279, 282, 353). My point, then, is not to dispute a source but to suggest that only against a background rich in reference and free from reductive equations does Isabel Archer's own carriage ride assume its fullest irony. For she does flee from her husband, across France, through the night. But the carriage of her dreams is now a railway carriage, and she is alone, and the man whom she flees to is dying, and "the arms . . . or at any rate . . . the hands" (515) that eventually receive her are only Henrietta's. Isabel's situation is cruelest when we appreciate how popular the romantic dream is which has been annihilated.

What Isabel shares with fiction's heroines—and with Victorian women generally—is, however, much more than simply a penchant for romantic dreams.

ISABEL

I

Eyes not down-dropt nor over-bright, but fed
  With the clear-pointed flame of chastity,
  Clear, without heat, undying, tended by
    Pure vestal thoughts in the translucent fane
Of her still spirit; locks not wide-dispread,   5
  Madonna-wise on either side her head;
  Sweet lips whereon perpetually did reign
The summer calm of golden charity,
Were fixed shadows of thy fixed mood,
  Revered Isabel, the crown and head,   10
The stately flower of female fortitude,
  Of perfect wifehood and pure lowlihead.

II

The intuitive decision of a bright
  And thorough-edged intellect to part
    Error from crime; a prudence to withhold;   15
    The laws of marriage character'd in gold
Upon the blanched tablets of her heart;
A love still burning upward, giving light
To read those laws; an accent very low
In blandishment, but a most silver flow   20
    Of subtle-paced counsel in distress,
Right to the heart and brain, tho' undescried,
    Winning its way with extreme gentleness
Thro' all the outworks of suspicious pride;
A courage to endure and to obey;   25
A hate of gossip parlance, and of sway,

Crown'd Isabel, thro' all her placid life,
The queen of marriage, a most perfect wife.

III
The mellow'd reflex of a winter moon;
A clear stream flowing with a muddy one,   30
    Till in its onward current it absorbs
        With swifter movement and in purer light
        The vexed eddies of its wayward brother:
    A leaning and upbearing parasite,
    Clothing the stem, which else had fallen quite   35
With cluster'd flower-bells and ambrosial orbs
Of rich fruit-bunches leaning on each other—
Shadow forth thee:—the world hath not another
(Tho' all her fairest forms are types of thee,
And thou of God in thy great charity)   40
Of such a finish'd chasten'd purity.[87]

Having called Tennyson "the poet I had earliest known and best loved,"
(*MY* 87), James can find, as late as 1904, a Boston scene evoking the
Tennysonian refrain " 'long, unlovely street' " (*AS* 247).[88] As a literary
apprentice James not only reviews the Bard but also includes in both
Watch and Ward and *Roderick Hudson* direct quotations from Tennyson's most ambitious poem on the Woman Question—*The Princess*.[89]
After establishing how numerous James' early borrowings from Tennyson are, Giorgio Melchiori goes on to define the reason for these
borrowings.

> In making use here of the works of his predecessors James's purpose is
> not to comment ironically on their value as works of art but rather to
> show up the irony of the situations presented in them by contrasting
> them with a harsher reality . . . . in the case of Tennyson's poems . . .
> James regularly inverts the pathetic or optimistic conclusions.[90]

Whether James is consciously making a similar inversion with "Isabel" is
less important than the fact that Tennyson's poem raises virtually every
issue which Isabel Archer will confront throughout *The Portrait*. Line 39
of "Isabel" tells us (in case we hadn't guessed) that Isabel is a model
woman. Especially encouraged by "perfect wifehood" (12) and "a most
perfect wife" (28), we see that Tennyson has indeed painted the portrait
of a lady, the Perfect Lady of the Victorian ideal. His poem is, then, a
good place to begin studying James' critique of that ideal.

Tennyson defines the proper functions of the Perfect Lady in lines
13–24 and 30–33. Since Man's life out in the real world has left him
proudly suspicious (24) and soiled (30), Cloistered Woman's lucidity and
purity enable her to act as counselor and cleanser. What do these roles

cost woman? Virtually everything. "Isabel" is a paean to repression. The poem seems to begin in that middle ground beloved of Victorians. "Eyes not down-dropt nor over-bright" suggests that woman should be neither too cowed nor too volatile. The next forty lines, however, stress obsessively the subordinate state of womankind. As counselor her accent is "very low," her counsel "undescried"; she hates "sway." In fact her only extreme trait precludes any disruptive extremes—"extreme gentleness." Thus, although Tennyson recognizes woman's "head" and crowns it in line 10, the stanza ends with "lowlihead"; the crown reappears near the end of the next stanza too, but is again qualified reassuringly, this time by "placid." Subjugation is further enforced by Tennyson's insistence upon the essential staticness of woman's life. In lines 5–16 Isabel's spirit is "still," her lips "perpetually . . . calm"; "fixed . . . fixed" is her one "mood," and equally single-minded is her commitment to the "laws" of marriage. Tennyson may recognize the real nature of Woman's marital situation (the husband as proudly suspicious is clearly insecure and threatened), but he will not rock the boat. The "courage" which might drive Woman to action and change proves only passive, only "The courage to endure and obey." When "still" recurs in line 18, we see that the staticness which makes Woman an ideal counselor serves another function as well. Her light-giving love burns without heat. Woman's sexuality is as rigidly circumscribed in "Isabel" as her intellect and social mobility are. See how lines 2–4 establish her sexlessness—"chastity . . . without heat . . . pure." Her Heart is "blanched": no red here, only the white of purity. Rejecting *agape*, Tennyson stresses *caritas* in line 8 so that his Isabel can function not only as a Perfect Lady but as a type of God himself. What they share, we learn in line 40, is "charity."

The circumscribed nature of Woman's sexuality is also insisted upon in two highly conventional images which James adapts in *The Portrait.* "The mellow'd reflex of a winter moon." Diana, goddess of the moon and patroness of the hunt and of chastity, is obviously associated with Miss Archer, but critics who see the association only in terms of sexual coldness miss part of James' point. As a moon being, Isabel Archer, like Tennyson's Isabel, is representative not only of Victorian woman's proper sexual attitude but also of Victorian woman's actual sexual plight.

> "I would be the sun of my domestic world—nothing less. . . . My wife, to use a poet's comparison, should be the moon, whose light must reflect from me."

Woman is the lesser man, and all thy passions, match'd with mine,
Are as moonlight unto sunlight, and as water unto wine.

The first excerpt here is from Caroline Chesbro',[91] the second from "Locksley Hall" (95). Great writers no less than popular scribblers use sun-moon imagery to define the sexes—Man as aggressor, Woman as passive—and thus reinforce society's basically chauvinistic ideal. "Reflex" in "Isabel" means "reflection," but it also suggests that as her husband's reflection Woman is basically reflexive, fundamentally dependent upon the stimulus of another. By using reflection images with his Moon Lady, Henry James is less holding her frigidity up to ridicule than he is making Isabel part of a society which repressed sexuality so relentlessly. This repression also appears in the botanical images of Tennyson (and James). Taking up the highly conventional analogy of oak and ivy, Tennyson makes explicit what that analogy implies—that Woman is a "parasite" (34). With female inferiority once again established, the Bard can then, like a good Victorian, go on to credit Woman with *utile* and *dulce*. That the word "upbearing" in line 34 means not only "bearing flowers in an upward direction" but also "helping the Male bear up" (in several senses) is established by "The stem . . . else had fallen quite." But woman's beautiful fecundity never gets out of hand, for the rich fruit bunches lean on one another. The poem then ends reaffirming Woman's purity. "Chasten'd" is what has happened not only to Isabel but to the reader.

Virtually every aspect of Tennyson's poem—woman's role as moral counselor, her social and sexual circumspection, the images of moons and plants—reappears, as I have said, in *The Portrait of a Lady*. Henry James, like the Bard and nearly every writer and citizen of the period, is touched by the feminist controversy. As Gilbert Osmond is part of the Gentleman Question, Isabel Archer is born out of the Woman Question —that examination of female roles and rights which gains intensity in the 1860s and '70s and has been called "the trial of the institution of marriage." Historians tend to agree that increasingly among middle-class women in High Victorian times "there was a vague sensation of discontent and emptiness."[92] Such specific issues as woman's right to deeds of title and to a separate bank account, her need for greater freedom in matters of employment, birth control, divorce, and abortion—these and other issues sprang from a more general sense "that all was not well with the social fabric, that the actual bliss of Victorian monogamic matrimony was not up to theory."[93] The most popular orthodox authority on the domestic sanctities was Mrs. Sarah Stickney Ellis, who wrote *The Women of England, The Wives of England, The Mothers of England, The Daughters of England* and who began her epic endeavor by "premising that the women of England are deteriorating in their moral character."[94] Mrs. Ellis' orthodoxy shaped and reflected the 1840s and '50s, the formative years of Henry James (and of Gilbert Osmond). In the 1860s Mrs. Ellis is joined by Mrs. Linton, whose famous *The Girl of the Period* declaimed in a more strident voice the same conservative attitudes.

We used to think we knew to a shade what was womanly and what was unwomanly. . . . if this exactness of interpretation belonged to past times, the utmost confusion prevails at present. . . . Men and tradition say one thing, certain women say another thing.

(2:110–11)

Those certain women who shamelessly opposed Mrs. Ellis and Mrs. Linton were all the more "certain" when a spokesman of special stature appeared on their side. "It is Mill's views, above all, which . . . made contemporary novelists realize that if they were to keep in tune with the times, their ideas of marriage and celibacy, and indeed of women as a whole, would have to undergo some sort of reassessment."[95]

Novelists had, in fact, been reassessing woman's situation at least since the fiction of Charlotte Brontë. Her unprecedentedly homely heroines perform such unconventional acts as declining marriage with a cleric bound for the mission fields or finding dignity and purpose in a life of spinsterhood. Still more unheard of was what Charlotte's friend Mrs. Gaskell was tolerating. In *Ruth* the "unfortunate" is treated sympathetically and survives long enough to serve society in exemplary fashion. Mrs. Gaskell sounds her challenge immediately: "it is well to know what were the chains of daily domestic habit" (2). The chains of orthodox attitudes are then subjected to white-hot satire. The adoring mother of Ruth's seducer says, " 'of course . . . it was my wish to be as blind to the whole affair as possible' " (88). Accordingly, she assumes in the face of all the evidence that this lower-class girl must have seduced her susceptible darling, and, "handsomely" leaving fifty pounds behind, Mrs. Bellingham "rescues" her sickly but potent son and abandons Ruth forever. These and other enormities of social orthodoxy shake the Reverend Mr. Benson. "Into whole labyrinths of social ethics Mr. Benson's thoughts wandered" (116). No wonder some of Mrs. Gaskell's "friends" never spoke to her again.

In the fiction of the 1860s, feminist ideas flourish. Plain heroines become the rage; young women are marrying older men, as Henry James notes in an 1865 review (*NAR* 280) and as Isabel Archer soon demonstrates with Osmond. In addition

there was a growing emphasis during the 1860's on misalliances and marital troubles. . . . "Emancipated women"—nonconformist or discontented with the ordinary domestic and social round—were especially conspicuous during the 1860's.

(R. Colby, 272, 264)

In particular, four new writers emerge in shocking fashion.[96] All are women. Mrs. Gaskell's heretical sympathy for the "unfortunate" is compounded by Mrs. Henry Wood. *East Lynne* opens with a Daughter-Wife-Mother to delight even Mrs. Ellis; suddenly this Isabel flees with a vile seducer to an untoward pregnancy. But the real shocker comes when she survives the apparently heaven-sent train wreck and returns as governess to the very children she abandoned! Mrs. Wood clearly expects us to pity the wretch and to feel indignant that the seducer is " 'not liable in justice' " (192). What followed *East Lynne* can hardly be spoken of.

> The tender fascination of those soft and melting blue eyes; the graceful beauty of that slender throat and drooping head, with its wealth of showering flaxen curls; the low music of that gentle voice; the perfect harmony which pervaded every charm.... "I saw that she was a perfect lady."[97]

That this archetypical heroine is actually a murderess makes the novel and stage versions of *Lady Audley's Secret* (1862) one of England's all-time popular successes. Next comes Ouida, who "set out to shock her public with unspeakable improprieties."[98] And then there is Rhoda Broughton. Adding to irreverence a witty style, *Cometh Up as a Flower* (1867) presents sympathetically the subversive situation of a wife-heroine who " 'is unfaithful to him [her husband]; if not in deed, at least in heart and thought' " (385).

Probably most disconcerting to orthodoxy was not such profligacy itself, nor even the tendency of major writers to question once-hallowed moral assumptions.[99] The real danger appears again in Mrs. Gaskell. When the Reverend Mr. Benson's kindness to Ruth is attacked with the traditional argument that " 'the world has decided how such women are to be treated,' " Benson replies, " 'I take my stand with Christ against the world' " (347). Christianity provided the individual with chapter and verse against Repressive Authority. The example of Jesus defying the clerical establishment, befriending adulteresses, and inspiring the lower classes—all this could well provide common ground for an alliance of Christians with the secular radicals of John Mill.

Could indeed. But except for F. D. Maurice and his followers, it tends not to happen. Orthodoxy is less threatened, finally, by feminist writers than it had feared. Years later Rhoda Broughton says of her long life: "I began my career as Zola, I finish it as Miss Yonge." Miss Broughton finished, in fact, largely where she began. For all its irreverence, *Cometh Up as a Flower* builds to a melodramatic climax so conventional that Lermontov had scorned it forty years before.

> "She will marry a monster out of submissiveness ... and will start persuading herself that she is miserable, that she loved only one man ... but that Heaven had not wished to unite her with him because he

wore a soldier's coat, although under that thick grey coat there beat a passionate and noble heart."

(102)

Lapsing from radicalism to melodrama is, in fact, endemic to most feminist fiction. Charlotte Brontë's ultimate satisfaction with masterly males is well documented; the unfortunates in *Ruth* and *East Lynne* succumb, eventually, to the mandatory early death; and that blond villainess, Lady Audley, is finally caught, humbled, and shut away. Why these writers, and particularly Charlotte Brontë and Mrs. Gaskell, settle for the dreariness of conventional endings, cannot be explained by any simple theory of intimidation by editors or readers. Feminist novelists are attempting a precarious balance. Their heroines desire, not man's place, but man's guidance so that they might achieve self-fulfillment. Their complaint is not that men prevent them from becoming geniuses, but that men prevent them from developing their potential, whatever it may be. These women want a mentor, but not a master. Frances Henri continues teaching after her marriage, but she also continues calling her husband "Monsieur." One of Mrs. Gaskell's spirited young ladies refuses to be lectured like a child, yet "she liked to be lectured" by her future husband (*R* 215).

In so delicate a balance we find that coalescence of opposites which great art frequently achieves. That Victorian feminists rarely achieve great art (except for Charlotte Brontë and Mrs. Gaskell) cannot be attributed simply to problems of technique. These novelists are understandably tentative about how much to demand for womankind because, as we shall see, they are opposing the immense authority of attitudes long-standing and widely held. Moreover, feminists know that the ultimate sanction of their temerity can be used against them.

> For herself [the good woman], she has no doubts whatever, no moral uncertainties. The path of duty is as plain to her as are the words of the Bible, and she loves her husband too well to wish to be his rival or to desire an individualized existence outside his. . . . There are two ways of dealing with pinching shoes. The one is to wear them till you get accustomed to the pressure . . . the other is to kick them off and have done with them altogether. . . . the one is emblematic of Christian patience, the other of Pagan power.
>
> (Mrs. Linton, 2:149, 1:167)

Especially with its Pauline origins and inclinations, Protestantism can hardly ignore "Wives be subject to your husbands." Moreover, all brands of Christianity in the nineteenth century preach primarily patience, not radicalism, to the oppressed—whether the oppressed are Negroes in America or women of the world. Since the lamb to the slaughter became the Paschal Lamb, Jesus' example of quiescent triumph combines with social pressures to make most Victorian feminists hesitant indeed about seeking beyond their mentors for a personal truth.

Feminist issues appear in both the reviews and the fiction of Henry James. His reviews take up repeatedly the problem of creating heroines. "Edith . . . is, we suppose, the heroine of the story, inasmuch as she has the privilege of expiring on the corpse of the hero" (*Na* 1877, 44).[100] No more satisfied with the Lady Audley alternative to the conventional heroine, James denies that "the only escape from bread-and-butter and commonplace is into golden hair and promiscuous felony" (*Na* 1875, 17). As early as 1867 he mentions a possible alternative to these polar simplicities: "high-toned, free thinking heroines" (*Na* 450).[101] The key here is "free thinking." Victorians agree with rare unanimity that American women are, for good or ill, markedly freer than their European sisters. Hear the admiration in Fanny Kemble's words: "it is difficult to imagine society existing at all under more absolute conditions of freedom for its female members than the women of the United States now enjoy."[102] American women could hold title to property and thus secure it from their husbands' creditors; these women had freer access to higher education, particularly medicine; they could travel and voice opinions in ways rarely practiced in Europe; even Mrs. Linton admitted that American women were freer—freer to shirk motherhood and be gaudy. Here, then, is James' alternative to the simplicities of Lady Audley and expiring Edith. Especially with the hallowed precedent of Shakespeare's Portia ("the very type and model of the young person intelligent and presumptuous" [*AN* 49]), James espouses "the delicate, nervous, emancipated young woman begotten of our institutions and our climate, and equipped with a lovely face and an irritable moral consciousness" (*Na* 1875, 12).

Such a heroine allows James to introduce various feminist topics into his fiction. In 1867, for example, one of his young women says " 'yes, they are cruel times. . . . they make one doubt of all one has learnt from one's pastors and masters' " (*CT* 1:241). Another early heroine says in best Lucy Snowe fashion, " 'if you think I'm afraid of never marrying, you're mistaken. One can be very happy as an old maid' " (*CT* 2:120–21). Particularly as the crucial decade continues, the feminist topics which concern James chiefly are freedom and knowledge.

"We women are so habitually condemned by fate to act simply in what is called the domestic sphere, that there is something intoxicating in the opportunity to exert a far-reaching influence outside of it."

"Why should I suffer the restrictions of a society of which I enjoy none of the privileges?"

"I had tried to get some insight into the position of woman in England. . . . she told me the position of a lady depended upon the rank of her father. . . . that proves to me that the position of woman in her country cannot be satisfactory."

(*CT* 3:85; 4:290, 449, 450)

Since what characterizes the American girl is her questioning of accepted attitudes, a novelist studying the American girl finds himself necessarily at the heart of the Woman Question. " 'I have to pretend to be a *jeune fille*. . . . no American girl is a jeune fille; an American girl is an intelligent, reasonable creature' " (*CT* 4:369). James does not accept this self-congratulatory definition as uncritically as his heroine does, of course. On the other hand, he and Howells do agree with another James character (and with foreign commentators on America since colonial times)[103] that the " 'prime oddity of ours . . . [is] the liberty allowed to young girls' " (*CT* 3:158). The fact of liberty, and the consequent freedom to transform and even invert traditional roles, might make the American girl seem special. In fact, however, they make her representative. Conservative critics of the 1850s and '60s proclaim ceaselessly that things are topsyturvy: woman's desire for freedom means that the Venerable Mother is being replaced either by the coquette prone to free love or by the working woman inimical to housework. Mrs. Linton sees this inversion of roles as characteristic, moreover, of the fiction of the 1860s.

Our later novelists, however, have altered the whole setting of the palette. Instead of five foot ten of black and brown, they have gone in for four foot nothing of pink and yellow. Instead of tumbled masses of raven hair, they have shining coils of purest gold. Instead of hollow caverns whence flash unfathomable eyes eloquent of every damnable passion, they have limpid lakes of heavenly blue; and their worst sinners are in all respects fashioned as much after the outward semblance of the ideal saint as they have skill to design.

(1:49)

Such an inversion is not exceptional in American life. It is the way of things, as a foreign visitor in a James tale establishes in 1877.

"I have often noticed that contradiction in American ladies. You see a plump little woman, with a speaking eye and the contour and complexion of a ripe peach, and if you venture to conduct yourself in the smallest degree in accordance with these *indices*, you discover a species of Methodist—of what do you call it?—of Quakeress? On the other hand, you encounter a tall, lean, angular person, without color, without grace, all elbows and knees, and you find it's a nature of the tropics! The women of duty look like coquettes, and the others look like alpenstocks!"

(*CT* 4:385)

And so, as he makes a Europeanized American into the most subversive dandy of the century, Henry James makes the American girl not only the center of his fiction, but also the representative Victorian woman on both sides of the Atlantic. By putting his New World heroine in Old World situations, James can analyze extensively the experiences which popular fiction treated tentatively and obliquely. " 'Surely thoughts are free' "—the cry of beset womanhood in *East Lynne*—reverberates throughout James' work, for he concentrates upon that ordeal of consciousness which is the ultimate concern of serious feminists.

Although one type of heroine, like Amy or Laura, is happy to gain the requisite wisdom of the heart through the conventional medium of domestic labors, another type of heroine (often her author is orthodox in other matters) hungers to seek out knowledge more directly. Knowledge and freedom and the pride that makes women aspire to these male prerogatives are very much characteristic of Ellen in *The Wide, Wide World* and Edna in *St. Elmo.* When Ellen wishes she knew " 'a great many things . . . French, and Italian, and Latin, and music, and arithmetic, and chemistry . . . a great many things' " (146), her ambition is opposed by those who, like the appropriately named Miss Fortune, believe, " 'it doesn't do for women to be bookworms' " (146). (Art here is mirroring life with a vengeance, for Mary Somerville—world renowned for her *Mechanism of the Heavens*—"was once urged by her future sister-in-law to give up this 'foolish manner of life and studies and make a respectable and useful wife to her brother.' ")[104] Woman's aspirations are also criticized as prideful. For her determination to achieve eminence in scholarship, Edna is repeatedly told, " 'your pride is your only fault' " (*StE* 186). Although the pride that drives such young women does often need some moderating, popular authors clearly espouse their heroines' ambitions and clearly recognize the necessary relation of knowledge to freedom and proper pride.

Isabel Archer's quest differs from Edna's in one important respect, however. Isabel seeks *experiential* knowledge. We have seen James satirize the notion of her as a "prodigy of learning" (46), and he parodies the scribbling women in the persons of the American Corinne and of Lady Pensil, the dramatist. Isabel herself admits that she does not want to write books (47).[105] What she does want (despite her fears) is to know the great world. In this respect she resembles, not Edna, but another type of heroine—women like Emma Bovary (or Hildegarde in *The Initials*). Isabel thus combines two conventional but distinct heroine types. Like Emma Bovary in her direct experience of life's attractions and wile, Isabel resembles Edna in seeking out knowledge with a self-consciousness which Emma lacks. This mixture endows Isabel with a complex typicality that prompts our interest and sustains our sympathy. James thus achieves his dream of "a great American novel, in which the heroine might be infinitely realistic and yet neither a schoolmistress nor an outcast" (*PoP* 334). Schoolmistress and outcast: Edna and Emma. Isabel is neither and yet both.

This mixture of character types is symptomatic of the mixed nature of Isabel's quest.

> What was she going to do with herself [Ralph wonders]? This question was irregular, for with most women one had no occasion to ask it. Most women did with themselves nothing at all; they waited, in attitudes more or less gracefully passive, for a man to come that way and furnish them with a destiny. Isabel's originality was that she gave one the impression of having intentions of her own.
>
> (59)

What does Isabel intend to do? Daniel Touchett recognizes the inequity which feminists consider basic to Victorian life. " 'I have had very good opportunities—better than what a young lady would naturally have' " (52). Isabel, like most Victorian women and contrary to the charges of chauvinists, does not want to unsex herself. " 'I don't think I want to see it [life] as the young men want to see it. . . . I am not in the least an adventurous spirit. Women are not like men' " (139, 140). On the other hand, Isabel "gave an envious thought to the happier lot of men, who are always free to plunge into the healing waters of action" (355). Saying repeatedly that she does not wish to begin life by marrying, Isabel believes " 'there are other things a woman can do' " (139). But what? Daniel Touchett's legacy provides her with part of the answer. "To be rich was a virtue, because it was to be able to *do*, and to do was sweet. It was the contrary of weakness. To be weak was, for a young lady, rather graceful, but, after all, as Isabel said to herself, there was a larger grace than that" (195). What Isabel can do as an heiress is defined for her by Lydia Touchett. Having said earlier that " 'an unmarried woman—a girl of your age—is not independent. There are all sorts of things she can't do,' " Lydia now says, " 'you can do a great many things if you are rich. . . . You can go and come . . . I mean of course if you will take a companion' " (149, 203). So what does Isabel do? " 'I wander about as if the world belonged to me, simply because—because it has been put into my power to do so' " (284). Her wandering is largely directionless, her power largely powerless. Isabel may need a companion, a guide, but to what end? In *The Portrait*, as in most Victorian fiction, the relation of Heroine and Guide is crucial. How self-sufficient is the Victorian woman whom wealth and nationality free from superficial restraints? How free does this woman want to be? How free *can* she be? Isabel Archer displays both a tendency to rely upon herself and a need to trust more experienced heads. This mixture, like her mixture of types and the mixed nature of her quest, means that her need for guide figures is especially great. "Her thoughts," the narrator tells us, "were a tangle of vague outlines, which had never been corrected by the judgement of people who seemed to her to speak with authority" (47). Studying the guide figures who shape her courtship and marriage will provide another perspective on both the quality of Victorian life and the nature of Isabel's and James' commitment to form.

Many of fiction's most didactic moments concern the education of young women. America's first best-seller stated expressly

> [this little tale] may, I flatter myself, be of service to some who are so unfortunate as to have neither friends to advise, or understanding to direct them, through the various and unexpected evils that attend a young and unprotected woman in her first entrance into life.[106]

Nearly a century later Henry James makes inescapable his own Orphan-Heroine's place in the tradition of young women who need guidance. "Isabel waited, with a certain unuttered contentedness, to have her movements directed" (240). For all her brashness, Isabel fears, as she admits to Ralph, the poisoned cup of experience; she is seeking, like us all, for direction. Conventionally Heroines in this situation face one of two alternatives. Often, as in *The Guardian Angel* and *Le Roman*, the Heroine meets a highly qualified guide who preserves her virtue by word and interference. At the other melodramatic extreme is the vicious guide like Mrs. Jukes who advises, not what is best for the heroine, but what is most advantageous for some Byronic male. If this extreme is obviously too crude for *The Portrait*, The Allwise Guide is impossible for epistemological reasons. Truth is too precarious, and has to be rewon by each consciousness too often, for James to feel completely easy even with omniscient narrative, let alone with an omniscient mentor. (Parodying muscular Christianity, James introduces the Clerical Guide, only to dismiss this alternative irrevocably. "The Vicar of Lockleigh ... had been a mighty wrestler, and ... he was still, on occasion—in the privacy of the family circle as it were—quite capable of flooring his man. . . . her [Isabel's] imagination was a good deal taxed to think of him as a source of spiritual aid" [73].) James once again mixes conventions—providing his Orphan-Heroine with highly qualified guides, who all fail.

Closest to motherless Isabel should be her father. Mr. Archer, however, belongs to a long line of inadequate fathers which includes men who mean well but cannot control their daughters (Judge Merlin in *Ishmael*), men who substitute ironic commentary for proper attention (Mr. Bennet in *Pride and Prejudice*), and men who are actually cruel (Capt.

Montgomery in *The Wide, Wide World*). Although James' gentle, comic tone precludes any luridness, the case against Mr. Archer is made seriously, for crotchety Lydia Touchett is not the only character "taking him to task for the manner in which he brought up his three girls" (25). James adds the corroborating weight of "a few very harsh critics [who] went so far as to say that he had not even brought up his daughters. They had had no regular education" (31). Isabel's profligate father is, in fact, made to share responsibility for her romantic unworldliness. When she, like a good heroine, says, " 'I don't know anything about money,' " Lydia replies, " 'Yes, that's the way you were brought up—as if you were to inherit a million' " (26).

Lydia, in turn, seems the natural replacement for Mr. Archer once he (and the nearly perfect Guide Figure, Daniel Touchett) are dead. Lydia's counterpart in *Le Roman*, Baroness de Ferjeux, takes the guide role seriously. " 'Je protégerai l'innocence sacrifiée' " (27). Bringing Isabelle from the provinces to the *grand monde*, the Baroness " 'était ma providence, mon ange tutélaire, et se promettait de me servir de chaperon dans le monde' " (73). Lydia Touchett is not derelict in any simple sense. She remonstrates when Ralph and Warburton treat Isabel more freely than they would an English girl (62–63). On the other hand, Lydia errs at both extremes. Not only has she "fallen into gratuitous and exaggerated scruples" (128), but she chaperones her niece as she nurses her son—at her own convenience. "Mrs. Touchett now inclined to the belief that her niece should stand alone" (261), now being the very time that Isabel's inheritance makes her most prey to ravishers. Lydia even admits that refusing to " 'meddle' " in Isabel's marriage " 'was not considerate—it was convenient' " (309, 310).[107]

Instead of meddling, Lydia hands Isabel over to another guide, the all-knowing Madame Merle. Even to this obvious shirking of duty we can have no simple response, however. Ralph approves his mother's action. " 'Since you wish to see the world you couldn't have a better guide' " (233).[108] Where Madame Merle guides Isabel is, of course, to Osmond. Again our judgment is complicated, however, for we cannot simply pigeonhole Madame Merle as the Bad-Duenna type. When Countess Gemini's conversation becomes too intimate, Madame Merle silences her and sends Pansy away (250). We not only admire this conventional defense of innocence but presume that Madame Merle was doing the same for Isabel earlier when she removed the Countess physically by "passing her arm into the Countess Gemini's, as if to guide her course to the garden" (240). "As if," again. We do not know for many pages why Madame Merle keeps the Countess away from Isabel; and when we do finally learn, the extent of Madame Merle's failure as guide is qualified by her enormous loss as mother.

There are no "as if"s with Henrietta Stackpole. She is the quintessential Guide Figure. "Without parents and without property," Henrietta "had adopted three of the children of an infirm and widowed sister, and was paying their school-bills out of the proceeds of her literary labour" (49). Henrietta is, in fact, *too* conventional. Her melodramatic imagination and jingoistic espousal of Caspar prevent her from influencing Isabel much. Another woman is very influential, however.

> "When first I got an idea that my brother had designs upon you, I thought of writing you, to recommend you, in the strongest terms, not to listen to him. Then I thought it would be disloyal, and I hate anything of that kind. Besides, as I say, I was enchanted, for myself; and after all, I am very selfish."
>
> (329)

Countess Gemini resembles earlier duennas in James, for she, like Madame Grandoni and Madame Stramm (Nora's guide in Europe), has married a worthless European who abuses her. In turn, the difference between Countess Gemini and Madame Grandoni indicates how far James has come since *Roderick Hudson*. Now the guide fails to provide advice at the proper times, and eventually provides it less from concern for the innocent than from spite and the desire to shock and be important.

Isabel's peril should still not be extreme, however, for she has one last guide. In consigning Isabel to Madame Merle, Ralph has in fact placed her in Gilbert Osmond's hands. Osmond repays the favor by replacing Ralph as cicerone—guiding Isabel through his villa as Ralph had earlier done through the richer rooms of Gardencourt and the Florentine galleries. Isabel, who desires "to have her movements directed" (240), finds in Osmond "the kindest of *ciceroni*. . . . [He later] directed her steps into the garden" (243, 244). Conventionally the husband assumes the paternal responsibility of defending the woman against the world, so Isabel seems to have found the right man. As "her father had kept it [the disagreeable] away from her," Osmond has already vowed that " 'Pansy will never know any harm' " (31, 237). Isabel in more independent moments can claim that " 'I don't need the aid of a clever man to teach me how to live' " (146), but her more conservative side is impressed by Osmond's care of Pansy. " 'Papa left directions for everything' " (293).

James thus uses conventional Heroine-Guide relations for unconventional ends. The long list of derelict guides calls further into question the quality of Victorian life. What are we to think of a world which can produce only tyrannical guides like Gilbert Osmond or insufficient guides like Mr. Archer, Lydia Touchett, Madame Merle, Henrietta, Countess Gemini? We wonder, as we never do in popular fiction, whether society is any longer capable of its sacred responsibility to defend its most valuable, if headiest, innocents.[109] The buck cannot stop here, however. With his "imagination of disaster," James virtually assumes—and what an American assumption it is—that society will be inadequate. This assumption is the backdrop before which the drama of the "free" girl must be played out. We wonder less whether the free girl will fail than what she will do afterwards. Once she can answer the question " 'would you have listened to Ralph?' " with " 'not if he had abused Mr. Osmond' " (310), we must recognize that Isabel would not have heeded anyone's advice. Her headstrongness prompts what almost never befalls conventional Impulsive Heroines. An irrevocable act. Yet Isabel's willfulness does not justify our dismissing her as some critics have done. By establishing the inadequacy of her numerous guides and of her early training, James qualifies her failure and tempers our judgment. We forgo righteous severity and appreciate both the value of what is lost and the inevitability of that loss. In this unconventionally dark situation a new Guide enters in the second half of *The Portrait*. Isabel herself. Her attempt to provide Pansy with the Guide which she herself lacked is what allows us another perspective upon the nature of "form."

Critics have severely questioned Isabel's adequacy as Guide. To appreciate—intellectually, let alone emotionally—her predicament, we readers of the 1970s must recognize certain attitudes and pressures of the 1870s. We must confirm what reading Tennyson's "Isabel" seemed to indicate: that Isabel Archer is, despite her apparent emancipation, a representative Victorian woman—in ways which Victorian readers would have perceived immediately. H. E. Scudder, in fact, perceived it as soon as *The Portrait* appeared.

> Our admiration is increased when reflection shows that, individual as Isabel is in the painting, one may fairly take her as representative of womanly life today. The fine purpose of her freedom, the resolution with which she seeks to be the maker of her destiny, the subtle weakness into which all this betrays her, the apparent helplessness of her ultimate position, and the conjectured escape only through patient forebearance,—what are all these, if not attributes of womanly life expended under current conditions?
>
> (*AM* 1882, 126)

Modern critics have failed to appreciate Isabel's representative role because they have failed to understand the "current conditions" which James absorbed from his milieu and incorporated in his novel.

To appreciate these "conditions" and thus Isabel's role in *The Portrait*, let us begin with a basic fact. From girlhood a Victorian woman was lectured relentlessly about her inferiority, her genetic inferiority, to men. Early in *The Daughters of England*, Mrs. Ellis establishes the attitude essential for young females. "As women, then, the first thing of importance is to be content to be inferior to men" (5). When the young woman reaches marriageable age, Mrs. Ellis' next installment is ready, but the message in *The Wives of England* has not changed. "One important truth sufficiently impressed upon your mind will materially assist in this desirable consummation—it is the superiority of your husband, simply as a man" (10). And concerning marriage itself, Mrs. Ellis, good Christian that she is, could hardly speak in stronger terms. "The wife should endeavor, before every other earthly thing, and next to the salvation of her soul, to obtain and keep her husband's confidence" (38).

By the 1870s there is, of course, some increase in woman's freedom. Young ladies are now enjoying more strenuous physical exercise and, according to one magazine, "archery delights many."[110] Moreover, "a coaching revival comes" in 1871; *The Graphic* defines "the fashionable beauty," as "a huntress . . . she drives a pair of horses like a charioteer."[111] As a fashionable beauty of Diana's company, Miss Archer

> drove over the country in a phaeton. . . . Isabel enjoyed it largely, and, handling the reins in a manner which approved itself to the groom as "knowing," was never weary of driving her uncle's capital horses through winding lanes and by-ways.
>
> (60)

In light of such increased freedom, Irene Clephane goes on to ask the crucial question, "What, then, remained of the mid-Victorian rigidities?" Answer: "the girl of the 'seventies kept to fundamental taboos. . . . union at the altar must be regarded as unbreakable, whatever the unhappiness it brought" (4). We can hardly overestimate the pressures on a Victorian woman. As late as 1857, for instance, "reformers" were petitioning Parliament to institute the death penalty for adultery. Until 1873 English law denied even the possibility of a wife's gaining custody of children over three years old. In America in the 1870s, reaction to the Woodhull affair helped generate a climate of opinion characterized by "Comstockery." The Comstock Act itself extended the term "obscene" to books with pages on birth control. "Purity authors had begun to monopolize marriage manuals and extolled frigidity in the female 'as a virtue to be cultivated, and sexual coldness as a condition to be desired.' "[112] The general atmosphere was so hostile that it "literally destroyed the possibility that feminism would be able to generate a body of theory adequate to its later needs."[113] Nor did things improve much in the '80s. When prostitution in England was made illegal in 1885, for example, no penalty was included for being a procurer. Even in the 1890s there were fewer than six hundred divorces a year in all of England.

As an American with a particularly free-form upbringing, Isabel Archer has managed to avoid some mid-Victorian rigidities. Linked by her carriage passion to the freest decent element of the 1860s and '70s, she indicates how free a Victorian lady can be who is not a "blue" or a "Modern Man Hater" and does not want to join the "Shrieking Sisterhood." Her very role as Victorian wife, however, shows Isabel to her horror that she must either forgo her essential identity or else "assail this grey preëminence of man."[114] With all her freedom Isabel thus functions particularly well to indicate where woman's freedoms end. To evaluate Isabel's conduct with her husband, we must recognize how expressly James is presenting her marriage as a paradigm of Victorian woman's situation. Let us begin with this passage:

> [1] Her mind was to be his—attached to his own like a small garden-plot to a deer-park. [2] He would rake the soil gently and water the flowers; he would weed the beds and gather an occasional nosegay. [3] It would be a pretty piece of property for a proprietor already far-reaching. [4] He didn't wish her to be stupid. [5] On the contrary, it was because she was clever that she had pleased him. [6] But he expected her intelligence to operate altogether in his favor, and so far from desiring her mind to be a blank, he flattered himself that it would be richly receptive. [7] He had expected his wife to feel with him and for him, to enter into his opinions, his ambitions, his preferences; and Isabel was obliged to confess that this was no very unwarrantable demand on the part of a husband. [8] But there were certain things she could never take in. [9] To begin with, they were hideously unclean. . . . [10] that she should turn the hot light of her disdain upon his own conception of things—this was a danger he had not allowed for.
>
> (398–99)

First, compare James' sentences 4 through 7 with the following.

> It should not be necessary for her to *talk much*. . . . An attentive listener is generally all that he requires; but in order to listen attentively, and with real interest, it is highly important that we should have considerable understanding of the subject discussed.
>
> Men do not care for brains in excess in women. They like a sympathetic intellect which can follow and seize their thoughts as quickly as they are uttered. . . . Neither do they want anything very strong-minded. . . . it is companionship, not rivalry, still less supremacy, that they like in women.
>
> "My wife should have talent enough to be able to understand and value mine, but not sufficient to be able to shine herself. . . . I want feeling, affection, devotion myself—a domestic woman, who would think my approbation sufficient for her happiness."

These three passages were written almost exactly a quarter-century apart—1842, 1868, 1893. As the work of Mrs. Ellis, Mrs. Linton, and Ann S. Stephens,[115] they voice orthodoxy's attitude toward the female mind. The similarity of the three passages indicates how little the orthodox attitude changed over Victoria's long reign; the similarity with James' passage suggests how paradigmatic a Victorian woman Isabel Archer is. Her admission that Osmond's orthodox demands are "not very unwarrantable" presages her later assertion that "when one had to choose, one chose as a matter of course for one's husband" (498). In fact, one of the most touching aspects of the Woman Question is how little freedom most women actually seek. Mary Wollstonecraft, for example, is no less radical because she says, "the conclusion which I wish to draw is obvious; make women rational creatures, and free citizens, and they will quickly become good wives and mothers."[116] Wollstonecraft's commitment to the rights of exceptional women does not prevent her from seconding what would be orthodoxy's basic ideal. "I consider that women in the common walks of life are called to fulfil the duties of wives and mothers" (68). Much of her critique is, in fact, directed against women who violate the traditional domestic ideal.

> Cold would be the heart of a husband . . . who did not feel more delight at seeing his child suckled by its mother than the most artful wanton tricks could ever raise. . . . I have then viewed with pleasure a woman nursing her children, and discharging the duties of her station. . . . Her paternal affection, indeed, scarcely deserves the name, when it does not lead her to suckle her children.
>
>   (65, 66, 72)

Forty years later, Caroline Norton succeeds in changing the very law of England so that divorced mothers can qualify for custody of their infant children. Yet so ready is Mrs. Norton to accept woman's basic lot, so chary is she of altering the basic marital situation, that she defends herself from John Mitchell Kemble's hysterical attack by saying that "She had not written any . . . work advocating sexual equality. She insisted that her pamphlet . . . and her novel *The Wife* contained nothing whatever subversive to the doctrine of female subordination."[117] Finally, at the end of the 1860s, John Mill's passionate defense of woman's equality includes the generalization that

> when a woman marries, it may in general be understood that she makes choice of the management of a household, and the bringing up of a family, as the first call upon her exertions, during as many years of her life as may be required for the purpose.[118]

Isabel Archer is no crusader. Her admission that " 'if I were afraid of my husband, that would be simply my duty. That is what women are expected to be' " (464)[119] clearly echoes the conservative attitudes in the Ellis-Linton-Stephens passages. But the Norton-Stone-Mill passages indicate how strongly the conservative instinct for traditional domestic arrangements remains in even crusading feminists. For most nineteenth-century women, as for Isabel Archer, the question is not whether they might become radical "new women," but whether they can accommodate their desire for orthodox marriage with their need for the minimal freedom necessary for an individual identity.

Isabel's dilemma becomes more complicated and still more representative when we compare sentences 1–3 and 8–10 with

> her mind was beside his as the vase of cut flowers by the side of the rugged tree. . . . but . . . on all points which touched the heart he looked up to her as infallible and inspired.

Kingsley here in *Yeast*[120] and James with his garden-plot metaphor are, like Tennyson in "Isabel," using plant images to depict sexual relationships. James' metaphor differs from the others in important ways, however. Osmond's raking and watering are more starkly (even sadistically) chauvinistic than either Kingsley's vase and trunk or Tennyson's stem and fruit. Tennyson, as we saw, was ready—after establishing Woman as "parasite"—to grant her efficacy, to credit her with "up-bearing" the Male. Kingsley is still more orthodox in making woman a ruler as well as a subject. Gilbert Osmond, however, refuses to acknowledge here or anywhere in *The Portrait* that transfer of authority, that hegemony of the female heart, which Kingsley includes with his image and which most Victorians paid enthusiastic lip service to. Kingsley's recognition of woman's moral superiority is as conventional as his assertion of man's mental superiority. Mrs. Ellis says,

> [A wife should seek] that cultivation and exercise of the conversational powers which is most conducive to social enjoyment, and most productive of beneficial influence. . . . [woman's mind is good] only as a means of doing greater homage to her husband, and bringing greater ability to bear upon the advancement of his intellectual and moral good.
>
> (*Women*, 45; *Wives*, 36–37)

Now Gilbert Osmond is clearly one with Mrs. Ellis and orthodoxy in desiring an intelligent and agreeable wife. Yet just as clearly Osmond refuses to accept what Mrs. Ellis and Charles Kingsley consider the other side of the coin. Woman's heart corrects man's head. When Isabel practices this moral criticism, Osmond draws back offended. His very manhood is threatened, for, as James has already established, the desire to make a perfect wife presupposes the fact of phallic hegemony.

If, however, she were only wilful and high-tempered, the defect
might be managed with comparative ease; for had one not a will of
one's own that one had been keeping for years in the best condition—
as pure and keen [NB] as a sword protected by its sheath?

(281)

The sadism here becomes actual on the very page of our ten-sentence
passage.

She had pleaded the cause of freedom . . . of quite another ideal. Then
it was that her husband's personality, touched as it had never been,
stepped forth and stood erect. . . . It was her scorn of his assumptions
—it was that that made him draw himself up.

(398, 399)

Failure to educate a perfect wife results in that threat to Paternal
Authority which ultimately constitutes a threat to malehood itself.
Countess Gemini recognizes (if unconsciously) the situation when she
contemplates Isabel asserting herself against Osmond. "It seemed to her
that if Isabel should draw herself up she would be the taller spirit of the
two. What she wanted to learn now was whether Isabel had drawn
herself up; it would give her [the Countess] immense pleasure to see
Osmond overtopped. . . . if she had wished to see Osmond overtopped,
the conditions looked favorable now" (414, 498). The real issue in our
passage from *The Portrait* is that male hegemony which determines
woman's restricted status in "Isabel" and *The Princess* and which surfaces
repeatedly in the chauvinistic passages of *Yeast*. Ultimately the point is
not that Tennyson and Kingsley revere what Osmond contemns, but that
he makes express what they cloak in conventional images and sentiments. Osmond's sadistic sexuality is the inevitable manifestation of a
Paternal Ideal which Tennyson and Kingsley and most Victorian males—
for all their protestations about woman's moral superiority—are committed to deeply. In Gilbert Osmond, James portrays The Man of the
Period who feels offended at and threatened by woman's self-assertion.
The Victorian Male wants power without chastening, he wants the *utile*
without the *dulce*.

How we react to his wants depends significantly upon James' technique
here. Rather than resort to express statement, James uses conventional
materials which encourage conventional expectations. Knowing the
orthodox relation of large and small plants, of head and heart, Victorian
readers of sentences 1–8 would have approved of Osmond's intellectual
hegemony. Isabel's moral reactions in sentence 9 would then have
signaled that the second half of the head-heart interaction was underway,
right on schedule. But that Osmond rejects his wife's admonitions, that
he refuses to be chastened and improved—James needs no express
statement to indicate the impropriety of such conduct. The breaking of a

traditional pattern, the thwarting of a conventional expectation, makes our reading experience active. Our need to discover what went wrong with the pattern helps us to recognize what has gone wrong with Isabel's marriage and, by implication, with Victorian marriage generally. Isabel's orthodox submission to man's mind has not earned her orthodox moral freedom. Her outrage comes not only from the uncleanness of Osmond's ideas but from his refusal to acknowledge either her right to judge or the worth of her judgments. Gilbert Osmond is thus hoist on his own orthodoxy. The very code which he enforces against Isabel's intellectual freedom proceeds to convict him for denying her moral freedom. In turn, orthodoxy is hoist too. Mrs. Ellis can maintain that "the most delightful [women] . . . point the plainest moral" (*Women* 11), but this maxim presumes what is unlikely—that males who are pampered intellectually will tolerate a sudden reining in, a sudden accusation of inadequacy. J. S. Mill speaks for many feminists and for many orthodox but suffering wives when he notes that

> the almost unlimited power which present social institutions give to the man over at least one human being . . . offers to him a license for indulgence of those points of his original character which in all other relations he would have found it necessary to repress and conceal.
>
> (166)

Even Coventry Patmore will admit

> For what man ever yet had grace
> Ne'er to abuse his power and place?

Now such honesty Patmore will not sustain, of course.

> And, though in time he'll treat you worse,
> He'll love you more, you need not doubt.[121]

But the real situation is "as a fashionable physician of the day so neatly put it to the mother of an engaged daughter: 'Tell her nothing, my dear madam, for if they knew they would not marry.' "[122] Without mounting a soapbox or waving a placard, Henry James makes us experience what honest Victorians knew—that the ideal of Victorian marriage, the dream of reciprocal mastery, was culpably remote from the social reality.

To her horror, Isabel thus discovers what Victorian orthodoxy denied —fundamental opposition between the supposedly complementary head and heart of the marital union. "It was a strange opposition, of the like of which she had never dreamed—an opposition in which the vital principle of the one was a thing of contempt for the other" (391). In revealing this untoward opposition of head and heart, James is not only dissecting Victorian life; he is also practicing one of his basic methods of social commentary throughout *The Portrait*. What orthodoxy proclaimed as complementary, James shows at least potentially opposed. (He also comments by the opposite technique. What orthodoxy separated as polar, James shows essentially intermixed. Besides mixing the supposedly polar roles of Dandy and Father in Gilbert Osmond, James questions another orthodox polarity with Isabel. "Women were classified into polar extremes. They were either sexless ministering angels or sensuously oversexed temptresses."[123] Yet the Isabel who ministers angelically to Ralph Touchett can respond to the passionate kiss of Another Man and can inflict pain upon her husband quite vampishly, as we will see.) Showing opposition where orthodoxy proclaimed compatibility, James goes beyond the head-heart split and explores two supposedly complementary roles. Catharine Sedgwick says in *The Linwoods*, "All a woman need know is how to take good care of her family and of the sick."[124] Not only is Isabel Archer forced to choose between family and nursing, but James prepares us early in *The Portrait* for such an unconventional split. When Ralph says, " 'you ought to be a good nurse,' " Isabel admits, " 'I don't think I am. . . . I am said to be too theoretic' " (44). Isabel is clearly the Heroine type, and Heroines are unquestionably Good Nurses; yet Isabel is not.

To indicate how serious the fissures in Victorian monolithic homelife are, James even questions the compatibility of two roles conventionally considered so homogeneous that they were often hyphenated. Wife-Mother. The effect of Isabel being a *step*mother begins to be clear when we understand what being a Step-Mother involved. In this role the Victorians did, of course, allow for tension. Since the Step-Mother's bond was only to the Husband, she was often cruel to his children. The solution:

> "The character of the *step-mother* (in general deemed an odious one) I will allow to be the most difficult to fill of any allotted to our sex," admitted Caroline Wentworth [in *The Step-Mother*]. By devoted care of the children of her husband's first marriage, Mrs. Wentworth's conduct proved that even the dangers of this difficult office might be overcome by tact and sympathy.
>
> (Brown, 152)

Easy enough. Just treat his children nicely, and all will be perfect. That the Step-Mother's role could actually be excruciatingly self-dividing— that her special commitment to the Husband and the children's special relation to the Father could in fact make this role *the* paradigm of Victorian woman's plight—James begins to establish when Pansy says, " 'You will be my stepmother. . . . They are always said to be cruel; I think you will never be cruel' " (328).[125] Accusations of cruelty are soon in the air, however.

When Pansy kissed him [Osmond], before going to bed, he returned her embrace with even more than his usual munificence, and Isabel wondered whether he meant it as a hint that his daughter had been injured by the machinations of her stepmother.

(443)

Since the point of view is not omniscient and since Isabel at best *wonders* whether a *hint* is meant, James avoids any luridness. Are accusations in the air because Isabel has an uneasy conscience or because Osmond is legitimately angry or because one or both of them is giving way to histrionic tendencies? For certain some critics find Isabel quite a Wicked Step-Mother. Before we examine the evidence against her, we should note how James keeps open the alternative possibility—that Isabel may be the Kind Step-Mother whom Pansy anticipates.

Isabel is contrasted with another woman whom Osmond has procured as Pansy's stepmother. Mother Catherine belongs to the legion of females, clerical and otherwise, who do the Byronic man's bidding. After Pansy in her first scene calls each nun " 'Mamman,' " and after the narrator refers expressly to "Mother Catherine" (215), a contrast between clerical- and step-mothers is established.

"Perhaps some day," added Madame Merle, "you will have another mother."
"I don't think that is necessary," Pansy said.... "I have had more than thirty mothers at the convent."

(218)[126]

To make convincing the threat to Pansy and the contrast with Isabel, James avoids luridness determinedly. He makes his heroine—whose congenital tendency to melodrama is, in this case, exacerbated by her Protestant background—admit twice (505, 510) that the convent is a clean well-lighted place, without thumbscrews or racks. Also Mother Catherine disagrees with Osmond about Pansy's returning to the convent. These and other complications allow James, in turn, to encourage our conventional distrust of convents and their keepers. Isabel finds the place a "prison" (505). Mother Catherine resembles Madame Merle,[127] " 'has a most coquettish little toilet-table' " (507), and speaks with "the authority of the church" (510). James' point is not that Mother Catherine is actually villainous or even that her institution is necessarily harmful; Catherine does, however, embody an alternative which is cruel for Pansy. Thus Isabel profits by the contrast. If anyone is to be the Kind Step-Mother, it must be she. Her success at replacing Catherine seems confirmed later when Pansy and Warburton cast her in the most benign of Romish roles—"Madonna" and " 'guardian angel' " (433, 442). But is she?

Guardian Angel and Step-Mother: duty to the child and duty to the husband. This tension is endemic to Victorian family life, despite orthodoxy's pretensions. Reconciling her two roles becomes most difficult for Isabel when Warburton arrives to court Pansy. To judge Isabel's conduct fairly, neither to white-wash her nor to ignore the pressures of 1870, we must accept as our premise the immense authority of the Victorian husband's will. Isabel clearly draws back from the sordidness which Mrs. Ellis condemns:

> We have all heard of such a thing—perhaps some of us have seen it—as a mother making a party with her children to oppose the wishes or authority of their father.
>
> (*Mothers*, 79)

Isabel has, in fact, come already to a recognition which is straight out of Mrs. Ellis.

> If she had not deceived him in intention she understood how completely she must have done so in fact.
>
> (*PL* 392–93)
>
> At the same time that you have been deceived, it is more than probable that you have been deceiving.
>
> (*Wives*, 7)

Especially after disappointing Osmond so often, Isabel is understandably intent upon pleasing him about Pansy's marriage. Critics sentimentally ignore Victorian psychology when they expect Mrs. Osmond to second Pansy's choice of Ned simply because Miss Archer had always proclaimed her own freedom.[128] If Pansy's feelings could change, and if her father's candidate could love her in return, then the marriage to Warburton would not be monstrous. Neither Isabel *nor the reader* can know with certainty beforehand that these two conditions are impossible. Only after discovering Warburton's real love does Isabel meet again with Pansy and find that the Wife-Mother roles can no longer be reconciled.

To maintain the husband's confidence is, we saw, woman's highest earthly duty; yet Mrs. Ellis, following Rousseau, Maria Edgeworth, and many other authorities, also maintains that counseling the Ignorant Innocent is woman's special province (*Mothers* 15). When Isabel attempts to avoid a complete break between Wife and Mother by answering Pansy's plea for advice with " 'that's for your father; you must get his advice,' " Pansy responds right out of Mrs. Ellis. " 'A lady can advise a young girl better than a man.' " When Isabel then replies, " 'I advise you, then, to pay the greatest respect to your father's wishes' " (432), how are we to react?

James says expressly that Isabel is arguing "hypocritically.... pusillanimously" (433). He will not let us simplify her conduct. Throughout the novel Isabel's conservative instincts have prompted sententia as righteous and cold as Osmond's own.

"Be a good child . . . give pleasure to your father. . . . you are right to obey . . . . I hope it may never be my fortune to fail to gratify my husband's [taste]. . . . I would rather hear nothing that Pansy may not."

(293, 294, 319, 329)

In her scene with Pansy, Isabel is torn by contrary emotions of heart-felt affection and wifely obedience—emotions reflected in James' expression "said the Madonna, with unusual frigidity" (433). Countered at every turn by Pansy's arguments, Isabel finds herself in a struggle which she does not really want to win and yet cannot simply concede. As a woman horribly divided, she embodies the anguish of the Victorian Mother-Wife.

Isabel was grateful for the dimness of the room; she felt as if her face were hideously insincere. She was doing this for Osmond; this was what one had to do for Osmond! . . . it still clung to her that she must be loyal to Osmond, that she was on her honour in dealing with his daughter.

(433, 435)

His daughter. Isabel's stepmotherhood is emblematic of how completely *his* the Victorian children are in times of parental disagreement, let alone legally. As J. S. Mill observes,

They are by law *his* children. He alone has any legal rights over them. Not one act can she do towards them or in relation to them, except by delegation from him. Even after he is dead she is not their legal guardian, unless he by will has made her so.

(160; Mill's italics)

When Isabel attempts to follow *his* directive instead of responding with the effortless self-sacrifice which stage Mothers display (and which some critics seem to expect), she is revealing the reality of Victorian marriage. Only if James makes us feel the husband's immense authority can Isabel's final choice of Mother over Wife be fully convincing and admirable.

For Isabel does, finally, refuse to encourage Warburton's suit. Even when he comes to say good-bye, the right word from her would make him stay. Wife would triumph over Mother. Isabel's own farewell from Pansy dramatizes, in turn, her choice of Mother over Wife. As Pansy kneels to Isabel, we witness no simple tableau, but rather a complicating mixture of conventional scenes. When the child kneels to the Mother, it is traditionally for help and consolation; when the child kneels before the Step-Mother, it is usually in fear or remonstrance. And Pansy?

"Ah, Mrs. Osmond you won't leave me!" . . .
"I won't desert you," she said at last. "Good-bye, my child."

(513)

From "his daughter" to " 'my child', " from Step-Mother to True Mother. The effect of Isabel choosing *caritas* over the old-school ideal of submission appears dramatically. "Isabel descended, and when she reached the bottom the girl was standing above" (513). This scene clearly echoes Isabel's earlier image of *Osmond* looking down upon her from above. Disobeying her husband has thus not freed Isabel from over-towering tyranny; it has only handed her over to another tyrant. Love in each case imposes its heavy commitment.

Accepting this second commitment does not mean that Isabel fits, at last, into a single, conventional role. In the inevitable revelation scene, Countess Gemini expects Isabel to be the Deceived Wife and rave against the Other Woman. But Isabel pities Madame Merle. When the Countess says, " 'you don't take it as I should have thought' " (504), Isabel is feeling less that she has been used than that Madame Merle is a mother who has lost her child. James escapes the maudlin here by once again superimposing conventional scenes: between the Outraged Wife and the Commiserating Mother operates a tension which makes Countess Gemini realize, " 'I have made you ill' " (505).

Isabel's unconventional complexity of insight also transforms other aspects of the traditional Mother role. As interpreter of signs, for example, she seems as orthodox as Mrs. Montgomery of *The Wide, Wide World* when she "read[s] the meaning of" Pansy's blushes (512). Isabel has also been able to interpret properly other conventional situations.

His [Ned's] manner and appearance had not the dignity of the deepest tragedy. . . . But she suddenly felt touched; her own unhappiness, after all, had something in common with his, and it came over her, more than before, that here, in recognizable, if not in romantic form, was the most affecting thing in the world—young love struggling with adversity.

(403)

Unlike Osmond whose cosmopolitanism makes him treat young love cynically, and unlike Madame Merle, who " 'always see[s] too much in everything' " (483), Isabel can now appreciate what is simple. She is not attempting to make Ned and Pansy into more than they are (as she once did with the Misses Molyneaux, and with Gilbert Osmond). "She now perceived that Pansy's ambiguities were simply her own grossness of vision" (374). When Bantling touchingly describes Ralph's deathbed situation, Isabel can transcend the social whirl and recognize the timeless fact of suffering. "Even in the crowded, noisy station this simple picture was vivid" (519). On the other hand, Isabel's insights have by no means become reductively conventional.

> Mrs. Touchett of course followed the tradition that ladies, even married ones, regard the marriage of their old lovers as an offence to themselves. Isabel's first care therefore was to show that however that might be in general, she was not offended now. But meanwhile, as I say, her heart beat faster; and if she sat for some moments thoughtful . . . it was not because she had lost an admirer. Her imagination had traversed half Europe; it halted, panting, and even trembling a little, in the city of Rome. She figured herself announcing to her husband that Lord Warburton was to lead a bride to the altar, and she was of course not aware how extremely sad she looked while she made this intellectual effort.
>
> (527)

Warburton has, in fact, prompted intricate reactions from Isabel ever since he reappeared as Pansy's suitor.

> "How much you [Osmond] must wish to capture him." . . . a momentary exultation took possession of her—a horrible delight in having wounded him; for his face instantly told her that none of the force of her exclamation was lost. Osmond expressed nothing otherwise, however; he only said, quickly, "Yes, I wish it very much."
>
> (437)

Surely Isabel is experiencing here emotions not acknowledged in *The Wives of England*. Her delight in hurting Osmond (like her response to Caspar's kiss later) complicates the orthodox polarity of angel and vamp. Moreover, Isabel feels special delight here with Osmond because she knows—having already talked with Ralph—that Warburton loves *her*. Her responses to Warburton are, in turn, more ambivalent than Mrs. Ellis would allow.

> [Isabel] "But he is really in love?"
> [Ralph] "Very much, I think. I can make that out."
> "Ah!" said Isabel, with a certain dryness.
>
> (427)

Thinking Ralph means that Warburton loves Pansy, Isabel has apparently succeeded, like a good wife, in satisfying Osmond's wishes. Why then the dryness? Is she disappointed because her husband has prospered at the expense of her daughter, or because her long-time suitor has at last got over her? Is the Wife role incompatible not only with Mother but also with Heroine? Ralph confirms the oddness of her " 'Ah' " when he replies, " 'you said that as if you were disappointed.' " And so, when Isabel, on page 527, thinks again of Lord Warburton, her reaction is prompted by much that is complex both in their long relationship and in her various roles. Returning mentally to Rome, Isabel reenacts her earlier, ecstatic vision of Italy. Not necessarily jealous in any conventional sense, she feels nonetheless a sorrow related to her fateful dismissal of her British suitor. She may not long to marry him now, and may not even regret her earlier refusal; but surely her sadness is prompted by more than fear of Osmond. In Warburton's marriage Isabel sees how far she has come from the days of the ceremony of innocence, when she could dismiss a peer and dream of Italy.

We come again to Isabel's final rejection of Caspar and final affirmation of form. Isabel returns to her husband and suffers, but she is no more the Long-Suffering Wife than she was, in any simple sense, a Step-Mother. Like many beset heroines Isabel chooses the "straight" path,[129] but unlike them her path is not without deviousness. Isabel, in serving Pansy, is serving herself. Doing her duty in this case allows Isabel, like Ellen in *The Wide, Wide World*, to have her woodcocks and eat them too. Henry James, unlike Susan Warner, expects us to see how complex the motivation is. Recognizing with Caspar's kiss her potential for passionate sexuality, Isabel controls that dangerous impulse by returning to a marriage forever dead to passion. Her reaffirmation of marriage cannot, then, be seen simply as the triumph of duty over the powers of sexuality; doing what society advocates allows Isabel to repress what she (and society) fear. The very convenience of this act, its inevitable self-service, is what assures Isabel permanent ambivalence. In the years to come, she will be Wife-Mother, and yet more, and less.

Ambivalence, on the other hand, does not deny stature to Isabel. By precluding facile heroics, James makes possible a genuine, if moderated, heroism. He precludes not only Long-Suffering Wife, but also Christian Martyr. No religious sanction, no pious unction, lubricates the gears of suffering and the eyes of the reader. In *The Portrait*, we find not the religious apotheosis of *Ruth* but the wearing grind of secular nada. The very absence of heavenly reward is, in fact, what gives dignity and pathos to Isabel's continued commitment to the conventional virtues of patience and service. Mrs. Linton's definition of what "is essentially a mother—that is, a woman who can forget herself" (1:310), sounds simple-minded because Mrs. Linton does not sustain the possibility that diverse and even subversive impulses might contribute to the self-forgetful state. The issue is not whether we disagree with orthodox ideals; we simply cannot experience those ideals as simplistically as orthodoxy requires. Henry James, on the other hand, can write a story about a wife who flees from a cruel husband to nurse a young man dying across the Alps—and completely approve of this conduct in "At Isela" (1871). Having his heroine in *The Portrait* return to her husband is not a failure of nerve or a retreat into orthodoxy because James insists simultaneously upon the convenience of submission and upon the enormity of Victorian family life. He indicates the pain and degradation which Victorian wives suffer from male power drives even as he reveals that these wives can feel delight in their husband's disappointments and can feel sexual passion for other men. In all, Isabel, by conforming to and yet differing from society's ideal, compares favorably with society—with promiscuous Countess Gemini, dry Lydia Touchett, simple Henrietta, polished Madame Merle. In such a setting, Isabel stands out, not as ideal perfection, but as distinctly preferable to anyone else in her glittering wasteland. Sustaining simultaneously the traditional role and its denial, she achieves Madame Merle's synthesis while avoiding her duplicity, and thus achieves what mystery is for Henry James. " 'I knew she could play any part.... I didn't understand that she would play two at the same time' " (310).

Thus, with characterization, as with style, James makes us experience that coalescence of opposites which is his ideal of form. Compare his metaphor about form and content in style—"the flesh is indetachable from the bones"—with his belief that a human relationship involves "the *form* ... that clothes the naked fact."[130] As an idea becomes fully significant only when it achieves that stylistic form which is its specific articulation, so characters remain mere naked facts until they enter upon that form which is a relationship. Style redeems the overly general; a relationship redeems the atomized character. Style introduces those qualifications and contradictions which allow an idea to apply to a human condition and reader; a formal relation provides the character with expectations and standards and responsibilities and possibilities which then help define what he is and is not. Thus, in characterization, as in style, *form* provides that otherness, that qualification, which adapts the idea or the individual to our human condition. When Gilbert Osmond says, " 'a woman's natural mission is to be where she is most appreciated,' " Isabel replies, " 'the point is to find out where that is' " (244). Where that is, according to James, is a relationship, a meaningful form. When Isabel opts for "form," she is thus affirming more than marriage in its sacramental sense. She is manifesting the worth of conventional roles as forms. To appreciate her action fully, we must see Isabel's final scene with Caspar in light of her book-long relations with her guide figures. Specifically we must recognize that the last sixty pages of *The Portrait* present Isabel's last meetings with each of her major guides. In each scene a character tries to reduce the moment to melodrama, and in each scene Isabel eventually escapes from a conventional role and proceeds on to the next guide. We have already seen, for example, that Osmond as the Outraged Husband tries to force Isabel into the role of either Adulteress or Obedient Wife; leaving *him* ossified in a conventional role, Isabel goes on to Countess Gemini, who tries to cast her as Outraged Wife. We have also seen how, in her scene with Ralph, Isabel is the one who oversimplifies—" 'This is not death, dear Ralph.' 'Not for you—no' " (530)—and must be brought beyond conventional attitudes to a profounder awareness of human union and love. Despite her development through these scenes, Isabel has not achieved full adulthood, even with Ralph. Her cry " 'Ah, my brother!' " (532) indicates how much openness she has achieved with a male, but it also indicates that she has not gone beyond a brother-sister relation. A scene with Caspar is inevitable. How much Isabel still has to learn when she comes to England is evident as she confronts—before Ralph or Caspar— another of her guides. "Then Isabel stood there in the crowd, looking about her. . . . She had a sudden perception that she should be helped" (517). And Henrietta appears, with Bantling. Importantly here, the one whom Isabel depends upon chiefly is the stalwart male. "Her eyes rested on [Bantling]. . . . it was not in the power of the multitude that pressed about him to make him yield an inch of the ground he had taken. . . . [she remained] looking at Mr. Bantling, whom she had never thought so interesting" (518). Waiting, as she did with Osmond, to have her movements directed, Isabel says to Bantling and Henrietta, " 'I will do whatever you wish' " (520).

After Ralph's death, Isabel still needs help. To be her guide is exactly what Caspar proposes. " 'I can help you. . . . trust me. . . . [Ralph] left you . . . to my care' " (541). Clearly Caspar is converting the moment into the conventional melodrama situation of Dominant Male protecting Helpless Female. Although Isabel's conservative instincts crave such protection, James prevents us from sharing her inclination, for he uses against Caspar the conventions which Caspar tries to use with Isabel. Caspar's subsequent " 'trust me. . . . trust me. . . . trust me' " (543) echo down to us from a thousand melodramas. The words are traditionally the Seducer's, however. " 'Let me help you. . . . If you will trust me, I will do my very best for you. I will give you my best advice. . . . What I advise is this. Come with me into this little inn.' " Speaking here for all Seducers is Bellingham in *Ruth* (41, 57), a novel which not only presents the heroine tempted to carnality but also surrounds her with numerous inadequate guides. To further undermine Caspar, James also enlists the literary tradition through direct allusion. Caspar's Miltonic " 'the world is all before us' " echoes, as critics have noted, Isabel's earlier use of the line and functions to place Caspar at a stage of naive romanticism which Isabel has long since moved beyond. Caspar also says, " 'we can do absolutely as we please' " (543). Not only does this sentence glitter with the hyperbole which we have seen Isabel weaned from (and which Caspar remains committed to throughout the scene—" 'I see the whole thing. . . . it's so easy. . . . you have nothing to consider' " [542, 543]). Caspar's sentence also calls down upon him the immense moral force of James' favorite Victorian sage, Matthew Arnold. "Doing as One Likes" is caustically examined not only in *Culture and Anarchy* but throughout *The Portrait of a Lady*. " 'Doing what you like' " (285) is what Osmond once called " 'triumphant' " and what Isabel, even then, could see through. " 'To triumph, then, it seems to me, is to fail! Doing what we like is often very tiresome' " (286). Another spokesman for absolute self-fulness is Osmond's sister. " 'I understand still less why you shouldn't do as you like' " (499). And so, when Caspar Goodwood shares with Countess Gemini not only the initials CG but also the simplistic ethic of absolute self-fulness, the Arnoldian echo warns us of their limitations.

We need the warning, for Caspar's proposal is trickier than it looks. His appeal is twofold: to Isabel's conservative need for protection, and to that passion which she has always believed herself capable of and which she feels unmistakably with Caspar's lightning kiss. What makes this twofold appeal tricky is not its dual nature as such (security and passion seem in fact an apparently ideal blend), but the fact that the two appeals are in this case incompatible. While Caspar is ostensibly offering to lead Isabel forward into a new reality of passional intimacy, he is in fact leading her back into the old world of stage roles and words. Caspar is finally much more like Osmond than he or anti-Isabelite critics want to imagine. While Caspar is advocating the unhallowed act of adultery, he is engaged in that stereotyping and that moral simplification which characterize both melodrama *and* orthodoxy's attitude toward sexual relations. He cannot see Isabel except in stereotypic terms—" 'I swear, as I stand here, that a woman deliberately made to suffer is justified in anything in life—in going down into the streets, if that will help her!' " (543)—and thus he cannot lead her out of Osmond's old world of stage roles. And of words. We must remember that Caspar, for all his plain-style directness, has ever been a man associated with words. Whereas Isabel rejoices because she finds in Florence realities "which had hitherto been great names to her" (228), Caspar during one proposal scene looks not up at Isabel but down into his hat, "his eyes fixed upon the name of his hatter" (145). Words, in turn, *are* roles when an individual is made into a generic noun. Offering help just when Isabel "had wanted help . . . had not known where to turn" (544), Caspar is in fact reducing Isabel to a conventional role and a generic noun— Submissive Woman.

Isabel is, in turn, at her most representative when she is experiencing Caspar's twofold appeal. Both as conventional heroine and as the

American woman liberated by upbringing and wealth, Isabel experiences a basic fact of womanly life—that men take liberties with liberated women, and that these liberties are finally similar to the liberties men take with Helpless Heroines. Throughout *The Portrait* men have treated Henrietta with a familiarity which they feel warranted by her emancipated profession and which she reacts strongly against each time.[131] Isabel's repeated expressions of fear and her consistent feeling of defensiveness derive in no simple sense from "frigidity."[132] Women *are* beset by male power drives, especially when the culture has canonized those drives as Authority. Above all Isabel cannot let herself become the woman whom the culture identifies as Woman.

> "We have no natural place here. We are mere parasites, crawling over the surface. . . . A woman, it seems to me, has no natural place anywhere; wherever she finds herself she has to . . . crawl."
>
> (*PL* 181)

Madame Merle is referring here to expatriate American women, but "parasite" is what Tennyson said expressly and what the hallowed oak-ivy metaphor implied inescapably about all women. Madame Merle and Countess Gemini and Lydia Touchett prove what happens when a woman wanders without any natural place. To join them is what Caspar's offer of the whole world involves for Isabel. Her rejection of his proposal-proposition is thus as complex as the offer itself. The "straight path" (544) which Isabel takes leads directly away from the man who has repeatedly been called "straight."[133] By apparently embracing the culture's role of Faithful Wife, Isabel is in fact both acting out Victorian woman's terrible dilemma and achieving for herself an individuality beyond social stereotypes. To combine the conventional and the individual is her task, her hope. She must avoid that extreme individualism which has cut Lydia Touchett off so completely from the human community that Lydia is finally dry and eccentric and alone; Isabel must, on the other hand, avoid that extreme commitment to social roles which has denied Pansy any real individuality. To commit herself to society, but on her own terms and with the opportunity of further growth, means that Isabel has moved beyond her need for Male-as-Protector, and has become at last her own guide.

By simultaneously accepting and transcending the form of a conventional role, Isabel makes for herself a natural place in the social wasteland. Rather than being the garden plot to some male's deerpark, she becomes an occasion for her own growth, and for the growth of others. She thus answers the question which Caspar's irresponsible romanticism cannot. What of Pansy? In turn, Isabel's affirmation of conventional roles makes all her disappointed dreams less bitter for us. Her suffering has meant more than knowledge. It has meant knowledge efficacious in the world.

"I am not at all helpless. There are many things I mean to do."

(*PL* 462)

Simply to mean well, may be the mere impulse of a child or an idiot; but to know how to *act* well . . . is the highest lesson which the school of moral discipline can teach.

(*Wives* 23)

Mrs. Ellis is moving here. And in the face of all society's inadequacies and her own, Isabel, exhibiting woman's conventional ability to act under duress, is moving too. She, and Henry James, have managed to reaffirm the value of what we never actually doubt but often are distanced from—the traditional virtues of courage and patience and family affection which may sound hollow in the mouths of politicians or from the pages of advice books, but which are, we know, the profoundest features of the intricate melodrama which is our lives. We return to our beginnings, and yet see things anew. The process of arriving at this point has been sufficiently intricate that we can respond to a conventional role—respond not with the simplicity of a popular audience reacting to that role directly, respond only after contradictions and reversals, but respond. Through art we thus take part in one of the important actions. As Henry James could say as early as 1871:

It does indeed seem as if a certain sense that once flourished and was mighty had now passed out of the world. . . . oh, for some such high view of facts as would suggest that tho' eclipsed this sense, this need, were not lost. . . . Narrow optimism, however, is as bad as narrow pessimism, and if the love of beauty as the Renaissance possessed it, is dead, let us sing a splendid requiem. . . . Then we shall have the satisfaction of at least having kept up the tradition.

(*HJL* 260, 261)

3

Style, Character, and Social Commentary

Hatred is a failure of imagination.

Graham Greene

"When *I* use a word," Humpty Dumpty said, in a rather
scornful tone, "it means just what I choose it to mean—neither
more nor less."
"The question is," said Alice, "whether you *can* make words
mean so many different things."
"The question is," said Humpty Dumpty, "which is to be master
—that's all."

Lewis Carroll

"Ah!" he said. "Love, that terrible thing!"

Djuna Barnes

One sketches one's age.

Henry James

Be good, sweet maid, and let who will be clever.

Charles Kingsley

Having traced their origins and parallel development, we can now
study style and characterization as they interact. *Washington Square* is a
particularly appropriate text because style and character work in sustained harmony here for the first time in James' novelistic career. His
growth is, in fact, manifest in the very subject of the novel—which is
tradition itself. James has freed himself sufficiently from slavish commitment to convention that he can examine such commitment critically.
Washington Square thus involves more than even Richard Poirier claims
for it, more than a comment upon the act of writing. That act is seen as
part of the larger social endeavor of living in the nineteenth century.

That it is difficult to define the effects—and thus the meaning—of
Washington Square becomes clear when we read the novel's best critic.

[Dr. Sloper] is right, and the novel does nothing to convince us until after the trip to Europe that Catherine is not stolid, tedious, and dully sweet. In this, James and Sloper are in essential agreement. Naturally, James's sentiments cannot ever appear to be exactly the same as the Doctor's. . . . we naturally feel that they [critical remarks] are less cruel said behind her back, as it were, by James, than to her face by her father. But these matters are simply a part of the necessary difference between the kinds of personal revelation possible to the author, and those that can be made by a character in a novel which is omnisciently narrated. . . . James's comedy in the early chapters is like Dr. Sloper's: that of a highly witty man who would refuse to be intimidated, by sentimental reasons, from enjoying the comic possibilities of Catherine's deportment. Indeed, before her affair with Townsend becomes passionate enough to reveal the hidden depths of her character, she offers little else to an agile mind than a subject for ironic pleasantries.

(Poirier, 172, 173)

In *The Comic Sense of Henry James*, Poirier achieved more than an excellent book on a major author; he demonstrated in especially convincing fashion how much the meaning of fiction, like the meaning of poetry, depends upon our experience of the text. To Jacques Barzun's contention that Dr. Sloper is "a being for whom the melodramatic epithet of 'fiend in human form' is no longer sayable but still just," Poirier rightly replied, "Mr. Barzun sees what James is saying, but he gives no indication that he has experienced the way in which it is said" (168). Barzun is being melodramatic because he is defining Sloper in terms of a priori categories, not in terms of the more qualified, humane experience of reading James' novel. Poirier's ability to define the cause of such critical extremism makes all the more unfortunate his failure to avoid extremism himself. In the excerpt above, Poirier fails to capture the complexity of our reading experience because he interprets *Washington Square* both too tough-mindedly and too tidily.

Poirier's determination not to sentimentalize Catherine is healthy, but his tough-minded reading is itself finally sentimental. For it also simplifies the situation. By equating Dr. Sloper too completely with the Jamesian narrator, Poirier tends to overrate our commitment to Sloper and to overstate our sense of Catherine's limitations.[1] Poirier neither notes how often James separates himself from Sloper early in the novel nor acknowledges how adversely we react to a father treating his daughter as a novelist treats his puppets. We find ourselves reacting to Poirier's analysis as we do to Sloper's: whatever their factual accuracy, both analyses lack the sympathy which James elicits page by page. In fact Poirier calls Catherine "stolid," whereas James says that "people who expressed themselves roughly called her stolid" (23).

Poirier's analysis is also, at the other extreme, too tidy. Making a neat division between Catherine before and after the European trip, he posits too sudden a reversal in our attitude toward her. "She becomes interesting," he says, "at about the point when Catherine and her father leave for Europe" (175). Has she really not been interesting before this? There is, in fact, no moment so early in the novel that we feel "she offers little else to an agile mind than a subject for ironic pleasantries." Without denying Catherine some development, we must recognize that the techniques which control our responses after the European trip have been operating from the beginning of the novel to help redeem the daughter and undercut the father. By studying both of these processes, we can take up the issue which critics continue to disagree about. Was James correct in titling his novel *Washington Square* rather than, say, *Catherine* or even *Fathers and Daughters?* In other words, is his book *social* in any serious sense?[2] How James' style helps us recognize that the Heroine's plight involves the operation of her whole milieu and indeed the operation of convention itself: this is what we must finally understand.

"There is another passage in the same book [*Th
Ambassadors*] about the hero sitting *there* (in th
Luxembourg Gardens) against the pedestal of som
pleasant old garden-statue.... Go into the sa
Luxembourg Gardens to look for my right garden
statue (composing with other interesting objects
against which my chair was tilted back. Do bring m
something right, in short, from the Luxembourg."

"... some view, rightly arrived at, of Notre-Dam
would also serve—if sufficiently bedimmed and re
fined and glorified; especially as to its Side on th
River and Back ditto."

"Look out *there* [in the Place de la Concorde] fo
some combination of objects that won't be hack
neyed ... some fountain or statue or balustrade o
vista ..."

James to Coburn, quoted in *Alvin Langdo
Coburn, Photographer* (New York, 1966)

Catherine

On the first page of *Washington Square,* James begins establishing the doctor's limitations, and the narrator's and reader's distance from him. The doctor's name is Sloper. Slop, Slope, Sloper: from Sterne's inadequate physician to Trollope's clever cleric, to James' physician-father.[3] Again using traditional names for his own purposes, James creates a lineage which does not immediately doom his doctor but which should make us immediately wary. Then the narrator's wit appears for the first time. The victim of the epigram is not Catherine, however. "There was nothing abstract in his remedies—he always ordered you to take something" (13). The blow is not lethal; James is merely exercising upon his physician a most traditional satire. But the epigram does prevent any complete association of Sloper either with James or with us. Why would the novel begin undercutting not Catherine but her father, and why would its succeeding pages establish *his* limitations, unless James wants us to respond to Sloper's initial criticism of Catherine with less than wholehearted participation, with ambivalence and even sympathy for the girl? We need not deny or minimize Catherine's limitations in order to suggest that they are more than offset by Sloper's own. Let us focus now upon three ways in which James' style—in the many pages before the European trip—establishes the doctor's inadequacy and the daughter's worth.

1

One aspect of style in *Washington Square* is how characters reveal their true natures through uses and abuses of language. Dr. Sloper, for example, uses words as his supposed antithesis, Morris Townsend, does, because both men are finally rhetoricians.*

He walked with her through the devious ways.

They followed this devious way, and finally lost the path.

(102, 139)

Morris and Lavinia, Sloper and Catherine. The straight way becomes devious because Morris and Sloper exercise upon their impressionable women a power not sufficiently tempered by human sympathy.[4] Both

*For more on rhetoricians in *Washington Square,* see chapter 1, pp. 49–51.

men are feared by Catherine and her aunt (81, 158); both men judge Lavinia "a goose" (22, 137). Morris' courtship differs from the doctor's own, not in Townsend's insistence upon wealth, but in his lower standards in other matters. A large dowry had been indispensable for Sloper too (14).

To indicate how manipulative these men actually are, James shows that the Rhetorician resembles two other conventionally cold-blooded types—the Scientist and the Rake. We cannot entirely condone even a doctor's taking notes (48), speaking of and thinking in " 'categories' " (76, 77, 87), and espousing geometry (123); but for a suitor to be so calculating seems unpardonable.

> Doctor Sloper's opposition was the unknown quantity in the problem he [Morris] had to work out. . . . in mathematics there are many shortcuts, and Morris was not without a hope that he should yet discover one. . . . "He will never give us a penny; I regard that as mathematically proved."
>
> (129, 160)

An even more sinister bond between the men appears when

> he had passed his arm round the girl's waist and taken a kiss. . . . he drew her toward him and kissed her. . . . he put his arm round her tenderly, soothingly; and then he kissed her. . . . he had pressed her in his arms.
>
> (65, 73, 109, 118)[5]

The similarity between Morris the Dandy-Rake (in the first and last quotations) and Sloper the Paterfamilias (in the second and third) presages James' more sophisticated fusion of these two types in Gilbert Osmond. Like *The Portrait*, *Washington Square* shows that the Father resembles his supposed antagonist, the Rake, because both types use male attractiveness and authority to control impressionable women.

Moreover, both men control Catherine as much by their words as by their embraces. Having studied in chapter 2 the rhetorical prowess of Morris and Sloper, we can concentrate now upon the effects of their style.

> The doctor delivered himself of these remarks slowly, deliberately, with occasional pauses and prolongations of accent, which made no great allowance for poor Catherine's suspense as to his conclusion.
>
> The Doctor enjoyed the point he had made.
>
> (73, 111)

James encourages our traditional distrust of rhetoricians not only by emphasizing Sloper's savored cruelty, but by rendering Catherine's responses complexly.

Catherine, with her forehead touching the window-panes, listened to this exchange of epigrams as reservedly as if they had not each been a pin-prick in her own destiny.

(41)

Since Catherine's many limitations make her (as we will see later) anything but the Fair Heroine or even the "new" Homely Heroine of the 1860s, she can be silent and long-suffering here and still seem more than conventional. Verbal sharpness cuts the heart. Thus wit becomes a moral issue, and the word "sharp" a moral index. Morris speaks "sharply" (122) and the "cold and sharp" alpine atmosphere (140) reflects Sloper's conduct there. As the victim of their sharpness, Catherine, in turn, needs to defend herself. "She would have liked also, in denying it [Sloper's joke], to be a little positive, a little sharp. . . . But Catherine could never be sharp" (44).

Catherine's lack of sharpness does not mean that "she offers little else to an agile mind than a subject for ironic pleasantries." For several reasons. Catherine is *not*, for one thing, a completely hapless loser in the battle of words. After an early reply that leaves her father "staring" (44), Catherine manages two subsequent remarks which (however inadvertent) are pointed enough to earn from him the title of "epigram" (109, 111). Moreover, Catherine can catch up those talkers whose smoothness skids them into overstatement.

[Arthur] "He [Morris] doesn't know many people here, but he's very sociable, and he wants to know every one."
"Every one?" said Catherine.
"Well, I mean all the good ones."

(37)

Admittedly Arthur is a foil for Morris, but James shows that Catherine can also handle the exaggerations of her melodramatic suitor.

[Morris] "I certainly would rather have you easily than have to fight for you."
"Don't talk about fighting; we shall not fight."

(67)

Besides these infrequent verbal successes, James also makes us recognize redemptive qualities in Catherine's apparent dullness. Her silence, for example, is sometimes intentional.

[Lavinia] "My dear Catherine, you know very well that you admire him." . . . It might very well be that she admired him—though this did not seem to her a thing to talk about.

It seemed to her that there would be something of impudence in making a festival of her secret.

(40, 54)

Silence becomes an act of decorum, probity, reverence. And even when
Catherine's silence does derive from an inability to reply, we are not
inclined to sport much with one who was "wishing so much and
expressing so little. . . . nursing the thoughts that never passed her lips"
(73, 144). Repeatedly what James stresses is not the inadequacy of
Catherine's wit, but her moral superiority in defeat.

> Catherine blushed, for she felt *almost* as if they were making sport of
> her. . . . Of course she would have liked to take it [Sloper's witty ques-
> tion] as a joke—as her father *must* have meant it. . . . [She spoke]
> in a voice so timidly argumentative that it *might* have touched him.
>
> (39, 44, 71; my italics)

The italicized words indicate that Catherine responds to viciousness
with a generosity which does not derive simply from obtuseness. Her
plight as victim seems especially touching because of the moral worth of
the person victimized. When "she regarded it [Morris' love], very
naturally, as a priceless treasure" (65), the "very naturally" atones for a
multitude of foibles. The way that Morris and Sloper play with
Catherine is "very natural" only in the most Darwinian sense.

> "Shall I find you just the same when I come back?" she asked; though
> the question was not the fruit of scepticism.
> "The same—only more so," said Morris, smiling.
>
> (136)

Catherine does not catch Morris' double entendre because she cannot
imagine that anyone would sport at such a moment. Her inadequacy here
seems a moral achievement. And Dr. Sloper is thus pierced with his own
epigram. For Morris' verbal cleverness here and elsewhere establishes his
worth according to Sloper's own criterion—" 'You are good for nothing
unless you are clever' " (19).[6]

2

A second function of James' style might itself be called rhetorical.
He presents Sloper's judgments of Catherine—and Sloper's arguments on
behalf of those judgments—in ways which necessarily affect our response
to them.

> [Sloper] often said to himself that, such as she was, he at least need
> have no fear of losing her. I say "such as she was," because, to tell the
> truth—But this is a truth of which I will defer the telling.
>
> (17)

James' control of tone is important. Knowing that the misogyny inherent
in Sloper's judgment of Catherine must not damn him completely this
early in the novel, James the rhetorician tantalizes us here, exciting our
interest but deferring any complete explanation as we must defer any

complete judgment. In fact, Sloper's misogyny is sufficiently qualified by his ability to appreciate his exceptional wife that the doctor escapes seeming monstrous. He does not, however, seem as attractive as Poirier makes him.

> [Catherine was] of a sex which rendered the poor child, to the Doctor's sense, an inadequate substitute for his lamented first-born.
>
> (16)

Besides the sympathy obvious in his expression "the poor child," James adds the phrase "to the Doctor's sense" in order to suggest that other men's senses might well be different. Ours are, and promise to continue so. For Sloper, who "had never been dazzled, indeed, by any feminine characteristics whatever" (18), could only compensate for his misogyny enough to judge Catherine fairly *if* he knew himself better than he does. "You would have surprised him if you had told him so; but it is a literal fact that he almost never addressed his daughter save in the ironical form" (33). Without minimizing the accuracy of some of Sloper's subsequent judgments, James manages to keep us differing consistently with him.

For one thing, Sloper is repeatedly wrong. His judgment "that Catherine was not wise enough to discover that her aunt was a goose" (22) is followed immediately by Catherine's kindly but astute analysis of Lavinia's limitations.[7] Sloper's judgment seems particularly inadequate because it is *he* who cannot make proper distinctions regarding Lavinia.

> Doctor Sloper's manner of addressing his sister Lavinia had a good deal of resemblance to the tone he had adopted toward Catherine.
>
> (34)

Resembling Lavinia is, in fact, characteristic of Sloper himself. Although Poirier attributes this resemblance to the doctor's decline after the European trip, the resemblance actually appears early in the novel. What Sloper shares with Lavinia is inadequacy of judgment. "Both she and her brother . . . exaggerated the young girl's limitations" (22).

Sloper's errors of judgment mount with the pages. Assuming Catherine too simple to fib, "with all his irony, her father believed her" when she denies remembering Morris' name (35). Sloper's imperviousness *is* penetrated soon, however. Having made the judgment that " 'decidedly . . . my daughter is not brilliant,' " the doctor immediately receives from her the reply that leaves him "staring; he wondered whether his daughter were serious" (44). Before the European trip, Catherine again turns the tables. "This striking argument gave the Doctor a sudden sense of having underestimated his daughter" (132). Sloper's realization here is important because it indicates more than his limitations as a judge. "It [the striking argument] displeased him—displeased him deeply" (132). Worse than

simplistic, Sloper is morally intransigent; he does not wish to be forced to
see more in Catherine than he had assumed there.

The inadequacy of the doctor's judgments is emphasized stylistically
by his reliance upon taglines. We have already seen, for example, that
Sloper's tidy " 'not brilliant' " is undercut by the retort that leaves him
"staring." Soon we find him relying with equal confidence upon " 'absolutely unattractive' " (47), "a simpleton" (54), and " 'a weak-minded
woman' " (58). Although the extreme nature of these judgments would,
of itself, make us dubious, the narrator has encouraged our disassocia-
tion from Sloper by providing more intricate evaluations.

> She was not ugly; she had simply a plain, dull, gentle countenance.
> The most that had ever been said for her was that she had a "nice" face;
> and, though she was an heiress, no one had ever thought of regarding
> her as a belle.
>
> (20)

"Not ugly . . . plain, dull, gentle . . . 'nice' . . . heiress . . . [not] a belle" :
compared with such qualification, the bald tag " 'absolutely unattractive' " seems inadequate, and even gross. Likewise, compare "a simpleton" and " 'a weak-minded woman' " with

> she was so *quiet* and *irresponsive*. People who expressed themselves
> roughly called her *stolid*. But she was *irresponsive* because she was
> *shy, uncomfortably, painfully shy*. . . . she sometimes produced an
> impression of *insensibility*. In reality, she was the *softest* creature in
> the world.
>
> (23; my italics)

The contrast of Sloper's taglines with Catherine's modest complexity
appears especially sharp when a single word is the focus. "He had told
her that she was a heartless daughter. Her heart was breaking; she had
heart enough for that" (117). By repeating "heart" twice in six words,
James emphasizes its presence here as Catherine has established her
heartfelt concern for her father throughout the novel. What we experience here is less the accuracy of Sloper's judgment than the cruelty of his
attempt to fix his daughter in a formulated phrase.

3

Our early sense of the mixed natures of Sloper and Catherine is
confirmed by a third, and particularly effective, way in which James uses
style. With Dr. Sloper James repeatedly presents positive traits *after*
traits more questionable.

> He passed in the best society of New York for a man of the world—
> which, indeed, he was, in a very sufficient degree.
>
> (14)

We must not overstate the amount of distancing here. The narrator's final words confirm Sloper's cosmopolitanism unquestionably. But did James need *all* the words of the sentence to make that confirmation? Compare his sentence with

He was, indeed, to a very sufficient degree, a man of the world.

"Passed for" introduces the possibility that what passes for cosmopolitanism in America might well not pass muster in London or Paris.[8] The very fact that the narrator must add a clause supporting the American opinion indicates how tenuous the initial attribution is. Now the narrator's support does, as I say, establish Sloper's cosmopolitanism finally. But the complexity of our experience remains. We cannot unring a bell. No subsequent remark can entirely undo an initial statement because reading is an experiential, not an arithmetic, process. Later words may qualify our initial response significantly, but they cannot eradicate it entirely. Upon this experiential fact, James' presentation of Sloper depends heavily.

Here, for example, are the next two sentences on page 14.

I hasten to add, to anticipate possible misconception, that he was not the least of a charlatan. He was a thoroughly honest man.

By the very mention of charlatanry, James forces us to consider Sloper in light of the vice traditional with doctors. James raises the issue by denying charlatanry, of course, and then further denies it by the subsequent affirmation. But see how different our response would be if the passage read simply, "he was also a thoroughly honest man." James does not *need* to mention charlatanry. Nothing previous has suggested it, and the strongest affirmation of Sloper's probity would be the unimpeachable "he was a thoroughly honest man." By anticipating "possible misconception," James assures that we will experience that misconception momentarily.

For a man whose trade was to keep people alive he had certainly done poorly in his own family; and a bright doctor who within three years loses his wife and his little boy should perhaps be prepared to see either his skill or his affection impugned. Our friend, however, escaped criticism . . . all criticism but his own, which was much the most competent and most formidable.

(16)

Here a misconception is prolonged before it is corrected. Again James could have presented the issue less damningly—by *beginning* with the fact that Sloper escaped criticism, and by omitting or at least minimizing any suggestion that he lacked "skill" or "affection." Our questioning of Sloper's adequacy is, however, basic to James' tactic in the opening pages of *Washington Square.*

By making us immediately question Dr. Sloper's adequacy, James equips us to deal with Sloper's wit before it is visited upon Catherine. Such preparation does not, of course, prevent our enjoying the wit. Poirier rightly senses how taken we are with the doctor's *mots*. What Poirier does not account for is the intricacy of our response. Because we have from the very beginning been less than completely one with Sloper, we tend to be more immediately sensitive to the cruelty and inadequacy of his remarks. To sustain our uneasy mixture of attraction and repulsion, James structures dramatic scenes as he does the narration— placing Sloper's admirable moments *after* ones more damning.

> [Lavinia] "Do you think it is better to be clever than to be good?"
> "Good for what?" asked the Doctor. "You are good for nothing unless you are clever." . . .
> "Of course I wish Catherine to be good," the Doctor said next day; "but she won't be any less virtuous for not being a fool."
>
> (19)

Sloper's second statement is sober, judicious, concerned. It could easily have answered Lavinia's initial question. By intervening the epigram " 'you are good for nothing unless you are clever,' " James makes us experience first the superficiality of Sloper's epigrammatic mind. The doctor's second statement can qualify, but it cannot remove, our impression of moral irresponsibility. Had James not wanted to convey this damning impression, he need only have omitted the epigram.

> "Is it possible that this magnificent person is my child?" he said. . . .
> "I am not magnificent," she said, mildly, wishing that she had put on another dress.
> "You are sumptuous, opulent, expensive," her father rejoined. "You look as if you had eighty thousand a year."
> "Well, so long as I haven't—" said Catherine illogically . . .
> "So long as you haven't you shouldn't look as if you had. Have you enjoyed your party?"
>
> (33)

How could she enjoy it, especially since this dressing down occurs "in the crowd"? Sloper's final question is sincere, of course: he wants his daughter to have a good time. Because Catherine and we experience the sharpness of his reprimand first, however, the question cannot atone completely. We are ultimately struck less by Sloper's fatherly concern than by this father's willingness to hurt his daughter publicly.[9] We react this way especially because we have already encountered:

> her great indulgence of it [taste] was really the desire of a rather inarticulate nature to manifest itself; she sought to be eloquent in her garments, and to make up for her diffidence of speech by a fine

frankness of costume. But if she expressed herself in her clothes, it is certain that people were not to blame for not thinking her a witty person.

(24)

Although the verdict here is damning and just, the reading experience is complicated by James' presentation. The negative judgment comes *after* the redeeming side of the case. James is thus using with Catherine the same basic tactic as with her father—only in reverse. And the effects which he achieves are likewise opposite. We encounter the positive aspects *before* the negative, and are thus predisposed toward Catherine. Although the narrator's wit flashes in finally to emphasize the limitations of her wit, we do not feel with Poirier that "she offers little else to an agile mind than a subject for ironic pleasantries." James has already established touchingly *why* she overdresses. That reason seems ultimately more important than the aesthetics of her clothes.

This tactic of placing Catherine's positive traits before her negative ones occurs in dramatic scenes.

"Excuse me," he [Morris] added; "you see I am natural myself."
And before she had time to think whether she excused him or not—which afterward, at leisure, she became conscious that she did—he began to talk. . . .
"I sing a little myself," he said; "someday I will show you. Not to-day, but some other time."
And then he got up to go. He had omitted, by accident, to say that he would sing to her if she would play to him. He thought of this after he got into the street; but he might have spared his compunction, for Catherine had not noticed the lapse.

(43)[10]

Twice Catherine's limitations are manifest. She should not have excused Morris' " 'natural' " self-praise, and she should have noted his "lapse." In both cases, however, our initial response increases our sympathy for Catherine. She has no "time to think" because Morris immediately follows his rhetoric with more rhetoric; and, in the second instance, the vanity that prompts his promise to sing and the inconsiderateness that prompts his "lapse" in etiquette, contrast him emphatically with his humble and considerate interlocutor. Once again, Catherine's limitations, though real, are not sufficient to prevent our initial response from being, with modification, our final one. Hers are basic virtues. The major inadequacy lies with those who attempt to demean and deceive her.

James' tactic of beginning with the positive or negative trait which, despite the subsequent appearance of its opposite, is finally primary to the character—this tactic helps shape our reactions to the conduct of Sloper and Catherine throughout the first half of *Washington Square*. As we encounter the second trait, we find it qualifying a response already present in our consciousness. We thus experience that coalescence of opposites which James' early novels had merely asserted. Our two-sided response flowers, in turn, into a commitment to Catherine which is prompted by the very conflicting nature of the evidence and which I will call "moral."

> *Washington Square* differs from *Roderick Hudson* and *The American*, however, in that its melodrama is significant more to the psychological than to the moral life of its characters. . . . Sloper is corrupted precisely because he believes in them [circumstances].
>
> (Poirier, 182)

Does "corrupted" relate to the "psychological" or to the "moral" life? Compared with *The Golden Bowl* or even *The Portrait*, psychological exploration is not extensive in *Washington Square*. The characters here are too consistently types. I raise Poirier's distinction between the psychological and the moral because these fashionable categories help us recognize the actual alternatives which James offers. We can agree with Poirier that we "care more for the problem of Dr. Sloper than for the chance to call him a fiend or a villain" (182) and yet can still find *Washington Square* evoking response ultimately moral—because the moral has nothing to do, finally, with calling people fiends or villains. Our alternatives are actually the moral and the moralistic. By his technique of counterpointing positive and negative traits, James prevents our simplifying the characters moralistically into villains or saints. That we can see both sides does not mean, however, that we are reduced, as Poirier says, to "a mood which can only be called contemplative" (169). The consistent emphasis of the counterpointing prompts from us a degree of sympathy for Catherine which is, in fact, a moral preference. We escape moralism because we do not respond in terms of a priori standards. Experiencing the reality which James presents, we respond in favor of life, in favor of Catherine. And thus morally.

> All the centuries of a nation are
> the leaves of the same book.
> *Ernest Renan*

Society

As we increasingly recognize Dr. Sloper's limitations and Catherine's worth, we come also to recognize that James is concerned here with more than a domestic struggle.

> We are reminded [by Laurence Oliphant's *The Tender Recollections of Irene Macgillicuddy*] that there *are* types—that there is a good deal of local color—that there is a considerable field for satire. Only, why should it be left to the cold and unsympathetic stranger to deal with these things? Why does not native talent take them up . . . and show us, with the force of real familiarity, both the good and the evil that are to be found in Fifth Avenue?

James wrote this barely a year before he began work on *Washington Square* (*Na* 1878, 357). By making us experience complex moral responses to his characters, James can generate comparably complex evaluations of their society. Style contributes as importantly to this second process as to the first. Without insisting upon too absolute a correspondence, we can find in the tightly controlled antitheses and balances of Dr. Sloper's urbane prose a stylistic equivalent of the social control which genteel norms exercised in Catherine's New York. Any criticism of these norms and style is complicated, however, by the fact that the Jamesian narrator uses and clearly enjoys the same urbane, controlled style that Sloper does. Assured of moderation by the extent of his implication, James explores the larger forces at work in Catherine's situation. He examines the standards of the genteel America of which he and his novel are a part.

1

First, the narrator's prose.

> Mrs. Montgomery brushed away her tears, and blushed at having shed them.

> [Catherine] felt miserably helpless and hopeless.

> (91, 112)

The strict parallelism of "blushed . . . brushed" and "helpless . . . hopeless" boxes potentially volatile subject matter into sharply defined

segments. The artfulness is obvious enough to direct our attention away
from the subject matter and onto the surface of the prose itself. This same
effect occurs when Sloper's son dies despite "the mother's tenderness and
the father's science" (16). Although the involvement of both parents is
touchingly evident, the balanced syntax asserts the controlling, distancing frame of art. We cannot mistake for reality the artifact which James is
constructing. This success is, in turn, what makes form a thematic issue
in *Washington Square*. The very control achieved by balanced syntax
and other self-conscious devices[11] calls them into question morally.

Stylistic control becomes thematically important because Dr. Sloper
attempts to order events very much as the Jamesian narrator does.
Balanced syntax is repeatedly involved. How can we indict Sloper
without implicating the narrator? How can we convict either and absolve
society? Let us begin answering these questions by defining how style
affects our response to Sloper's efforts at control.

> He was curious and impatient, for he was sure she was going to speak
> of Morris Townsend; but he let her take her own time, for he was
> determined to be very mild.
>
> (69)

The balanced syntax functions here, not to assure the narrator's control
of a tense moment, but to indicate Sloper's determination *to* control it.
The exactness of the syntactic balance—"he" and "for" clauses paralleling
"he" and "for" clauses—reflects his success. This genteel control Catherine attempts to emulate.

> He was so quiet; he was not at all angry; and she, too, must be quiet.
> But her very effort to be quiet made her tremble.
>
> (73)

Like her father's passage, Catherine's has four clauses. The first and
third, with their "he . . . quiet . . . she . . . quiet," reflect in their syntax
Catherine's attempt at control. Her failure is suggested syntactically too.
The clause which breaks the parallelism and stands autonomous is the
one that reveals Catherine trembling uncontrollably, as her father never
would.

In the pages that follow, syntax continues to reflect Catherine's
attempt to conform to her father's genteel standards.

> She would try to appear good, even if her heart were perverted; and
> from time to time she had a fancy that she might accomplish something
> by ingenious concessions to form, though she should persist in caring
> for Morris.
>
> (117)

By using the main clauses for Catherine's hopes and the minor clauses for
her discordant emotions, James emphasizes how torn she is. Moreover,

that the dissonant feelings appear in *minor* clauses reflects both the discordant nature of these feelings and her inability to assimilate them entirely. Catherine's hope for success here, somewhat devious as it is, derives from a very genteel view of the world.

> If she were only good enough, Heaven would invent some way of reconciling all things—the dignity of her father's errors and the sweetness of her own confidence, the strict performance of her filial duties, and the enjoyment of Morris Townsend's affection.
>
> (94)

Since God is in his heaven, all will, after appropriate suffering, be ordered for the godly. Including the syntax. Catherine's dream of integrating fractious elements is mirrored in the syntactic balance after the dash where phrases relating to Sloper and Morris are made parallel with Catherine's own and thus with one another.

A version of this harmony is realized when Catherine reenters the alpine coach.

> In it sat her father, rigid and silent; in silence, too, she took her place beside him.
>
> (142)

The chiasmic structure here is virtually perfect.

(*A*) In it   sat her father   (*b*) rigid and silent (11 syllables)
(*a*) beside him   she took her place   (*B*) in silence too   (11 syllables)

Especially since the theme of the sentence is the deployment of father and daughter, their integration seems complete. One problem does obtrude, however. Unlike the passage from page 94 where Catherine's dream came true in harmoniously parallel phrases, the clauses on page 142 are mirror-imaged: not *AbaB*, but *AbBa*. And Catherine and her father are, in fact, diametrically opposed. Despite their superficial congruence, they hold views of Morris as polar as a photograph and its negative. Thus this one sentence reflects in its syntax both the surface and the core truths about Sloper's use of genteel constraints.[12] He can force Catherine into a kind of conformity, but true harmony and coherence cannot be achieved by fiat and cannot, finally, be achieved by Sloper.

Whether Catherine can achieve harmony is a question that remains even after her father's death.

> She calmed herself with a great effort, but with great rapidity.
>
> From her own point of view the great facts of her career were that Morris Townsend had trifled with her affection, and that her father had broken its spring.
>
> (180, 190)

In time Catherine has indeed achieved that ordering of emotions, that stability of vision and control of syntax, which the genteel tradition espoused. Clearly, however, James is not advocating in any easy way the standards of Dr. Sloper.

> Nothing could ever alter these facts; they were always there, like her name, her age, her plain face. Nothing could ever undo the wrong or cure the pain that Morris had inflicted on her, and nothing could ever make her feel toward her father as she felt in her younger years.
>
> (190)

For order Catherine pays the price of resigning herself to sequential time. She passes from her father's impossible rigidity to the equally hopeless rigor of later life. Her reality is as fixed as the syntax on page 190. Repeating three times the inexorable "nothing could ever," James establishes the link between her name which no man will now change and the men who assured that questionable stability. Order has cost Catherine life itself.

2

By sharing with Dr. Sloper the style of wit and control, James can comment from the inside upon life in Washington Square. James does not title his novel *Catherine* or even *Fathers and Daughters* because he wants us to see in Catherine's domestic struggle the operation of her entire milieu. Dr. Sloper is, as we have seen, singled out by New Yorkers as a shining light. He is in fact their representative man. His wine cellar and cigars and carriage horse are exactly as they should be. Moving uptown with the fashionable tide, Sloper chooses a house which "exactly resembled" its neighbors (26). Bowden does not exaggerate the importance of this house when he says, "with its reference to the neighboring houses, it seems almost a condemnation of a whole class of men" (41). Almost, indeed. By implicating all fashionable New York through the house of its representative man, James is adopting the practice of a social critic whom he has known since the 1850s—George William Curtis.[13] In the once-celebrated *Potiphar Papers*, Potiphar moves uptown with the fashionable tide.

> "Bless my soul! Mr. Potiphar, your house is just like your neighbor's."
> I know it. I am perfectly aware there is no more difference between my house and Croesus' than there is in two ten-dollar bills of the same bank. He might live in my house and I in his without any confusion.[14]

Dr. Sloper's response to Catherine's social ineptness is strongly affected by his place in society. The scarlet dress not only offends his taste; it embarrasses him. " 'You shouldn't look as if you have' " eighty-thousand a year because people will talk. In failing to live up to her mother, Catherine is failing to come up to the norm of Genteel Womanhood. It is this social failure that her father cannot forget or forgive. Nor does the rest of New York society uphold—with the exception of Mrs. Almond—any worthier values. Young men Catherine's age cannot deal with her, whereas shallow Marian Almond is the belle of the ball and weds early.

> [Sloper] "I must do the young men of New York the justice to say that they strike me as very disinterested. They prefer pretty girls—lively girls—girls like your own. Catherine is neither pretty nor lively."
> [Mrs. Almond] "Catherine does very well; she has a style of her own—which is more than my poor Marian has, who has no style at all."
>
> (47)

By turning Genteel canons of taste upon Catherine's style, Dr. Sloper is actually denying to life its personal element. This denial, in turn, contributes to our awareness that gentility, for all its fastidiousness (or rather because of it), is actually gross. Society's representative man speaks to Catherine with "a dreadful ugliness" (111); later, his words "seemed a rather gross way of putting it" (143). Lavinia's attempts at repartee are rightly termed " 'pugilism' " (155) and she eventually prompts from Morris, " 'surely women are more crude than men!' " (164). Morris himself cannot talk, however, for he too speaks "crudely" and admits, " 'I certainly say it distinctly enough—brutally and vulgarly enough' " (162).

Recently John Lucas has discussed the grossness of gentility in *Washington Square*.[15] Lucas' reading differs from mine sufficiently that a brief explanation of our differences will, I hope, help clarify the function of society in James' novel.

> They [Morris, Lavinia, Sloper] see themselves called on to play parts created by their self-conscious awareness of what their society requires of them.
>
> (39)

Lucas' Marxist-oriented interpretation exaggerates the social determinism in *Washington Square*. James is less concerned with how society conditions Morris, Lavinia, and Sloper, than he is with how these characters condition Catherine. That "Morris is the inevitable product of the society which tries to exclude him" (41) is simply not the attitude which the novel encourages us to take. Who is trying to exclude Townsend? The name towns-end, plus Morris' Byronic wanderings, suggest that he is indeed an outsider. But society hardly excludes him.

Townsend is admitted to the Almonds' upper-class party, and then to eminent Dr. Sloper's house, and table. Sloper says expressly (and we believe him) that he objects to Morris, *not* because the young man is trying to make his way up in society—as Sloper knows he himself did—but because Morris is finally worthless. Morris will not use his marriage to foster his talents, as Sloper did. Where in the novel does James suggest that Morris' worthlessness is society's doing?

Lucas' interpretation of Morris, and of Lavinia and Dr. Sloper,[16] is determined in part by his healthy reaction against two prevailing critical tendencies. One is to minimize the social aspect of *Washington Square*.

> Richard Poirier quotes this letter [to Howells] . . . only to argue that it supports his case that "the public status of characters in *Washington Square* depends not at all on their social place or nationality, and is wholly a matter of their similarity to stock characters in stage melodrama and the fairy tale." My own feeling is that the novel itself everywhere contradicts Poirier's thesis, and that if characters *do* become like stock types in stage melodrama and fairy tale—and I agree that they do—it is because they see themselves called upon to play parts created by their self-conscious awareness of what their society requires of them.
>
> (39)

James' intention is actually somewhere between Lucas and Poirier here. Lucas introduces a stage of complexity which the novel does not depict, for he has the characters turning themselves into types. Rather, James *begins* with recognizable types. Then—this is what Poirier undervalues— James uses the types to examine society.

Lucas is also reacting against a critical tendency which we have already discussed. The tendency to judge fiction moralistically. By stressing how completely society has shaped the characters, Lucas can preclude the attribution of evil, "not, anyway, unless we are prepared to see their inadequacies as evil" (58–59). We can share Lucas' wariness of moral taglines without, however, straying from the reading experience. "James's aloof distaste for the society he presents. . . . a kind of ironic ruthlessness" (42): Lucas' expressions here fail to account for the bond which James establishes with society by the very fact that his narrator shares with Sloper the style of genteel wit. Instead of showing that society makes individuals into types, James assumes that we are all social beings. Moralistic terms like "evil" and "fiend" are inappropriate to *Washington Square, not* because we see Morris and Sloper as helpless products of society, but because we cannot avoid seeing each man as one of us. In Sloper's right-wrongness—he is right about Morris' character and intentions, and yet wrongs Catherine horribly—we see the paradoxical quality of our human nature. Lucas fails to capture our reading experience because he allows us, as moralistic critics do, to stand finally outside the novel. Only by making us see the degree of our commitment to the value system which prompts Sloper's *mots* and our enjoyment of them, only by implicating us in the atrocious treatment of Catherine, can James comment upon his society and yet escape the vitiating extremes of tagline moralism and social determinism.

James also transcends "ironic ruthlessness" by showing that Catherine, for all her large awkwardness, is ultimately genteel in the finest sense. Recognizing grossness in others, she does not reply in kind. When her father says, " 'you won't think me cruel,' " Catherine can only recognize "possibilities which made her feel sick" (73); when she is told at Morris' house that he has gone, " 'I asked no more questions; I was ashamed' " (178). Years later Catherine achieves with Morris the admirable limitations of a moderated vision. " 'I forgave you years ago, but it is useless for us to attempt to be friends' " (205). She even manages in later years to appreciate the flourishes of genteel style in Morris' despicable letter. On the other hand, Catherine ends no paragon. Having challenged society in her timid way, she returns to that society and is characterized increasingly by the word "rigid."[17] As maiden aunt and perennial fixture, she has become a part, at the cost of ever being whole. How then are we to interpret Catherine, and James' social commentary, finally?

In the last sentence of *Washington Square* James' style combines with his handling of character type to transcend melodrama and carry us to high intensity of feeling.

> Catherine, meanwhile, in the parlor, picking up her morsel of fancy-work, had seated herself with it again—for life, as it were.
>
> (206)

What is the difference in effect if we remove from this sentence its last three words? The basic contrast—"fancy-work" versus "life"—would remain, and also the resulting pathos of a life reduced to trivia. The "as it were," for which pundits deride James, is important here, however.

> He is a mouse, as it were.
> He is a little timorous, as it were.

"As it were" can create two different effects simultaneously. It both encourages us to discount the way an idea has been expressed and also affirms the basic veracity of that idea. It says to the reader of my examples above: put in whatever way, metaphoric or literal, the fact of the timidity remains. "As it were" is a type of understatement which finally *emphasizes* the sentence's point by indicating that other words would not alter that point significantly.

The "as it were" in James' sentence softens the extreme quality of the contrast between fancy-work and life. The resulting urbanity of tone precludes the stridency and righteousness of "fiend in human form"; it keeps the last sentence of the novel in tune with the preceding two hundred pages.[18] On the other hand, by establishing that Catherine's plight could have been expressed by a less dramatic contrast, "as it were" functions to emphasize the core truth of that contrast. Regardless of how facts are verbalized the reality remains—for life Catherine has only trivia. "As it were" increases poignancy by preventing her plight from seeming merely "melodramatic."

"As it were" constitutes, then, a double triumph. It manifests James' transcendence of the genteel tradition, and Catherine's triumph over us. First, James. *Washington Square* has often been called the fine flowering of the genteel tradition in America, for James' novel manifests the clarity, urbanity, precision, and, above all, the moderation which genteel spokesmen espoused. The most admirable aspect of the book's moderation—the way we are brought to recognize the humanity of paradoxical Sloper's right-wrongness—is just what saves *Washington Square* from being, finally, a genteel novel. James cannot finally abide within the restraints of genteel values. By the very act of using a genteel epigrammatic style to demonstrate the limitations of genteel epigrams and standards, James achieves a stylistic paradox analogous to the thematic paradox of Sloper's right-wrongness. Seeing Sloper two-sidedly saves James from the fundamental error of Sloper's genteel society—the error of seeing individuals only one-sidedly, only in terms of types. Stereotyping Catherine violates her in either of two ways. Society's basic concern is whether she fits in, whether she is the Beautiful Heroine like her mother (or even the Homely-But-Vivacious-Heroine of the next generation). Concluding no, society takes no more serious interest in her. Catherine fares little better, however, with those particular socialites who do see her as a Heroine. To Lavinia, Catherine is a stage Damsel made real; to Morris, she is the Heiress to snare; to Sloper, she is the Young Person to be controlled by Victorian Paternity.

That Catherine is more than a type, that she is a homely and unvivacious Heroine-Heiress-Young Person who is also a human being, James establishes by providing her with conventional traits which he then transforms. In our Maiden's Missive-to-her-Beloved, for example, we recognize a genuineness and intensity absent, say, from Morris' more conventional epistles. " 'I am punished enough, and I don't understand. Dear Morris, you are killing me' " (175). Thus when Catherine at the end assumes the traditional pose of the Heroine-with-her-knitting, we recognize the difference between the conventional significance of this gesture—tranquility, productivity, stability—and her life as it will actually be.

Or rather will not be. The poignancy of our recognition here establishes the greatness of James' art in *Washington Square*. It places him not only beyond the genteel endeavors of Bayard Taylor or T. B. Aldrich, but even beyond the supposedly iconoclastic efforts of Rhoda Broughton. With Catherine we find out what it is really like to be a homely girl in a world which goes by the book.

Art and life thus come together. Seeing society see Catherine as Heroine involves us in an issue fundamental to literature and to society— the propriety of convention. How does a person, as artist or as citizen, undertake the dangerous act of interpreting life in terms of forms sanctioned by the past? How can Convention not be fatal? By 1880 James has come far enough to avoid fatal forms in his art by writing a novel about their fatal effects. The act of writing becomes part of living in the nineteenth century because James' very theme is how society makes the same conventional forms fatal in daily life. Transforming conventions allows James to comment upon tradition as he becomes part of it.

James' transcendence of both the moral limitations of genteel society and the artistic limitations of genteel fiction can also be seen as Catherine's triumph over us. Our laughter at her—and sometimes it has been *at* her—has meant a failure of imagination. We can smile at the wit of "Catherine . . . was, after all, a rather mature blossom, such as could be plucked from the stem only by a vigorous jerk" (49), because we fail to imagine all the pain which a jerk like Morris may well inflict. The novel encourages our short-sightedness, of course, so that we may be brought gradually from our basic social cruelty to a growing awareness of the humanity that exists within objects of society's easy satire and outside the stereotypes of society's limited caste. Catherine triumphs in the end because she has really changed so little. She gains in awareness and courage, but basic integrity and worthiness were hers from the beginning. She, finally, develops less than we because she has less need to. And in her triumph, Catherine carries us ahead with her—probably not, however, for life as it will be.

4 🐛

Style, Character, and the Process of Portraiture

There is no greater work of art than a great portrait.

Henry James

How do you develop enough grace to capture a thief more graceful than yourself.

Norman Mailer

And, Sir, as to metaphorical expression, that is a great excellence in style, when it is used with propriety for it gives you two ideas for one.

Samuel Johnson

If the young man had believed in repetition, of what might he not have been capable? What inwardness he might have attained!

Kierkegaard

Love is a long close scrutiny.

John Hawkes

The interaction of style and character, the alchemy of genre and personal elements: these two, related processes have been our subjects throughout, and they are so now. Despite the success of *Washington Square*, James' crucial decade does not, cannot, climax there. In 1881 he achieves for the first time in his career a sustained, if qualified, mastery of a last technique essential to his subsequent fiction. Using recurrent syntactic patterns with a "rounded" character, he conveys the illusion of mental process.[1]

To understand the relation between this process and portraiture, we must begin by realizing that "portrait" can mean two quite different things. Gilbert Osmond's passion to make life into art reaches its acme, as several critics have noted, in this portrait.

Framed in the gilded doorway, she struck our young man as the picture of a gracious lady.

(339)

Ned does not mean his observation critically, but we see in the generalized phrase "a gracious lady" the regularizing effect of Osmond's passion. That Isabel is clearly not at her best here, that she seems quite lifeless and dead at her soirée, does not make Osmond's portrait a failure in any simple sense, however. It rather indicates the operation of an aesthetic which values surface perfection over what James calls "the constituted consciousness" (*FN* 116).

> Osmond had given her [Isabel] a sort of tableau of her position as his daughter's duenna.
> "I like to think of her [Pansy] there, in the old garden, under the arcade.". . . He contemplated awhile the picture he had evoked, and seemed greatly pleased with it.
> (407, 490)

Osmond's static portraits fix life in the amber of convention. But even when the artist's intention is more benign, an excessive concern with surface will prevent him from reaching the heart of the matter.

> "Descriptive" writing, to our English taste, suggests nothing very enticing—a respectable sort of padding, at best. . . . The prejudice, we admit, is a wholesome one, and the limits of verbal portraiture of all sorts should be jealously guarded.
> In spite of the elaborate system of portraiture to which she [Emma Bovary] is subjected, in spite of being minutely described . . . she remains a living creature, and as a living creature she interests us.
> (*FrP* 34, 204)[2]

"Living . . . living." Believing experience to be not static but processive, James praises *Madame Bovary* for "the process of her history" (*FrP* 205). There are for James, then, two types of portrait: the static setpiece and the processive rendering of inner life, "the picture of a gracious lady" and *The Portrait of a Lady*. By 1881 he has brought to the static setpiece a refinement beyond Osmond's rigid tableaux,[3] but James cannot, finally, fulfill himself in a mode so essentially static. Since Isabel's saving grace is her ability to move maddeningly, redeemingly, from one revelation to the next, James must generate in our consciousnesses an analogous movement if we are to be moved to sympathy for her. Once again, then, James' problem is primarily technical. How to create moving pictures. Unlike the devices studied earlier, James' internalized portrayals of character do not fully realize the inherent potential of this technique. Appropriately, the novel which caps a decade so mixed is itself mixed, transitional.

This mixed quality is what determines my procedure in this chapter. Mental process passages in *The Portrait* must be studied in the context of that ongoing technical development which has preceded 1881 and will continue after it for a quarter-century. Specifically, we must see how

James' early renderings of the mind resemble popular practice, and how his own techniques are fully realized for the first time in *The Ambassadors;* within this context we can then define the strengths and weaknesses of mental process passages in *The Portrait* itself.[4] This procedure does not make *The Portrait* merely a way-station to *The Ambassadors.* Since all artifacts constitute what the artist could and could not accomplish technically at a particular time, it is precisely *not* to make an earlier work into something else that we must distinguish it from later efforts. The act of comparison does, however, attest to a sense of continuity. Between 1882 and 1901 James' technical concerns are various, but he never ceases laboring to present what Hyacinth, Fleda, and Maisie knew. Then, in 1901, James, chastened, complicated, disillusioned, challenged by his many experiments, begins the trilogy which will constitute the supreme rendering of what compelled him most. "You see I still, in presence of life (or of what you deny to be such,) have reactions—as many as possible. . . . that I note and 'enjoy' (grim word!) noting" (*LL* 2:361). This famous declaration to Henry Adams is really a confirming of James' commitment to Isabel, Strether, Maggie, William James, and all who suffer to know. Seeing Isabel in light of Strether is to acknowledge her place in a splendid family of the mind.

> ... but the wonder was his own.
>
> *G. K. Chesterton*

1871 and 1901

1

Gordon Taylor defines accurately the limitations of popular renderings of the consciousness. "Since these [moral] values are fixed and since the nature of reality is never in doubt, how her [Mrs. Stowe's] characters perceive reality is relatively unimportant" (26). In a fixed universe the characters, choosing between absolute extremes, enact a kind of psychomachia.

> He of course had no imagination, which, as we know, should always stand at the right hand of charity; but he had a good store of that wholesome discretion whose place is at the left.

> It was to him as if he saw the hereditary demon of the Morvilles watching by his side, to take full possession of him.

In the first passage here* Henry James indicates his early commitment both to conventional psychology and to popular techniques for rendering it. Since consciousness is more a moral reflex than a self-generating process, the technique best suited to rendering that reflex is personification.

> Conscience also asked . . . . conscience had hardly time to whisper . . . . conscience presently began to whisper . . . . said conscience again . . . . said conscience . . . . conscience said . . . . conscience pricked her . . . . said conscience.

Here in *The Wide, Wide World*[5] it may reach an absurd extreme, but the technique of personifying conscience is little more effective in *Watch and Ward* when we encounter "the easy breathing of her [Nora's] conscience" (587), or when Nora "had challenged conscience" (689). James' novel seems especially old-fashioned because he also personifies so many other mental states.

> Discretion told him . . . . If imagination should lead her a-wandering, gratitude would stay her steps . . . . let silence combine with absence to plead for him . . . . love and doubt fared in company . . . . joy, bursting in, had trampled . . . . joy had taken up the words . . . . [Discretion] had

*W&W 234 (also quoted by Taylor); HR 1:269.

been shut up in a closet . . . . It was love, and not indifference, that had pulled the wires.

(234, 323, 427, 586, 588 [twice],
589, 695)

Such limited techniques are not the only ones which popular writers use to render mental processes, however. Taylor seems not to give the devil his due because he does not—despite his admission that *Uncle Tom's Cabin* may be a "perhaps extreme" example of conventional practice (7)— suggest how much of James' later technique is rooted in popular fiction. Particularly James' use of the colloquial.

The newly developing realistic dialogue had suggested to James a way to render the mind at work . . . . were it not for the punctuation and some slight syntactical clues, one could not distinguish the tongue's utterance from the mind's flow.

(Bridgman, 97, 98)

That popular fiction also uses colloquial style to render mental processes Taylor recognizes, even as he is denying any real colloquialism to *Uncle Tom's Cabin.*

A trace of *erlebte Rede*, or use of the character's idiom in a third-person statement recording his mental process, appears in the word "niggers." . . . By setting Haley's epithet off from the formal diction and elaborate periods with which she controls the passage, Mrs. Stowe minimizes the idiomatic flavor and hence the element of direct representation. The thought remains formally attributed to the character's mind, rather than represented directly from it.

(9)

In establishing how popular authors use colloquial style to render the consciousness, we must avoid sweeping claims. Taylor is right that conventional novels never *sustain* the illusion of mental process. They lack two essential qualities: thoughts must seem self-generating, and the process open-ended. Nowhere do the scribblers attain the flow of Lambert Strether's mind or the depths of Molly Bloom's. Since popular practice, for all its limitations, does have much to teach young James, however, let us look briefly at the other side of the coin. Not only psychomachia but also colloquial diction and syntax render characters' thoughts in popular novels.

To achieve what Bridgman calls "the mind talking to itself" (100), popular novelists resort to devices traditional to dialogue. Besides actual quotation marks—" 'All in vain, kind Charlie,' said he to himself" (*HR* 2:31)—there are frequent questions and exclamations.

What was it? who was it?—The old newsman! Ellen was sure. Yes— she could now see his saddlebags.

This, then, must be Lady Keith!—but no sign of recognition?
                                                          (*WWW* 355, 521)
Was it only an ordinary service of friendship? . . . Was it not a
positive return of good for evil? Yes, evil!

                                                          (*HR* 2:174)

Such humble beginnings are genuinely, if only momentarily, colloquial.
They are also perennial. In 1881 James is still relying consistently upon
quoted thoughts, questions, exclamations. Chapter 42, for example,
presents in less than a full page:

> Did all women have lovers? Did they all lie, and even the best have
> their price? Were there only three or four that didn't deceive their
> husbands? . . . What was coming, what was before them? That was
> her constant question. What would he do—what ought she to do?
> When a man hated his wife, what did it lead to?
>
>   (*PL* 398, 399)[6]

And then there is always:

> What am I? Am I single? Am I married? Am I a widow? Can I marry?
> Have I married? May I marry? Who am I? Where am I? What am I?—
> What is my name? What is my condition in life? If I am married, to
> whom am I married? If I am a widow, how came I to be a widow, and
> whose widow came I to be? Why am I his widow? What did he die of?
> Did he leave me anything? if anything, how much, and is it saddled
> with conditions?—Can I marry again without forfeiting it? Have I a
> mother-in-law? Have I a family of step-children, and if so, how many,
> and what are their ages, sexes, sizes, names and dispositions? These are
> questions that rack me night and day.

Here, four years before *The Portrait*, W. S. Gilbert parodies in *Engaged*
the brainless litanies of introspective heroines.[7] And, at least by implication, he does more. We see unmistakably that the illusion of mental
process cannot be effectively sustained if a writer merely borrows,
untransformed, the questions and exclamations of dialogue. Recognizing
both the limitations of these devices and their popularity with all grades
of novelists, we can go on to discover that the scribblers themselves
could do better.

The appearance of italics in mental process passages marks, as
Bridgman notes, an important stage in the stylistic development of James
and Mark Twain (94, 99). Our humble popular writers had long since
been using italics for the same purpose, however.

> She *must* go on, and the necessary preparations for the morrow *must*
> be made. . . . she *could* not love him less. . . . yes, she *had* been
> hypocritical.

Is James' famous chapter 42 readily distinguishable from its popular kindred?* The scribblers also foster the illusion of thinking by combining a character's own words with a syntax which suggests process.

> "My old gentleman!" cried Ellen, as she sprang to open it [the door]. No,—there was no old gentleman, but a black man. . . .
>
> (*WWW* 55)
>
> A carriage—her color came and went, but it was only some of the guests; another—the Brownlows.
>
> (*HR* 2:40)

The expression "only some of the guests" and the repeated "old gentleman" are clearly the heroine's own words; the syntax, with its fragments, suggests the dartings of the girls' minds.

> He saw that it [the boat] contained a gentleman and lady, English— probably his cousins themselves.

Prophetic of Strether's revelatory moment with *his* boating couple, this passage from *The Heir* (2:122) presents a consciousness moving processively. We follow the optical focus—from boat, to boaters, to their nationality, to their probable identity. This self-generating quality, and the open-endedness fostered by "probably," indicate considerably more sophistication than Taylor credits the popular tradition with. They also qualify Bridgman's thesis that James discovered his mental process techniques in his own realistic dialogue. In fact, compare Bridgman's summary with the popular practice which we have seen:

> James's late work is particularly marked by colloquial signs such as simple words, repeated words, parallel structures, emphasis by italics, emphasis by punctuation, and discursiveness.
>
> (99)

That all these traits appear in the scribblers' examples above and can be documented many times over in other texts is not surprising once we understand why the mind's ruminations—particularly in scenes of "meditation"—received such perennial attention in fiction. Novelists make central to their books what is central to their readers' lives. And most Victorian readers are earnestly Protestant. The inner life, with its self-examination, conversion experience (and even its handy metaphor of sudden illumination), is a primary concern of both pious texts and pious Christians. Adding to introspectiveness the perennial popular craving for sentiment, we find understandable indeed the frequency of scenes with heroines meditating before windows or in darkened chambers.

Descended from the introspective, stern Calvinism of his grandfather and from the gentler but no less introspective Swedenborgianism of his

*WWW 62; *HR* 2:315; *PL* 395.

father, Henry James, Jr., could hardly help sharing the scribblers' concern with consciousness. He differs from these novelists, however, in the nature of his concern. Free of sectarian constraints, James can take the potentially volatile situation of Protestant self-analysis, and secularize it. His chief interest is not the conscience judging between sheep and goats, but the consciousness attempting to understand its processive experience. By freeing the spirit from straight ways and foregone conclusions, James opens Pandora's box and, with Sigmund Freud, helps initiate the modern period.

A sense of James' link to and differences from popular psychology helps us, in turn, to understand his debt to conventional ways of rendering that psychology. The scribblers' use of colloquial diction and syntax does not mean that James learned his practice solely from them; I said before that our awareness of popular techniques *qualified* Bridgman's thesis because I wanted to suggest how much of later James was abiding in the literary air around him.[8] The scribblers do with their colloquial techniques what they did with their best devices of style and characterization: they do not sustain them. The illusion of self-generated and open-ended process is rarely maintained beyond a sentence. Popular novelists do not join colloquial moments together into moving pictures because they do not see experience as processive; they fear to set our minds in motion because such motion will, most likely, lead us astray. Instead, the epiphanies of popular characters are momentary confirmations of static, enduring truths. Since Jamesian epiphanies are inevitably qualified by the next instant, James must, once again, transform his tradition. Conversant with what the scribblers do best—convey single moments of awareness colloquially—he manages eventually to create an ongoing epic of consciousness.

2

James' late style is probably too large a subject for a whole book, let alone for part of one chapter. Fortunately, critics, especially in recent years, have devoted enough study to certain features of that style—its abstractness, its parenthetical interpolations, punctuation, repetition, verb tenses—that I can presume the importance of these features and turn directly to the tactic which contributes so much to sustaining the illusion of mental processes in *The Ambassadors.*

> Thanks to his constant habit of shaking the bottle in which life handed him the wine of experience, he presently found the taste of the lees rising as usual into his draught. His imagination had in other words . . .

> He wasn't there to dip, to consume. . . .

Could even the most devoted Jamesian state what the master is trying to convey here?

> Thanks to his constant habit of shaking the bottle in which life handed him the wine of experience, he presently found the taste of the lees rising as usual into his draught. His imagination had in other words already dealt with his young friend's assertion.
>
> He wasn't there to dip, to consume—he was there to reconstruct.
>
> (117, 68)

Especially in context the additional clauses shed considerable light upon our initial darkness. Why, then, does James allow darkness at all? In each case, a mystery is created, and then solved. On page 117 James gives us a metaphor and then a literal statement; on page 68, a negative and then a positive.[9] Simply omitting the metaphoric and the negative elements, James could have avoided mystery. Mystery occurs, then, not because Strether's specific thoughts are themselves inscrutable, but because James knows that he can successfully create the illusion of Strether thinking only if he can generate an analogous process in us. The very presence of an initial metaphor or negation will impel us farther into the passage for elucidation. The eventual literal or positive statement does not, in turn, function as a simple authorial explanation. We escape our initial puzzlement only by joining the metaphoric and literal or negative and positive elements together in our minds. Our minds are made to move, to jump like a spark across a dark gap. We ourselves create that relationship, that connection, which is meaning.

This explanation is not precise enough, however. My spark analogy implies too complete an illumination. Imagine rather that the two elements—metaphoric and literal, or negative and positive—are two colored discs which overlap but do not coincide completely. Where the discs overlap, meaning happens. But meaning remains partial because the two elements do not, cannot, coincide completely. No two clauses can mean precisely the same thing because no two words, let alone groups of words, can be exactly synonymous. There must always be intractable margins where the discs fail to coincide. Thus any act of elucidation, any attempt at explanation, introduces new obscurity; ambivalence happens as meaning does. We are forced to acknowledge two different relations simultaneously.

James' tactic for conveying the illusion of mental processes and for generating an analogous process in us is, then, to create a mystery and then to solve it partially. Two basic ways of doing this are the metaphoric-literal and the negative-positive patterns. Recurring on virtually every page of the late novels, these patterns do not become mechanical or intrusive because James augments them with variations and with a third pattern.

> Strether hadn't had for years so rich a consciousness of time—a bag of gold into which he constantly dipped for a handful.
>
> (77)

Varying the metaphoric and literal components by reversing them, James achieves a quite different effect. The mystery here occurs in the *second* half of the sentence.[10] We recognize a similarity between a consciousness of time and a handful of gold, but the metaphor—worth, like all pictures, a thousand words—is not exhausted by this similarity. Rather, the image multiplies similarities and, worse still (or better), introduces differences which complicate Strether's mental state and our attitude toward it. Does, for example, gold's traditional association with corruption enter here to suggest the dangers of Strether's dalliance with time? Are we also made wary by the bag image which indicates that time may well be less inexhaustible, more terminal than Strether seems aware of? Does "for years" indicate that Strether is returning to the naive romanticism of his first trip to Paris, when he came with his bride and his dreams of promise? These and other questions receive no definite answers, of course. By increasing our sense of mystery at the *end* of the sentence, the literal-metaphor pattern impels us on for meaning to the next and successive sentences. The pattern also increases our general awareness that even the simplest statement may reveal sudden depths when seen from another perspective.

Besides variation,[11] James also relies upon a third pattern.

> He was conscious of how much it was affected, this sense, by some-
> thing subdued and discreet in the way she had arranged herself
> for her special object and her morning walk—he believed her to have
> come on foot; the way her slightly thicker veil was drawn—a mere
> touch, but everything; the composed gravity of her dress, in which,
> here and there, a dull wine-colour seemed to gleam faintly through
> black; the charming discretion of her small compact head; the quiet
> note, as she sat, of her folded, grey-gloved hands.
>
> (181)

Here the general notion of "something subdued and discreet" is followed by particular details, the veil, dress, head, hands. This general-particular pattern creates a mystery—what is the something?—and then encourages us to find a solution by defining the word "something." Since a definition itself involves words which need defining, James uses the general-particular pattern to launch us as ambassadors on voyages of discovery.

Many of the best narrative moments[12] in *The Ambassadors* (and in the late works generally) occur when James combines all three of his basic patterns. Here is one example.

> Suddenly, however, on this particular day, he felt a particular fear
> under which everything collapsed. He knew abruptly that he was
> afraid of himself—and yet not in relation to the effect on his sen-
> sibilities of another hour of Madame de Vionnet. What he dreaded
> was the effect of a single hour of Sarah Pocock, as to whom he was
> visited, in troubled nights, with fantastic waking dreams. She loomed

at him larger than life; she increased in volume as she drew nearer; she
so met his eyes that, his imagination taking, after the first step, all, and
more than all, the strides, he already felt her come down on him,
already burned, under her reprobation, with the blush of guilt, already
consented by way of penance, to the instant forfeiture of everything.
He saw himself, under her direction, recommitted to Woollett as
juvenile offenders are committed to reformatories. It wasn't of course
that Woollett was really a place of discipline; but he knew in advance
that Sarah's salon at the hotel would be. His danger, at any rate in such
moods of alarm, was some concession, on this ground, that would
involve a sharp rupture with the actual.

(211)

Combining his basic patterns, James moves beyond single, momentary
revelations to the illusion of sustained process. The general notion of a
"fear" is defined by successive particularizations, which include both the
negative-positive ("it wasn't . . . but he knew") and the literal-metaphor
("committed to Woollett as . . . offenders . . . to reformatories") patterns. We learn in this synthetic passage, as in the whole novel and
in our daily experience, that meaning comes only through continually
reestablished relations, through an ongoing process of definition and
redefinition.

Our progress through the passage on page 211 is particularly representative of late James because our motion has not been linear. We
encounter an initial notion—Strether's "fear"—and then we move, not
on to other events, but around this core notion, ending again with
Strether's fear. Since we now know that the fear is of the danger of a
concession, we have not simply gone around in circles. Back where we
started and yet farther on toward understanding, we have moved rather
in a gyre. This motion, assured by the fact that all three basic patterns
depend upon repetition, assumes special importance in *The Ambassadors*
because a circling motion characterizes the whole novel. The gyre of
James' artistry expands from the small circuit of a metaphoric-literal
sentence, to larger synthetic passages (211), to sequences which circle for
pages,[13] to the *medias res* opening of the majority of the chapters, to the
very plot of the novel which begins with Strether's arrival in Europe and
ends with him using his return ticket. These motions have generated in us
so analogous a process that we finally experience Strether's passage as an
epic of our own consciousness.

To make a novel which mirrored in its every aspect the mental
processes which are its subject, involved thirty years of stylistic commitment. Between this achievement and *Watch and Ward*, James first
sustained the illusion of mental process in a novel which still owed much
to its predecessors.

> "If I lived in your room, I should
> be afraid at night."
>
> *Raskolnikov*

1881

Epistemologically *The Portrait* is the most sophisticated of James'
novels to date.

> "She chiefly communicates with us by means of telegrams, and her
> telegrams are rather inscrutable.... 'Changed hotel, very bad,
> impudent clerk, address here. Taken sister's girl, died last year, go to
> Europe, two sisters, quite independent.' Over that my father and I
> have scarce stopped puzzling; it seems to admit of so many inter-
> pretations."
> "There is one thing very clear in it," said the old man; "she has given
> the hotel-clerk a dressing."
> "I am not sure even of that.... Does it mean that they have been left
> well off, or that they wish to be under no obligations? Or does it
> simply mean that they are fond of their own way?"
> "Whatever else it means, it is pretty sure to mean that."
>
> (13)

Inscrutable indeed, this lady who intimates that she is bringing to Europe
a girl who "died last year." Lydia's mysteries should be solved when the
authoress herself explicates the text.

> [Ralph] "What you meant, then, in your telegram, was that her
> character was independent."
> "I never know what I mean by my telegrams."
>
> (42)

Lydia Touchett's telegram, appearing less than ten pages into *The
Portrait*, establishes the novel's epistemological issues with a clarity and
concentration which make critical neglect of this passage particularly
surprising.[14] James is presenting a paradigmatic situation—the act of
exegesis—and is repeating for our attention the word "meant." That
word recurs at least 258 times in the novel; the specific act of text analysis
occurs with six telegrams and several letters.[15] Moreover, analyzing the
"meaning" of *written* words is only part of our task. Like Lydia's
telegram, dialogue consistently short-circuits.

217

[Caspar] "Some day? You mean as long a time hence as possible."
[Isabel] "Oh no; I don't mean all that."
"What *do* you mean."

(470–71)

Such confusion of "meaning" spreads, of course, into the speakers' mental processes. Pondering Osmond's protracted embrace of Pansy,

Isabel wondered whether he meant it as a hint. . . . "I haven't the least idea what you mean," said Isabel.
"You have played a very deep game." . . . looking down at her thoughtfully, in his usual way, which seemed meant to let her know that she was not an object, but only a rather disagreeable incident, of thought.
"If you mean that Lord Warburton is under an obligation . . ."

(443)

Since so much talk ends without ever establishing "meaning," the process of exegesis continues on after disquieting silence ensues. "She wondered what Madame Merle had meant by no one being the wiser. . . . did Madame Merle suppose that she was capable of doing a deed in secret? Of course not—she must have meant something else" (290, 291).

So sophisticated an epistemological context challenges James' technical resourcefulness. He responds by mixing old and new techniques. Critics who have discussed this mixture tend to divide sheep from goats too neatly: chapter 42 looks toward the future, whereas most of the rest of the book is traditional. Actually, nothing establishes the extent of James' maturation better than the fact that techniques apparently new with *The Ambassadors* recur *throughout* the 550 pages of *The Portrait*. In turn, vestiges of early practice appear in chapter 42, as we saw when Isabel reels off a string of questions like any Beset Maiden, including W. S. Gilbert's. These, and other vestigial elements in the novel contrast unfortunately with James' more advanced techniques and with the sophisticated epistemological context. Faced with this mixture, let us begin with the vestiges of creation.

1

Devices which seemed antiquated in *Watch and Ward* appear in *The Portrait* with surprising frequency. For instance, the incredible personification "curiosity, even on tiptoe, expired before it reached them [windows]" (210) is but one of several in 1881.[16] Equally archaic is:

"I never exhibited the smallest preference for anyone else."
"For any one but yourself," X mentally observed; but the reflection was perfectly inaudible.

"I never sacrificed my husband to another," Y continued, with her stout curtness.

"Oh no," thought X; "you never did anything for another!"

A. "Do you live here—in the mountains?"

B, *aside*. "Does she think I'm a goatherd?" (*Aloud.*) "No, I live just now at Geneva."

A. "Well, you *are* peculiar, anyhow!"

B, *aside*. "So are you, if you come to that."

I have omitted proper nouns in order to stress how similar these passages are in their reliance upon that heavy gambit, the stage aside. The broadly comic situation in *Daisy Miller: A Comedy in Three Acts* may justify the device in our second example.[17] But in the more serious situation of Madame Merle's talk with Lydia Touchett (191–92), the aside introduces a crudeness appropriate to a stage villainess and woefully inappropriate to Madame Merle's elegant if devious consciousness. Acknowledging the wisdom of Wayne Booth's admonition not to discount techniques simply because of their antiquity, we can still call stage asides and most personifications "vestigial" because they mar the dramatic moment so obviously.

A different type of equally harmful archaicness occurs when

How could he tell her that he had recognized his own coat of arms on a carriage . . . —that he had questioned the currier . . . and discovered that the same uncle [was on his way] . . . that he dreaded their discovering Hildegarde's being with him . . . and that, to avoid a chance meeting, he had wandered about . . .

(*In* 387)

But the sense that it was his last chance, that he had loved her and lost her, that she would think him a fool whatever he should say, suddenly gave him a lash.

(*PL* 471)

That novelists who wanted to present the mind talking to itself tended to choose the mode of classic indirect discourse is understandable, but unfortunate. The final effect is decidedly *un*colloquial. The "that" pattern calls attention to itself, emphasizes the ordering role of the narrator, and replaces the flow of consciousness with the clanking of gears.

She [Madame Merle] had once said that she came from a distance, that she belonged to the old world, and Isabel never lost the impression that she was the product of a different clime from her own, that she had grown up under other stars. Isabel believed that at bottom she had a different morality. . . . Isabel suspected that her friend had esoteric views. She believed, with the presumption of youth, that a morality . . .

> She [Countess Gemini] was ashamed to say how seldom she had been
> allowed to go there [Rome]. . . . She went whenever she could; that
> was all she could say . . . . She was convinced that society was infinitely
> more interesting in Rome . . . . She heard a great deal about her sister-
> in-law.
>
> (299, 413)

Here archaic and advanced techniques in *The Portrait* contrast sharply.[18]
Both passages begin with dialogue presented in indirect discourse. On
page 299 the indirect discourse then continues on to render Isabel's
thoughts. The insistent "that"s and the barrage of mental-process verbs
("never lost the impression . . . believed . . . suspected . . . believed")
diminish considerably our sense of Isabel's presence. Where Countess
Gemini, on the other hand, stops talking in indirect discourse and starts
talking to herself is not only hard to determine but finally immaterial.
Whether "convinced" is what she says or what she is, the colloquial flow
of her all too free mind commits us to her.

A last, lingering difficulty we can approach best through Elizabeth
Drew's statement that "we enter [besides Isabel's] the consciousness of
Ralph and Madame Merle and Gilbert Osmond, but not, I think, of any
of the others" (229). Such an "I think" is noteworthy, not because it
constitutes the demonstrable error of a distinguished critic, but because it
seems to represent what most readers think. I know of no critic, despite
the extensive concern with mental process in *The Portrait*, who has
begun to suggest how wide-ranging James' point of view shifts are in this
novel.[19] In fact we enter the consciousnesses of every major character
and of several minor ones. Besides Ralph, Isabel, Madame Merle, and
Osmond, there is, for example, the Countess Gemini, who sustains off
and on for three pages a colloquial meditation upon herself, Isabel, and
Henrietta (413–15). We also enter the Countess' mind on pages 497–98.
Caspar Goodwood's thoughts are rendered very colloquially on pages
424, 466–67, and 468; both Daniel and Lydia Touchett are focused on
(51–52, 255, 535); likewise Ned Rosier (335, 338, 341–42), Henrietta
Stackpole (152, 449, 467), and Lord Warburton (275–76). Even Isabel's
sister, the conciliatory Lily, dominates the stage for a paragraph. "She
thought it would be so natural for Isabel to come home and take a house
in New York—the Rossiters', for instance, which had an elegant conservatory and was just around the corner from her own" (296).

Besides suggesting the extent of James' viewpoint shifts in *The Portrait*,[20] my intention is not, of course, to judge the technique harmful per
se. James continues these shifts in his later fiction, and uses them at times
with great effectiveness in *The Portrait*. Passing too readily among
consciousnesses can, however, cause a difficulty in 1881 which is largely
absent by 1901. The difficulty appears in the difference between Isabel

analyzing Warburton's intentions (355) and Ralph analyzing his own
(358–59). Isabel is sitting with Warburton. Ralph . . . Ralph is nowhere.
"It probably will not be surprising to the reflective reader that Ralph
Touchett should have seen less of his cousin since her marriage. . . . there
was a difference, as Ralph often said to himself—there was a difference."
Ralph's ruminations float in the void; we get no real sense of *him*
thinking, although the individual sentences are themselves quite adequately processive. The same difficulty occurs when we contrast Isabel's
thoughts on page 290 with Osmond's ten pages earlier. Isabel is thinking
about Pansy, in the girl's presence, in her house. But "in general Osmond
took his pleasures singly. . . . at present he was happy" (280). In general
. . . at present: the absence of a dramatic context makes Osmond's passage seem less a record of his mind thinking than a narrative summary of a
character's thoughts.[21] We may even wonder whether James is at times
guilty of what he excoriated others for—appropriating a character's
consciousness in order to introduce background and other materials.

   2

   Whatever their particular defects, James' vestigial techniques
share one thing in common. They fail to make our minds move. Indirect
discourse techniques which are too stiff and viewpoint shifts which are
too random fail to make us experience the mystery inherent in *The
Portrait*'s epistemological situations. Such failures mark the novel as a
stage in James' development, but they are not the paramount feature of
his mixed practice in 1881. To determine how successful James' new
techniques are at generating mystery, at making our minds move, we
must define the status of chapter 42. Although this chapter contains the
highest concentration of James' new techniques, his success in *The
Portrait* depends upon the consistency with which he can render the
illusion of mental process *throughout* the novel. To demonstrate the
range, as well as the intensity, of James' practice, I have chosen the
majority of my examples from outside chapter 42.
   In the complex epistemological situations of *The Portrait*, the general-
particular pattern functions consistently to show characters taking one
notion and gradually proceeding to some "meaning." Here is the pattern
in chapter 42.

   He said to her one day that she had too many ideas. . . . he had really
   meant it. The words were nothing, superficially; but when in the light
   of deepening experience she looked into them, they appeared por-
   tentous. He really meant it—he would have liked her to have nothing
   of her own but her pretty appearance. . . . What he meant was the
   whole thing—her character, the way she felt, the way she judged.
                                                                            (395)

We find here both of the qualities essential to creating and sustaining the illusion of mental processes. The thoughts seem self-generating, and the process open-ended. Thoughts seem self-generated because the generalization—"that she had too many ideas"—spawns successive particularizations which define and redefine it; "too many ideas" is the opposite of "pretty appearance," is her character, feelings, judgments. This self-generating process seems, in turn, open-ended because we are really experiencing not what Osmond's statement "means" in any absolute sense but what Isabel thinks it may mean. We are prompted to follow both Isabel's analysis of meaning and what *that* means. "Too many ideas" is not defined exhaustively with "judged" because we realize that Isabel does not know herself well enough yet to evaluate Osmond's words and her own ideas fully.

To indicate that this self-generating and open-ended process, supposedly quite special to chapter 42, appears consistently throughout *The Portrait*, we could study the general notion of "eccentric" as applied to Lydia Touchett (27) or "ambition" and Isabel (107). Instead, let us focus upon the word which probably generates the general-particular pattern more frequently than any other—a word which critics have acknowledged in late James (it appeared in the excerpt from page 181 of *The Ambassadors*) but which is already basic to James' practice by 1881.

> She felt that something had happened to her of which the importance
> was out of proportion to the appearance; there had really been a
> change in her life. What it would bring with it was as yet extremely
> indefinite; but Isabel was in a situation which gave a value to any
> change. She had a desire to leave the past behind her. . . . This desire,
> indeed, was not a birth of the present occasion; it was as familiar as the
> sound of rain upon the window.
>
> (30)

"Something." It is so useful to James because it suggests the initially indeterminate quality of a dawning awareness. As the character gropes toward increased "meaning," James introduces a word so bereft of denotation that we must seek definitions for it—and encounter terms which themselves need defining. "Something" is "out of proportion," is "change," is "desire." In the process we also experience the mysteries provided by negative-positive and literal-metaphoric elements: "change was not . . . it was . . . familiar as the sound of rain." Although we could multiply examples of how "something" generates the illusion of open-ended process throughout *The Portrait* (27, 393, 400, 411, 495), let us go on to the other two basic patterns.

The more highly developed of these by 1881 is the negative-positive.

> She found herself near a rustic bench, which, a moment after she had
> looked at it, struck her as an object recognized. It was not simply that

she had seen it before, nor even that she had sat upon it; it was that in this spot something important had happened to her—that the place had an air of association. Then she remembered . . .

(539)

Dialectically the mind moves. Defining the object of perception first by what does not make it significant, the negatives ("not . . . nor") function as though removing barriers to sight, to the significant fact that "something important had happened to her" here. Now Isabel is looking, not simply at the physical bench, but at "something." Defining *that* as "air of association" triggers in turn the whole stream of association which is memory. And the flow is on.

The negative-positive pattern is most successful when the self-generating quality of the dialectic does not depend upon a process of physical seeing and when open-endedness derives from more than the mere continuation of the passage.

She wished, therefore, to hold fast to justice [P]—not to pay herself by petty revenges [N]. To associate Madame Merle with her disappointment would be a petty revenge [P]—especially as the pleasure she might derive from it would be perfectly insincere [P]. It might feed her sense of bitterness [P], but it would not loosen her bonds [N]. It was impossible to pretend that she had not acted with her eyes open [N]; if ever a girl was a free agent, she had been [P]. A girl in love was doubtless not a free agent [N]; but the sole source of her mistake had been within herself [P]. There had been no plot, no snare [N]; she had looked, and considered, and chosen [P].

It was her conviction, at least, that she deceived him, and made him say to himself that he had been misinformed. But she also saw, so she believed, that he was not disappointed [N], as some other men, she was sure, would have been [P]; he had not come to Rome to look for an opportunity [N]. She never found out what he had come for [N]; he offered her no explanation[N]; there could be none [N] but the simple one that he wanted to see her [P]. In other words, he had come for his amusement [P].

(374, 454–55)

That both passages continue on for some length is not the chief cause of their open-endedness. On page 374, dialectical processes bring Isabel close to the real truth. Once she hits upon the definition of herself as "free agent," that notion prompts its opposite, as though responding to the impossibility of human freedom in Rome. So she qualifies: no girl in love is free. Close enough here to reach out and touch the more specific and sinister cause of her entrapment, Isabel fails. The positive statement which the negative prompts only returns her to herself as "sole source." Isabel's naive, egoistic belief in freedom is still strong enough to divert the train of thought which has taken her as far as "no girl in love is free."

The process on page 374 thus remains open-ended because we realize that Isabel will have to return to the notion of herself as free agent—return until she achieves enough freedom of thought to reveal how little freedom of action we all tragically have. On pages 454–55, the mental processes are also incomplete. Cued by James' "it was her conviction" and "so she believed," we recognize how self-serving Isabel's dialectic is here. Caspar is not disappointed (N); he is only seeking amusement (P). By postponing until after this rationalization the direct comment that "Isabel followed up this induction with a good deal of eagerness, and was delighted to have found a formula that would lay the ghost of this gentleman's ancient grievance," James can use the facile flow of her logic, the absence of any implicating reversal like "no girl in love is free," to make us experience her words *as* rationalizations. The very quality of the negative-positive pattern tells us that Isabel will have to face once more her relations with Caspar.

Even when Isabel does think again about her relationships, she does not reach any kind of complete propositional "truth." James must maintain open-endedness because no one moment, however splendid, can constitute the character's complete apotheosis or the author's final word.

> It was not her fault [N]—she had practiced no deception [N]; she had
> only admired and believed [P]. . . . She knew she had too many
> ideas [P]; she had more even than he supposed, many more than she
> had expressed to him when he asked her to marry him [P]. Yes, she *had*
> been hypocritical [P].
>
> (391, 395)

Isabel can move from the righteous self-exoneration of "It was not her fault" to the honesty of "Yes, she had been hypocritical" because she allows her dialectical processes enough freedom to take her and us on to painful awareness. By achieving this dialectical flow Isabel is, in fact, putting herself into harmony with reality as it is. "These intimations contradicted the spirit of the present hour" (517). Moving in contradictions, experience belies the sophistries and short-sightedness of the present moment. Thus the very fact that Isabel reaches new awareness about herself means that still greater awareness abides ahead. Since each revelation is less a benediction than a promise, we move on with her to that next negation which is the next affirmation.

Or the next image. Dialectic can also be fostered by metaphor, as Austin Warren has shown with James' dialogue. "Dialectic . . . is a cerebral process, pursued by two or more minds, in contrapuntal movement of thesis, antithesis, synthesis."[22] A process similarly processive, but usually not controlled consciously, can also occur *within* one mind.

She was not indifferent to her husband's sister, however; she was
rather a little afraid of her. She wondered at her; she thought her
very extraordinary. The Countess seemed to her to have no soul [L];
she was like a bright shell, with a polished surface, in which something
would rattle when you shook it [M]. This rattle was apparently the
Countess's spiritual principle [L]; a little loose nut that tumbled about
inside her [M]. She was too odd for disdain, too anomalous for
comparisons [L].

                                                                                              (414)

Like so many mental-process situations, this one begins with a negative-
positive sequence which establishes the dialectical flow of the character's
consciousness and generates a comparable flow in us. Then, after "not
indifferent" is explained as "afraid . . . wondered" and the cause of these
emotions is tentatively defined as "very extraordinary . . . no soul," the
inadequacy of such propositional explanations prompts a metaphor.
"Like a hard, bright shell." This movement from literal to metaphoric
sustains the dialectical flow of consciousness and is continued by
Isabel's subsequent elaborations—"polished surface" and "rattle." After
the explanation required by this metaphor has in turn generated a
further complexity of image (a "loose nut"), we come to Isabel's startling
realization that the much-metaphored Countess is "too anomalous for
comparisons." The literal-metaphoric pattern is thus open-ended, necessarily. As no two words can be exactly synonymous, no analogical
relation—no comparison involving the literal-metaphoric sequence—can
sum up a character adequately. We are impelled on, to seek further
definition in experience.

How our search is most frequently fostered by the literal-metaphoric
pattern appears clearly in one last passage.

Apart from this, Mrs. Touchett had a great merit [L]; she was as
honest as a pair of compasses [M]. There was a comfort in her stiffness
and firmness [L]; you knew exactly where to find her [P], and were
never liable to chance encounters with her [N]. On her own ground she
was always to be found [P]; but she was never over-inquisitive as re-
gards the territory of her neighbor [N]. Isabel came at last to have a
kind of undemonstrable pity for her [L]; there seemed something so
dreary in the condition of a person whose nature had, as it were, so little
surface [M]—offered so limited a face to the accretions of human contact [L-P]. Nothing tender, nothing sympathetic, had ever had a
chance to fasten upon it [L-N]—no wind-sown blossom, no familiar
moss [M]. Her passive extent, in other words, was about that of a
knife-edge [M].

                                                                                              (204)

Again an image to be explored is embedded in a negative-positive dialectic, and again the image cannot fully sum up the character. Like the best moments throughout *The Portrait*, our exploration here extends beyond one image to those generated by the mind's process. From compass, to various circumscribed planes ("where to find her . . . ground . . . territory . . . surface . . . face"), to visual proofs of fruitful contact with life's planes ("blossom . . . moss"), and then to the opposite of fruitful contact—the knife edge. Sharpness is basic to a compass point but was initially played down here in favor of other traits ("stiffness . . . firmness"). Protruding suddenly, sharpness points up Lydia's chief inadequacy. Especially since the narrator has already told us that "the edges of her conduct were so very clear-cut that for susceptible persons it sometimes had a wounding effect" (20), we see that Isabel on page 204 has moved to James' awareness. Without attaining anything like complete knowledge of Lydia Touchett, we do experience that surfacing of sudden truth which characterizes mental process at its truest.

Finally, it is in concert that the three syntactic patterns and the various types of definition work most effectively. For a representative example we could return to the great "garden-plot" passage from chapter 42, or could study the famous paragraph which presents Caspar's kiss. Instead, let us choose a passage which has not received proper attention. Riding north to dying Ralph, Isabel meditates:

> The past and the future alternated at their will, but she saw them only in fitful images, which came and went by a logic of their own. It was extraordinary the things she remembered. Now that she was in the secret, now that she knew something that so much concerned her, and the eclipse of which had made life resemble an attempt to play whist with an imperfect pack of cards, the truth of things, their mutual relations, their meaning, and for the most part their horror, rose before her with a kind of architectural vastness. She remembered a thousand trifles; they started to life with the spontaneity of a shiver. That is, she had thought them trifles at the time; now she saw that they were leaden-weighted. Yet even now they were trifles, after all; for of what use was it to her to understand them? Nothing seemed of use to her to-day. . . . To cease utterly, to give it all up and not know anything more—the idea was as sweet as the vision of a cool bath in a marble tank, in a darkened chamber, in a hot land. . . . if her spirit was haunted with sudden pictures, it might have been the spirit disembarrassed of the flesh. There was nothing to regret now—that was all over.
>
> (516)

"A logic of their own": Richard Bridgman uses this expression to define the essence of colloquial processes. "Talk moves through a series of discursive units observing a logic of its own" (20). The elemental motion of such logic cannot be generated by authorial assertion. James' assertions of process here—"fitful images . . . started to life with the spontaneity of a shiver . . . haunted with sudden pictures"—would contrast with and thus emphasize the staticness of the passage *unless* style were making Isabel's mind seem actually in motion. Fortunately for James, such motion is just what we are experiencing. The general notion of "the things she remembered," for example, needs defining. We get "something" and "the truth of things." Apparently, however, none of these three "thing"s refers to the same thing. "Something" relates, not to the remembered "things," but to being "in the secret"; and "the truth of things" is defined by the general-particular pattern as "relations . . . meaning . . . horror."

We then return to "remembered," and the "things" are called "trifles." Defining trifles by the "shiver" image and then, dialectically, denying that the things are trifles ("they were leaden-weighted"), Isabel's mind proceeds on to another dialectical reversal, and then short-circuits. "Yet even now they were trifles . . . nothing seemed of use. . . . not [to] know anything [was sweet] . . . . nothing to regret." The "thing"s are thus continuing to pile up, and to mean little. Lest this passage in its frustrating abstractness mean too little to us, James interweaves patterns of literal-metaphoric relations. These metaphors emerge and fade, fitful images indeed, generating one another and yet so obliquely that we experience more flight than link. Moving from eclipse to architecture, for example, seems a very free association—clear only when we realize that the middle term, "imperfect pack of cards," relates to eclipse through their mutual thwarting of processes and to architecture through the suggestion of a house of cards. From architecture to the eastern bath images is another long jump, especially since architecture is associated with horror and the bath with pleasurable escape. We then see that escape is itself a horror because it constitutes the self-destruction which the initial horror impelled Isabel toward.

These self-generating processes seem open-ended not only because the passage continues, but because Isabel must. She must resist her morbid defeatism if she is to achieve the life-affirming commitment essential to Jamesian resignation. The way to this affirmation will be through a fuller understanding of the "thing"s of our passage—the past and its lessons. Thus, as we experience Isabel on page 516, we sense that her mental processes cannot rest yet, not here. We are especially confident that she will continue because she has recently displayed a significant new power.

> She [Madame Merle] had not proceeded far before Isabel noted a
> sudden rupture in her voice, which was in itself a complete drama.
> (508)

Sensitive from the first, Isabel has learned through her suffering to become a good Jamesian. She can recognize, even in the midst of intense confrontation, that the paramount events abide behind and cause the "plot" of a scene or of a villainess. This ability to perceive simultaneously the surface and the depths, and to recognize the primacy of the latter—is the ultimate attainment. Isabel manages it through her suffering, James achieves it by rendering that suffering formally, and we, beneficiaries of them both, may even for the moment experience a comparable wisdom.

> Be generous and delicate and
> pursue the prize.
>
> *Henry James*

Epilogue

To end with *The Portrait* as a splendid yet mixed achievement: there could be no other way. Recognizing, with James' help, the endlessness of relations, we draw our circle as we can. What gets included—techniques for style and characterization and mental process, plus the Victorian "variety and picturesqueness" which Joseph Warren Beach describes (207)—all this means that the range of felt life combines with the range of felt consciousness to make *The Portrait* the last great Victorian novel even as it announces the advent of modern fiction. In turn we recognize an analogous process of transformation and emergence in the crucial decade itself. The protagonist here, of course, is Henry James. Exploring his characters' explorations has brought James his own self-knowledge. In a decade of maturation which not only introduces virtually every theme and formal issue of his long career but also constitutes a paradigm of the novelist's development in the Victorian period, James lives out his belief that the life of the individual is the greatest adventure of all. James thus stands for what a younger contemporary would later defend so splendidly. "Why do they praise so much the soldier in battle. A man may display as reckless a courage by entering into the hell of himself." For all the differences between himself and William Yeats, Henry James, with his passion for style and his imagination of disaster, would have agreed.

Notes

Preface

1. Joseph J. Firebaugh, "Coburn: Henry James's Photographer," *American Quarterly* 7 (1955): 215–33.

2. From these letters Leon Edel quotes passages which do not appear either in Coburn's autobiography (*Alvin Langdon Coburn, Photographer* [New York, 1966]) or in James' discussion of the photographs in his Preface to *The Golden Bowl* (*AN* 331–35). We can only hope, therefore, that some or all of the missing letters will eventually appear in the fourth volume of the *Henry James Letters*, which Edel is now editing.

3. Quoted by Nancy Newhall in her introduction to *Alvin Langdon Coburn* (Rochester, 1962), 12.

4. Coburn, 52.

5. The photograph "Notre Dame" was later published by Coburn in *Camera Work* 1908, no. 21, p. 30, and has been reproduced in *Camera Work: A Critical Anthology*, ed. Jonathan Green (New York, 1973), 155.

6. Coburn, 54.

Introduction

1. As early as 1874, James establishes that "the books translatable were books of matter, and the books untranslatable books of *manner*" (*Na* 1874, 321).

2. Henry Fielding, *The Life of Mr. Jonathan Wild the Great* (New York, 1962), 132.

3. Henry James, *The Ambassadors* (Boston, 1960), 66.

4. Leo Spitzer, *Linguistics and Literary History* (Princeton, 1948), 11.

5. Seymour Chatman summarizes these and other objections by various critics in his "Editor's Introduction" to *Literary Style: A Symposium* (Oxford, 1971), xiii, xiv. Howard S. Babb also details some difficulties in his "Introduction" to *Essays in Stylistic Analysis* (New York, 1972), 4–5.

6. M. A. K. Halliday, "Linguistic Function and Literary Style: An Inquiry into the Language of William Golding's *The Inheritors*," in Chatman, 330–65.

7. Fritz Martini, "Personal Style and Period Style: Perspectives on a Theme of Literary Research," *Patterns of Literary Style*, ed. Joseph Strelka (University Park, Pa., 1971), 90–115; Louis T. Milic, "Rhetorical Choice and Stylistic Option: The Conscious and Unconscious Poles," in Chatman, 80; Carl H. Klaus, "Reflections on Prose Style," in *Contemporary Essays on Style*, ed. Glen A. Love and Michael Payne (Glenview, Ill., 1969), 57.

8. Roland Barthes, "Style and Its Image," in Chatman, 9. Klaus, at the end of his essay, also discusses ways in which the artist is formed by his materials. Josephine Miles sums up the whole dilemma of choice: "So we have the confluence in a literary text of ready-made forms and associations from the language, with those from the literature in general, and with those from specific genres of usage in particular" ("Style as Style," in Chatman, 25).

9. Charles Muscatine, *Chaucer and the French Tradition* (Berkeley, 1957); Jonas A. Barish, *Ben Jonson and the Language of Prose Comedy* (Cambridge, Mass., 1960); Richard Bridgman, *The Colloquial Style in America* (Oxford, 1966); Morris W. Croll, *Style, Rhetoric, and Rhythm* (Princeton, 1966); besides the volume cited above, see also Leo Spitzer's *Essays on English and American Literature* (Princeton, 1962).

10. Bradford Booth, "Form and Technique in the Novel," in *The Reinterpretation of Victorian Literature*, ed. J. E. Baker (Princeton, 1950), 67–96.

11. Caroline Ticknor, *Hawthorne and His Publisher* (Boston, 1913), 141.

12. Frank Kermode, *The Sense of an Ending* (Oxford, 1966), 17.

13. For the most educated guesses about sales in the nineteenth century, see Frank Luther Mott's *Golden Multitudes* (New York, 1947), James D. Hart's *The Popular Book* (Oxford, 1950), and Richard D. Altick's *The English Common Reader* (Chicago, 1957). Just to suggest the kind of profits which Hawthorne knew he was missing out on: Fanny Fern received the unheard-of figure of $100 a column for her stories in Bonner's *Ledger*, where she appeared weekly for almost fifteen years! Bonner also paid $20,000 to print a novel in the *Ledger:* not Hawthorne's or Melville's, but Henry Ward Beecher's.

14. Mott, 215.

15. A. Holder-Barell, *The Development of Imagery and Its Functional Significance in Henry James's Novels* (New York, 1966), 21.

16. Robert Colby, *Fiction with a Purpose* (Bloomington, Ind., 1967), 9.

17. In America, *Atlantic Monthly* published *Watch and Ward* (August–December 1871) and *The Portrait of a Lady* (November 1880–December 1881). The last number of *The Bostonians* appeared in *The Century* issue for February 1886.

18. I do not include "plot" as a separate category here because popular fiction blends character types so completely with their "situations" that discussing one involves discussing both.

19. Karl Kroeber, *Styles in Fictional Structure* (Princeton, 1971), 7.

20. Eliot and Dickens, Hawthorne and Twain, Flaubert and Turgenev, not only transform received materials; they frequently transform the same materials that we see James use. What we discover with him, then, is not a unique achievement, but rather his own version of that personalization which marks every great writer's career and works.

21. Mark Twain and Charles Dudley Warner, *The Writings of Mark Twain*, Author's National Edition (New York, 1898), 10:200–201.

22. For good summaries of these changes, see Lewis Mumford's *The Brown Decades* (New York, 1931) and Jay Martin's *Harvests of Change* (Englewood Cliffs, N.J., 1967).

23. William Dean Howells, *Heroines of Fiction* (New York, 1901), 1:40.

24. Quoted by Alan Bott in *Our Fathers* (London, 1931), 5.

25. Robert Falk, *The Victorian Mode in American Fiction, 1865–1885* (East Lansing, Mich., 1964), 19.

26. Edmund Wilson, "The Chastening of American Prose Style: John W. De Forest," in *Patriotic Gore* (Oxford, 1962), 638.

27. W. N. Brigance (*A History and Criticism of American Public Address* [New York, 1943]) cites Champ Clark's belief "that oratory was falling into disuse, particularly on the floor of Congress" (1:136). In general, simplicity increased after the Civil War because most political speeches were written to be read (see S. B. Harding's *Select Orations* [New York, 1909], xxii). In particular, so famous an orator as Samuel Gompers relied very much upon plain style.

28. E. G. Parker, *The Golden Age of American Oratory* (Boston, 1857), 8, 9.

29. Larzer Ziff, *The American 1890s* (New York, 1966). Discussing the St. Louis

labor conference of 1892, Ziff says, "what is striking about the imagination which thus reveals itself is the way in which the serious radical remedies of the platform are cushioned by a preamble that rings the familiar high-flown changes on biblical rhetoric" (81–82). The preamble's author was no infiltrating establishmentarian: he was Ignatius Donnelly.

30. E. D. Jones (*Lords of Speech* [New York, 1937]) is probably correct when he says that "of all the eloquent speakers America has produced, the most gorgeous rhetorician was Robert G. Ingersoll" (149), but Jones does go on to suggest how complex Ingersoll was, by quoting Ingersoll himself on style. "[The great orator] knows the greatest ideas should be expressed in the shortest words—that the greatest statues need the least drapery" (158). And so, consistent with this aesthetic but in virtually diametric opposition to his own floweriness and to his contemporary reputation, Ingersoll espouses, not Everett at Gettysburg, but Lincoln. "The speech of Lincoln will never be forgotten. It will live until languages are dead and lips are dust. The oration of Everett will never be read" (158). For the mixed nature of postwar style there is no better example than the theory and practice of fighting Bob Ingersoll.

31. R. T. Oliver, *History of Public Speaking in America* (Boston, 1965), 425.

32. Jones, 199.

33. Ibid., 117.

34. Ziff quotes Grant's Paducah proclamation: "I am here to defend you against this enemy, and to assert and maintain the authority and the sovereignty of your government and mine. I have nothing to do with opinions. I deal only with armed rebellion and its aiders and abettors. You can pursue your usual avocations without fear or hindrance" (73). Lincoln's reaction was, "the man who can write like that is fitted to command in the West."

35. This excerpt from *Ladies' National Magazine* is quoted on the title page of Baroness von Tautphoeus' *The Initials* (Philadelphia, 1854).

36. "Prescott's style at first shunned the flexibility encouraged by European romanticism and showed more of the eighteenth century English emphasis upon clarity, use of balance, antithesis and metaphor, and abstention from 'low diction.' . . . As he went on writing, he simplified it [his style] a great deal and he repudiated more and more consciously the eighteenth century theory that there is only one good style. . . . In style, his [Parkman's] predilection for the 'direct' and 'manly' made him both less eighteenth century and less romantic than the other literary historians, as little disposed to balance and antithesis as to glossy adjectives and hyperthyroid verbs" (*Literary History of the United States*, ed. R. E. Spiller et al., rev. ed. [New York, 1953], 531, 537). Motley, though least regenerate of the three, is clearly more personal and creative than, say, Jared Sparks, or even Bancroft.

37. Quoted by David Levin in his excellent *History as Romantic Art* (Stanford, 1959), 254.

38. Spiller et al., 530.

39. Ibid., 527.

40. Edel notes a call by Motley announcing this kindness in February, 1877 and dinner with Motley in the winter of 1876–77 (*E*2:283, 330).

41. "The Jesuits in North America in the Seventeenth Century," *Na* 1867, 450–51; "The Old Régime in Canada," *Na* 1874, 252–53. In her excellent "Henry James Criticism: A Current Perspective" (*ALR* [1974], 155–68), Adeline R. Tintner notes the presence of Gardiner's *The History of the Great Civil War* in "The Given Case" and of Gibbon's *The Decline and Fall* in "Glasses," and urges further study of James and the historians.

42. Prescott wrote short stories for a literary society and then literary criticism for the *North American Review*; Motley did literary criticism for the same magazine and

two novels; Bancroft reviewed both Cooper and Scott for the *North American Review* (collected in *Essays from the N.A.R.*).

43. David Grimsted, *Melodrama Unveiled* (Chicago, 1968), 149. For England, see Michael R. Booth, *English Melodrama* (London, 1965), 157.

44. J. O. Bailey, *British Plays of the Nineteenth Century* (New York, 1966), 331.

45. Frank Rahill, *The World of Melodrama* (University Park, Pa., 1967), 267; John Geoffrey Hartman, *The Development of American Social Comedy from 1787 to 1936* (Philadelphia, 1939), 21.

46. Bailey, 354.

47. For developments in rendering mental process see Gordon O. Taylor's *The Passages of Thought* (Oxford, 1969) and my chapter 4. The increasing colloquialization of American prose is studied by Harold C. Martin ("The Development of Style in Nineteenth-Century American Fiction," in *Style in Prose Fiction: English Institute Essays 1958* [New York, 1959], ed. Harold C. Martin) and by Richard Bridgman. Interestingly, while Bridgman joins James with Twain as the two major innovators of colloquial style in the later nineteenth century, Wilson separates James from those who achieve the new "language of responsibility" (650) and joins him with Henry Adams as one who "in keeping the old-fashioned long rhythms . . . has used them for a new kind of impressionism; in returning to the old embroidery, he has varied it with an imagery less formal" (665).

48. David Lodge, *Language of Fiction* (New York, 1966), 168.

49. John Tomsich, *A Genteel Endeavor* (Palo Alto, Calif., 1971).

50. *The Writings of Mark Twain,* Author's National Edition, 23:312–13.

51. Defending himself against William's barbs, Henry confesses to "a constant impulse to try experiments of form" and acknowledges how long such experiments have occupied him; he replies nonetheless that "it is something to have learned how to write, and when I look around me and see how few people (doing my sort of work) know how (to my sense) I don't regret my step-by-step evolution" (*LL* 1:66).

Chapter One

1. James himself refers to the "half-remembered novels, devoured in infancy" (*LL* 1:28).

2. James refers to these popular authors in the following places. Louisa May Alcott (*Moods, NAR* 1865, 276–81; *Eight Cousins, Na* 1875, 250–51). Mary Elizabeth Braddon (*Lady Audley's Secret, Na* 1865, 593; in this same review James mentions *Aurora Floyd*, and says that he has read "half a dozen" of Miss Braddon's novels since *Aurora Floyd*). Charlotte Brontë (*Jane Eyre, AM* 1866, 491, and *Na* 1867, 410; James refers to "Miss Brontë's heroines" in *CT* 1:108; he has also read Mrs. Gaskell's *Life of Miss Brontë, Na* 1866, 247; as late as 1915, James mentions *The Professor, AM* 1915, 27). Mrs. E. R. Charles (*The Schönberg-Cotta Family, Na* 1865, 344–45; *Diary of Mrs. Kitty Travylyan* is also mentioned in this review; *Winifred Bertram and the World She Lived In, Na* 1866, 147–48; in this review James refers knowledgeably to "the author's preceding work"). Mrs. D. M. M. Craik (*A Noble Life, Na* 1866, 276; here James also mentions *John Halifax, Gentleman* and "Miss Mulock's tales"). Maria S. Cummins (*The Lamplighter, SB* 77). Mrs. R. H. Davis (*Waiting for the Verdict, Na* 1867, 410–11; in this review, James indicates that he has also read "a number of short stories" by Mrs. Davis; *Dallas Galbraith, Na* 1868, 330–31; James mentions *Margaret Howth* disparagingly in an 1870 *Atlantic* review, 251. Maria Edgeworth (James refers to her in *Nation* reviews of 1866 and 1868 [128 and 334], to her "infantine heroines" in *FrP* 64, and to *The Parent's Assistant* in 1878 [*Na*, 403]). Mrs. Frances Eliot (*The Italians: A Novel, Na* 1875, 107). Mrs. T. Erskine (*Wyncote, Na* 1875, 202). Mrs. E. Gaskell (*Wives and Daughters: A Novel, Na* 1866, 246–47; in this review James also

refers to *Cranford* and to Mrs. Gaskell's "tales"). Mrs. C. Jenkins (*Within an Ace, Na* 1875, 202; that James also knows other novels of Mrs. Jenkins is clear when he says that she "has done very much better things than *Within an Ace*"). Anne E. Manning (*The Household of Sir Thomas More* and *Jacques Bonneval; or The Days of the Dragonnades, Na* 1867, 126–27). Miss Hannah More (mentioned in an 1868 *Nation* review, 334). Mrs. Oliphant (*White Ladies, Na* 1875, 201; James is also aware of her "half-dozen works a year pace"). Ouida (*Signa: A Story, Na* 1875, 11; "she began several years ago writing unmitigated nonsense" indicates that James had read at least some of that nonsense). Miss Elizabeth Stuart Phelps (James refers disparagingly to *Hedged In* in the 1870 *Atlantic* review [251] and mentions Miss Phelps again in an 1875 *Nation* review [228]). H. E. Prescott (*Azarian: An Episode*, plus *The Amber Gods, The Rim*, and *Sir Rohan's Ghost* are all discussed in James' *NAR* review of 1865, 268–77). Mrs. Radcliffe (*The Mysteries of Udolpho, Na* 1865, 593; James unquestionably knew the rest of Mrs. Radcliffe's major novels). Mrs. A. M. C. Seemuller (*Emily Chester, NAR* 1865, 279–84; *Opportunity, Na* 1867, 449–50). Elizabeth Stoddard (*Two Men: A Novel* is the subject of a review written for *NAR* and never published [see Joseph Kraft's "An Unpublished Review by Henry James," *Studies in Bibliography* 20:267–73]; *The Morgesons*, mentioned in the same review). Mrs. Stowe (James mentions her in reviews as early as the *NAR* piece of 1864 [583]; his famous description of *Uncle Tom's Cabin* as "a wonderful 'leaping' fish" occurs in *SB* 160; in an 1866 letter he says, "I have been re-reading two or three of her books and altho' I see them to be full of pleasant qualities, they lack those solid merits wh. an indistinct recollection of them had caused me to attribute to them" [*HJL* 64]; yet in 1869, homesick in Italy, he can call *Old Town Folks* "a work of singular and delicious perfection" [*HJL* 130]; in the 1875 *Nation* James discusses *We and Our Neighbors*, and mentions "some of her tales" [61]. Miss Thackeray (*Miss Angel, Na* 1875, 201; in this review James refers familiarly to the "usual finesse" of her touch). Baroness von Tautphoeus (*The Initials*, see note 8). Miss L. B. Walford (*Mr. Smith, Na* 1875, 202). Susan Warner (James mentions *The Wide, Wide World, Na* 1865, 344). Mrs. Henry Wood (James knows her as early as the 1864 *NAR* review [584], and surely knows both the novel and play versions of *East Lynne*). Mrs. A. D. T. Whitney (*The Gayworthys: A Story of Threads and Thrums, NAR* 1865, 619–22). Charlotte Yonge (*The Heir of Redclyffe*, see note 8; *The Daisy Chain, Na* 1865, 344).

3. Thomas Bailey Aldrich (James praises his style "in verse as well as in prose," *Na* 1875, 12–13). Bulwer-Lytton (in the 1864 *NAR* review James mentions Bulwer's "several historical tales" [584]). Wilkie Collins (*Woman in White, Na* 1865, 593; knowing much of Collins' work from *Household Words* and elsewhere, James mentions him in both the 1865 *Nation* review of M. E. Braddon [593] and the 1870 *Atlantic* review of Disraeli [251]). Frederick Swartwout Cozzens [alias Richard Haywarde] (mentioned in an 1860 letter [*HJL* 29]). George William Curtis (in *Literature* for 11 June 1898, James mentions reading Curtis—probably the *Potiphar Papers*—in the fifties [667]). Benjamin Disraeli (*Lothair, AM* 1870, 249–51; James is clearly familiar with Disraeli's other novels). J. W. De Forest (*Honest John Vane, Na* 1874, 441–42); James also mentions in this review "several interesting novels by De Forest"). A. J. Froude (*Short Stories on Great Subjects, Na* 1867, 351). Julian Hawthorne (*Idolatry, AM* 1874, 746–48; here James also summarizes the earlier novel, *Bressant*). Oliver Wendell Holmes, Sr. (although James does not mention *Elsie Venner* and the *Autocrat* until 1915 [*AM*, 25], he had surely read these plus *The Guardian Angel* immediately upon their publication). Charles Kingsley (besides reviewing *Hereward* [*Na* 1866, 115–16], James mentions in other reviews *Westward Ho!, Hypatia, Two Years Ago, Yeast, Alton Locke* [*Na* 1865, 21–23; 1875, 61; 1877, 60–61]; in the 1878 "An International Episode" a character compares scenery to " 'the

coast scenery in Kingsley's novels' " [CT 4:271]; for James' admiration for Kingsley, see Introduction, p. 7). Henry Kingsley (*The Hillyars and the Burtons: A Story of Two Families*, Na 1865, 21-23). G. A. Lawrence (*Guy Livingstone*, Na 1875, 61, and 1876, 372). Captain Marryat ("several of the productions of..." [*EL* 133]). "Ike Marvel" (in the 1898 *Literature* article James mentions Marvel among his readings in the fifties [667]). James Payn (in 1902 James recalls *Lost Sir Massingberd* [*Illustrated London News* 1898, 500]). George S. Phillips (in 1865 James wrote and *NAR* never published a review of *The Gypsies of the Danes Dike* [HJL 58]). Charles Reade (James mentions *The Cloister and the Hearth* in the 1864 *NAR* review [584] and in the 1867 *Nation* review of historical novels [127]; in 1866 he refers to "the much abused *Griffith Gaunt*" [Na 128]; *Never Too Late to Mend* and *Put Yourself in His Place* appear in 1865 *Nation* and 1870 *Atlantic* reviews [22; 251]; James was reading Reade early, in *Once a Week* [JF 91], and was still mentioning him in 1915 [*AM* 29]; for James' great if qualified admiration for Reade see chapter 2, n. 96). Henry D. Sedley (*Marian Rooke*, Na 1866, 247-48). Bayard Taylor (in his 1875 *NAR* review of *The Prophet* James says that Taylor "has written a good deal of almost everything" [188-94]; in the *Harvard Library Bulletin* [11:245-59] Edel confirms that James also wrote a review of *John Godfrey's Fortunes* which *NAR* never published). T. A. Trollope (*Lindisfarne Chase: A Novel*, *NAR* 1865, 277-78). Artemus Ward (James mentions him in an 1869 letter [HJL 131] and in CT 2:294). George Whyte-Melville (in 1913 James mentions Whyte-Melville's "jolly rubbish" as he recalls "the fashionable trash of Victorian times" [E. Stone, *The Battle and the Books* (Athens, Ohio, 1964), 78]).

4. In many cases James has read the works before 1876 but mentions them only between 1876 and 1881. Frank Lee Benedict (*St. Simon's Niece*, Na 1876, 32). William Black (in the 1878 *Nation* review of *Macleod of Dare*, James also mentions *Madcap Violet, Princess of Thule, The Three Feathers, Adventures of a Phaethon* [387-88]). Rhoda Broughton (*Joan*, Na 1876, 372; here James also mentions *Cometh Up as a Flower*). Charles H. Doe (*Buffets*, Na 1876, 32-33). Mrs. Annie Edwards (*Leah: A Woman of Fashion*, Na 1876, 33). Julia Constance Fletcher (*Kismet*, Na 1877, 341; *Mirage*, Na 1873, 172). Mrs. Gore (" 'reading Mrs. Gore is no proof of intellect' " [CT 4:273]). Julian Hawthorne (*Garth*, Na 1877, 369; in this review James also mentions *Bressant* and *Idolatry*). Helen Hunt Jackson (*Mercy Philbrick's Choice*, Na 1876, 372). J. G. Lockhart (*Adam Blair* is mentioned in *Ha*, 102-3). Laurence Oliphant (*The Tender Recollections of Irene Macgillicuddy*, Na 1878, 357). Edmund Yates (James mentions him in a *Nation* review in 1876, 32).

Finally, here are some other indications of the breadth of James' early reading. He dipped (with varying degrees of frequency) into *Chambers's Journal, The Illustrated London News, Godey's Lady's Book, The Charm, The Boston Token and Atlantic Souvenir*, plus *British Chronicle, Knickerbocker Magazine, Every Saturday, Pall-Mall, Advertiser*, and *Wood's Household Magazine* (*Cornhill* 1902, 500; *Century* 1888, 220; *SB* 65, 83; *Ha* 42; HJL 30, 33, 76, 118, 261, 334). He refers familiarly to the " 'Rollo' books," to the "fashionable novels," to "a potential heroine of Miss Burney," to "the sensation writers" (Na 1875, 251 and HJL 26; Na 1867, 411; CT 2:260; Na 1865, 410).

In all these listings I have been very conservative, listing only titles which I could document definitely. James surely read more. I agree, for instance, with Oscar Cargill (*The Novels of Henry James* [New York, 1961]) that James had read all of Holmes, and more Wilkie Collins than the specific references indicate. He also received a generous dose of "popular" techniques from his voluminous readings in George Sand, Hugo, Balzac, and Dickens.

5. Cargill, 16. Cargill has been particularly effective in demonstrating James'

knowledge of and debt to French popular (and great) writers. Among the popular ones, James' favorites are About, Cherbuliez, Droz, Loti, and Sand.

6. Herbert Ross Brown, *The Sentimental Novel in America, 1789–1860* (Durham, N.C., 1940), 361. That the popular novels' tendency to simplify experience was shared by stage melodramas, both Grimsted and Michael Booth confirm. "The melodrama as mirror of contemporary life disfigured facts ludicrously by forcing and transforming them into the pattern of the moral and intellectual tenets of the age. . . . The world of melodrama is thus a world of certainties where confusion, doubt, and perplexity are absent" (Grimsted 203, Booth 14).

7. Quoted by Theophil Spoerri in "Style of Distance, Style of Nearness," in Babb, 66.

8. Both *The Heir of Redclyffe* and *The Initials* are mentioned in *Watch and Ward* (415, 326). Felix Alan Walbank (*Queens of the Circulating Library* [London, 1950]) says that "hardly any book in the language has been accorded the reception that *The Heir of Redclyffe* did. . . . among soldiers in hospital during the Crimean War *The Heir of Redclyffe* was the book most in demand" (21). James expresses his admiration of *The Heir* as early as 1865. Discussing "semi-developed novels," he says, "occasionally, like the 'Heir of Redclyffe', they almost legitimate themselves by the force of genius. But this only when a first-rate mind takes the matter in hand" (*Na* 1865, 344). For recent essays on *The Heir*, see K. Tillotson's "The Heir of Redclyffe" in *Mid-Victorian Studies* (London, 1965), 49–55, and Vineta Colby's *Yesterday's Woman* (Princeton, 1974), 193–201. To *The Initials* Howells devoted a whole chapter in *The Heroines of Fiction* (James himself receiving only one). Howells observes that "not to have read 'The Initials' was in their day to have left one's self out of the range of intellectual conversation and almost of human sympathy" (2:138). In 1907 James lists *The Initials* among " 'stories of real life' " which he "very early . . . began to prefer" (*EL* 132). In 1909 he is still remembering the "dear old rococo Munich of the 'Initials' (of my tender youth)" (*LL* 2:142). Near the end of his life James can recall "my conscious joy in bringing back to my mother, from our forage in New York, a gift of such happy promise as the history of the long-legged Mr. Hamilton and his two Bavarian beauties, the elder of whom, Hildegarde, was to figure for our small generation as the very type of the haughty as distinguished from the forward heroine (since I think our categories really came to no more than those)" (*SB* 78–79). Helen Waite Papashvily (*All the Happy Endings* [New York, 1956]) notes that "*St. Elmo* won an audience that places it securely among the ten most popular novels ever published in the United States" (156). *The Wide, Wide World* did even better. Before *Uncle Tom's Cabin* "the greatest achievement of any of the lady novelists, by the twin tests of copies sold and tears coaxed, was *The Wide, Wide World*. . . . In England the book had a reception unequalled by any previous American novel" (E. Douglas Branch, *The Sentimental Years* [New York, 1934], 131; Papashvily, 2). James' 1865 reference to *The Wide, Wide World* is not entirely complimentary, for he is detailing the limitations of the "realist" school; but he does put Susan Warner among very distinguished company. "For an exhibition of the true realistic *chic* we would accordingly refer that body of artists who are represented in France by MM. Flaubert and Gérome to that class of works which in our literature are represented by the 'Daisy Chain' and 'The Wide, Wide World' " (*Na* 1865, 344).

Plot summaries. *The Heir of Redclyffe* (2 vols., 725 pages): Guy Morville, while still underage, becomes Baronet of Redclyffe; he is the ward of the Edmonstone family, which includes three sisters, Laura, Amy, Charlotte, and their invalid brother, Charlie; Philip Morville, cousin to the Edmonstones and second in line for the Redclyffe baronetcy, has given up a promising career in school and is currently an army officer. After mastering his terrible temper and graduating from college (and various heroic exploits), Guy marries Amy and honeymoons with her on the Continent. Philip in the meanwhile has been endlessly critical of Guy and yet has engaged in that infamous act, the concealed engagement, with Laura. On the Continent, Philip falls dangerously ill. He is nursed back to health by Guy and Amy (who is now pregnant), but, in the process, Guy catches the fever and dies, a perfect Christian, aristocrat, husband. Guy's death brings to Philip awareness of his wrongs to Guy and Laura. Although Philip marries Laura and works hard at Redclyffe and in parliament, he never finds Guy's perfect peace.

The Initials (402 pages): Hamilton, a younger son, is traveling in Germany when he receives a letter signed only by the puzzling initials A.Z. In the process of tracing out the mystery he meets those "perfections of German beauty" Hildegarde and Crescenz. After Hildegarde's temper is calmed by a series of events—the admonitions and death of her father, the suite and suicide of infamous Raimund, Hamilton's flirtations with Crescenz and Mrs. Berg, a nearly compromising trip with Hamilton—she marries Hamilton and they forsake sterile English upper-class life for Bavarian rural joys. Finally, for the sake of their children's education, they return to England, perfect, of course.

St. Elmo (564 pages): A classic Byronic villain, St. Elmo was once perfect but has been made cynical by the perfidy of his true love and of his best friend; he now wanders the globe prodigiously and returns home occasionally to subdue his wolflike hounds and tantalize the community. On one such return he finds that his mother has taken in an orphan, Edna Earl. The novel traces Edna's rise to the pinnacle of worldly fame as an author, and the steady degradation of St. Elmo to such depths of love for her that he even becomes a cleric. Having already rejected Gordon Leigh because his mind was not equal to hers, and Douglass G. Manning because he was only intellectual, Edna allows St. Elmo's cleric-hood to convince her of his reform, and consequent perfection, and they marry.

The Wide, Wide World (581 pages): Coming to her aunt's home (her mother is near death and her father quite heartless), Ellen Montgomery learns to curb her temper and pride before the aunt, Miss Fortune. After the influence of the paragons Alice (who dies) and John (her brother), Ellen returns to England and chastening experiences in strict Scotland. In the end she sails again for America, presumably to marry John.

Finally, a brief summary of *Watch and Ward* (86 pages in *Atlantic Monthly*'s double-column pages; the novel was drastically, though insufficiently, revised by James in 1878 and never again printed in his lifetime. Leon Edel brought out the 1878 version in 1959 (Grove): After the young bachelor, Roger Lawrence, is refused for the third and last time by Miss Morton, he encounters the suicide of a man whom he had briefly met earlier in the evening, Mr. Lambert. Lambert's now orphaned daughter, Nora, age 11, strikes Roger's good heart, and he raises her, with the scarce dreamed of hope that she will turn out to be a perfect wife. Nora's early homeliness flowers into eventual beauty and upon her return from Italy with Mrs. Keith (the former Miss Morton, now widowed and Roger's confidante), she *is* perfect. In the meantime, however, she has attracted two men, her cousin George Fenton and Roger's cousin, Hubert. During Roger's long illness, Hubert and Nora grow very close, but Mrs. Keith finally calls Hubert's bluff and he flees. In her unhappiness Nora refuses Roger's proposal. She then imagines their whole life has been a perfidy, and flees to New York. After Fenton tries to hold her for ransom and Hubert reveals his long-time fiancée, Nora and Roger meet in the street, and live happily ever after.

9. Viola Hopkins Winner, *Henry James and the Visual Arts* (Charlottesville, 1970), 6. Darrel Abel (*American Literature* [Great Neck, N.Y., 1963]) notes that "American superlatives" were an acknowledged national trait (247). Readers who overstress James' fastidiousness fail to heed (among many things) his reaction during the first

moments of his return to London in 1869. "The immensity was the great fact, and that was a charm; the miles of housetops and viaducts" (*Century* 1888, 219–20).

10. Constance Rourke, *American Humor* (New York, 1931), 192. Taking issue with Miss Rourke, Richard Poirier locates the source of James' exaggerated language in English literature, particularly Swift (*The Comic Sense of Henry James* [Oxford, 1960], 67–68). For recent corroboration of Rourke's position, see Caroline G. Mercer's "Adam Verver, Yankee Businessman," *NCF* 22 (1967): 251–69. "There can be little doubt that James knew a great deal about American humor in literature and life and what it represented, whether in popular journalistic, or more sophisticated forms" (252–53).

11. D. W. Jefferson, *Henry James and the Modern Reader* (New York, 1964), 163.

12. Charlton Laird, *Language in America* (Englewood Cliffs, 1970), 354, 355.

13. Interestingly, in Rhoda Broughton's first novel we find, " 'you'd thank me to "absquatulate," as the Yankees say' " (*CUF* 163). Not only is such diction sufficiently in the air before James' crucial decade that even a young Englishwoman can appropriate it, but she associates that diction, not with the frontier, but with Yankees.

14. Rahill, 172; Grimsted, 207.

15. J. M. S. Tompkins, *The Popular Novel in England, 1770–1800* (London, 1932), 187.

16. Samuel Richardson, *Clarissa Harlowe*, vol. 8, Letters LXI and LXXI, in *The Works of Samuel Richardson*, ed. E. Mangin (London, 1811), 283–84, 321.

17. Concerning acting, James says that "Madame Ristori . . . seem[s] very often to exaggerate, to grimace, to tear a passion to tatters" (*SA* 29); concerning criticism, James calls attention to "Mr. Lathrop's rather too emphatic way of putting it" (*Ha* 92). In his many criticisms of "perfect" characters in fiction, James concentrates upon popular authors. "The author [Mrs. Seemuller] has aimed at the creation of a perfect woman. . . . Heaven preserve us from any more radical specimens of this perfection!" (*NAR* 1865, 280); " 'John Halifax' was an attempt to tell the story of a life perfect in every particular" (*Na* 1866, 276). Major novelists also do not escape James' censure. He criticizes Adam Bede as "too good," a figure of "perfect righteousness" (*AM* 1866, 486, 488); he also reproves Meredith, Daudet, and Whitman for stylistic exaggeration.

18. Jane Austen dislikes "pictures of perfection," George Eliot believes that "it will not do to wait for perfection," and Cooper contends that "the supreme folly of the hour is to imagine that perfection will come before its stated time."

19. Roger exaggerates Fenton's potential limitations ("Roger had made up his mind that he would be outrageously rough and Western") and so is disappointed to find him "a pretty fellow enough" (329). Fenton, in turn, overestimates Roger's age and simplicity (330); Fenton's "friend," Mrs. Paul, later overreacts with Nora (696–703).

20. *In*: 10, 70, 79, 83, 89, 101 (twice), 112, 116, 118, 125, 137, 172, 186, 187, 188, 190, 224, 259 (twice), 275, 311, 341, 346 (twice), 349, 358, 382. *RH*: 21 (twice), 83, 88, 121, 129, 132 (twice), 136, 146, 154, 161, 173, 178, 180, 182, 207, 215, 223, 290, 305 (twice), 306, 307, 308 (twice), 309, 325, 345 (twice), 348 (twice), 370, 419, 432, 446, 456, 479. I have concentrated on *Roderick Hudson* because it, unlike the very brief *Watch and Ward*, is approximately the length of the popular novels. Also the larger novel has elicited sweeping praise, not only from F. R. Leavis (*The Great Tradition* [New York, 1963], 130), but from Yvor Winters, who says, "as a full-length and objective portrait of an uncommon but still recognizable type, the book is in its fashion superb" (*In Defense of Reason* [Denver, 1947], 328). In this chapter and the next, I attempt to show that immaturity of technique—both quantitatively and qualitatively —is what prevents the portrait of Roderick from being convincing, let alone superb.

21. Though Isabel's good looks are affirmed by most of the characters (Daniel Touchett, 18; Caspar, 33; Ralph and Warburton, 40; Madame Merle, 188; Countess

Gemini, 328), even so enamored a swain as Lord Warburton can recognize that "Miss Archer had neither a fortune nor the sort of beauty that justifies a man to the multitude" (96). "Isabelle la sérieuse," in Cherbuliez' *Le Roman* is presented unqualifiedly as " 'la plus belle fille de l'univers' .... 'classique' .... '[avec] les plus beaux cheveux de France et de Navarre'" (16, 23, 24).

22. *HR* 1:3, 37, 43, 96, 124, 147, 159, 160, 167, 196, 204, 206, 212, 226, 248; 2:214, 223, 241, 264, 280, 287, 288, 293. *In:* 6, 11, 15, 19, 31, 44, 52 (twice), 54, 68, 72, 78, 94, 97 (twice), 125 (twice), 135, 142, 146 (twice), 147, 160, 161, 167 (twice), 171, 173, 181, 193, 197, 212, 215 (twice), 216, 229, 246, 251 (twice), 259, 262, 272 (twice), 275, 282, 292, 298, 316, 327 (twice), 331, 335, 347, 350, 351. *RH:* 8, 13 (twice), 16, 17, 23, 29, 37, 38, 39, 46, 50, 62, 87, 93, 95, 97, 100, 106 (three times), 120, 127, 153, 156, 161, 164, 169, 172, 177, 180–81, 204 (twice), 205, 215, 219–20, 220, 221, 226, 234, 264, 266, 267, 311, 320, 325, 330, 332, 347, 370, 391 (twice), 392, 394, 409, 411, 414 (twice), 422, 423 (twice), 424, 427, 430 (twice), 433, 436–37, 437, 440, 457, 464.

23. "Exquisitely," 15; "hideous," 17; "high," 61; "tremendous," 10; "utter," 20; "remarkable," 20; "consummate," 7.

24. I have estimated the length of each novel as: *Watch and Ward*, 50,000 words; *Roderick Hudson*, 143,000; *The American*, 120,000; *The Portrait of a Lady*, 225,000; *The Heir of Redclyffe*, 250,000; *St. Elmo*, 200,000; *The Wide, Wide World*, 290,000; *The Initials*, 250,000. In tables 1'–4' are the actual figures, from which I computed the frequency per 100,000 words.

TABLE 1'

	W&W	RH	Ame	PL
extraordinary	3	38	14	25
fantastic	0	19	8	2
magnificent	0	37	19	10
passionate	52	70	15	41
terrible	8	29	30	15

TABLE 2'

	W&W	RH	Ame	PL
absolute	6	24	8	23
excellent	10	23	22	31
exquisite	3	15	11	20
extremely	20	57	69	78
remarkable	3	20	23	31

TABLE 3'

	W&W	RH	Ame	PL
immense	5	28	22	55
perfect	25	72	61	162

TABLE 4'

	PL	StE	HR	WWW	In
extraordinary	25	6	5	7	31
fantastic	2	12	2	1	1
magnificent	10	7	9	1	6
passionate	41	18	28	36	47
terrible	15	15	19	7	4
absolute	23	12	24	15	16
excellent	31	0	34	29	45
exquisite	20	12	8	7	1
extremely	78	8	39	27	66
remarkable	31	12	12	13	26
immense	55	1	3	3	4
perfect	162	37	69	88	103

25. Richard Chase, *The American Novel and Its Tradition* (Garden City, 1957), 120; Ralph Barton Perry, *The Thought and Character of William James* (Boston, 1935), 1:370. James' awareness of exaggeration appears clearly in early letters. 'The latter [Turner] is assuredly great: but if you wish to hold your own against exaggeration, go to see him at the National Gallery. . . . I do, for instance, believe in criticism, more than that hyperbolical speech of mine would seem to suggest" (June 1869 and March 1873, *EL* 57, 73). When he wished to criticize another aspect of Henry's practice, William was capable of seeing that his brother was trying to fight free of popular extravagances. "I fancy this rather dainty and disdainful treatment of yours comes from a wholesome dread of being sloppy and gushing and over-abounding in power of expression, like the most of your rivals in the *Atlantic*" (Perry 1:264).

26. Edel notes how James came to use "smothering extravagances" in delicate situations to "be candid while relying on the vanity of his correspondents to read only that which would please them" (*EL* 233, 22); in *Henry James: A Reader's Guide* (Ithaca, 1966), S. Gorley Putt observes that James "never, to his very end, gave up the joys of eloquent mock-hyperbole" (41); Edwin T. Bowden says of *The Reverberator* that "the constant tone of slight exaggeration makes the novel a welcome comic variation" (*The Themes of Henry James* [New Haven, 1956], 38); for Peter Buitenhuis, "hyperbole is the main source of humour" in "The Point of View" (*The Grasping Imagination* [Toronto, 1970], 121); Poirier likewise finds exaggeration a key to James' comic method (191), while Charles Thomas Samuels finds that in *What Maisie Knew* "the prodigious round of mating that we witness merely exaggerates James's point for comic effect" (*The Ambiguity of Henry James* [Urbana, 1971], 184).

27. C. Willett Cunnington, *Feminine Attitudes in the Nineteenth Century* (London, 1935); J. A. and Olive Banks, *Feminism and Family Planning in Victorian England* (Liverpool, 1964); Judith H. Montgomery, "The American Galatea," *CE* 32 (1971): 890–99; Martha Vicinus, "Introduction: The Perfect Victorian Lady," in *Suffer and Be Still* (Bloomington, Ind., 1972).

28. George Watterston, *Glencarn*, and John Neal, *Keep Cool*, both quoted by Brown, 112, 291. An equally dubious praise of womanly perfection is quoted by John S. and Robin M. Haller (*The Physician and Sexuality in Victorian America* [Urbana, 1974]). In 1846 the physician John A. Smith proclaimed, "there emerges, as the crowning act [of evolution], the most elaborate and most perfect form and model of beauty, human eyes have yet beheld—THE CAUCASIAN FEMALE BUST" (2).

29. Quoted by John Killham, *Tennyson and "The Princess"* (London, 1958), 114.

30. John Ruskin, "Of Queens' Gardens" in *Sesame and Lilies* (New York, 1970), 51.

31. The failure to hold out against the consolation of perfection is what makes even so innovative a writer as Charlotte Brontë finally "popular." In *Villette*, for example, we find " 'wise people say it is folly to think anybody perfect' " (28). Accordingly a suitor is condescended to because " 'he thinks I am perfect' " (85), and Lucy Snowe can even admit " 'Full well, do I know that Dr. John was not perfect' " (190). Yet Dr. John *is* all too perfect. His chin is "perfect," and he has "perfect knowledge of Villette" (90, 191). Despite the innovations which Charlotte Brontë did achieve, we end each of her novels dissatisfied with the all too conventional virtues which they sustain and the consolations which they offer. Likewise with Rhoda Broughton's novels, which continue many of Charlotte Brontë's explorations. After all the delightfully dis-respectful jabs at orthodoxy which Nell begins with, *Cometh Up as a Flower* deteriorates into an enforced marriage, final separations of the lovers, and early death. For more on the limited radicalism of popular fiction, see chapter 2, pp. 157–58.

32. He also fulfilled this role in Victorian life. "Guy Morville . . . became the model for hundreds of youths growing up to manhood. . . . [particularly] William Morris

... Edward Burne-Jones ... Dante Gabriel Rossetti, and the Pre-Raphaelite group of which he was the leading spirit" (Amy Cruse, *The Victorians and Their Reading* [Boston, 1935], 51, 52).

33. There can be no melodramatic black-white distinction between *Roderick* and *The American*. James does not use "perfect" (or any of his techniques) with consistent perfection in *The American*, and he did not fail consistently with them in his first two novels. I have tried throughout to acknowledge both his early successes and his later failures. My distinction between *Roderick* and *The American*, then, is a matter of degree. In the earlier novel, James may use "perfect" complexly, but he does not do so consistently. Aware of imperfection he nonetheless proclaims perfection. And all his other hyperbole—his "utterly"s and "extremely"s—lack a context to moderate them sufficiently. In *The American*, hyperbole is generally used well, with lapses appearing at points of greatest stress; in *Roderick*, the lapses are into effectiveness. I mark a dividing line at *The American*, because it is the first James novel in which, despite obvious romantic, archaic, and melodramatic aspects, I become seriously concerned with the characters' fates.

This same qualification obtains for most of the stylistic features which I study. I have, for example, discussed the deleterious effect of "perfect stillness" and "perfect consciousness" in early James and popular fiction. These expressions recur in *The Portrait*, often without sufficient redeeming transformation. The same thing can be said for the saccharine expressions which I discuss in chapter 1, section 2; for static portraiture in chapter 4, section 1; for personification in both chapters 1 and 4; and for various aspects of mental process rendering throughout chapter 4. Only by fully acknowledging the transitional quality of *The Portrait* can we fully appreciate how great an art work it is.

34. "The discriminating observer we have been supposing might, however, perfectly have measured its [Newman's face's] expressiveness, and yet have been at a loss to describe it."

35. Our sense of inadequacy may derive partly from the failure of Claire as a dramatic presence, which readers have rightly criticized; but our response also results, at least in part, from James' ability to evoke and control our skepticism about perfection.

36. Although some critics have interpreted the opening of *The Portrait* as an "idyll," others have noted its greater complexity. Charles Feidelson ("The Moment of *The Portrait of a Lady*," *Ventures* 8 [1968]: 47–55) finds all so ailing "that the immemorial order he [James] admires is incapable of supporting anything but a tea party"; Thomas F. Smith notes the tension between richness and the shortness of time ("Balance in Henry James's *The Portrait of a Lady*," *Four Quarters* 13 [1964]: 11–16); Philip M. Weinstein correctly says that the idyll is limited by sickness, unsuccessful marriage, and aspiration qualified by failure (*Henry James and the Requirements of the Imagination* [Cambridge, Mass., 1971], 38); and, in contrast to Laurence B. Holland's sense of the perfect form of chapter 1 (*The Expense of Vision* [Princeton, 1964], 46–48), Richard Poirier, quite incredibly, finds that "the total effect is close to the mock epic.... The diction ... has a fastidious pomposity.... his eager discriminations ... give an excessive and correspondingly satiric note to the ritualized feelings that are at the same time being commended" (191). For other comments on this chapter see William J. Maseychik's "Points of Departure from *The American*" in *Henry James* (ed. Tony Tanner [London, 1969], 116–27) and Sheldon W. Liebman's "The Light and the Dark: Character Design in *The Portrait of a Lady*," *Papers on Language and Literature*, 6 (1970): 163–79.

With the second tea (83), the ceremony of innocence is over, for now the location is inside, and the occasion is death—the death of the genial *genus loci* who presided over the earlier ceremony. The motion of time and change is relentless throughout the book (35, 352, 356, 371, 417, 449, 509, 524).

37. Also: " 'You want to drain the cup of experience.' 'No, I don't wish to touch the cup of experience.' . . . 'You want to see, but not to feel,' said Ralph. 'I don't think that if one is a sentient being, one can make the distinction.' . . . 'You evidently expect that a crowned head will be struck with you.' 'No, that would be worse than marrying Lord Warburton' " (139).

38. Pansy is called "perfect" at least nine times (212, 214, 249, 341, 343, 404 [twice], 408, 433).

39. As early as *Roderick Hudson,* James introduces a somewhat comparable rejection of perfection itself when Christina Light criticizes Mary. " 'He [Roderick] doesn't like perfection; he is not bent upon being *safe*' " (347).

40. " 'When I say she exaggerates I don't mean it in the vulgar sense.' . . . Certainly she had fallen into exaggerations. . . . 'she was prone to exaggeration' " (232, 363, 371). The first and third "she" is Madame Merle. As the second "she," Isabel receives justified criticism at the time when she is trying hardest to achieve the social surface which Madame Merle and Osmond worship—after her marriage but before her discovery of Pansy's parentage.

41. I agree with Weinstein that Roderick is a failure dramatically (13). But this failure is symptomatic of the whole popular mode of presenting character and thus it illuminates Jamesian and popular practice in ways which Weinstein does not discuss.

For James' presentation of intellectual and social prowess, let us examine Roderick's development. Intellectually, Roderick makes vast strides with extreme rapidity. "In a short time he had almost turned the tables and become in their walks and talks the accredited source of information. . . . He had divined their logic and measured their proportions, and referred them infallibly to their categories. . . . A single glimpse of a social situation of the elder type enabled him to construct the whole" (83, 82). Such assertions we find as irritatingly irresponsible here as we do when E. D. E. N. Southworth says that Ishmael's "thirsty intellect drank up the knowledge. . . . Ishmael was perfect in his recitation" (246) or when Balzac does not demur from his narrator's assertion that Louis Lambert's " 'était la plus riche mémoire, la tête la plus fortement organisée, le jugement le plus sagace que j'aie rencontrés' " (588) or when Augusta Jane Evans says that St. Elmo's "lordly, brilliant intellect would have lifted him to any eminence he desired" (79–80). How far James comes by 1881 is clear when we meet that prodigy of learning, Miss Isabel Archer of Albany, N.Y. "Among her contemporaries she passed for a young woman of extraordinary profundity; for these excellent people never withheld their admiration from a reach of intellect of which they themselves were not conscious, and spoke of Isabel as a prodigy of learning, a young lady reputed to have read the classic authors—in translations" (46). Isabel is intelligent enough to warrant our full interest, of course, but from her history of German thought she brings back only the roses of a straying imagination. Thank heaven.

The intellectual power which helps bridge the gap between the study and the social realm of dinner table and parlor is the ability to speak foreign languages. Such skill must therefore be mastered by all popular protagonists. Philip "began to translate it [*I promessi Sposi*] fluently, and with an admirable choice of language" (1:34); Guy's French "was daily becoming more producible" (2:115); both St. Elmo and Edna Earl are masters of tongues numerous and exotic. James resorts to such facile affirmations with Roderick. Although the sculptor does, we are told, destroy the sense of many lines, "he picked up Italian without study, and had a wonderfully sympathetic accent" (206). By 1881 the dominant male again speaks Italian, but the added complexity of James' presentation enables us to believe in Gilbert's skills and to recognize in his limited success the necessary failure of his quest for cosmopolitan conventionality. "He used the Italian tongue, and used it with perfect ease; but this would not have convinced you that he was an Italian" (212).

Socially, characters manage in several ways to be "perfectly" irresistible. To "chatter captivatingly," for example, is the boyish and girlish power of so many protagonists. As Roderick "chattered away half the night in Roman drawing-rooms" and, sitting with Rowland on various occasions, "talked so much amusing nonsense. . . . and chattered for an hour" (94, 134, 246), so Guy "was quite confidential with Mrs. Edmonstone, on whom he used to lavish, with boyish eagerness, all that interested him" (*HR* 1:31) and Ellen's "tongue ran very freely, for her heart was completely opened to him" (*WWW* 54). For James, moreover, the problem is not merely that Roderick is too winsome and arch. "He talked the most joyous nonsense. . . . Roderick talked so much amusing nonsense. . . . She talked irresistible nonsense" (*RH* 129, 134, 214). Thus the novel's only real character, Christina, is reduced to Roderick's winsomeness and then reduced further to virtual nonexistence, because James not only resorts to popular fatuity, but does so indiscriminately. In *The American*, all seven appearances of "chattered" are seriously qualified: Valentin as " 'a great chatterer' " is distinctly, if attractively, superficial (92, 259); the others who chatter emptily in society are worse still—Dora Finch (39), the young marquise (323), and various party guests (97, 99, 211). Isabel's vividness of speech is only mentioned as chattering twice in passing (51, 179); the other two appearances are qualified and effective. Pansy "entertained her like a little lady—not chattering, but conversing" (291); Ralph, dying, " 'doesn't chatter as he used' " (525).

As a social success, Roderick "took to evening parties as a duck to water" (92). Although he is sufficiently Byronic that James must make him a bit volatile, Roderick does not go beyond the safe confines of boyish overenthusiasm. "But it remained as true as before that it would have been impossible, on the whole, to violate ceremony with less of lasting offense. . . . He was impulsive, spontaneous, sincere; there were so many people at dinner-tables and in studios who were not, that it all seemed worth while to allow this rare specimen all possible freedom of action. If Roderick took the words out of your mouth . . . he did it with a perfect good conscience" (92, 93). Isabel is also a good talker. But only after 360 pages of experiencing her words and wit and logic and illogic do we encounter "of old she had a great delight in good-humoured argument, in intellectual play (she never looked so charming as when in the general heat of discussion she had received a crushing blow full in the face and brushed it away as a feather)" (363). Especially when we recognize here Ralph's natural tendency to sweeping statement and his intense affection for Isabel, we see James' mature use of a basically popular technique. The claims for Isabel pass beyond assertion and succeed in moving us because the dramatic reality confirms and vivifies them. Ralph's evaluation is experientially true because Isabel is.

42. Isabelle also has "infatigable attention" (193) and her father is "infatigable" (8); Edna Earl labors so "that the hours passed unheeded" (237), and eventually weeks likewise ("she did not close her eyes for a week" [521]); Ishmael possesses "indestruct-able vitality" (303–4); Louis Lambert is capable of a "singulier temoignage de force" (524). Although it is not important to the main action of the novel, a vestige of this type of hyperbole appears in *The American* when we are told that Newman could work all night "without a yawn" (1).

43. Critics have made too much of point of view in James' early novels. Point of view cannot take precedence over reader response. Granted that James can recognize his characters' tendency to extreme statement: if these extremes render the reading experience distasteful, then the fact that the character, not the author, makes the statement, is immaterial. When Roger exclaims, " 'poor little disfathered daughter,— poor little uprooted germ of womanhood'" (239), James simply cannot have anticipated the extent of our disaffiliation. In *Roderick Hudson* the point of view issue is complicated by Rowland Mallet. Although some critics, following James in the Preface, attempt to make Rowland the reflecting center of the novel, other critics have

wisely taken the novel at its face value. Cornelia Pulsifer Kelley (*The Early Development of Henry James* [Urbana, 1930]), and D. W. Jefferson are correct in assuming that James in the Preface tended to reread the early novel in light of his much later experiments with point of view. Gordon Taylor sums up well my belief that Rowland does not function consistently apart from James: "Rowland's perceptions of this reality tend to dissolve into James's.... The actual movements of his consciousness are diluted by abstraction and by frequent blending into the solution of James's presence as an author"(52). Although there are times when Rowland clearly speaks for himself and when he displays traits which James intends us to examine critically, I will not distinguish him from James in those many judgments for which Rowland is clearly, and solely, James' spokesman.

44. Dramatic effectiveness is even more difficult to achieve, and even more crucial, when the protagonist is not active like statue-sculpting, mountain-climbing Roderick, but is reactive, passive. All too predictably, however, James resorts to assertion. The language he applies to Roger in *Watch and Ward* seems exaggerated for several reasons. Sometimes it contradicts our previous experience. Since Roger in the first few pages wears lavender gloves, carries "in all weathers a peculiarly neat umbrella," is given to " 'fussing' over his health" and proves inadequate before Miss Morton and ineffectual before Mr. Lambert, we are indeed surprised when the night air "restored the *healthy* tone of his sensibilities" (234, my italics). Likewise, since Roger has been deceiving Nora for ten years, we cannot respond properly when James twice calls Roger's face "honest" (333, 424). Not only innocent Nora (" 'I've seen people without a quarter of his goodness' " [580]) but also reliable "objective" observers call Roger "good." The experienced German widow says via Nora that " 'you are the one good man she ever heard of' " (426). Miss Sandys even goes so far as to repeat one of the standard encomia of popular fiction: as Guy was " 'too good for this world' " (*HR* 2:356), so Roger's " 'spirits were too good for this life' " (701). Since Miss Sandys knows of Roger's plan to marry Nora, she makes her evaluation in light of his sustained deception of his ward. Thus we are supposed to accept her absolution. Not only can we not forget Roger's deception, but his very kindnesses to Nora are less dramatically real than his repeated foolishness. He does not seem "good."

Still more at variance with our experience of Roger is his intermittent Byronism. Because much ado is made about hereditary madness in Guy's family, we can believe that Guy harbors a "murderous impulse" (*HR* 1:271) or even that "never had Morville of the line felt more deadly fierceness" (267); and because our early experience of Roger confirms the narrative assertions that he is "placid" (417) and because the following quotations lack any apparent undercutting by James, we find only ludicrously incongruous Roger's "fierce discomposure" (335), "his passionate vexation" (336), his "unwonted force" (424), "the intenser heat of his passion" (697), "the furious irresponsibility of his passion ... a reckless personal need" (700). Carefully hidden offstage he even becomes "violent" (697). Comparison with Mephistopheles may be appropriate to that swarthy outcast, St. Elmo (79), but it is hopeless with Roger (424). We smile at Hildegarde's "perfectly crimson ear" (*In* 215) as we do when Roger "turned a furious crimson" (338). We may believe that Raimund was " 'perfectly desperate' " (*In* 298) because we have already seen his messy suicide, but we cannot believe either Roger's own claim that he is " 'a desperate man' " or even the reliable Miss Sandys' sense of him as " 'an image of suicidal despair' " (698, 701).

Even when James' assertions do not contradict our previous experience, however, the language is often so exaggerated that Roger seems ludicrous. When Roger is happy, it is "with solemn glee" (240), "in broad enchantment" (246), or because Nora is "divinely amiable" (320). Especially since we never find Nora very enchanting, the language here makes Roger all too closely resemble the ecstatic heroines of popular fiction. In sadness, Roger is equally extreme. Things seem "intolerably bitter" (236), "an ... awful impiety" (241), "fatally confounded" (327). Overripe in themselves, these expressions, like those with the active characters, become mechanical and repetitious. As Roger "was seized with a mad desire" (327), so Nora "felt a passionate desire .... felt an indefinable need of protesting .... felt horribly deluded" (580 [twice], 689). The extent of the formula here cannot be fully appreciated, however, until we see that Rowland in *Roderick Hudson* also "felt an irresistible kindness" (28), "felt an almost overmastering reluctance" (117), "felt a sore sense of wrath" (125), "felt a kind of dumb anger" (193), "felt an irresistible compassion" (200), was "seized with a strong desire" (427), and, "felt an immense desire" (466). Thus emotion is denied by the very language that asserts it. Instead of intense inner drama we meet formulaic assertions of intensity.

45. When, for example, Madame Merle says to Isabel, " 'you are an exquisite creature,' " it is clearly a preamble to the enormous qualification, " 'I wish you had a little money' " (188); when the narrator notes that "her imagination was remarkably active" (46), his "remarkably" goes beyond praise of her insightfulness and emphasizes her tendency to romantic, girlish, capricious fancy. Likewise with indefatigability. Even in the early stages of *The Portrait*, Isabel's energy is not rendered so facilely as Roderick's was. "She was really tired; she knew it, and knew that she should pay for it on the morrow; but it was her habit at this period to carry fatigue to the furtherest point, and confess to it only when dissimulation had become impossible. For the present it was perfectly possible" (42). A Roderick-figure does appear in *The Portrait*, however, and receives the chastisement which the reader was forced to supply in *Roderick Hudson*. " '[Osmond] Are you not tired?' '[Mother Catherine] We are never tired.' 'Ah, my sister, sometimes,' murmured the junior votaress" (215). Fatigue is particularly important in *The Portrait* because it becomes an issue between Isabel and Osmond. The first time they meet he says, " 'you must be very tired,' " and she replies, " 'no, indeed, I am not tired; what have I done to tire me?' " (236). Osmond later says revealingly, " 'I should like to see you when you are tired and satiated' " (284). The man who prefers "little" women wants Isabel just tamed enough to accept his jaded vision obediently. His plan's eventual failure is foretold in her admission, " 'I am horrid when I am tired' " (286). Marriage to Osmond does take its toll, and the admission of various types of fatigue echoes through Isabel's conversation. " 'I am very tired .... I am very tired of his name .... I am very weary of it all' " (443, 444, 475). In danger of losing completely that spiritual elasticity which once gave her strength, Isabel in the Forum "rested her weariness upon things that had crumbled for centuries and yet were upright still" (477). As we will see in chapter 4, Isabel's danger on the ride to Ralph is that she will die spiritually, that her fatigue will sink her into final despair. Why she does not, we will discuss then. For now we must recognize how carefully James has examined that trait of indefatigability which he once—like a popular novelist—bestowed so facilely upon his main characters.

46. F. O. Matthiessen, *American Renaissance* (Oxford, 1941), 21–22. (James, incidentally, uses "out-Heroding Herod" in 1874 [*CT* 3:327].) In his explanation of Emerson's almost religious reverence for oratory, Matthiessen gives us a good sense of what "eloquence" meant to most sensitive, educated men of the period.

47. Quoted by Brown, 93.

48. Rahill, 259–60.

49. Jerome Hamilton Buckley, *The Victorian Temper* (Cambridge, Mass., 1951), 109.

50. William Makepiece Thackeray, *Letters and Private Papers* (Cambridge, Mass., 1945), ed. Gordon N. Ray, 2:282; quoted in part by Françoise Basch in *Relative Creatures* (New York, 1974), 242. For more on Thackeray as preacher, see Praz' *The*

Hero in Eclipse in Victorian Fiction (London, 1956), 207, 209. The other major Victorians took their preaching no less seriously, of course.

51. Matthiessen, *Renaissance*, 22.

52. Near the end of his life James can still recall "forever mounting on little platforms at our infant schools to 'speak' The Raven and Lenore and the verses in which we phrased the heroine as Annabell*ee* . . . falling thus into the trap the poet had so recklessly laid for us" (*SB* 60). In *St. Elmo* we are treated to an elocution contest (183) as well as to orations which Edna writes and then recites (189); in the children's magazine *Pansy*, part of the daily regimen is "elocution lessons" (Papashvily, 188).

53. Putt, 40. As late as 1887, James is praising *Denise* for "an uttered homily" nearly four pages long (*SA* 208).

54. Tony Tanner, *The Reign of Wonder* (Cambridge, 1965), 129.

55. *W&W* 235, 422, 580, 581, 697, 703, 706 (twice), 707; *RH* 40, 76, 95, 105, 240, 253 (twice), 254 (twice), 275, 327, 386, 391 (twice), 424, 461, 473. Not all these are used unqualifiedly, of course, but the commitment of both novels to eloquence is complete.

56. An asserted but not experienced eloquence is Hubert's. "Hubert Lawrence had an excellent gift of oratory. . . . His utterance seemed to Nora the perfection of eloquence" (422). Lest we attribute his eloquence simply to Nora's infatuation, James shows the whole congregation responding similarly (422). Thus Hubert may be vain but he is not misrepresenting his powers when he says, " 'a certain gift comes to me. They call it eloquence. . . . they seem to like it' " (581). James' practice here is unlike George Eliot's or Herman Melville's, for we hear and thus experience the eloquence of Dinah Morris and Father Mapple. James follows the tactic of popular writers who merely *assert*. In *Adam Blair*, the protagonist possesses a "noble and energetic strain of eloquence. . . . more powerful, under any circumstances, it could scarcely have been" (35, 58); of one of Blair's fellow clerics we are told, "not one that heard Dr. Muir pray that day, would have wished the duty to have fallen into other hands" (16). St. Elmo's first sermon as a minister moves everyone even more than all the other sermons throughout the book have done. Since the laity also are allowed moments of eloquence, various Jamesian ranters imitate numerous popular brethren. In *Le Roman* one character wants "lui parler, la sermonner" (145), and Max is called "éloquent" four times (154, 168, 215, 224). In *The Initials*, Hamilton "was so eloquent on the theme given him, that he not only convinced Major Stultz that he had been mistaken, but induced him even to banter. . . . [later] he spoke long and eloquently, and made an evident impression" (187, 198); in *St. Elmo*, such " 'men of . . . resistless eloquence' " (91) are ideals; in *Wide, Wide World*, nature herself is our " 'eloquent' " teacher (499). Our difficulty in responding to all such eloquence is even greater when the authors are referring not to words but to gestures or tones. As Hubert's face "turned most eloquently pale" (*W&W* 706), the pastor in *St. Elmo* "had never seen a countenance half so eloquent" as Edna's (115); as Edna's "countenance was eloquent with humble gratitude" (553), Nora can make "a gesture of eloquent simplicity" (706) and fill her voice with an "all-eloquent tremor of tone" (*W&W* 707).

57. Devendra P. Varma, *The Gothic Flame* (New York, 1957), 40. So great is the nineteenth century's debt to the eloquence of the eighteenth century that C. J. Furness can say of elocution textbooks, "the same gestures were being used in 1880 that had been prescribed in 1780" (*The Genteel Female* [New York, 1931], 152).

58. Quoted by Vineta Colby (*The Singular Anomaly* [New York, 1970], 183) from Henry Logan Stuart's *Fenella*.

59. Matthiessen cites the Tocqueville sentence in *American Renaissance*, 20.

60. Tompkins, 101.

61. Likewise in Reade's *Griffith Gaunt*, Catherine, pleading for her life in court,

"had noted down the exact order of her topics, but no more" (London, 1903 [1866], 303). Inspiration also surpasses premeditated eloquence in Mrs. Gaskell's *Ruth*, for the Reverend Mr. Benson, having labored mightily on a funeral oration for Ruth, "put the sermon away, and opened the Bible" (452).

62. Quoted by Vineta Colby (*Yesterday's Woman* [Princeton, 1974], 156) from Hannah More's *The Repository Tales*.

63. Lavinia draws her ideas of eloquence from Mr. Penniman whom she calls " 'one of the most eloquent men of his day' " (98) and whom James has already undercut as "a poor clergyman, of a sickly constitution and a flowery style of eloquence" (17).

64. Even in *The Portrait* the style is not completely consistent. Mrs. Touchett is supposedly the plain-style speaker, but try to distinguish her from Madame Merle when pages 181–82 are compared with page 203.

65. For other mentions of Johnson see *CT* 2:227; *W&W* 580; *Na* 1866, 276, 1873, 24; *FrP* 66; *Na* 1878, 384; *Ha* 53, 133–35; *PL* 117; *HJL* 416. For a good, if brief, discussion of James and the eighteenth century, see E. Stone, 52.

66. Quoted by Branch (106) from *Harper's* "Easy Chair" for January 1853.

67. In his personal library James owned John Forster's two-volume *The Life and Times of Oliver Goldsmith* (London, 1854).

68. H. Montgomery Hyde, *Henry James at Home* (New York, 1969), 6.

69. For an excellent discussion of post–Civil War America's veneration of the English and American eighteenth century, see John Tomsich's *The Genteel Endeavor* (Stanford, 1971)—especially the chapters on Norton and Stedman, and the observation that "when they [reformers] spoke positively about American politics, they were likely to be thinking nostalgically of the age of John Quincy Adams, their golden age of political virtue" (87).

70. Laird, 305. Laird also notes that Brown's rival, Samuel Kirkham, outsold Brown but made few, if any, serious contributions. The last version of *The Grammar of Grammars* which Brown revised was 1857; at about this time, "Professor George P. Marsh was preparing his *Lectures on the English Language*, which . . . announced the new study of language in the New World" (305). William Dwight Whitney's *Language and the Study of Language* appeared in 1867. For theories of grammar and language in England during this same time see Hans Aarsleff's *The Study of Language in England, 1780–1860* (Princeton, 1967).

71. As early as 1870 William James notes "the resemblance of Hawthorne's style to yours and Howells's" (Perry, 1:316).

72. Nathaniel Hawthorne, *The English Notebooks*, ed. R. Stewart (Oxford, 1941), xxxvii.

73. Stewart xxviii; Frederick C. Crews, *The Sins of the Fathers* (Oxford, 1966), 12.

74. Altick, 253; Fred Lewis Pattee, *The Feminine Fifties* (New York, 1940), 55.

75. Mott, 43.

76. For an extended, if idiosyncratic, discussion of the nineteenth century's use and vulgarization of eighteenth-century style, see Q. D. Leavis' *Fiction and the Reading Public* (London, 1932).

77. James Sutherland, *A Preface to Eighteenth Century Poetry* (Oxford, 1948), 84, 140.

78. Jean H. Hagstrum, *Samuel Johnson's Literary Criticism* (Minneapolis, 1952), 85.

79. Extensive use of generalization also came to James through some "great" novelists and through the "literary" historians. "Like Cooper and Scott, they [the historians] were interested in generalizing about such subjects as 'national character,' and in illustrating through minor characters such abstracted traits as 'remarkable resolution,' 'intrepidity' (especially the intrepidity of an occasional woman), and chivalric generosity" (Levin, 15).

80. Samuel Johnson, *Rasselas* in *Samuel Johnson*, ed. Bertrand H. Bronson (New York, 1952), 505; Alexander Pope, "An Essay on Criticism," in *Pastoral Poetry and Essay on Criticism*, ed. E. Audra and A. Williams (New Haven, 1961), 2:209; *W&W* (243–44, 589); *St.E*, (506), *WWW* (339).

81. "Heart" is especially hallowed by mid-Victorian times because it is sanctioned not only by the eighteenth-century love of formula and sentimentality but also by romantic practice. "Romantic poets were fond of expressing certain human acts in such a way as to make a human organ (ear, eye, voice, heart) the grammatical subject of the sentence. Instead of 'The prisoner looked out the small window,' the romantic poet is likely to say 'The prisoner's eye peered out the small window' " (Lubomír Doležel, "Toward a Structural Theory of Content in Prose Fiction" (in Chatman, 97). Debating the relative powers of the "heart" and the "soul" is, as Brown notes, a perennial feature of sentimental fiction (79).

82. For statistics on the use of words in James and popular novels, see page 66. James' other favorite formulas are "soul" (18 appearances in *W&W*), "dozen" (17), "half a dozen" and "half an hour" (14), "hundred" (13).

83. In *Lady Audley's Secret* we find "a sharp tussle" (339); in *East Lynne*, "one sharp tussle for liberty" (403); and in *Cometh Up as a Flower*, "a bitter weary tussle" (339). In early short stories James stages at least two tussles (*CT* 2:351, 412).

84. Rahill, 68.

85. M. Booth, 135.

86. Nathaniel Hawthorne, *The House of the Seven Gables* (Boston, 1964) [1851], 15, 135, 178, 250 (twice), 251.

87. *W&W*: 235, 237, 238, 240, 241 (thrice), 242, 243 (twice), 245 (twice), 246 (thrice), 320, 323 (thrice), 325 (twice), 326 (twice), 327, 331 (twice), 339, 416 (thrice), 417, 418, 420 (twice), 427, 429 (twice), 577 (twice), 578, 582, 584, 588, 594, 696, 700, 708. *W&W*: 235, 238, 239, 240 (twice), 243, 246, 320, 323 (twice), 326, 330, 331, 332, 336, 419, 424, 427, 577, 579, 582, 584, 590, 592 (thrice), 696 (twice), 698 (twice).

Noun entities are most harmful at heightened moments. After Fenton says, " 'Is that hospitality? If that's the way they understand it hereabouts, I prefer the Western article!' " we read, "This passionate outbreak, prompted in about equal measures by baffled ambition and wounded sensibility, made sad havoc with Nora's strenuous loyalty to her friend" (*W&W* 334). The transitional "this passionate outbreak" functions like a noun entity: it attempts to encapsulate the dialogue, to sum it up in a word. It succeeds, of course, only in deadening Fenton's outburst. Then, the entities "baffled ambition and wounded sensibility" prove too neat and too neatly juxtaposed to actually suggest a mental state, even George's. Since the cliché verb "made havoc with" cannot be sufficiently disguised by the qualifier "sad," the *action* of the sentence is also unconvincing. An entity, "strenuous loyalty," then finishes off the quotation, and the reader. Lest we attempt a comeback, here is the next sentence. (The italics are mine and indicate the appearance of the devices which we have been studying in this section.) "Her *sense of infinite property in her cousin—the instinct of free affection alternating more gratefully than she knew* with the *dim consciousness of measured dependence*—had become in her *heart* a sort of *boundless and absolute rapture*" (334).

88. *HR*: 1:9, 11, 57, 71, 73–4, 97, 280, 308; 2:91, 173, 192, 237, 264, 322, 363. *W&W*: 236, 237, 242 (twice), 320, 415, 420, 424, 429, 582 (twice), 699, 707.

89. James Boswell, *London Journal, 1762–1793*, ed. Frederick A. Pottle (New York, 1950), 135.

90. At its worst, the popular tradition suffers for its sins, of course. "Said Ellen, her eyes watering" (*WWW* 231). Euphemism actually distorts the moment here, for Ellen is not suffering from watery eyes. She is weeping.

91. Again, here are the actual totals.

TABLE 5'

	W&W	RH	StE	HR	WWW	In	Ame	PL
personification	39	18	32	20	25	8	7	9
formula: "heart"	70	67	305	143	293	39	43	51
formula: "pretty"	62	49	49	51	69	76	71	60
entity: girls, women	76	28	93	30	11	22	4	23

92. Vernon Lee, *The Handling of Words* (London, 1927), 243.

93. This last image and the one from NY 334 show, of course, that James' revisions entail more than simply a technical advance. He is seeing Rowland more complexly and is using a more complex technique to make us experience a comparably sophisticated insight. He is doing the same thing when he takes the 1876 sentence, "he [Rowland] used to reflect that during those days he had for a while been literally beside himself," and adds, "even as an ass, in the farmer's row of stalls, may be beside the ox" (285, NY 314).

94. *PL* 7, 19, 40, 166, 393–94, 457, 501, 502, 529, 530.

95. James also uses circumlocution to emphasize, with varying degrees of sharpness, that other characters never reach Ralph's full awareness. Although James' sting is gentle when he refers to the "conjugal chamber" (29) and "the conjugal mansion" (450) of overly serious Lily, he hits harder with Lydia Touchett. "For what is usually called social intercourse she had very little relish; but nothing pleased her more than to find her hall-table whitened with oblong morsels of symbolic pasteboard" (55). Capable of seeing through the vacuity of "what is called social intercourse," Lydia nonetheless enjoys "oblong morsels of symbolic pasteboard." Not "calling cards." Not what they are—signs of callers—but what they symbolize—her own importance. In its hollowness the circumlocution "oblong morsels of symbolic pasteboard" suggests the hollowness of Lydia's life and thus the limitations of her two-sidedness.

Not all James' circumlocutions in *The Portrait* have thematic significance. Some seem genteel conventions—calling Italian "the Italian tongue" (212), or referring to Isabel in the opera box as "the more attractive of its occupants" (275). Some seem positively coy—calling March "the windy month" (485) or referring to enlistment age as "old enough to wear shoulder straps" (108). Whatever humor is intended here seems arch.

96. Does the fact that James expressly used the word "epithet" five times in *The Portrait* (70, 106, 220, 478, 540) indicate his increased awareness of this device *as a device?* Matthiessen notes that James in the revisions *adds* epithets "to characterize the world of which she [Isabel] is part. . . . Where James had written 'the nineteenth century,' he was later to call it 'the age of advertisement' " (*Henry James: The Major Phase* [Oxford, 1944], 161).

Many epithets in *The Portrait* are fresh enough to be wryly comic: "The conciliatory Lily" (30, 295), "the cheerful Lily" (297), "the quick-fingered Henrietta" (76), "the sociable Bunchie" (92), "Miss Annie Climber, the young lady of the continental offers" (154). Other epithets derive interest from the character who coins them, as when Pansy conceives of Isabel as "the elegant Miss Archer" (326) and Warburton deems Ned "the melancholy youth" (409). When the epithet "the master of Gardencourt" recurs (456), it takes us a moment to realize that Ralph, not Daniel, is being referred to; with this recognition comes immediate comparison with Daniel, and thus we sense Ralph's grandness, and also, possibly, a generational decline from father to son, his inevitable fate.

One other epithet indicates clearly James' evolution. "Rustic" is a word, like "oaten," which tends to appear in overly conventionalized pastoral situations. It appears that way, for example, with Roderick's drinker:

his back was slightly hollowed, his head thrown back, and both hands raised to
support the rustic cup.

(16)

Compare this rustic cup with Isabel's rustic bench.

At the end of a few minutes she found herself near a rustic bench, which, a moment
after she had looked at it, struck her as an object recognized. It was not simply that
she had seen it before, nor even that she had sat upon it; it was that in this spot
something important had happened to her. . . . Then she remembered that she had
been sitting there six years before. . . . she overcame her scruples and sank into the
rustic seat.

(539–40)

"The rustic cup": "The rustic seat." The difference between the two "the"s, and thus
between the two "rustic"s, marks James' triumph over epithets and entities and over the
larger tendency to generalize fiction into statement. Isabel's bench we know well
enough, have experienced sufficiently, that the "the" refers directly to it; there is no
movement on to a type, as Pope does with his epithet The Man of Ross or as James did
with his entity "the female charm." On the other hand, "the rustic cup" does belong to
this earlier tradition. Since we have no experience of the cup specific enough to make it
"the" cup, Roderick's statue loses particularity and interest, passes into the general, the
literary. One of the paradoxes of James' crucial decade is precisely that he becomes a
literary master by becoming less "literary."

97. By 1876 James, reviewing *Mercy Philbrick's Choice*, can criticize the vagueness
of the noun entities "poetic temperament" and "artistic temperament" (*Na* 372). One of
the revisions of *Roderick Hudson* indicates well that minimum particularity which
entities need to function effectively in James' fiction. He changes " 'success is only
passionate effort' " to " 'achievement's only effort passionate enough' " (*RH* 78; *NY*
85). " 'Passionate effort' " and " 'effort passionate enough' ": we move from a
generalized idea to a particular experience qualified as life is qualified.

In James' revisions the entity "maternal conscience" becomes "a conscience that
worked in the most approved and most punctual fashion" (*NY* 249); and "Roderick
was peculiarly inscrutable" (322) becomes "Roderick's reflecting surface exhibited, for
the time, something of a blur" (*NY* 353). In 1874, James could say that Roderick
"looked . . . with the eye of the sculptor" (23), and could still say in 1881 that Madame
Merle's "touch was that of an artist" (159). The latter affirmation he makes convincing
in revision by replacing the easy entity with "she touched the piano with a discretion
of her own" (*NY* 1:245). In *The American* Newman is both the author and the butt of
undercutting entities. Having used the hallowed expression " 'the proud consciousness
of honest toil,' " Newman then rephrases it, " 'of having manufactured a few wash
tubs' " (95)—in order to show himself aware of the hard reality that underlies
traditional American verities. He does not, however, recognize the inadequacy of
other verities which he assumes universal. "Newman found it impossible to convince
him [Valentin] of certain time honored verities" (98). The wit here does not entirely
assuage our apprehensiveness because Newman is depending upon such verities—
upon the word of gentlemen, for instance—to assure his future happiness.

98. The revisions indicate this maturity too. As *The Wide, Wide World* presents "the
airy travellers" (126) and *Adam Blair* "the little airy bed-chamber" (63), so James in
Roderick Hudson gives us "these airy adventurers" (233). Since he is presenting not
birds but Roderick and Christina atop the Coliseum, James in 1907 calls them what
they are—"these high climbers" (*NY* 258).

In turn, *The Portrait* is not completely free of sacchariness. "The windy month
expressed itself in occasional puffs of spring" (485); "London does not wear in the
month of September its most brilliant face" (128); "sunshine rested on the walls . . .

washing them, as it were, in places tenderly chosen" (73); "the doctors had whispered to Ralph that another attack would be less easy to deal with" (58).

99. Isabel later fails twice with Warburton. "Isabel stopped; it seemed to her there would be a certain flatness in the utterance of her thought. 'I know what you are going to say. You hoped we should always remain good friends.' This formula, as Lord Warburton uttered it, was certainly flat enough.... 'Please don't talk of all that'; a speech which barely seemed to her an improvement on the other" (268); " 'I want to marry,' he added, more simply. 'It ought to be very easy,' Isabel said, rising, and then blushing a little at the thought that she was hardly the person to say this" (356). We continue to hold out hope for Isabel, however, because she, unlike Osmond and Madame Merle, who "always paid, in public, a certain formal tribute to the commonplace" (344), is determined to "try to understand—she would not simply utter graceful platitudes" (236–37).

100. W. K. Wimsatt, Jr., *The Prose Style of Samuel Johnson* (New Haven, 1941), 15–49.

101. H. C. Martin, 126.

102. Guy passes from hero to villain and back to hero without ever acquiring the gray of our common mortality: in favor, he so surpasses his violent forebears that " 'it is wolf and lamb, indeed' " (*HR* 1:167); out of favor, his marriage to Amy "would have been uniting a dove and a tiger" (1:327).

103. Thirty-seven times here; in *The Heir*, twenty-nine. Levin finds this same penchant in the American historians—"all four used the same technique of simplified contrasts" (102).

104. Reade, *Griffith Gaunt*, 34, 123; Wood, *East Lynne*, 187; Baroness von Tautphoeus, *In* 75.

105. Martha Banta (*Henry James and the Occult* [Bloomington, Ind., 1972]) and Sallie Sears (*The Negative Imagination* [Ithaca, 1968]) deal well with simultaneous effects in James' later work. Donald L. Mull in his recent *Henry James's 'Sublime Economy'* (Middletown, Conn., 1973) is particularly effective with the paradoxes and contradictions in early James.

106. Recently Philip Grover (*Henry James and the French Novel* [New York, 1973]) has suggested that an instinct for contrast was one of James' legacies from Balzac. Grover quotes from the Preface to *Roderick Hudson* where James describes searching for "some more or less vivid antithesis.... I required my antithesis—my antithesis to Christina Light" (*AN* 8, 18). Grover's concern with contrasts of setting and character does not carry him on, however, to study James' stylistic use of antitheta.

107. Quoted by E. Stone, 20.

108. The belief that "piety pays dividends" is, according to Margaret Dalziel, a tenet "most apparent in evangelical periodicals" (*Popular Fiction 100 Years Ago* [London, 1957], 157).

109. He makes a similar improvement with the "partly-partly" formula. Repeatedly in the early novels we encounter such tidy expressions as "partly because he wished to please the two women and partly because he was strangely pleased himself" (*RH* 59); in *The Portrait* James often leaves one of the poles indeterminate. "... an animation partly due perhaps to the fact that she perceived her sister-in-law to be engaged in conversation" or "a kind of cynical directness which seemed also partly an expression of fatigue" (480, 487).

110. "Mr. Archer had a remarkably handsome head and a very taking manner (indeed, as one of them had said, he was always taking something)"; "he wished she would ask something of him. But Isabel asked nothing but questions"; "Rome, as Ralph said, was in capital condition"; " 'I take no hints. But I took a message.' ... 'You took it?' "; "Gilbert Osmond's rich devices"; " 'my wife has declined—declined to

do anything' " (31, 52, 265, 349, 376, 483). Besides the sexual puns which I have quoted, there are such other gems as Madame Merle's admission, " 'my dear, I am a horror' " (179) and Ralph's chauvinistic, patronizing, " 'I understand Henrietta as well as if I had made her' " (190). Henrietta's enigmatic relationship with Bantling is made still more suspect by the narrator's diction. "The two had led a life of great intimacy. . . . really in a manner quite lived together" (201). Recently Sheldon W. Liebman has effectively discussed various ways in which language becomes unreliable and meanings shift in *The Portrait* ("Point of View in *The Portrait of a Lady*," *ES* 52:136–47).

111. The "half-half" construction appears barely half as many times in the much longer *Portrait* (11 vs. 6). Or compare Gloriani as "half-Italian, half-French" with Osmond—"if he had English blood in his veins, it had probably received some French or Italian commixture" (211). Generally James uses words like "mixture" with enough syntactic complexity that the style doesn't seem to deny mixture ("mixed with it now was an audible strain of bitterness" [75]). Occasionally, to be sure, we do still meet "an odd mixture of the indifferent and the expressive" (236).

112. Many critics have noted that the word "form" occurs frequently in the latter pages of *The Portrait*. Besides appearances on pages 313 (twice), 323, 324, 353, 355, 376, 382, 393, 397, 401, 403, 409, 427, 429, 436, 441, 447, 465, 467, 491, 496, 543, 544, "form" is particularly important in the following passages: "Her notion of the aristocratic life was simply the union of great knowledge with great liberty; the knowledge would give one a sense of duty, and the liberty a sense of enjoyment. But for Osmond, it was altogether a thing of forms. . . . he [Caspar] had spoken with a visible effort to control himself, to give a considerate form to an inconsiderate state of mind. . . . 'why should you go through that ghastly form?' " (397, 471, 543). Linked to men who use form for selfish ends, and prey to the limitations of both men, Isabel preserves the form of her marriage. Why, is a question that every serious reader must ask. For the most extensive discussions of "form," see Holland, 43–54; Tony Tanner, "The Fearful Self: Henry James's *The Portrait of a Lady*," *Critical Quarterly* 7 (1965): 205–19; Frederick J. Hoffman, "Freedom and Conscious Form: Henry James and the American Self," *Virginia Quarterly Review* 37 (1961): 269–85; Philip Rahv, "The Heiress of All the Ages," in *Image and Idea* (New York, 1949), 51–76.

113. I very much agree with Cargill that "the difficulty readers have had with Isabel's actions comes largely from the mistaken assumption that James presented her as an ideal type—a notion fostered largely by the dubious assumption that she is drawn wholly from his cousin, Minny Temple" (106).

114. Matthiessen, *The Major Phase*; Dorothy Van Ghent, *The English Novel* (New York, 1953); D. Stone, *Novelists in a Changing World*. See also V. F. Blehl, S. J., "Freedom and Commitment in James's *The Portrait of a Lady*," *The Personalist* 42 (1962): 368–81; John Rodenbeck, "The Bolted Door in James's *Portrait of a Lady*," *MFS* 10 [1964–65]: 330–40.

Chapter Two

1. Joyce Tayloe Horrell, "A 'Shade of Special Sense': Henry James and the Art of Naming," *AL* 42 (1970): 212. In summing up the conventional aspects of the plot of *The Portrait*, Leon Edel goes on to add the crucial qualification. "At moments the story [*The Portrait*] verges on melodrama when it isn't pure fairy-tale; a rich uncle, a poor niece, an ugly sick cousin, who worships her from a distance, three suitors, one heiress, and her final betrayal by a couple of cosmopolite compatriots into a marriage as sinister as the backdrop of a Brontë novel: of such time worn threads is this book woven. And yet to say this is to offer a gross caricature of a warm and human work" ("Introduction" to *The Portrait of a Lady* [rev. ed., Boston, 1963], ix; also quoted by Cargill [97]). A few of the many other commentators upon this aspect of James' work

are F. R. Leavis (*The Great Tradition*), Leo B. Levy (*Versions of Melodrama* [Berkeley, 1957]), Manfred Mackenzie ("Ironic Melodrama in *The Portrait of a Lady*," *MFS* 12 [1966]: 7–23), Marjorie Perloff ("Cinderella Becomes the Wicked Stepmother: *The Portrait of a Lady* as Ironic Fairy Tale," *NCF* 23 [1969]: 417–33), Peter Brooks ("The Melodramatic Imagination," *Partisan Review* 39 [1972]: 195–212).

2. Elsie dies on the threshold of her twenty-first year; virtually all lives in the novel are overshadowed by one sorrow or another; and one of the basic elements of the book is the beloved teacher's attempt to guide the future career of a young medical student.

3. Howells, 2:181–82. Although Howells is actually referring to Tess, his words are truer still of popular characters.

4. Robert Bechtold Heilman, *Tragedy and Melodrama* (Seattle, 1968), 178.

5. Praz, *Hero*; Peter Conrad, *The Victorian Treasure-House* (London, 1973). In *Yesterday's Woman* Vineta Colby gives some attention to painting and popular fiction. Another important pictorial influence upon Victorian daily life, and thus upon popular Victorian fiction, was the fashion book. In *The Heir*, "the young ladies ranged themselves in imitations of the book of fashions" (1:122).

6. For popular multiplication of this very gesture, see *St. Elmo*:

leaning her elbows on the window-sill, Edna rested her face in her palms . . . . leaning her face in her palms, rested her elbows on the ground . . . . head leaned wearily on his shrunken hand . . . . resting her elbow on her knee, dropped her face on her hands . . . . knelt with his face shrouded in his hands . . . . resting her arms on the black marble, she laid her head down upon them . . . . leaned his elbow on the side of the pew . . . and rested his temple on his hand.

(48, 65, 190, 356, 403, 439–40, 507)

Repeating other gestures is also very common in early James:

laying a kindly hand on his shoulder . . . . patting him kindly on the shoulder . . . . laying an almost paternal hand on the little painter's yellow head . . . . laid his hand on his arm . . . . laid his hand on his other arm . . . . laid his hand affectionately on his friend's shoulder . . . . laid his hand on Roderick's shoulder . . . . laying his hand on Roderick's arm . . . . laid his hand on his arm . . . . laid her hand on his arm . . . . laid one hand on her arm.

(24, 113, 132, 183 [twice], 200, 203, 277,
287, 386, 400)

7. Quoted by Tompkins (83) from *The Pupil of Pleasure*.

8. The heroine's speed afoot often gets amusing, especially during those instant changes of clothes which occur at crisis moments in popular and Jamesian fiction. "Nora made it the work of a single moment to reach her own room [which is upstairs] and fling on her bonnet and shawl, of another to descend to the hall door" (*W&W* 705); "running up to her room, she [Edna] tied on her hat and walked rapidly across the park [from the second floor, no less]" (*StE* 277). Downright funny are the bloopers that occur with these gestures. "Nora was removing her bonnet before the mirror. . . . as she spoke, she caught Hubert's eye in the glass. He dropped it and took up his hat" (*W&W* 423); "wandering listlessly about the room, her eye fell on the Saturday-evening paper" (421); "she seemed to see Roger's bent, stunned head in the street" (596). None of these, however, can match my two favorites from *The Wide, Wide World*: "she stooped her lips to the trough" and "Mrs. Marshman also stooped down and kissed herself" (112, 294).

9. M. Booth, 135; the Hallers, 105, 204. In the plastic arts, the tradition of Hogarth is carried on, though with real differences, by Cruikshank and other great Victorian illustrators, including Thackeray himself. See particularly John Harvey's *Victorian Novelists and Their Illustrators* (London, 1970).

10. Papashvily, 2.

11. Michael Davitt Bell, *Hawthorne and the Historical Romance of New England* (Princeton, 1971), 8.

12. Edward Bulwer-Lytton, *Pelham* (Lincoln, Neb., 1972), 415, 454.

13. The total figures are:

TABLE 6'

	W&W	RH	StE	HR	WWW	In	Ame	PL
fling-spring	16	39	38	34	61	57	7	7
burst	6	13	2	16	54	17	6	10

14. In 1878 James can delete from the 1871 text of *Watch and Ward* the intrusive ending of "Nora answered with a faint, grave smile, and stood looking at him, *invoking by her helpless silence some act of high protection*" (695; my italics). James does of course continue to use the older, more direct narrative commentary in *The Portrait*. Poirier discusses well the effect of these commentaries at their best; at their worst they can remain intrusive, as when Ralph "even blushed a little—his blush being the sign of an emotion somewhat acute" (157).

15. "Guy's brows drew together again, and his eyes glanced as if he was much inclined to resent the remarks" (*HR* 1:35); "Fenton spoke loud and fast, as if to deepen and outstrip possible self-contempt" (*W&W* 699).

16. Table 7' follows:

TABLE 7'

	W&W	RH	StE	HR	WWW	In	Ame	PL
gesture	4	22	6	9	2	7	9	4
attitude	1	36	1	1	4	0	13	38

Of the other, more assertive type of generalized posture, I find only two in *The Portrait:* "a gesture of apology" (9) and "his hat in the attitude of *ennui*" (275).

17. Worse off still, of course, are those characters who have become their poses so completely that they cannot diverge from them even into deceit. Ned and Pansy, for example. After his rejection, Ned appears in widely separated scenes, "in the attitude of a young man without illusions. . . . such an attitude, today, could belong only to Mr. Edward Rosier" (409, 486). Whether he can ever be anything more than the slightly comic swain languishing for his porcelain shepherdess, we doubt. And she? "She only looked toward it [approbation] wistfully—an attitude which, as she grew older, made her eyes the prettiest in the world" (375). Pansy is not self-consciously striking a pose. But neither can she exist outside the postures of her rarefied milieu; like "pretty," the "attitude" shows the enormity of making a human being into an art object.

18. Alexander Welsh establishes the death angel as an iconographic figure in the Victorian literary and pictorial arts, and mentions Isabel Archer; he does not, however, discuss James' complex use of the death angel with Isabel and the ambivalence of our response to her (*The City of Dickens* [Oxford, 1971], 184, 192–93). For popular examples of the heroine as death angel, see Isabel in *East Lynne* smoothing her dying son's path to paradise (435, 441, 443), or Nell doing the same for her father in *Cometh Up as a Flower* (340, 343), or Gulnare nursing the Corsair (II xii). In his early fiction, James himself has a heroine who "knelt . . . like a consoling angel" (*CT* 2:134); and, of course, Nora hurls herself upon her knees beside Roger's sick bed and cures him marvelously. For instances of heroines as complex angels, Charles Reade is a gold mine; for a recent study of woman as Fair Angel, see Susan Gorsky's "The Gentle Doubters: Images of Women in Englishwomen's Novels, 1840–1920" in *Images of Women in Fiction*, ed. Susan Koppelman Cornillon (Bowling Green, Ky., 1972), 28–54.

19. Leo Levy's "The Comedy of *Watch and Ward*" (*Arlington Quarterly*, 1 [1968]: 86–98) suggests how much variation James is making on character types and situations. Especially after my comparison with *The Initials*, I should add that Roger clearly differs from the more traditional hero, Hamilton, in many ways, and Nora, as uncapricious and orphaned, is by no means identical with Hildegarde.

20. Helene E. Roberts, "Marriage, Redundancy or Sin: The Painter's View of Women in the First Twenty-five Years of Victoria's Reign," in Vicinus, 67.

21. Battle images, particularly swords and guns, for example. Hubert wars twice with Mrs. Keith. He begins the campaign strongly enough for phallic imagery. With "a sudden watchful quiver in his eye, like a sword turned edge outward" (587) he faces Mrs. Keith. Man enough for this, "she unsheathed one of her own steely beams, and for a tenth of a second there was a dainty crossing of blades" (587). The outcome: "Hubert made her a little bow" in defeat (588). In their second battle, Hubert signifies his retreat from the field of life by retreating "to the window" (589), the station conventionally associated with the Heroine-as-Perceiver. Disparaging this unmanliness with the word "tickled" (589), Mrs. Keith presses her advantage. "She had dragged a heavy gun to the front; she determined to fire her shot" (590). This phallic image has been denied to Hubert earlier in the novel: "he fought the Devil as an irresponsible skirmisher, not as a sturdy gunsman planted beside a booming sixty-pounder" (415). Like Hubert, George attempts to do battle. "Fenton shot her a glance of harsh mistrust" (704). Soon he too is routed and must hang his head, like Hubert (705).

Very briefly, here are some other examples of James reversing sexual roles and symbols. Most of the women, for example, have men's names in *Watch and Ward*. Nora's last name is Lambert, her music teacher's is Murray, her guide-figure's maiden name was Morton and now is Keith; George's mistress is Mrs. Paul. Another instance is portals, gates, doors. Traditionally female symbols, these are applied to men in various complex and even disconcerting ways before the novel ends. Or the fact that the word "potent" occurs twice as often with women as with men. When Hubert admits, " 'I had the wit to see, but I lacked the courage to do' " (586), he sums up the inadequacies of his sex and one theme of *Watch and Ward*.

22. Among many instances in *Watch and Ward*, here are a few. Roger makes little headway either in the realm of thought or action. "Roger fretfully meditated, but generally with no great gain of ground . . . . Roger rose to his feet [when Miss Morton tells of her engagement] like a man who has received a heavy blow and springs forward in self-defense. But he was indefensible, his assailant inattackable. He sat down again and hung his head" (330, 236). Even at the climactic moment of the book when Nora is in danger, "when at last he reached Hubert's dwelling, a sudden sense of all that he risked checked his steps . . . . So he turned heavily back to the Fifth Avenue" (700). One of the few things that Roger can do is put action off on women. "He weighed the proprieties for a week, and then he determined the child should choose for herself. . . . at last Roger felt that he must speak of his love. He walked away to the farther end of the terrace. . . . It was not for him to talk, but for her to perceive!" (242, 321). Fortunately for him, Nora and other women *can* act when they have to. "It made a hideous whirl about her; but she felt that to advance in the face of it was her best safety. . . . His address she well remembered, and she neither paused nor faltered" (705, 706). The contrast between women who can act and men who cannot, is made expressly. "Nora collected herself as solemnly as one on a death-bed making a will; but Roger was still in miserable doubt and dread" (709). And so, what is said of Roger during his illness will be true of him for life. " 'I verily believe she saved him' " (589).

23. F. W. Dupee maintains that *"Watch and Ward* is strewn with images so palpably and irresistibly erotic as to imply a whole resonant domain of meaning beyond anything he could have intended (*Henry James* [New York, 1951], 61); Edel and Gale agree, and J. A. Ward finds "no suggestion that his [Roger's] calculated education of Nora is either immoral or neurotic" (Edel, "Introduction," *Watch and Ward* [New York, 1957], 6, 7, 9; Robert Gale, "Freudian Imagery in James's Fiction," *The American Imago,* 11:188; Ward, *The Search for Form* [Chapel Hill, 1967], 60). Oscar Cargill, on the other hand, maintains that "half a century ago any Yankee boy would have seen this business, without the benefit of Freud, as erotic, and one cannot believe that it would have been differently interpreted a generation earlier" (12). I wholeheartedly agree, especially if the Yankee boy was a twenty-nine-year-old cosmopolite. Putt seconds Cargill (33), as does the best article on *Watch and Ward,* Levy's "The Comedy of *Watch and Ward."*

24. In his 1873 review of Cherbuliez, James says that he has been reading the Swiss novelist since 1862 ("Cherbuliez's *Meta Holdenis," NAR* 461–68). James is still referring to Cherbuliez in the Notebooks in 1898 and 1899 (267, 292) and in the autobiographical volumes of both 1913 (*SB* 327–28) and 1914 (*NSB* 12). Mentioning Cherbuliez at least six times in early letters (*HJL* 75, 83, 264, 274, 348, 447), James says in 1868, "I do adore that man" (83). Only with *Meta Holdenis* does James begin to voice substantial reservations about Cherbuliez.

Recently, Joseph L. Tribble established many connections between *Le Roman* and *The Portrait of a Lady* ("Cherbuliez's *Le Roman d'une honnête femme:* Another Source of James's *The Portrait of a Lady," AL* 40 [1968]: 279–93). After noting the similarity between the names of the femmes fatales—Madame Merle and Madame Mirveil—Tribble then makes the necessary qualification. Unlike the heroines and villains of the two novels, the femmes fatales, except for their names, differ quite completely. Serena Merle is middle-aged and controlled, Emmeline de Mirveil is young and histrionic. Such differences disappear if we compare Emmeline, not with Madame Merle, but with Christina.

After *Le Roman* appeared in 1866, an unsigned American translation was published by Gill in Boston in 1874.

25. Christina enters the novel dramatically, walking through the Ludovisi Gardens with her mother and the Cavaliere in attendance; Malombré enters equally dramatically, walking through the woods and attended by two servants. Malombré's poodle, unlike Christina's, is black and wears his ribbon, not as a decoration, but as a bandage.

26. Malombré's role of perceiver (he is repeatedly called "Argus") is restricted to obsessive spying upon Mme Mirveil; Christina's perceptions involve her in the larger issues of social and psychological life (" 'I am an observer!' " [255]).

27. On page 87 we meet a young lady with "a pair of extraordinary dark blue eyes"; on page 154, we meet a young lady with "deep gray eyes." In each case, the young lady is, alas, Christina. James' descriptions are so conventional that he simply fails to concentrate upon those details which are so indispensable to great fiction. He did the same thing in *Watch and Ward,* for Hubert's eyes there are initially "a cool gray" (245), but later "intense blue" (586).

28. Rahill, 51.

29. Joseph H. Friend, "The Structure of *The Portrait of a Lady," NCF* 20 (1965): 89.

30. Quentin Anderson, *The American Henry James* (Rutgers, 1957), 188; Robert W. Stallman, *The Houses That James Built* (East Lansing, 1961), 27. Juliet McMaster ("The Portrait of Isabel Archer," *AL* 45 [1973]: 50–66) seems to be following Anderson when she says that "one is tempted to see Osmond's name as suggesting

finally an ossified world, a world of death and rigidity." Concerning Osmond's first name, Martha Banta suggests that "his Christian name implies the nebulous 'bright wish' on whose validity she [Isabel] has risked everything" (175).

31. Eino Railo, *The Haunted Castle* (London, 1927), 152, 158.

32. For other discussions of James' names see Robert Gale, "Names in James," *Names* 14 (1966): 83, 108; David Galloway, *Henry James: The Portrait of a Lady* (London, 1967), 26; Maxwell Geismar, *Henry James and the Jacobites* (New York, 1962), 272; Clare R. Goldfarb, "Names in *The Bostonians*," *Iowa English Yearbook* 13 (1968): 18–23; Arnold L. Goldsmith, "The Poetry of Names in *The Spoils of Poynton*," *Names* 14 (1966): 134–42; J. T. Horrell, "A 'Shade of Special Sense'"; E. Stone, 115–26; my "Strether and the Transcendence of Language," *MP* 69 (1971): 116–32; J. M. Backus, " 'Poor Valentin' or 'Monsieur le Comte': Variation in Character Designation as Matter for Critical Consideration (in Henry James's *The American*)," *Names* 20 (1972): 47–55; E. J. Hinz, "Henry James's Names: Tradition, Theory and Method," *CLQ* 9:557–78.

33. "Mrs. Montgomery," with an unfeeling husband, perseveres courageously on behalf of her daughter in *The Wide, Wide World* and in *Washington Square* "Mrs. Montgomery" exhibits comparable courage when the daughter is not her own and the unfeeling male is her brother. Ladies named "Morton" and "Keith" appear in *St. Elmo* and *The Wide, Wide World.* "Sandys" was a well-known artist who exhibited in the Academy, and was published in *Cornhill* in the 1860s; on the other hand, since James revised this name in 1878 to "Sands," he may have named his "Miss Sandys" after the famous George. The name "Valentin" not only appears with traditional amorous associations in *Two Gentlemen of Verona* and *Love for Love,* but also takes on tragic overtones when a youth duels to his death over female honor in *Faust;* James' Valentin combines these amorous and fatal associations. Nora's last name, "Lambert," suggests *Louis Lambert,* which James had read by 1871; an artist named Lambert appears in *Christopher Kirkland,* the famous novel by Mrs. Linton, whom James praises politely in the crucial decade (*EL* 171–72); in another novel of the sixties which James knew, *Cometh Up as a Flower,* we find "that female Daniel Lambert" (258); and a more remote Lambert is the lover in a celebrated turn-of-the-century burlesque (*The Elegant Enthusiast* by Lady Harriet Harlow). Whether or not James knew this last Lambert, his giving to the heroine a man's name (genius-artist-lover in the tradition) emphasizes Nora's power and self-sufficiency.

34. "Pansy" was also the nickname of the magazine's founder, Isabella MacDonald Alden (1841–1930), who had "Probably one of the longest careers in American letters" (Papashvily, 186); this Isabella, incidentally, came from upstate New York. For James and some of his readers, the name Pansy had one other association with children. To honor Hawthorne's memory, the *Atlantic* for August 1864 published "Pansy and Doctor Dolliver." The motherless girl, "dwelling in an uncheerful house," is three.

35. Bowden, 56; Rahill, 233.

36. Cargill suggests that the "Ralph" in George Sand's *Indiana* may also be an influence here. A man named "Touchit" does appear in Thackeray's *Lovell the Widower.*

37. The author is even more famous. Theodore Hook appears in *Vanity Fair* and *Pendennis* as Wagg. *Gilbert Gurney* was, in fact, a chief source for *Pendennis,* which, in turn, James expressly mentions in his early fiction.

38. Matthew Gregory Lewis, *The Castle Spectre* (London, 1798). Lodowick Carlell, *The Tragedy of Osmond, the Great Turk* (Berkshire, England, 1926). Lewis, at most, took only the name from the earlier play, however, for Carlell's Osmond is a model servant. In Mozart's *The Abduction from the Seraglio,* the servant Osmond is comic, but he is seriously committed to the ideal of wifely purity established by his culture.

39. Rahill, 203. The question of James' exact knowledge and use of this element of the literary tradition is impossible to determine. He knew Monk Lewis' work well; he also knew Gilbert Stuart, and read both *The Wide, Wide World* and the *London Journal*. It seems probable that James in his playgoing saw *Lucy Leslie*. That he knew *Osmond, the Great Turk* or *Lucy Osmond* is less likely. Since determining James' sources precisely is an impossible task, our chief efforts must be toward defining as fully as possible the literary tradition into which James unquestionably dipped at times.

40. Railo notes the association of Matilda and Constance (252), but not Madame Merle's link to both.

41. Mario Praz, *The Romantic Agony* (Oxford, 1933), 191.

42. Cargill has used both etymology and literary history to increase our understanding of Madame Merle's complexity. In French "merle" means "blackbird," and by extension "liar"; since Madame Merle is fair, Cargill also suggests the white blackbird of DeMusset's "Histoire d'un merle blanc" (91).

43. Other examples abound. Lady Audley is called "bewitching" and is associated with "witchcraft.... sorcery" (78, 192). Griffith Gaunt says to Kate, " 'I think you are a witch' " (97). In *East Lynne* a maid is named "Marvel" and in *Cometh Up as a Flower* we find handwriting crabbed "as Merlin's charm" (183).

44. Praz, *Agony*, 261.

45. Peter L. Thorslev, Jr., *The Byronic Hero* (Minneapolis, 1962), 81.

46. In fact she is, if anything, an object lesson in how to age attractively. See how adequately Madame Merle fulfills the Older Woman type which Eliza Lynn Linton praises fulsomely. "A woman of ripe age has a knowledge of the world, and a certain suavity of manner and moral flexibility, wholly wanting to the young.... [who] are generally without pity.... Her figure is still good—not slim and slender certainly, but round and soft.... She has still her white and shapely hands" (*The Girl of the Period* [London, 1883], 1:204, 205, 208). James reviewed Mrs. Linton in 1868 (*Na* 332–34).

47. Perry Miller, *Nature's Nation* (Cambridge, Mass., 1967), 251.

48. John B. White, *Foscari, or The Venetian Exile* (Charleston, 1806), 9.

49. Mihail Lermontov, *A Hero of Our Time* (Garden City, N.Y., 1958), 56, 202.

50. Ellen Moers, *The Dandy* (New York, 1960), 34. Barbey d'Aurevilly renders this maxim as "to be perfectly dressed one must not be noticeable." He even goes so far as to say, "one may be a Dandy in a ragged coat.... the clothes matter not at all" (*The Anatomy of Dandyism*, trans. D. B. Wyndham Lewis [London, 1928], 28, 78).

51. After we see Roderick "passing his hand through his abundant dark hair" and after "he tossed his clustering locks" (19, 194), James says that Roderick "gave a toss to his clustering locks which was equivalent to the signature—Roderick Hudson" (233). A signature is just what the gesture is *not*, because a signature is personal, characteristic. Roderick's hair fits him all too completely into a tradition begun in the eighteenth century and extending to Rhett Butler, Elvis Presley, and the Beatles. See particularly in *Pelham* a character "thrusting his large hand through his lank light hair" (65), and in *East Lynne* "Richard described a peculiar motion of his [the villain's], the throwing off his hair from his brow" (269).

52. "He lives, nor yet is past his manhood's prime, / Though seared by toil, and something touched by time" (*Lara*, I iv). In *The Heir*, Philip, as we saw, ages prematurely and never achieves stable health and proper "moderation." In *Watch and Ward*, marriage makes Roger ever younger, whereas "Hubert Lawrence, on the other hand, has already begun to pass for an elderly man" (710). Because of his suffering, Adam Blair's hair "had become tinged with untimely grey (like that of the Royal Sufferer of Carisbrooke)" (238).

53. Mr. Lambert's "eyes [were] as lurid as coals" (233); Byronic Hubert's "blue eyes

flashing cold wrath .... his eyes flashed" (590, 594); and poor Roger's eyes "glowed like living coals" (697) when he is supposedly Byronic. Roderick has "his usual luminous, unshrinking looks" and "a sinister spark in his eye" (183, 383).

54. Likewise, in *The Heir*, Amy can be saved only by obeying Guy's command to let go of the branch and take his hand. Even in *Roderick Hudson*, James complicates the conventional situation, for Christina, unlike Amy, Gwendolen, or Isabel does not perpetuate her domination by marrying the cliff-prone suitor.

55. Holmes speaks up for such boyish theatrics. "The Swiss youth climb the sides of the Alps to find the flower called the *Edelweiss* for the maidens whom they wished to please. It is a pretty fancy, that of scaling some dangerous height before the dawn, so as to gather the flower in its freshness, that the favored maiden may wear it to church on Sunday morning, a proof at once of her lover's devotion and his courage" (*EV* 231).

56. The image used with Osmond's egotism—"hidden like a serpent in a bank of flowers" (396)—echoes not only Genesis and Milton, but such popular examples as " 'among my flowers there is a snake' " in *Pelham* (45), " '[his] note, coiled like a snake among the flowers' " in *Vanity Fair* ([Boston, 1963], 278), and "[the seducer] like a serpent behind the hedge" in *East Lynne* (175).

Osmond is prideful enough (" 'I have never, no never, seen anyone of Osmond's pretensions' " [251]) to imagine a divine origin for himself (" 'he has always appeared to believe that he is descended from the gods' " [251]). Grandcourt and Max, more overtly Byronic in their infernal pride and in their knack of finding abysses, (*DD* 98, *LR* 66), get their vast knowledge also in the conventional way—through worldwide travel and hair-raising exploits. Grandcourt "had been everywhere, and seen everything .... 'tiger-hunting or pig-sticking. I saw some of that for a season or two in the East. Everything here is poor stuff after that' " (*DD* 100, 81). Max, who speaks "en homme du monde qui a beaucoup vu," says, " 'demain je partirai pour l'Afrique, je chasserai le lion dans l'Atlas' "; he even threatens to reach Richmond before the American Civil War ends because " 'je suis curieux de voir un siège de près. Une belle mort, voilà ma dernière fantaisie' " (*LR* 45, 158, 394). All of this could have come straight out of *St. Elmo*. Osmond, on the other hand, has attained the demonic control which great knowledge affords, while remaining immured in his poor, private life. He neither wears the conventional "diamond ring" (118) of Grandcourt nor utters "de hautains défis" (128) like Max. At each point, James sufficiently transforms the tradition that we can take it seriously.

57. In popular literature the fall is commemorated over and over. Ishmael's stepmother says of his father, " 'Oh, Herman! Herman! how could you fall so low?' " (173). Miss Merlin can, in turn, show woman's propensity for a Satanic career. " 'None other but the sins by which angels fell would have power to draw my soul down from heaven' " (*Ish* 516).

58. Such fury is a real possibility. "There was a moment during which, if she had turned and spoken, she would have said something that would hiss like a lash" (508). It would also hiss like a snake, for Isabel would have descended to Satanic revenge.

59. Besides complicating our response to Osmond, James postpones the tableau until after the marriage debacle so that we see Isabel's romanticization of Osmond not as the infatuation of a naive girl but as the disillusioned realization of a sadder but wiser woman. She thus avoids being Catherine as Osmond avoids being Morris.

60. Also, in part, because the villain shows steadily more conscience. "It was in this type of play [domestic drama] that disquieting symptoms made their first appearance: a decline in that primitive integrity of evil, which distinguished the villain in his prime, and the emergence of an incipient moral sense that spelled decadence" (Rahill, 209).

61. Albert Camus, "The Dandies' Rebellion," in *The Rebel* (New York, 1956), 84; Praz, *Agony*, 378; Levin, 19. For his generous help with dandies and with Byronism generally, I am grateful to Jerome J. McGann, who would be a great dandy if he were not a great deal more.

62. To recognize Byron as a Dandy is not necessarily to equate Byronism and Dandyism, although Moers' contention that the two "isms" are "mutually exclusive" is probably too sweeping (51). Moers points to *Rouge et Noir* where Korasoff lectures Julian on the superiority of the Dandy to the Byronic mode. Moers also states, however, that in France, "Anglomania made the dandy and the romantic one and the same, though the two had scarcely met at home" (121). In England romanticism was introspective—which was very foreign to Dandyism. Yet M. W. Rosa (*The Silver Fork School* [New York, 1936]) is correct that Bulwer's decision to give the Dandy his own voice in *Pelham* made the figure more introspective and thus Byronic. Moers also acknowledges *Paul Clifford* as the "original demonstration that criminals could be dandies and dandies criminals" (83). Bulwer's *Paul Clifford* and G. A. Lawrence's *Guy Livingstone* in turn set the pattern for many other criminal dandies. Thus, what is important for Henry James is the fact that after the initial heyday of Brummell and romanticism (where much of Dandyism and much of romanticism were far apart indeed) the Dandy and Byronic figures shared sensitivity, boredom, and subversiveness to such a degree that later writers drew upon them both for villainous characters.

63. Although his chapter does not lead in this direction, Holland does note that "Osmond's view is at once more conservative in its deference to older social patterns . . . and more radical in his means to attain them. . . . He is the genteel embodiment of 'convention' in a strikingly modern version recognizable since 1789: convention become conscious and deliberate" (38, 39).

64. Charles Baudelaire, *The Essence of Laughter*, quoted by Maurice Beebe in *Ivory Towers and Sacred Founts* (New York, 1964), 133.

65. Moers, 267. Moers finds comparable contradictions in Stendahl—"outspoken liberal opinions and aristocratic prejudices" (139).

66. Likewise Trebeck, England's first Dandy in fiction, pursues women for their money; unlike Osmond, Trebeck is simply a villain and is punished accordingly. Even Thackeray's capacity to feel the attractions of that Old Regency Dandy, Wagg, does not prompt any very radical examination of values in *Pendennis*.

67. Others who have discussed Osmond and Grandcourt are Oscar Cargill (87) and George Levine ("Isabel, Gwendolen, and Dorothea," *ELH* 30 [1963]: 244–57); recently John Halperin (*The Language of Meditation* [Devon, England, 1973]) has emphasized verbal echoes which link the two characters (121, 129).

68. In turn, Osmond's role as Paterfamilias saves him from too close a connection with another conventional figure—that comic butt, the Yankee Fop. John G. Cawelti notes that "the Alger villains represent those vices particularly reprehensible to many nineteenth-century Americans: they have aristocratic pretensions and try to adopt the airs of the leisure-class" (*Apostles of the Self-Made Man* [Chicago, 1965], 121). Hartman goes on to establish that the same is true on the American stage. In the first native comedy to be produced professionally, Royall Tyler's *The Contrast*, "the caricature of an American whose god. is Lord Chesterfield reveal[s] the general antipathy felt" toward such continentalized fops (45); in succeeding plays, "at the end of each play they [snobs] turn out to be either blackguards or as in the case of a later play, *Fashion*, impostors. The reason for this character's presence was the opportunity for contrasting him with fine examples of American men and women" (136). In *The Portrait* the character closest to the Fop is, not Osmond, but Ned. Despite many similarities between the two, Osmond has a stature that Ned lacks; Isabel could never say of Osmond that he "was really so very flimsy" (383).

69. W. H. Auden, "Introduction" to *Intimate Journals*, quoted by Beebe, 134.

70. In *Watch and Ward*, Miss Morton's niece "kept her place beside her aunt" and Nora "retreated to a station beside Roger's knee" (235, 244). In *Villette* we find that "to stand by his knee . . . was the reward she wanted" (20). Her wants, moreover, derive from precedent, for already "she leaned on his knee . . . . took refuge on his knee" (9, 15). In *Ruth* the heroine remembers fondly "her childish meditations at her mother's knee" (34), and recalls that old Thomas " 'would take me on his knee' " (49). For James' use of the tableau of the girl at the adult knee, see *CT* 3: 124, 285. Twice youngsters stand "between his legs" but both times the youngsters are *boys* (*CT* 2: 101, 3:282). Rowland holds Cecilia's little girl between his knees (3), but here the little girl is *very* little. This innocuous gesture takes on very different significance when James makes the single transformation of substituting a daughter of marriageable age.

71. Papashvily is probably correct when she speculates that "with the exception of Mark Twain's Huckleberry Finn, Elsie Dinsmore is probably the best-known character ever to appear in American fiction" (170).

72. At other times Miss Broughton can manage enough distance to write of "a sweet benedictory smile, which seems to say, like the 'heavy father' in the fifth act of a melodrama, 'Bless you, my children' " (*CUF* 148). Major novelists also explore the "relations" of daughters and fathers—Bella and Mr. Wilfer, for example, or Dorothea Brooke's notion that "the really delightful marriage must be that where your husband was a sort of father" (*Middlemarch* [Boston, 1956], 8). In *Aurora Leigh*, the heroine feels "The stranger's touch that took my father's place"; before this Fair Stranger, Romney, can fully take the father's place by marrying the heroine, he parts from her to toil in the world and then "voice and look were now / More utterly shut out from me, I felt, / Than even my father's" (*Aurora Leigh* [New York, 1857], 18, 64). Gorsky notes that in popular fiction "the Ingenue often sweetly exchanges her father's arm for her husband's with no perceptible change in herself. . . . a husband twice his wife's age is not unusual" (Cornillon, 38, 39).

73. About Isabel's conventional aspects James leaves no doubt. "She had had everything that a girl could have: kindness, admiration, flattery, bouquets, the sense of exclusion from none of the privileges of the world she lived in, abundant opportunity for dancing, the latest publications, plenty of new dresses, the London *Spectator*, and a glimpse of contemporary aesthetics" (33).

74. Once again, however, Isabel's criticism redounds upon herself, implicating her and qualifying to some extent our judgment of Osmond. Osmond's reply to " 'Oh, Osmond, for a man who was so fine' " is " 'I was never so fine as you' " (445). With Isabel the word "fine" has also functioned throughout the novel in contradictory ways. Madame Merle is serious and we tend to agree when she praises Isabel as " 'that fine creature' " (263). On the other hand, Isabel's failure to judge Osmond correctly derives from her failure to understand the "fine." Having "never met a person of so fine a grain," Isabel assumes Osmond has " 'a fine mind' " (242, 321). Ralph immediately indicates her error. "She had invented a fine theory about Gilbert Osmond" (321). We, in turn, hold out hope for Isabel when she reaches Ralph's level of insight. "She asked herself if she had really married on a factitious theory, in order to do something finely appreciable with her money" (394). So rich in nuance and ambiguity is "finely appreciable" that it suggests effectively the various less-than-completely-flattering reasons why Isabel married Osmond. In the couple's final confrontation, his wish "to do something . . . refined" (491) indicates how cruel—and therefore how gross—is the type of refinement which she once idolized. When Isabel subsequently says, " 'very fine. No, I think it was rather rough' " (519), she is referring to her channel crossing, but we see in her words the power she has gained to distinguish differences.

75. *PL* 217, 291, 293, 326, 327 (twice), 328, 333, 339, 340, 341 (twice), 344, 346, 348, 357, 358, 368, 369, 371, 375, 378, 380, 383, 385, 404 (twice), 405, 407 (twice), 412, 432, 434, 435, 441, 442, 446, 451, 452, 488, 489, 490, 491, 501, 507 (twice), 510, 511, 520. The word "little" also functions in various other important ways. Ned's claim to be Pansy's proper suitor is established by the fact that he is not only "pretty," but also physically "little" (344, 346), and has " 'a comfortable little fortune' " (333). Osmond's implication in "little"ness is more damning. When he says of Pansy, " 'we will try and make up some little life for her' " (325), Isabel cannot yet imagine how repressively little a life he is imagining. Later Osmond teaches her when he incarcerates Pansy for " 'a little reflection' " (489) and thus reveals his determination that Pansy not only reflect the social ideal but also confine her aspirations to the little circle which her father prescribes. James even capitalizes on potential puns to show how "little" Osmond has become. Since we know how inadequate a suitor Lydia and Ralph judge him to be, we smile when we read "Osmond, at this moment, showed himself little at the Palazzo Crescentini" (313–14).

James' use of "little" is particularly important because he is again representative of Victorian practice, in fiction and in life. As Katharine Moore notes, " 'little' was a favorite term of endearment with many a Victorian husband" (*Victorian Wives* [New York, 1974], 17). Discussing Coventry Patmore's letters to his third angel-in-the-house, Moore says, "it is significant how often too the word 'little' occurs in these letters to Harriet" (17), for Harriet needed controlling as neither of Patmore's previous wives had. "Little" is also an important word for Dickens. Long ago Gissing examined Dickens' "little women" (*Charles Dickens: A Critical Study* [London, 1903], 190–93); recently Françoise Basch, discussing Mrs. Chirrup in "The Nice Little Couple," notes that "the adjective 'little,' referring to her, recurs eight times in six lines" (57). The Victorian passion for manageable wives is reflected in their overuse of the word "little," as though insisting would make it so.

76. Henry James, *Letters to A. C. Benson and Auguste Monod*, ed. E. F. Benson (New York, 1930), 7.

77. Richard D. Altick, *Victorian Studies in Scarlet* (New York, 1970); Jonathan Gathorne-Hardy, *The Unnatural History of the Nanny* (New York, 1973), esp. 291–302. For a sense of how frequently such domestic slaughters went unpunished, see Edward Van Every's *Sins of New York* (New York, 1930)—in particular, Polly Bodine's apparent guilt in the murder of her sister-in-law and nephew (61–71), and Benjamin Nathan's death at the hands of either his sons or his servants or both (124–41). For more on doctors, see the Hallers' discussion of "nineteenth-century terrorism," particularly 195–225. Their discussion of Victorian drug use, chilling in itself, is still more ghastly in light of Gathorne-Hardy's account of Nannies going beyond the laudanum-dipped sugar cube or even ether and quieting their little charges with doses from the gas jet (274).

78. Tomsich, 153; Mrs. Linton, 2:211. Tomsich comments upon another aspect of the conjugal situation when he says that "aggression underlay genteel behavior toward women in general, whether they were to be seduced outside marriage or confined by it to home and motherhood" (161). On the other hand, Mrs. Linton can also recognize that much of Victorian domestic horror derives from woman's failure to engage fully in domestic life. By relegating her children to a nurse, the Mother is betraying them into potentially very dangerous hands. "She [the Mother] does not remember that her children do not complain because they dare not. . . . [they lack] the protection of the glorified creature just gone to her grand dinner in a cloud of lace and a blaze of jewels; and the first lesson taught the youthful Christian in short frocks or knickerbockers is not to carry tales down stairs, and by no means to let mamma know what nurse desires should be kept secret" (1:15–16).

79. Moers, 160.

80. William Dean Howells, "Mr. Henry James's Later Work," *NAR* 1903, 137, reprinted in *Discovery of a Genius* (New York, 1961), ed. Albert Mordell, 206.

81. Edward Bulwer-Lytton, *England and the English*, quoted by V. Colby in *Yesterday's Woman*, 76. Bulwer's analogy recurs in *Aurora Leigh*. "We haggle for the small change of our gold, / And so much love, accord, for so much love, / Rialto-prices. . . . [if marriage be] a simple fealty on one side, / A mere religion—right to give, is all, / And certain brides of Europe duly ask / To mount the pile, as Indian widows do. . . . as the man's alive, / Not dead,—the woman's duty, by so much, / Advanced in England, beyond Hindostan" (101). Among Victorian novelists, Dickens and Thackeray inveigh with particular earnestness against England's marriage market.

82. Stephen Marcus, *Dickens: From Pickwick to Dombey* (New York, 1965), 32.

83. Quoted by Kathleen Tillotson in *Novels of the Eighteen-Forties* (Oxford, 1956), 276. James praises Trollope for making his villains mild and partially triumphant (*Na* 1866, 22, and 1868, 495).

84. Cargill's discussion of Isabel as a "mixed" heroine is probably the most extensive (79–86); Christof Wegelin (*The Image of Europe in Henry James* [Dallas, 1958]) gives a good analysis of the backgrounds of the American girl (56–78); besides the many critics who relate Isabel to Dorothea Brooke and Gwendolen Harleth, Holland notes James' apparent borrowings from *Adam Blair* (21–23) and Tribble from *Le Roman d'une honnête femme*. For the essays of Mackenzie, Perloff, and Brooks, see note 1.

85. Stallman uses the word "recast" to account for the differences between the two texts, but as a matter of fact Flaubert and James are actually referring to two quite different types of events. Emma dreams of a honeymoon: *daytime* carriage rides that move "slowly" through pastoral tropic lands and evenings *outside* the carriage "on the villa terraces, hand in hand." Even Emma's wild ride with Léon is during the daytime. James, as I try to show, is referring to romantic midnight flights across the countryside and away from husbands.

86. Tabitha Tenney, *Female Quixotism*, quoted by Papashvily, 31.

87. Alfred Lord Tennyson, *Tennyson: Poems and Plays*, ed. T. H. Warren and Frederick Page (Oxford, 1965), 6. All quotations from Tennyson will be from this edition.

88. According to H. Montgomery Hyde, "the earliest purchase among the books in the Lamb House Library would appear to be the *Poems* of Alfred Tennyson . . . given to Henry by his father during the family's stay in St. John's Wood in 1858" ("The Lamb House Library of Henry James," *Book Collector* 16 [19xx]:477–80). James is referring to this volume in 1869 when he describes Jane Morris as "[having] a mouth like the 'Oriana' in our illustrated Tennyson" (*HJL* 93). Throughout the early letters, expressions of Tennyson's echo repeatedly. " 'Stiller than chiselled marble'—Vide Tennyson"; "the ringing grooves of change"; "part of the 'dreadful past' as Tennyson says" (*HJL* 78, 201, 469). James mentions the *Princess* expressly in 1875 (*HJL* 482).

89. James reviews *Queen Mary* in 1875 for *Galaxy* (393–402) and *Harold* in 1877 for *Nation* (43–44); he quotes from *The Princess* on page 695 of *Watch and Ward* and on page 63 of *Roderick Hudson*.

90. Giorgio Melchiori, "Locksley Hall Revisited: Tennyson and Henry James," *REL* 6 (1965): 20. To indicate how complex James' attitude toward Tennyson had become, Melchiori quotes the passage from *The Middle Years* in which James states his reaction to hearing the Bard read what the young American novelist had asked especially to hear—"Locksley Hall." "What the case came to for me, I take it—and by the case I mean the intellectual, the artistic—was that it lacked the intelligence, the play of discrimination, I should have taken for granted in it" (106).

91. Caroline Chesbro', *The Children of Light*, quoted by Brown, 292.

92. Patricia Thomson, *The Victorian Heroine* (Oxford, 1956), 14.

93. Irene Clephane (and Alan Bott), *Our Mothers* (London, 1932), 15.

94. Mrs. Sarah Stickney Ellis, *The Women of England* in *The Family Monitor and Domestic Guide* (New York, 1850), 5. Since *The Daughters of England*, *The Wives of England*, and *The Mothers of England* are also bound in this one volume, page references to any of the four works can be located either in *The Family Monitor* or in the individual works published separately.

95. Thomson, 90.

96. For Henry James, Charles Reade was also an important contributor to the New Woman. James calls Hardy's Bathsheba Everdene "a young lady of the inconsequential, willful, mettlesome type which has lately become so much the fashion for heroines, and of which Mr. Charles Reade is in a manner the inventor—the type which aims at giving one a very intimate sense of a young lady's *womanishness*" (*Na* 1874, 424). Wayne Burns is quite right that Reade's Mrs. Gatty "reveals the features behind the veil of Victorian motherhood" and that Kate's indiscretions in *Griffith Gaunt* "represent a serious attempt to dramatize the impulses of the female heart that his contemporaries (as well as his sources) had overlooked or denied" (*Charles Reade* [New York, 1961], 128, 240). Although I cannot go so far as to accept Burns' claim that *Griffith Gaunt* "offers a more 'fundamental criticism' of accepted Victorian values than any other novel of the time" (311), I do agree that Reade, at his best, is a more effective critic than Charlotte Brontë or Mrs. Gaskell, let alone than the majority of scribblers.

Reade also shares with women novelists a trait which we will take up soon: he fails to sustain his radicalism. The end of *Griffith Gaunt*, for example, deteriorates; passionate and ambiguous Kate is reduced to a proper Victorian wife. Nor has Reade's radicalism been sustained throughout even the first two-thirds of the novel. He sounds like Mrs. Ellis when he berates Kate for not making her husband her most complete confidante. In general, what is radical about Reade is his uncovering of the passions; his ideas and beliefs are usually very conventional.

97. M. E. Braddon, *"Lady Audley's Secret,"* in *Murder by Gaslight* (New York, 1949), ed. Edward Wagenknecht, 21, 184.

98. Yvonne Ffrench, *Ouida* (London, 1938), 22.

99. We need only compare *Modern Love* with *Angel in the House* to see the dangers that major writers were drawn toward. In Thackeray's presentation of Helen Pendennis "the sacred emotion of mother-love is tentatively explored, and its seamier side ambiguously indicated" (Tillotson, *Novels*, 72). Even that antifeminist, Anthony Trollope, can earn Thomson's praise for not making Mrs. Trevelyan a Griselda. "My Lady Griselda, of late, indeed had fallen strangely out of favour with the novelist" (103). For recent work on Trollope and women, see Charles Blinderman's "The Servility of Dependence: The Dark Lady in Trollope," in Cornillon, 55–67.

100. James' sentence is witty surely, but a little severe for one who, barely two years earlier, gave us "before she reached her son, Mary Garland had rushed past her, and . . . had flung herself, with the magnificent movement of one whose rights were supreme, and with a loud, tremendous cry, upon the senseless vestige of her love" (*RH* 481).

101. James goes on to say that these heroines "are certain to do something utterly pedantic and unnatural and insupportable" (*Na* 1867, 450). What he dislikes, however, is the scribblers' handling of their heroines, not this type of heroine as such.

102. Quoted by Hazel T. Martin in *Petticoat Rebels* (New York, 1968), 28. There were some dissenters from Miss Kemble's opinion, of course, but these were restricted largely to the thirties and early forties. See Harriet Martineau's *Society in America*

(1837), and Mrs. Anna Jameson's *Winter Studies and Summer Rambles in Canada* (1838).

103. See Page Smith's chapter "Some Attributes of American Women: Foreign Perspectives," in *Daughters of the Promised Land* (Boston, 1970), esp. 83 and 86. For other discussions of the American Girl, see Rahv, Wegelin, Quentin Anderson, William Wasserstrom's *Heiress of All the Ages* (Minneapolis, 1959), and Ernest Earnest's new *The American Eve in Fact and Fiction, 1775–1914* (Urbana, Ill., 1974).

104. H. T. Martin, 31.

105. The history of German philosophy which sits unread on Isabel's lap may well be James' gentle parody of intellectual heroines like Lucy Snowe who contrast "my German" with the "needlework" of ordinary women (*V* 110). On the other hand, Isabel's desire not "to be thought bookish" (33) is real. As *The Portrait* progresses, "literature seemed a fading light" (93). To help us chart Isabel's quest for experiential knowledge, James contrasts her with the Countess Gemini and with Lydia Touchett. By judging Isabel "a prodigy of learning" (484), Countess Gemini recalls to our minds the narrator's earlier, parodic use of that expression and thus stresses how different Isabel's education throughout the book has been. Then, as Isabel leaves Osmond for the last time, the Countess appears with the question " 'you, who are so literary, do tell me some amusing book to read' " (497). How remote Isabel is now from the realm of words, how deeply she has entered the realm of suffering, is clear. "Isabel glanced at the title of the volume she held out, but without reading or understanding it.... 'My cousin, Ralph Touchett, is dying.' The Countess threw down the book" (497). When Ralph dies, Isabel is again questioned about books, this time by Lydia Touchett. "She [Isabel] had never been less interested in literature than today" (536). References to books thus help us follow one of the book's major movements—the emergence into mature consciousness of a sensibility initially confined all too completely to the romantic realm of words and melodramatic sentiments.

106. Susanna Rowson, *Charlotte Temple* (New Haven, 1964 [1791]), 35. Mrs. Rowson also wrote *Mentoria*, a volume expressly devoted to advising the Gentle Fair. In later life, Mrs. Rowson found still fuller expression for her didactic impulse by opening a posh finishing school.

107. Juliet McMaster connects Lydia's statement, " 'for a woman of my age there is no greater convenience ... than an attractive niece' " and her realization that Madame Merle " 'has made a convenience of me' " (58). McMaster also suggests the propriety of the name Touchett for a wand-waving fairy godmother, and links Lydia to similar figures in Dickens and Thackeray.

108. Ralph adds later that Isabel "had a great deal to learn, and would doubtless learn it better from Madame Merle than from some other instructors of the young. It was not probable that Isabel would be injured" (234).

109. Conventionally the Impulsive Heroine has at least one guide of unquestioned authority—Frances Henri's "Monsieur," Ruth's Mr. Benson, Ellen's Mr. John, Emma Woodhouse's Mr. Knightley. Unlike these men, Ralph begins with severe limitations. His ennui and fashionable cynicism in the opening chapters prompt him to consider Isabel an occasion for spectacle; her doings give him something to do. Eventually Ralph grows to a stature nearly equal to his father's; and we trust his judgment of Osmond. But Ralph's drawbacks do prevent us from dismissing Isabel entirely; he must bear with the other derelict guides some share in Isabel's trouble and society's failure.

110. Cunnington, 229.

111. Clephane, 3.

112. J. and R. Haller, 100.

113. William L. O'Neill, *The Woman Movement* (London, 1969), 29.

114. *The Princess*, 170.

115. Mrs. Ellis, *Daughters*, 26; Mrs. Linton, 1:132, 133; the Stephens passage is quoted by H. T. Martin (35) from "Women of Genius" in *Ladies' Companion* (1893) and differs from the other passages in that Stephens is critical of, rather than committed to, the orthodox attitude which she presents. As an example of this orthodox attitude toward woman's intellect in the fiction of the 1860s, here is *Lady Audley's Secret*: " 'I don't want a strong-minded woman, who writes books and wears green spectacles; but, hang it! I like a gal who knows what she's talking about' " (109). The force of this attitude is all the greater because it goes back, as Frank W. Bradbrook (*Jane Austen and Her Predecessors* [Cambridge, 1967]) and others have shown, to Doctor Gregory and various eighteenth-century advisers of the Gentle Fair.

116. Mary Wollstonecraft, *A Vindication of the Rights of Women* in *The Feminist Papers* (New York, 1974), ed. Alice S. Rossi, 85.

117. Quoted by Killham, 159. In his attack upon "An Outline of the Grievances of Women" (which he assumed Mrs. Norton had written), Kemble says, "if we were once to admit, and establish by law, the speculative doctrine of the equality of the sexes, of the 'co-equal rights of parents', the most dangerous and alarming practical consequences would speedily follow" (151–52).

118. J. S. Mill, "The Subjection of Women," in *Essays on Sex Equality*, ed. Alice S. Rossi (Chicago, 1970), 179.

119. Early in the novel James introduces the issue of female emancipation when Isabel answers Warburton's request for future meetings with " 'to enjoy that pleasure, I needn't be so terribly emanicipated' " (74). Her basically traditionalist view of marriage is repeatedly reaffirmed as her own marriage is deteriorating. "He was her master.... it still clung to her that she must be loyal to Osmond.... marriage meant that a woman should abide with her husband" (426, 435, 499).

120. Charles Kingsley, *Yeast, a Problem* (New York, 1888 [1850]), 169.

121. Coventry Patmore, *The Angel in the House* (London, 1863), 2:140, 186.

122. Cunnington, 213–14.

123. Peter T. Cominos, "Innocent Femina Sensualis in Unconscious Conflict," in Vicinus, 167.

124. Catharine Maria Sedgwick, *The Linwoods*, quoted by Brown, 282.

125. Earlier we experience this same dualism more subtly when Madame Merle's " 'she [Isabel] would make a charming stepmother' " (255) calls to mind the not so charming stepmothers of literature. In The Notebooks, Madame Merle "has no fear that she [Isabel] will be a harsh stepmother" (17). As late as 1893, interestingly enough, James can discuss the possibility of a play or a tale (eventually *The Other House*) in which a dying wife demands that her husband not remarry. "She had had a reason, a deep motive for her demand—the overwhelming dread of a stepmother. She has had one herself—a stepmother who rendered her miserable, darkened and blighted her youth" (139). Still later James creates the various stepmothers and guides of Maisie Farange, and later still that most mixed of stepmothers, Charlotte Stant Verver.

126. Pansy calls Catherine "Mother" again on page 489, and Madame Merle does so twice on 507.

127. Madame Merle and Mother Catherine are the only two characters called "Madame." Both share a trait almost always suspect in James' fiction and frequently so in popular novels—they are "plump." In James' early fiction, plumpness, especially of hands, is suspect or downright revelatory of moral softness (CT 2:402, 3:157, 4:111); Lady Audley's hands are "plump, white, and bejeweled" (58), and in *Villette* Charlotte Brontë associates both plump hands and a color invariably suspect in James—pink—with the sensual and wily Madame Beck (268). In a gesture innocent

and yet suggestive of the luridness often associated with clerical keepers, Madame Catherine, when confronted with red and white roses, chooses the red. Finally, a verbal ambiguity establishes how similar these women's attitudes can be. Madame Merle says of Catherine:

"She speaks delightfully of Pansy; says it's a great happiness for them to have her. She is a little saint of heaven, and a model to the oldest of them."

(507)

Who says, " 'she is a little saint of heaven' "—Catherine as quoted by Madame Merle, or Madame Merle of her own accord? Both women view Pansy so similarly that we cannot be certain. And the impossibility of certainty, the similarity of the two women, is James' point. He even uses a joke to emphasize his point (while the humor precludes our taking the words too literally and thus saves the scene from becoming melodramatic). When Madame Merle in defeat asks " 'will you let me remain a little,' " Mother Catherine replies, " 'you may remain always, if you like!' And the good sister gave a knowing laugh" (510).

128. Although Mackenzie's argument corresponds to Perloff's about Isabel's fostering of Warburton's suit, Mackenzie does see admirably the ways in which *The Portrait* sustains simultaneous oppositions. Isabel "is not, at the same time she is, an Innocent Betrayed" (20).

129. How convenient such a choice can be, James establishes in 1880. "Bernard was in that state of mind when it is the greatest of blessing to be saved the distress of choice—to see a straight path before you and to feel that you have only to follow it" (*Confidence* [New York, 1962], 137). In *Villette*, "I became a frequenter of this straight and narrow path" (102); in *Lady Audley's Secret* a male character discovers that " 'my path lies very straight before me'" (260).

130. *Harper's Bazaar* 1907, 356.

131. Ralph is so confident of his chauvinist evaluation of Henrietta that he repeatedly misinterprets her. Isabel tells him initially what Henrietta repeats later: " 'she told me you had said to her something that an American never would have said.' . . . 'I have never been spoken to in America as you have spoken to me' " (85, 110). The fault is not exclusively Ralph's, however. Warburton's " 'you had better come alone' " prompts from Henrietta the now familiar " 'would you make that remark to an English lady?' " (125). Since Warburton and Ralph have already treated Isabel as they would not have treated an English lady (61–62), Henrietta's question is very much to the point. When she urges that Ralph marry, and later when she asks him to invite Caspar to Gardencourt, Ralph's assumption that she is after him and/or Caspar is symptomatic of man's failure to understand and appreciate women. As Isabel says, " 'There is no generosity without sacrifice. Men don't understand such things' " (144–45).

132. Especially in light of what we have seen with Henrietta, Isabel's sense of male encroachment is not unjustified. That Caspar wants to "take complete possession of her" (106) and that Warburton, "a territorial, a political, a social magnate had conceived the design of drawing her into the system in which he lived and moved" (95) are the interpretations, not of a woman "frigid" in any simple sense, but of a woman who declines to be a Sheltered Heroine and feels instead that "she had a system and an orbit of her own" (95). Acknowledging in Isabel a certain sexual reticence, we must nonetheless recognize that her increasing defensiveness and fear are justified by the facts of social life, especially in the second half of *The Portrait*.

His [Warburton's] being in Rome at all made her vaguely uneasy . . . . she had ceased to be afraid of his renewing his suit . . . . morally speaking, she retreated . . . . she was afraid of him [Caspar]. She was ashamed of her fear . . . . [Warburton had been] something to be resisted . . . his reappearance at first menaced her . . . . covert observation had become a habit with her . . . allied to that of self-defense . . . . she had been afraid . . . . she was afraid to trust herself to speak . . . . the answer

frightened her .... "I have always to be defending myself" .... she was afraid ....
she had feared .... she felt afraid .... she had a constant fear .... "I am afraid"
.... "I am afraid" .... "afraid of myself" .... she was frightened .... "you have
made your wife afraid of you" .... "your wife was afraid of me this morning, but in
me it was really you she feared" .... "I am afraid—yes, I am afraid" .... she had a
constant fear .... she felt rather afraid .... "you [Caspar] have frightened me"
.... a feeling of danger .... she was afraid.

(PL 271, 277, 286, 302, 355, 385, 389 [twice],
390, 405, 441, 442, 448, 457, 463 [twice], 464,
470, 482, 483, 498, 529, 539, 540, 541 [twice])

133. Caspar is initially presented to us as "a straight young man from Boston"
(33). We subsequently learn that "his figure was too straight and stiff" (108). After
many months intervene, Caspar remains "straight" because time ossifies him. Later in
the novel he moves like a robot, complete in his monomania. "He had a habit of
looking straight in front of him, as if he proposed to contemplate but one object at a
time.... The people whom he passed looked back after him; but he went straight
forward" (452, 453). No wonder that Isabel, meeting him for the last time, "quickly
straightened herself" (540). Caspar's monomania is as oppressive as Warburton's
social system. In fact, Caspar attempts in the last scene to transform Isabel into a
conventional figure very like the one which being Warburton's wife would reduce her
to. The path of Isabel's individual destiny must be straight away from such a
straitjacket.

Chapter Three

1. I do not want to seem to overstate Poirier's connection of James and Dr. Sloper,
but our dissatisfaction with his pairing of the two derives partly from a certain
slipperiness that we feel, for example, when we read "before the terrible scene on the
Alps his [Sloper's] ironic observation of experience is, with some slight modification, James's own.... James's ironic voice and Sloper's are never, to repeat, exactly
the same because in the latter there is always a taint of direct cruelty, but they begin to
separate entirely at about the point when Catherine and her father leave for Europe
(169, 175). On page 169, we learn that the differences between James and Sloper are
"slight" until after the moment when, according to page 175, they have begun "to
separate entirely." No one could deny that James and Sloper share more in the early
chapters than in the later; I feel, however, that Poirier makes this connection
considerably closer and longer lasting than it is.

Recently, a position close to Poirier's has been presented by Gerald Willen. "His
[James'] narrator ... speaks for approximately half the novel from Dr. Sloper's point
of view" ("Preface," Washington Square, ed. Gerald Willen [New York, 1970], vii).

2. Among those who find the title suggesting a social dimension which James fails
to live up to, are such noted critics as F. O. Matthiessen ("the book might more
accurately have been called by her name" [The American Novels and Stories of Henry
James (New York, 1947), xi]) and F. W. Dupee ("it is not essential to Washington Square
that its scene is American" [63]). In so recent a major book as The Grasping
Imagination, Buitenhuis can say, "since the action is practically confined to drawing-
rooms, it can be divorced almost completely from local physical conditions. The title,
Washington Square, is consequently not particularly appropriate" (108). Likewise,
Donald Stone can refer to "images of Washington Square (so curiously missing in the
novel of that name)" [271]). Among those who find the title reflecting a basic social
concern in the novel are: Leon Edel (Henry James: Selected Fiction [New York, 1953],
xvi); Charles G. Hoffmann (The Short Novels of Henry James [New York, 1957], 26,
32); F. R. Leavis, 139; Robie Macauley (" 'Let Me Tell You about the Rich ...,' "
Kenyon Review, 27 [1965]: 649–50; S. G. Putt (Scholars of the Heart [London, 1962],

165, and *A Reader's Guide to Henry James*, 47); Rebecca West (*Henry James* [New York, 1916], 55).

3. The connection between the three names is not my discovery; I wish it were. I owe it to U. C. Knoepflmacher.

4. In "Doctor Sloper's Double in *Washington Square*" (*University Review*, 36 [1970]: 301–6), William Kenney notes some of the connections which I cite here.

5. Their phallic quality is emphasized when each man manipulates his "stick" around Catherine (42, 140); both also use the word "stick" with regard to constancy in women (126, 130, 157).

6. Morris "was saying clever things" on page 32, and Arthur " 'know[s] some people that call my cousin too clever' " (38). The word "bright" appears with both Morris and Sloper. The latter is "a bright doctor" whose "wife was a bright exception" (16, 18); of Morris, Lavinia thinks that "bright enjoyment was his natural element" (138). For a recent study of James' use of the word "clever," see Strother B. Purdy's "Henry James, Gustave Flaubert, and the Ideal Style," *Language and Style* 3 (1970): 163–84.

7. "Catherine, though she was very fond of her aunt, and conscious of the gratitude she owed her, regarded her without a particle of that gentle dread which gave its stamp to her admiration of her father. To her mind there was nothing of the infinite about Mrs. Penniman; Catherine saw her all at once, as it were, and was not dazzled by the apparition" (22). On the succeeding pages, James continues this contrast of Catherine and Lavinia, always to the young girl's advantage. Catherine catches Morris' name, which Lavinia missed (34–35); she is twice proved right about meeting him in the park (68, 70); she does not, like Lavinia and traditional heroines, make scenes (81). Moreover, Catherine's devotion to Morris, though all too great, escapes the complete submission which characterizes Lavinia's devotion. "Unlike her niece, Mrs. Penniman asked for no explanation. . . . and, unlike Catherine too, she made no attempt to contradict him" (52).

8. An almost identical contrast appears elsewhere in James' early work. Compare "a very active member of what she and her friends call society" and "[M. Doudan was] in a very sufficient degree a man of the world." The first quotation is from an early short story in which "she and her friends" are clearly being undercut for their social pretensions; the second is from a highly complimentary review of Doudan (*CT* 1:139; *Na* 1878, 64). James could easily have been as direct about Sloper as he is about Doudan, if he had not wanted to call Sloper's society momentarily into question.

9. We have a similar experience later when Sloper defeats his daughter in the library. James adds, "he was sorry for her, as I have said" (113), but we have already experienced both words—" 'if you see him [Morris], you will be an ungrateful, cruel child; you will have given your old father the greatest pain of his life' "—and deeds—"her hands were raised in supplication, but he sternly evaded this appeal. Instead of letting her sob out her misery on his shoulder, he simply took her by the arm . . ." Behaving "simply," Sloper fails to make the conventional gesture of love and, in turn, makes the gesture conventional to villains. Poirier finds Sloper being consciously, ironically melodramatic here. Catherine surely is not, however. The contrast of her gesture and her father's moves us deeply, and moves us even more, I feel, if Sloper's gesture is not spontaneous.

10. For other examples of positive traits preceding negative ones with Catherine, see: "Mrs. Penniman . . . [was] overlooking her [Catherine] at the piano, where Catherine displayed a certain talent, and going with her to the dancing-class, where it must be confessed that she made but a modest figure" (19); "She had succeeded, however, as she often failed to do when people were presented to her, in catching his name" (28–29); " 'Yes, Aunt Penniman would like that,' Catherine said, simply, and

yet with a certain shrewdness. It must, however, have been in pure simplicity, and from motives quite untouched by sarcasm, that a few moments after she went on to say . . ." (121).

11. Another example of balanced syntax controlling a volatile situation occurs when Catherine, waiting excitedly for Morris, "heard his voice at the door, and his step in the hall" (117). Among other self-consciously literary devices are alliteration ("plumping down into the paternal presence" [116]), direct narrative intrusions (James' use of "I" and "it will probably seem to the reader" and "as the French say"), and such other instances of control as when "passion" appears ("she had a passion") and then is defused by successive explanations ("for little secrets and mysteries—a very innocent passion" [20]).

12. Even with such disciplined counterpointing, James manages to keep his preferences evident. Of all the basic terms in the sentence, only one is not found in both clauses; only Dr. Sloper is called "rigid."

13. James mentions reading Curtis in the 1850s in an article in *Literature*, 11 June 1898, 677.

14. Quoted by Pattee, 265.

15. John Lucas, "*Washington Square,*" in *The Air of Reality: New Essays on Henry James*, ed. John Goode (London, 1972), 36–59.

16. Lucas argues that Sloper can drop his mask of irony only in the Alps because only there "he feels sufficiently remote from that social context which seemed to require of him a permanence of ironic posture" (46). Is misogyny required by Victorian society? Quite the opposite, one would feel. Surely Sloper is so revered and secure in society that conventional kindliness to a motherless daughter (of whatever girth) would bring him anything but contumely, would add to his plaudits as an exemplary Paterfamilias.

Intending to show that Lavinia is as socially conditioned as Sloper or Morris, Lucas actually makes a more accurate evaluation. "Her behavior springs directly from her desire to act out a chosen role" (43). Here the emphasis is more properly given: the novel does not show society making Lavinia act as she does; rather it encourages us to see that, acting as she does, Lavinia reflects social attitudes. Of course she reflects what conditioned her, but the question is one of the reading experience. Does the novel tend to emphasize Morris, Lavinia, and Sloper as products of society or as representative forces shaping (and misshaping) another character's life?

17. This fact is included in the argument of critics who find that Catherine actually *declines* morally; she refuses her father's deathbed request and then, still more perversely, refuses Morris years later. See Philip Roddman's "The Critical Sublime: A View of *Washington Square*" and David J. Gordon's "*Washington Square*: A Psychological Perspective" (in Willen, particularly 262, 269).

18. The intricacies of this sentence are by no means confined to its last words. Since "morsel," for instance, suggests a small bit of food as well as a small bit of cloth, we recognize how little Catherine has to nourish her. "For life," in turn, means in at least three ways: that Catherine has only a morsel to sustain her life; that Catherine has only that morsel for all the rest of her days; and that she has it for life-as-it-were, that is, for life if you can call this living. These various ideas are each quite melodramatic, but together they produce enough divergence of interpretation to be touchingly complex.

Chapter Four

1. Wayne Booth and John E. Tilford, Jr., among others, have established that "mental process" with James remains a mixed technique. It never becomes "stream of consciousness" because the narrator is never—or at least not for very long—absent.

Bridgman sums it up well when he says that "James expresses Isabel's thoughts in a blend of formal and colloquial elements" (99). Thus, I grant the importance of, but will not spend much time detailing, two often-debated aspects of James' mixed technique: the extent of the narrator's presence in a passage, and the extent to which a word is appropriate to a character's individual speech patterns.

Below are some important discussions of the labyrinthine issues of mental process and literary portraiture in James and elsewhere.

C. R. Anderson, "Person, Place, and Thing in James' *Portrait of a Lady*," in *Essays on American Literature in Honor of Jay B. Hubbell*, ed. Clarence Gohdes (Duke University Press, 1968); Joseph Warren Beach, *The Method of Henry James* (New Haven, 1918; rev. ed., Philadelphia, 1954) and *The Twentieth Century Novel* (New York, 1932); Wayne C. Booth, "Distance and Point-of-View: An Essay in Classification," *Essays in Criticism* 11 (1961): 60–79, and *The Rhetoric of Fiction*; Lawrence Edward Bowling, "What Is Stream of Consciousness Technique," *PMLA* 65 (1950): 333–45; R. Bridgman, *The Colloquial Style in America*; O. Cargill, *The Novels of Henry James*; Richard Chase, *The American Novel and Its Tradition* (Garden City, 1957); Seymour Chatman, *The Later Style of Henry James* (New York, 1972); Dorrit Cohn, "Narrated Monologue: Definition of a Fictional Style," *Comparative Literature* 18 (1966): 97–112; Elizabeth Drew, *The Novel: A Guide to Fifteen English Masterpieces* (New York, 1963); Edward Engelberg, *The Unknown Distance* (Cambridge, Mass., 1972); Charles Feidelson, "The Moment of *The Portrait of a Lady*"; John T. Frederick, "Patterns of Imagery in Chapter XLII of Henry James's *The Portrait of a Lady*," *Arizona Quarterly* 25 (1969): 150–56; Melvin J. Friedman, *Stream of Consciousness: A Study in Literary Method* (New Haven, 1955); Norman Friedman, "Point of View in Fiction: The Development of a Critical Concept," *PMLA* 70 (1955): 1160–84; P. Grover, *Henry James and the French Novel*; J. Halperin, *The Language of Meditation*; John Halverson, "Late Manner, Major Phase," *Sewanee Review* 79 (1971): 214–31; L. B. Holland, *The Expense of Vision*; Robert Humphrey, *Stream of Consciousness in the Modern Novel* (Berkeley, 1954); C. P. Kelley, *The Early Development of Henry James*; Arnold Kettle, *An Introduction to the English Novel* (London, 1953), vol. 2; Dorothea Krook, *The Ordeal of Consciousness in Henry James* (Cambridge, 1962); Robert Langbaum, *The Poetry of Experience* (New York, 1957); S. W. Liebman, "The Light and the Dark: Character Design in *The Portrait of a Lady*"; Percy Lubbock, *The Craft of Fiction* (New York, 1921); Harold T. McCarthy, *Henry James: The Creative Process* (New York, 1958); F. O. Matthiessen, "Henry James and the Plastic Arts," *Kenyon Review* 5 (1943): 533–50, and reprinted in *Major Phase*; Barry Menikoff, "The Subjective Pronoun in the Late Style of Henry James," *ES* 52 (1971): 436–41; A. R. Mills, "*The Portrait of a Lady* and Dr. Leavis," *Essays in Criticism* 14 (1964): 380–87; A. D. Moody, "James's Portrait of an Ideal," *Melbourne Critical Review* 4 (1961): 77–92; Elsa Nettels, "Action and Point of View in *Roderick Hudson*," *ES* 53 (1972): 238–47; R. Poirier, *The Comic Sense of Henry James*; C. T. Samuels, *The Ambiguity of Henry James*; Mark Schorer, "Technique as Discovery," in *Essays in Modern Literary Criticism*, ed. Ray B. West, Jr. (New York, 1952); Ora Segal, *The Lucid Reflector* (New Haven, 1969); F. E. Sparshott, "An Aspect of Literary Portraiture," *Essays in Criticism* 15 (1965): 359–60; F. Stanzel, *Die typischen Erzahlsituationen im Roman* (Vienna, 1955), translated by James P. Pusack in 1971 (*Narrative Situations in the Novel* [Urbana]); Victor H. Strandberg, "Isabel Archer's Identity Crisis: The Two Portraits of a Lady," *University Review* 34 (1968): 283–90; G. Taylor, *The Passages of Thought*; John E. Tilford, Jr., "James the Old Intruder," *MFS* 4 (1958): 157–64; D. Van Ghent, *The English Novel*; Stephen Ullmann, *Style in the French Novel* (New York, 1963); Ian Watt, "The First Paragraph of *The Ambassadors*: An Explication," *Essays in Criticism* 10 (1960): 250–74; V. H. Winner, *Henry James and the Visual Arts*.

2. Flaubert's characters do not always survive his passion for verbal portraiture, however. Why, James asks, "the mole on the Queen of Sheba's cheek and the blue powder in her hair? He has simply wished to be tremendously pictorial, and the opportunity for spiritual analysis has been the last thing in his thoughts" (*Na* 1874, 366). Other great writers whose love of surface prevents their portraying depths are Tennyson ("[scenes from his plays are] hardly more vivid and genuine than the sustained posturings of brilliant *tableaux vivants*" [*AM* 1875, 394]), Gautier ("poor Gautier seems to stand forever in the chill external air which blows over the surface of things" [*NAR* 1874, 418]), Swinburne ("the moral realm for Mr. Swinburne is simply a brilliant chiaroscuro of costume and posture. . . . ghastly in its poverty of insight" [*Na* 1875, 74]), the Goncourts ("as painters they are superior, as psychologists inferior" [*Fortnightly* 1888, 650]).

3. Wayne Booth and Bradford Booth have argued against the too easy assumption that using lucid reflectors is *the* way to write fiction. What I want to stress about James' practice in *The Portrait* is that he adds here a second kind of portrait, not that he "progresses" beyond the static kind. Not only do fine examples of the earlier type appear in *The Portrait*, but, as critics have noted, the "naturalistic" novels after 1881 actually return to many of the techniques which James, in *The Portrait*, seems to have "developed beyond." Ora Segal, following Beach, Andreas, and others, notes that "James still uses in *The Portrait of a Lady* the staple Victorian expository technique of block characterization. . . . He uses the introductory authorial report again in *The Princess Cassamassima*" (38); Wayne Booth notes the resemblance between the narrator in *The Bostonians* and the narrator of early Jamesian works (*Rhetoric of Fiction*, 58); for Donald Stone, James, using in the same novel static portraits and endings that do not change these initial images significantly, creates "characters [which] might be said to pre-exist . . . rather than to develop in the manner of James's more typical creations" (271). Stone also finds *The Tragic Muse* "the most stylistically conventional of his novels. . . . Sherringham is fatally conventional. . . . a fixed portrait" (308, 314, 315).

Recent critics have tended not to distinguish between two different types of portraits. Having defined portrait simply as "static," Michael Egan (*Henry James: The Ibsen Years* [London, 1972]) goes on to contrast such early static renderings with James' later "scenic" method. "James pursues with Homeric glee his extraordinary metaphor [Maggie's pagoda]. . . . James's prose has not simply evolved; it has undergone a complete transformation" (17). Granting what most critics have long recognized—that James' late imagery is more complex than his early, and that he does rely more upon a "scenic" method from the '90s onward—we might still wonder what we should attribute this sweeping (not to say Homeric) change to. Why, to that force which, so far as Egan can see, accounts for virtually everything of value in late James (including the water imagery!)—Henrik Ibsen. Yet see how James refers to *Hedda Gabler*: "the portrait of a nature . . . . the picture not of an action but of a condition." And these James quotations are from Egan's own pages (43).

4. Taylor in *The Passages of Thought* studies *The Portrait* and *The Ambassadors* in light of popular and early Jamesian practice. I retrace this ground not because I disagree with many of Taylor's insights, but because his treatment of James has, I feel, two important limitations. It does not do justice to popular techniques for rendering mental process; and, more important, it does not explore sufficiently James' actual *method* of presenting consciousness. Taylor does not really analyze James' style. Since the difference between a character's thoughts and a character thinking is that we are told of thoughts and are made to experience thinking, James' degree of success will necessarily depend upon the ability of his style to convey the illusion of process. To show how he moves to such technical mastery is my goal here.

5. *WWW* 12, 122, 167 (twice), 184, 255, 510, 575.

6. To indicate how extensive these vestigial techniques are in *The Portrait*, we might note that mental-process passages using quotation marks occur on pages 43, 59, 101, 159, 160, 176, 191–92, 237, 280, 300, 302, 330, 341, 373, 441, 484, 498. With exclamation marks, on pages 148, 163, 208, 293, 343, 373, 398, 399 (twice), 400 (twice), 433, 458, 468, 477, 479. At least seven times characters in mental-process situations ask three or more questions (103, 291, 324, 390, 398, 399, 430).

7. W. S. Gilbert, *Engaged,* in Bailey, 418.

8. That such mental-process techniques were, to some extent, also practiced by major nineteenth-century novelists is established by Dorrit Cohn. The four writers whom Cohn singles out are especially relevant to our study of James. "The first writer who made more extended use of the style [of narrated monologue] is Jane Austen.... Austen renders the rhythm of inner debate (rhetorical and highly self-conscious, to be sure) without letting the narrator's voice interfere. This happens at moments of inner crisis in several of her novels. Later in the century occasional examples can be found in most Victorian novelists, notably in Eliot and Meredith. In France, Flaubert is the first to make frequent and highly influential use of the style" (107). For an extended study of Flaubert's use of "free indirect style," see Ullmann's *Style in the French Novel,* 94–120.

9. How self-conscious James is about this process is clear in 1876 when he writes, "you see, the negative, with Benvolio, always implied as distinct a positive" (*CT* 3:379). Ian Watt briefly examines James' use of negatives in "The First Paragraph of *The Ambassadors*" in *Essays in Criticism.*

10. Alan Holder ("On the Structure of Henry James' Metaphors," *ES* 41 [1960]: 289–97) discusses this pattern. "The image follows a non-metaphorical expression, taking up in a parallel picture what has just been said in plain language" (290). Holder does not, however, deal with the creation of mystery. In fact, he says that "the plain statement is, in this case, necessary because the meaning of the metaphor would otherwise not be quite clear." I am arguing that no metaphor is ever quite clear in any sense which a one-sentence paraphrase could provide, and that the placement of the metaphor before or after the literal statement affects our experience considerably. R. W. Short ("Henry James's World of Images," *PMLA* 68 [1953]: 943–60) notes how "images create meaning without delimiting it" (945) and Priscilla Gibson ("The Uses of James's Imagery: Drama through Metaphor," *PMLA* 69 [1954]: 1076–84) shows convincingly how a metaphor repeated in different contexts changes in ways which suggest the evolution of a character's consciousness. Less convincing is John Halperin's recent argument that James' images are static and motion comes from the character circling around the image. For some other studies, see R. Gale, *The Caught Image;* Holder-Barell; Austin Warren, *Rage for Order,* 142–61.

11. Another variation is the positive-negative pattern. Although James also uses this type often, it does not seem to offer an analogous complexity. "There were some things that had to come in time if they were to come at all. If they didn't come in time they were lost for ever" (137). Emphasis from repetition and a definite sense of movement occur; but the final effect seems to move us toward cloture, toward establishing a single meaning. The negative seems to drive the final nail.

12. In "Strether and the Transcendence of Language" I discuss how Strether's own speech patterns provide much the same effect.

13. Early on page 72, for example, we meet the words "his confession"; not until well into page 73 do we learn "his confession was that he *had* ... agreed to breakfast out."

14. Recently D. Stone has mentioned this telegram, but briefly and in terms of the theme of independence (214).

15. Lydia's telegram is analyzed by Ralph, Daniel, and Warburton on page 13 and

by Lydia on page 42; after telegrams appear metaphorically (" 'You [Ralph] are as dismal as if you had got a bad telegram' " (126), Ralph does get (155) the all-too-clear telegram announcing that his father is dying; Lydia's telegram proposing to Isabel a journey (283) is also clear and cold; Isabel's next telegram (492), paralleling Ralph's on page 155, announces that *he* is now dying; after establishing the limitations of telegraphic truth (514), Isabel trusts in her wire to Henrietta (515). Besides the various letters which reveal the natures of Isabel and her suitors, Osmond writes to Countess Gemini "that she must be prepared to be very quiet. Whether or no she found in this phrase all the meaning he had put into it, I am unable to say" (414).

16. "His sensitive organ was really grateful for such grim favors. . . . London does not wear in the month of September its most brilliant face. . . . the mocking spirit, if it lurked in his words, failed on this occasion to peep from his eye . . . . that particular reflection . . . had not the assurance to present itself" (37, 128, 232, 448).

17. *James's "Daisy Miller,"* ed. William T. Stafford (New York, 1963), 53. In the early "Still Waters" (1871), Bruce McElderry finds no less than twenty-eight asides of the most melodramatic character ("The Uncollected Stories of Henry James," *AL* 21 [1949]: 286).

18. Lest this contrast seem to suggest that James' use of "that"s disappears entirely from his later novels or that such usage is necessarily obtrusive, see Watt's discussion of "that" in "The First Paragraph of *The Ambassadors.*" Although Bridgman correctly argues that the incorporation of oratorical cadences and syntactic runs is one more instance of the colloquialization of American narrative prose, he does not stress as I would the limited effectiveness of oratorical devices in most serious fiction. The heavy patterning often calls such attention to itself that we cannot feel much sense of intimacy with the character—especially when the character is not intended to seem grossly bombastic. Even when rendering a character's enthusiasm—"What had become of all her ardours, her aspirations, her theories, her high estimate of her independence, and her incipient conviction that she should never marry?" (325)—or a character's enthusiasm about a character's enthusiasm—"She struck him as having a great love of movement, of gaiety, of late hours, of long drives, of fatigue; an eagerness to be entertained, to be interested, even to be bored, to make acquaintances, to see people . . . to explore . . . to enter . . ." (362–63)—James makes us experience the intensity of intense thinking, but we do not in any full sense experience the thinking itself. Borne along by the mechanical repetition we are hypnotized or bludgeoned into a kind of inattention which ceases only when the repetitions do. Like riding a subway, we know we have traveled through experiences, but those experiences are not very real for us. James' love of incantatory rhythms—he came to enjoy Whitman enthusiastically—means that James will not give up entirely such sweeping periods. He will, however, vary their repetitions sufficiently that they draw us all the more into—rather than fence us off from—the character's consciousness.

19. By which I am not entering that other discussion—how many centers of consciousness the novel has (Feidelson arguing for three, Segal and others for two, some still clinging to the old notion of one). By the very fact that they are not major, many of the characters whose minds are entered do not function as centers of consciousness, for they do not provide major value systems for the novel. I have included viewpoint shifts among vestigial techniques because James has so much precedent for his practice. E. D. E. N. Southworth (and her peers) will use any character at any moment to convey whatever comes to mind. As a critic, James inveighed against this practice for decades.

20. Point of view shifting seems still more wide-ranging because James glides between and among consciousnesses within a single paragraph or sequence. We move, for example, from Ralph to Lydia and back to Ralph on page 253; from

Isabel to Countess Gemini and back to Isabel on 413–14; Caspar-Henrietta-Caspar, 466–67.

21. Studying James' gliding point of view, Bridgman, like Lubbock, does not find the shifting harmful. "In the course, then, of a fairly short passage a number of shifts in narrative manner have taken place, unsignalled and barely perceptible.... [James] entered Isabel's mind and at the level of mental speech moved from (1) the indirect, to (2) the direct and hence colloquial, to (3) a summary of thoughts" (98). It is when James moves to situations not anchored adequately in time and space that real problems begin.

22. Warren, *Rage*, 145. Warren also, of course, discusses metaphor as it appears in a "narrative of consciousness and inner soliloquy." This more uncontrolled process he calls "myth."

Index

277